BrT
4.20

D1490849

8615

TWENTIETH-CENTURY PHILOSOPHY:

THE ANALYTIC TRADITION

READINGS IN THE HISTORY OF PHILOSOPHY

SERIES EDITORS:

PAUL EDWARDS, Brooklyn College

RICHARD H. POPKIN, University of California, San Diego

The Volumes and Their Editors:

GREEK PHILOSOPHY: THALES TO ARISTOTLE
Reginald E. Allen

GREEK AND ROMAN PHILOSOPHY AFTER ARISTOTLE
Jason L. Saunders

MEDIEVAL PHILOSOPHY:
ST. AUGUSTINE TO OCKHAM
Father Allan B. Wolter

THE PHILOSOPHY OF THE SIXTEENTH AND
SEVENTEENTH CENTURIES
Richard H. Popkin

EIGHTEENTH-CENTURY PHILOSOPHY
Lewis White Beck

NINETEENTH-CENTURY PHILOSOPHY:
HEGEL TO NIETZSCHE

TWENTIETH-CENTURY PHILOSOPHY:
THE SPECULATIVE TRADITION
Peter Koestenbaum

TWENTIETH-CENTURY PHILOSOPHY:
THE ANALYTIC TRADITION
Morris Weitz

Twentieth-Century Philosophy: The Analytic Tradition

Edited and with an Introduction by

Morris Weitz

 The Free Press, New York
Collier-Macmillan Limited, London

PHILOSOPHERS DEPICTED ON THE COVER ARE,
READING CLOCKWISE, RUSSELL, MOORE, WITTGENSTEIN.

CONTENTS

GENERAL INTRODUCTION

It has become established practice in anthologies and histories of twentieth century philosophy to divide its analytic parts into (a) Realism, (b) Logical Analysis or Logical Atomism, (c) Logical Positivism, and (d) Linguistic, Ordinary Language, or Conceptual Analysis. In assembling this anthology, I follow this practice, except that I call the fourth phase Conceptual Elucidation, since the emphasis here is on the description of the roles of concepts, and not on their analysis. Practitioners of conceptual elucidation, such as the later J. Wisdom, L. Wittgenstein, G. Ryle, and J. Austin, are included primarily because in any sharp division of twentieth century philosophy into analysis and speculation, these philosophers obviously belong to the first tradition.

¶ REALISM

Realism as formulated in the twentieth century by G. E. Moore and Bertrand Russell, its founders and leading exponents, is the dualistic doctrine that mind and matter and universals and particulars are ultimate. Basic to this dualism, at least historically, is the theory of external relations. Both Moore and Russell defended this theory, especially against the attack upon it by F. H. Bradley, who had argued in *Appearance and Reality* (1893) that the theory and its complementary method of analysis are self-contradictory. Moore published his refutation of the view that all relations are internal and his defense that at least some relations are external in 1919-20 ("External and Internal Relations"). Russell launched his attack on internal relations as well as his justification of external relations somewhat earlier, in a series of books and essays. Much of his argument, especially his reduction of the axiom of internal relations to logical absurdity, is summarized in Lecture II of *Our Knowledge of the External World* (reprinted below).

Without a defensible theory of external relations, neither the in-

1

dependence of matter or of mathematics from the mind, nor analysis as a method of thought and discourse about the world could be vindicated. Russell's concern for science and mathematics made such a theory imperative. Although he set forth his theory as early as 1900, the best, succinct statement of the theory and of its implications for analysis and the foundations of Realism is in his article, "Some Explanations in Reply to Mr. Bradley," *Mind*, 1910:

I maintain that there are such facts as that x has the relation R to y, and that such facts are not in general reducible to, or inferable from, a fact about x only and a fact about y only: they do not imply that x and y have any complexity, or any intrinsic property distinguishing them from a z and a w which do not have the relation R. This is what I mean when I say that relations are external. But I maintain also . . . that whenever we have two terms x and y related by a relation R, we have also a complex, which we may call "xRy," consisting of the two terms so related. This is the simplest example of what I call a "complex" or a "unity." What is called analysis consists in the discovery of the constituents of a complex. A complex differs from the mere aggregate of its constituents, since it is one, not many, and the relation which is one of its constituents enters into it as an actually relating relation, and not merely as one member of an aggregate [p. 374].

Thus, according to Russell, analysis—"the discovery of the constituents of a complex"—is a legitimate philosophical procedure. A necessary metaphysical condition of analysis is the existence of independent unities whose constituents are terms and qualities in their (sometimes) external relations. Analysis as "relational thinking" can render experience and the commonsensical, scientific, and mathematical categories of physical object, space, time, causality, motion, and number intelligible. Dialectical argument of the Bradley variety that is designed to destroy the efficacy of analysis fails: Bradley's intuition is not a satisfactory alternative to the method of analysis in the understanding of the world.

That matter is not reducible to mind and that universals are not reducible to particulars is central in the early writings of Moore and Russell, as well as in much of the development of twentieth century Realism. Moore's "The Refutation of Idealism" (1903) (reprinted below), contains more than the title suggests in that it also argues for an epistemological realism regarding the object of empirical knowledge. Introspection of the sensation of blue, for example, reveals that blue is logically distinct from the awareness of blue, hence, that the first does not depend upon the second.

These objects of sensation, generally referred to as sense-data, are also claimed to be basic entities by Russell, who gave them a classic status in *The Problems of Philosophy* (1912). In that book, Russell sharply distinguishes between matter and mind and, like Moore in his later essays on sense-data, takes as the crucial problem the relation of sense-data to physical objects. Throughout their work, their confidence in the nonmental character of sense-data is matched by their hesitation in regard to the exact relation between these data and physical objects. The latter part of Moore's "A Defence of Common Sense" (1925) (reprinted below), gives some indication of just how difficult the problem has been to Realism.

Russell's *Problems* also presents the classic case for the reality of universals. That there is a timeless, spaceless realm of universals (or concepts, for Moore), is argued for on the basis of perception as well as of mathematics and logic. To deny universals or to reduce them to particulars is to reaffirm at least the one universal of resemblance, without which discourse is unintelligible. Once the relation of resemblance is recognized as ultimate, the logical motive for reducing universals to particulars collapses, and we are then able to postulate a whole realm of universal subsistent entities. In "On the Relations of Universals and Particulars" (1912) (reprinted below), Russell defends the dualistic view that there are particulars which have qualities or relations that are instances of universals.

Realism comprised other doctrines as well: on the nature of truth, belief, and value. It reaffirmed the correspondence theory of truth, it insisted on the externality of the relation between a complex object and a subject in belief, and it defended the view that goodness is a characteristic of that which is judged to be good no less than size and shape are qualities of material objects. Moore's *Principia Ethica* (1903) presents in its first chapter (reprinted below), among other things, the realistic argument for the existence of good as a non-natural property which can be known only by an act of intellectual intuition.

American philosophy in the early twentieth century paralleled English developments. In rebellion against Josiah Royce's Absolute Idealism, but also inspired by the philosophy of William James, American Realism, like the English variety, proclaimed the independence of material objects from mind. In 1912, *The New Realism* was published as a cooperative manifesto by a number of American philosophers, including R. B. Perry and E. B. Holt, in which both external relations and perception as an external relation between the act and the object of perception are advocated. Their identification of sense-data (or what they called "character-complexes") with things, and their thesis that a thing is a meeting place of the data we perceive, led to a revolt against their form of Realism. In 1920, *Essays in Critical Realism: A Cooperative Study of the Problem of Knowledge* appeared. D. Drake, G. Santayana, and A. O. Lovejoy led the attack. Perception, they claimed, contains three ingredients: the perceiving act, the given, and the object perceived. Arthur Lovejoy's *The Revolt against Dualism* (part of Chapter I of which is reprinted below) was the strongest defense of this representative theory of perception against the New Realists; nothing short of the representative theory, Lovejoy contends, can explain error, illusions, memories, and expectations. Only Critical, not New, Realism is compatible with philosophical reflection on the perceptual situation.

After *The Problems of Philosophy*, Russell became more sceptical in his philosophy. Realism gave way to Neutral Monism (the view that the mental and the physical are reducible to relations among neutral entities) and to fundamental doubts about Platonic entities as the ultimate denotata of mathematics and logic.

Moore, on the other hand, became more vociferous in his defense of Common Sense, especially against the attacks to which it had been subjected by previous philosophers. In 1924, Russell published a "personal statement" of his philosophy under the title of "Logical Atomism." In 1925, Moore chose as his personal statement, "A Defence of Common Sense." By then, Realism, although not abandoned altogether, gave way in Russell to Logical Analysis and, in Moore, to Common Sense.

¶ LOGICAL ANALYSIS

Although Russell was not the first to formulate the method of logical analysis in contemporary philosophy, he has been its leading advocate. He has variously referred to logical analysis as: the analysis of denoting phrases, the resolution of incomplete symbols, the method of dispensing with abstractions, and logical constructionism. All of these, at least for Russell, are variants on a set of techniques for the replacement of defective symbols.

Fundamental in Russell's logical analysis in his conception of logic. In Lecture II of *External World* (reprinted below), Russell sums up this conception, which had been his preoccupation from *The Principles of Mathematics* (1903), to *Principia Mathematica* (1910-13). Logic, he says in that lecture, has two continuous albeit distinguishable parts: a philosophical and a mathematical. The philosophical is concerned first with the forms that are abstracted from the linguistic and non-linguistic aspects of reality, and, second, with the foundations of mathematics. The mathematical part comprises the theorems deduced from the foundations.

Among the ultimate, i.e., irreducible, kinds of forms are names that designate particulars and propositions that correspond to facts. And among the ultimate kinds of propositions and facts are: atomic (e.g., "This is red"), molecular (e.g., "Either this is red or it is green"), existence (e.g., "There are green things"), general (e.g., "All trees are green"), completely general (e.g., "q⊃.pvq"), and negative (e.g., "Socrates is not alive"). There is a perfect isomorphism (i.e., one-to-one relation) between each of these propositions and its corresponding fact, such that in any program for the reconstruction of our discourse about the world, this isomorphism can function as the criterion of an ideal language.

Russell had already suggested in his early writings on denotation and description that these ultimate forms of propositions and facts are to serve as models in the analysis of language. In "On Denoting" (1905), for example, he pointed out that talk about "everything," "nothing," and "something" must be rephrased in their appropriate propositional contexts so that these denoting symbols disappear. His insight into the discrepancy between grammatical and logical form led to his famous "theory of descriptions," one succinct, informal statement of which is presented in Chapter 16 of *Introduction to Mathematical Philosophy* (reprinted below).

The theory of descriptions is primarily a technique for resolving propositions containing symbols of unreal or self-contradictory objects, which resolution preserves our robust sense of reality and still enables us to talk about these "pseudo-objects" intelligibly; derivatively, the application of the technique to all symbols whose meanings are not given in knowledge by acquaintance, hence incomplete symbols. Thus, "the present King of France," "the round square," and "the author of *Waverley*" are dealt with in the same way—by putting each of these descriptive phrases in an appropriate context and then resolving the whole proposition into another proposition in which the grammatical subject disappears. For example, "the author of *Waverley*" is enlarged to "The author of *Waverley* was Scotch"; which is then rephrased as "One and only one person wrote *Waverley* and whoever wrote *Waverley* was Scotch." Propositions about described objects are thus replaced by propositions involving values of propositional functions. In this way, a seeming subject-predicate proposition is transformed into an existential one. Philosophical analysis as resolution of the incomplete symbol, "the author of *Waverley*," thus reveals the real as against the apparent form of propositions about described objects.

Russell's theory of descriptions became extremely important after 1913 because it served as his model for the treatment of other symbols. Symbols for classes, numbers, points, instants, material particles, even ordinary objects, such as tables and persons, are transformed from names to incomplete symbols which, when put into their appropriate propositional contexts, can then be interpreted in terms of propositional functions, variables, and constants. In many books and essays, including *External World* (1914), *Analysis of Mind* (1921), *Analysis of Matter* (1927), as well as "The Relation of Sense-Data to Physics" (1914) (reprinted below), Russell applied analysis as resolution of incomplete symbols to the natural sciences, especially physics and psychology.

In 1929, F. P. Ramsey characterized Russell's theory of descriptions as a paradigm of philosophy. Russell's notion that one task of philosophy is the translation of grammatically misleading or defective expressions into their correct logical form became one of the major themes of analytic philosophy during the 1930s. Analysis, interpreted as logical translation, was advocated or practiced by all the leading analysts of the period: G. E. Moore, S. Stebbing, J. Wisdom, L. Wittgenstein, and G. Ryle. Ryle's "Systematically Misleading Expressions" (1931-32) (reprinted below), is a superb example of the influence of Russell's conception of philosophical analysis, although in its implied doubts about the *real* rather than merely *conventional* forms of language, the essay also points to the ensuing repudiation of analysis conceived as correct translation of incorrect expressions.

Although no selection from Wittgenstein's *Tractatus Logico-Philosophicus* (1921), is reprinted here, the importance and influence of that book require at least a short account of its main contributions to philosophy as logical analysis.

The *Tractatus* is a notoriously difficult book. While there is agreement on the general topics and theses of the work, there is vast and vehement disagreement about the exact meaning of the fundamental doctrines. That Wittgenstein discusses, among other things, the nature of language, logic, mathematics, and scientific laws, as well as the relation between language and the world and the proper function of philosophy is clear. That certain pervasive themes are proclaimed is also indisputable. Among these are: (1) traditional philosophical difficulties are the result of logical and linguistic misunderstandings; (2) these difficulties can be solved or avoided by the creation and stringent employment of an ideal language; (3) such a language, in its elements and structure, must be isomorphic with the reality it represents or pictures; (4) only propositions that do represent or picture have meaning, hence, that truth-value tautologies, logical constants, and mathematical propositions, although not nonsensical, are without meaning; and philosophical propositions about the relation between language and the world, including the propositions of logical atomism, that are basic to his theory of an ideal language, are nonsensical, consequently, that all the propositions of the *Tractatus* are nonsensical because they too try to describe this relation which can be shown but not described.

It may be undebatable that Wittgenstein advocates these theses, but the precise meaning of them, especially of an ideal language and the notion of the proposition as a picture, remains a matter of persistent dispute.

What seems clearest of all in the *Tractatus* is the role Wittgenstein assigns to analysis. The function of analysis is to resolve all descriptive, complex propositions about reality into their elementary ones, and these latter into their ultimate units of unanalyzable names and combinations of names, which represent and mean the ultimate simples—the logical atoms—of the world. Or, more briefly, the task of analysis is to make every statement an adequate picture of the reality it describes. As such, analysis is rooted in Wittgenstein's thesis of extensionality, i.e., that every statement is either a logically simple statement—an elementary proposition—or else a truth-function of such statements. Analysis is thus a form of linguistic transformation: the reduction of complex propositions, no matter what their grammatical form, to their atomic constituents and connections, which *show* their correct logical form. Analysis is presumably a legitimate philosophical procedure since it clarifies rather than confuses logical as distinct from grammatical form and because it does not transgress the limits of language. But it is not identical with philosophy, which has as its proper job the making clear of what can and what cannot be said. Once this task is completed, analysis can aid in the actual clarification. However, because philosophy itself is ultimately nonsensical, according to the *Tractatus*, and analysis rests upon philosophy, it is not immediately evident that analysis itself as a philosophical method is not also ultimately nonsensical.

¶ LOGICAL POSITIVISM

Logical Positivism, which in its variegated yet orthodox form lasted roughly from the beginnings of the Vienna Circle (1922) to the outbreak of the Second World War, was characterized by a number of radical, interrelated doctrines. Among these were: the verifiability theory of meaning, the rejection of metaphysics and theology, the emotive theory of moral judgments, the unity of science, the conception of language as a calculus, the conventionalistic interpretation of logic and mathematics, and the claim that legitimate philosophy consists solely of logical analysis. Most of these doctrines, it is generally agreed, stem from or were wrongly attributed to Wittgenstein's *Tractatus*.

The basic doctrine was the theory of meaning, according to which the cognitive meaning of a sentence is its method of verification: If a sentence is not verifiable—some positivists said directly verified, others, indirectly verified—or is not a truth-value tautology, it is cognitively meaningless. Carnap's "The Rejection of Metaphysics" (1935) (reprinted below) is a clear statement of the verifiability theory of meaning and of its philosophical implications.

Logic, mathematics, and the sciences, because they satisfy the verifiability criterion, however, were regarded as legitimate. Moreover, they can be conceived of as calculi, consisting of variables and constants and certain formation and transformation rules from which other sentences can be constructed or derived. "What is the syntax of these calculi?" suggested itself as a question that was neither meaningless nor scientific. The attempt to answer this question reconstituted itself to Logical Positivism as philosophical analysis. Philosophy was reconceived of as the systematic presentation of the logical syntax of the language of science.

This conception of philosophy had two important formulations: Rudolf Carnap, *The Logical Syntax of Language* (1934) and A. J. Ayer, *Language, Truth and Logic* (1936). In Carnap's verson, philosophy becomes the logical analysis of the sentences, terms, concepts, and theories of science, in which the analysis results in a purely formal, i.e., nonsemantical, theory of language. In Ayer's version, philosophy is identified with analysis, and analysis with contextual definition of the sort that Russell provided in his theory of descriptions, which Ayer takes to be *the* paradigm of philosophy. For both, as well as for all the logical positivists, philosophy as analysis is an activity of clarification of certain concepts, such as "matter," "mind," or "cause," and not a body of propositions that competes with science in the making of factual claims about the world.

As time passed, many of the leading logical positivists changed their views on some important matters, but there were equally important ones on which they stuck to the theories advocated earlier, such as the conventionalistic theory of mathematics and logic, represented by Hans Hahn's "Logic, Mathematics and Knowledge of Nature" (1933) (reprinted below); nor did any of them repudiate the emotive theory of ethical utterances. One of the most influential and authoritative statements of the emotive theory is the paper by C. L. Stevenson, "The Emotive Meaning of Ethical Terms" (1937) (reprinted below). The rise of Logical Positivism led to a renewed interest in methodological problems of the social sciences and history on the part of empirically minded philosophers. One of the most interesting and most widely debated theses in this area is that of C. G. Hempel—explaining a phenomenon in history no less than in the physical sciences consists in subsuming it under a general proposition. Details of Hempel's view are found in his "The Function of General Laws in History" (1942) (reprinted below).

¶ CONCEPTUAL ELUCIDATION

Historically, philosophy as the elucidation of concepts is rooted in the repudiation of analysis as the proper method of philosophy. Analysis, as practiced by Russell, Moore, their followers, and the logical positivists—i.e., as real, conceptual, or contextual definition, as reduction and translation of linguistic complexes into more simple units of discourse, or as logical syntax—is rejected, at first (during the 1930s and then after the war), by three of the great analysts themselves, Wittgenstein, Wisdom, and Ryle.

Why, then, we must ask to understand conceptual elucidation, was analysis rejected? Analysis as real definition, advocated by Russell, Moore, Wisdom, Stebbing, Ryle, and Wittgenstein, in their joint efforts to determine the ultimate simple entities or the real forms of facts is first challenged by Wittgenstein. His claim in the *Tractatus* that philosophy is an activity, not a body of propositions, implies the rejection of all ontological pursuits. In *Philosophical Investigations* (1953), Wittgenstein solidifies his repudiation of real definition by showing that traditional ontology is a series of excursions into the logical grammar of concepts rather than any exploration of reality. Indeed, traditional ontology is construed as a misdescription of the use of certain concepts.

Moore's theory of analysis as conceptual definition is rejected primarily because of the denotational theory of meaning implicit in the theory (i.e., linguistic expressions denote concepts which are their meanings). Here, too, Wittgenstein leads the attack which is, in large part, directed against the naming theory of his own *Tractatus*. What is retained of Moore's explicit theory of analysis is his distinction between understanding the meaning of an expression and knowing what it means in the sense of being able to give a correct analysis of its meaning (see "A Defence of Common Sense"). This distinction is transformed by Ryle and others into that of knowing how to use an expression and being able to say how we use it, where the latter is not defining the concept denoted by the expression but describing the function(s) of an expression and the conditions under which such functioning occurs.

That analysis is contextual definition or resolution of incomplete symbols and that Russell's theory of descriptions is *the* or even *a* paradigm of philosophy are also rejected. Basic to the theory is the concept of a logically proper name and the denotational theory of meaning. Russell's claim, e.g., that "the present King of France" is an incomplete symbol because it names nothing, hence has no meaning by itself, is repudiated primarily on the ground that the claim confuses the meaning with the use of a descriptive expression. P. F. Strawson, in "On Referring," *Mind* (1950), brings to a climax certain disaffections with Russell's theory of descriptions, already present in the early Wisdom, and presents his counterviews on descriptions and other referring expressions. Indeed, there is no other essay that illustrates as well as Strawson's the fundamental differences between philosophical analysis and philosophical elucidation of expressions or concepts.

Doubts about analysis as reduction or translation and about analysis as logical syntax take many forms. J. O. Urmson's "Logical Positivism and Analysis" (reprinted below) summarizes these doubts and points out how they led to the rejection of the rigid calculus view of language, with its implicit denotational theory of meaning and its explicit doctrine that the only legitimate uses of language are the stating of facts and of logical equivalences.

Central, however, in the rejection of contemporary analytic philosophy by the practitioners of conceptual elucidation is the theory of language implicit in or attributed to much of that philosophy. After the *Tractatus*, Wittgenstein and others began to question all the fundamental doctrines of this theory of language. That language has or that we must presuppose that it has an essence—i.e., a set of necessary and sufficient properties—and that language is a picture or a structurally isomorphic mirror of the world are denied. In the *Investigations*, the refutation is total and complete. Indeed, the whole theory is now seen as an illusion imposed upon language by language itself. If we turn the whole examination around, i.e., if we "look and see" how language functions, we find that language does not function as a picture or mirror, but—if a metaphor is needed—as an enormous toolbox, replete with the most diversified assortment of tools, practically none of which resembles those things in the world to which they may be applied. We also discover that words and sentences as such, i.e., independently of their specific uses, do not refer to or name anything; rather it is in the context of their employment that some words are used to name, others to classify, and still others to prescribe; and sentences are used variously to refer, describe, emote, persuade, etc. Meaning, too, it is seen, is not a relation between words and things, but must be construed as the rules, regulations, conventions, and habits that govern the actual use of expressions.

Once the notion of an ideal language is relinquished—"the picture that held us captive," as Wittgenstein puts it—the primary task of philosophy becomes that of the assemblage of reminders concerning the roles of certain expressions. Analysis gives way to the elucidation of concepts—to the description of the roles of certain concepts and the conditions under which these concepts function. Philosophy shifts from questions of the form, "What is the nature, analysis, or meaning of 'x' (e.g., 'cause,' 'mind,' 'pain,' 'knowledge')?" to questions of the form, "What does 'x' do in a language and how does 'x' do it?" Although there is disagreement among the practitioners of conceptual elucidation about its purpose—Wittgenstein and his strict followers holding that the sole purpose is to eliminate philosophical puzzlement, which is held to be the result of misunderstandings about the role of one or more expressions, whereas others, such as Ryle or Austin, allowing for logical descriptions of many key concepts regardless of whether they lead to pseudoproblems—all these philosophers (including those from whom selections are reprinted below) concur that an essential feature of proper philosophical activity is the detailed description of the actual workings of language, rather than the resolution of these workings into some unworkable schema of an ideal language. For them, the need to analyze—to replace defective expressions by correct ones —vanishes with the illusion they claim produced it.

REALISM AND COMMON SENSE

G. E. MOORE

GEORGE EDWARD MOORE (1873-1958), during his tenure at Cambridge University, was Fellow of Trinity College and later Professor of Philosophy. In 1940-42 he lectured at various universities in the United States. He was a Fellow of the British Academy and a recipient of the Order of Merit. Universally acknowledged as one of the founders and leading exponents of the method of analysis in philosophy, his influence has been great not only on philosophy but on the Bloomsbury literary circle as well. Among his important books are *Principia Ethica* (1903), *Philosophical Studies* (1922), and *Philosophical Papers* (1959).

"The Refutation of Idealism" (1903) is the first classic text of Realism. Although ostensibly a refutation of the doctrine that *to be is to be perceived,* which Moore took to be central in all arguments for the Idealist view that reality is spiritual, it is also a vindication of the common-sense notion that what is experienced is often distinct from and logically independent of our experience of it as well as a vindication of analysis as a method for discerning constituents of certain complexes in the world. Basic to Moore's refutation of Idealism is the rejection of the logical doctrine that all relations, including that of the object and subject of experience, are internal. Yellow and the sensation of yellow are not only distinct, but the latter also involves an external relation between consciousness which is mental and yellow which is not.

The Refutation of Idealism[1]

Modern Idealism, if it asserts any general conclusion about the universe at all, asserts that it is *spiritual*. There are two points about this assertion to which I wish to call attention. These points are that, whatever be its exact meaning, it is certainly meant to assert (1) that the universe is very different indeed from what it seems, and (2) that it has quite a large number of properties which it does not seem to have. Chairs and tables and mountains *seem* to be very different from us; but, when the whole universe is declared to be spiritual, it is certainly meant to assert that they are far more like us than we think. The idealist means to assert that they are *in some sense* neither lifeless nor unconscious, as they certainly seem to be; and I do not think his language is so grossly deceptive, but that we may assume him to believe that they really are very different indeed from what they seem. And secondly when he declares that they are *spiritual,* he means to include in that term quite a large number of different properties. When the whole universe is declared to be spiritual, it is meant not only that it is in some sense *conscious,* but that it has what we recognise in ourselves as the *higher* forms of consciousness. That it is intelligent; that it is purposeful; that it is not mechanical; all these different things are commonly asserted of it. In general, it may be said, this phrase 'reality is spiritual' excites and expresses the belief that the *whole* universe possesses *all the qualities* the possession of which is held to make us so superior to things which seem to be inanimate: at least, if it does not possess exactly those which we possess, it possesses not one only, but several others, which, by the same ethical standard, would be judged equal to or better than our own. When we say it is *spiritual* we mean to say that it has quite a number of excellent qualities, different from any which we commonly attribute either to stars or planets or to cups and saucers.

Now why I mention these two points is that when engaged in the

1. From *Philosophical Studies,* 1922, pp. 1-30. Reprinted by permission of Humanities Press, Inc., New York, and Routledge & Kegan Paul, Ltd., London.

intricacies of philosophic discussion, we are apt to overlook the vastness of the difference between this idealistic view and the ordinary view of the world, and to overlook the number of *different* propositions which the idealist must prove. It is, I think, owing to the vastness of this difference and owing to the number of different excellences which Idealists attribute to the universe, that it seems such an interesting and important question whether Idealism be true or not. But, when we begin to argue about it, I think we are apt to forget what a vast number of arguments this interesting question must involve: we are apt to assume, that if one or two points be made on either side, the whole case is won. I say this lest it should be thought that any of the arguments which will be advanced in this paper would be sufficient to disprove, or any refutation of them sufficient to prove, the truly interesting and important proposition that reality is spiritual. For my own part I wish it to be clearly understood that I do not suppose that anything I shall say has the smallest tendency to prove that reality is not spiritual: I do not believe it possible to refute a single one of the many important propositions contained in the assertion that it is so. Reality may be spiritual, for all I know; and I devoutly hope it is. But I take "Idealism" to be a wide term and to include not only this interesting conclusion but a number of arguments which are supposed to be, if not sufficient, at least *necessary*, to prove it. Indeed I take it that modern Idealists are chiefly distinguished by certain arguments which they have in common. That reality is spiritual has, I believe, been the tenet of many theologians; and yet, for believing that alone, they should hardly be called Idealists. There are besides, I believe, many persons, not improperly called Idealists, who hold certain characteristic propositions, without venturing to think them quite sufficient to prove so grand a conclusion. It is, therefore, only with Idealistic *arguments* that I am concerned; and if any Idealist holds that *no* argument is necessary to prove that reality is spiritual, I shall certainly not have refuted him. I shall, however, attack at least one argument, which, to the best of my belief, is considered necessary to their position by *all* Idealists. And I wish to point out a certain advantage which this procedure gives me—an advantage which justifies the assertion that, if my arguments are sound, they will have refuted Idealism. If I can refute a single proposition which is a necessary and essential step in all Idealistic arguments, then, no matter how good the rest of these arguments may be, I shall have proved that Idealists have *no reason whatever* for their conclusion.

Suppose we have a chain of argument which takes the form: Since A is B, and B is C, and C is D, it follows A is D. In such an argument though 'B is C' and 'C is D' may both be perfectly true, yet if 'A is B' be false, we have no more reason for asserting A is D than if all three were false. It does not, indeed, follow that A is D is false; nor does it follow that no other arguments would prove it to be true. But it does follow that, so far as this argument goes, it is the barest supposition, without the least bit of evidence. I propose to attack a proposition which seems to me to stand in this relation to the conclusion 'Reality is spiritual.' I do not propose to dispute that 'Reality is spiritual'; I do not deny that there may be reasons for thinking that it is: but I do propose to show that one reason upon which, to the best of my judgment, all other arguments ever used by Idealists depend is *false*. These other arguments may, for all I shall say, be eminently ingenious and true; they are very many and various, and different Idealists use the most different arguments to prove the same most important conclusions. Some of these *may* be sufficient to prove that B is C and C is D; but if, as I shall try to show, their 'A is B' is false the conclusion A is D remains a pleasant supposition. I do not deny that to suggest pleasant and plausible suppositions may be the proper function of philosophy: but I am assuming that the name Idealism can only be properly applied where there is a certain amount of argument, intended to be cogent.

The subject of this paper is, therefore, quite uninteresting. Even if I prove my point, I shall have proved nothing about the Universe in general. Upon the important question whether Reality is or is not spiritual my argument will not have the remotest bearing. I shall only attempt to arrive at the truth about a matter, which is in itself quite trivial and insignificant, and from which, so far as I can see and certainly so far as I shall say, no conclusions can be drawn about any of the subjects about which we most want to know. The only importance I can claim for the subject I shall investigate is that it seems to me to be a matter upon which not Idealists only, but all philosophers and psychologists also, have been in error, and from their erroneous view of which they have inferred (validly or invalidly) their most striking and interesting conclusions. And that it has even this importance I cannot hope to prove. If it has this importance, it will indeed follow that all the most striking results of philosophy—Sensationalism, Agnosticism and Idealism alike—have, for all that has hitherto been urged in their favour, no more foundation than the supposition that a chimera lives in the moon. It will follow that, unless new reasons never urged hitherto can be found, all the most important philosophic doctrines have as little claim to assent as the most superstitious beliefs of the lowest savages. Upon the question what we have *reason* to believe in the most interesting matters, I do therefore think that my results will have an important bearing; but I cannot too clearly insist that upon the question whether these beliefs are true they will have none whatever.

The trivial proposition which I propose to dispute is this: that *esse* is *percipi*. This is a very ambiguous proposition, but, in some sense or other, it has been very widely held. That it is, in some sense, essential to Idealism, I must for the present merely assume. What I propose to show is that, in all the senses ever given to it, it is false.

But, first of all, it may be useful to point out briefly in what relation I conceive it to stand to Idealistic arguments. That wherever you can truly predicate *esse* you can truly predicate *percipi*, in some sense or other, is, I take it, a necessary step in all arguments, properly to be called Idealistic, and, what is more, in all arguments hitherto offered for the Idealistic conclusion. If *esse* is *percipi*, this is at once equivalent to saying that whatever is, is experienced; and this, again, is equivalent, in a sense, to saying that whatever is, is something mental. But this is not the sense in which the Idealist *conclusion* must maintain that Reality is *mental*. The Idealist *conclusion* is that *esse* is *percipere*; and hence, whether *esse* be *percipi* or not, a further and different discussion is needed to show whether or not it is also *percipere*. And again, even if *esse* be *percipere,* we need a vast quantity of further argument to show that what has *esse* has also those higher mental qualities which are denoted by spiritual. This is why I said that *the* question I should discuss, namely, whether or not *esse* is *percipi*, must be utterly insufficient either to prove or to disprove that reality is spiritual. But, on the other hand, I believe that every argument ever used to show that reality is spiritual has inferred this (validly or invalidly) from '*esse* is *percipere*' as one of its premises; and that this again has never been pretended to be proved except by use of the premiss that *esse* is *percipi*. The type of argument used for the latter purpose is familiar enough. It is said that since whatever is, is experienced, and since some things are which are not experienced by the individual, these must at least form part of some experience. Or again that, since an object necessarily implies a subject, and since the whole world must be an object, we must conceive it to belong to some subject or subjects, in the same sense in which whatever is the object of our experience belongs to us. Or again, that, since thought enters into the essence of all reality, we must conceive behind it, in it, or as its essence, a spirit akin to ours, who think: that 'spirit greets spirit' in its object. Into the validity of these inferences I do not propose to enter: they obviously require a great deal of discussion. I only desire to point out that, however correct they may be, yet if *esse* is not *percipi*, they leave us as far from a proof that reality is spiritual, as if they were all false too.

But now: Is *esse percipi*? There are three very ambiguous terms in this proposition, and I must begin by distinguishing the different things that may be meant by some of them.

And first with regard to *percipi*. This term need not trouble us long at present. It was, perhaps, originally used to mean 'sensation' only; but I am not going to be so unfair to modern Idealists—the only Idealists to whom the term should now be applied without qualification —as to hold that, if they say *esse* is *percipi*, they mean by *percipi* sensation only. On the contrary I quite agree with them that, if *esse* be *percipi* at all, *percipi* must be understood to include not sensation only, but that other type of mental fact, which is called 'thought'; and, whether *esse* be *percipi* or not, I consider it to be the main service of the philosophic school, to which modern Idealists belong, that they have insisted on distinguishing 'sensation' and 'thought' and on emphasising the importance of the latter. Against Sensationalism and Empiricism they have maintained the true view. But the distinction between sensation and thought need not detain us here. For, in whatever respects they differ, they have at least this in common, that they are both forms of consciousness or, to use a term that seems to be more in fashion just now, they are both ways of experiencing. Accordingly, whatever *esse* is *percipi* may mean, it does *at least* assert that whatever is, is *experienced*. And since what I wish to maintain is, that even this is untrue, the question whether it be experienced by way of sensation or thought or both is for my purpose quite irrelevant. If it be not experienced at all, it cannot be either an object of thought or an object of sense. It is only if being involves 'experience' that the question, whether it involves sensation or thought or both, becomes important. I beg, therefore, that *percipi* may be understood, in what follows, to refer merely to what is *common* to sensation and thought. A very recent article states the meaning of *esse* is *percipi* with all desirable clearness in so far as *percipi* is concerned. 'I will undertake to show,' says Mr. Taylor,[2] 'that what makes [any piece of fact] real can be nothing but its presence as an inseparable aspect of *a sentient experience*.' I am glad to think that Mr. Taylor has been in time to supply me with so definite a statement that this is the ultimate premiss of Idealism. My paper will at least refute Mr. Taylor's Idealism, if it refutes anything at all: for I *shall* undertake to show that what makes a thing real cannot possibly be its presence as an inseparable aspect of a sentient experience.

But Mr. Taylor's statement though clear, I think, with regard to

2. *International Journal of Ethics*, October, 1902.

the meaning of *percipi* is highly ambiguous in other respects. I will leave it for the present to consider the next ambiguity in the statement: *Esse* is *percipi*. What does the copula mean? What can be meant by saying that Esse *is* percipi? There are just three meanings, one or other of which such a statement *must* have, if it is to be true; and of these there is only one which it can have, if it is to be important. (1) The statement may be meant to assert that the word 'esse' is used to signify nothing either more or less than the word 'percipi': that the two words are precise synonyms: that they are merely different names for one and the same thing: that what is meant by *esse* is absolutely identical with what is meant by *percipi*. I think I need not prove that the principle *esse* is *percipi* is *not* thus intended merely to define a word; nor yet that, if it were, it would be extremely bad definition. But if it does *not* mean this, only two alternatives remain. The second is (2) that what is meant by *esse*, though not absolutely identical with what is meant by *percipi*, yet *includes* the latter as a *part* of its meaning. If this were the meaning of 'esse is percipi,' then to say that a thing was real would not be the same thing as to say that it was experienced. That it was *real* would mean that it was experienced and *something else besides*: 'being experienced' would be *analytically essential* to reality, but would not be the whole meaning of the term. From the fact that a thing was real we should be able to infer, by the law of contradiction, that it was experienced; since the latter would be *part* of what is meant by the former. But, on the other hand, from the fact a thing was experienced we should *not* be able to infer that it was real; since it would not follow from the fact that it had one of the attributes essential to reality, that it *also* had the other or others. Now, if we understand *esse* is *percipi* in this second sense, we must distinguish *three* different things which it asserts. First of all, it gives a definition of the word 'reality,' asserting that word stands for a complex whole, of which what is meant by 'percipi' forms a part. And secondly it asserts that 'being experienced' forms a part of a certain whole. Both these propositions may be true, and at all events I do not wish to dispute them. I do not, indeed, think that the word 'reality' is commonly used to include 'percipi': but I do not wish to argue about the meaning of words. And that many things which are experienced are also something else—that to be experienced forms part of certain wholes, is, of course, indisputable. But what I wish to point out is, that neither of these propositions is of any importance, unless we add to them a *third*. That 'real' is a convenient name for a union of attributes which *sometimes* occurs, it could not be worth any one's while to assert: no inferences of any importance could be drawn from such an assertion. Our principle could only mean that when a thing happens to have *percipi* as well as the other qualities included under *esse*, it has *percipi*: and we should never be able to *infer* that it was experienced, except from a proposition which already asserted that it was both experienced and something else. Accordingly, if the assertion that *percipi* forms part of the whole meant by reality is to have any importance, it must mean that the whole is organic, at least in this sense, that the other constituent or constituents of it *cannot* occur without percipi, even if percipi can occur without them. Let us call these other constituents *x*. The proposition that *esse* includes *percipi*, and that therefore from *esse percipi* can be inferred, can only be important if it is meant to assert that *percipi* can be inferred from *x*. The only importance of the question whether the whole *esse* includes the part *percipi* rests therefore on the question whether the part *x* is necessarily connected with the part *percipi*. And this is (3) the third possible meaning of the assertion *esse is percipi*: and, as we now see, the only important one. *Esse* is *percipi* asserts that wherever you have *x* you also have *percipi* that whatever has the property *x* also has the property that it is *experienced*. And this being so, it will be convenient if, for the future, I may be allowed to use the term '*esse*' to denote *x alone*. I do not wish thereby to beg the question whether what we commonly mean by the word 'real' does or does not include *percipi* as well as *x*. I am quite content that my definition of '*esse*' to denote *x*, should be regarded merely as an arbitrary verbal definition. Whether it is so or not, the only question of interest is whether from *x percipi* can be inferred, and I should prefer to be able to express this in the form: can *percipi* be inferred from *esse*? Only let it be understood that when I say *esse*, that term will not for the future *include percipi*: it denotes only that *x*, which Idealists, perhaps rightly include *along with percipi* under *their* term *esse*. That there is such an *x* they must admit on pain of making the proposition an *absolute* tautology; and that from this *x percipi* can be inferred they must admit, on pain of making it a perfectly barren analytic proposition. Whether *x* alone should or should not be called *esse* is not worth a dispute: what is worth dispute is whether *percipi* is necessarily connected with *x*.

We have therefore discovered the ambiguity of the copula in *esse* is *percipi*, so far as to see that this principle asserts two distinct terms to be so related, that whatever has the *one*, which I call *esse*, has *also* the property that it is experienced. It asserts a necessary connexion between *esse* on the one hand and *percipi* on the other; these two words denoting each a distinct term, and *esse* denoting a term in which that denoted by *percipi* is not included. We have, then in *esse* is *percipi*, a *necessary synthetic* proposition which I have undertaken to refute. And I may say at once that, understood as such, it cannot be refuted. If the Idealist chooses to assert that it is merely a self-evident truth, I have only to say that it does not appear to me to be so. But I believe that no Idealist ever has maintained it to be so. Although this—that two distinct terms are necessary related—is the only sense which 'esse is percipi' can have if it is to be true and important, it *can* have another sense, if it is to be an important falsehood. I believe that Idealists all hold this important falsehood. They do not perceive that *Esse* is *percipi* must, if true, be *merely* a self-evident synthetic truth; they either identify with it or give as a reason for it another proposition which must be false because it is self-contradictory. Unless they did so, they would have to admit that it was a perfectly unfounded assumption; and if they recognised that it was *unfounded*, I do not think they would maintain its truth to be evident. *Esse* is *percipi*, in the sense I have found for it, *may* indeed be true; I cannot refute it: but if this sense were clearly apprehended, no one, I think, would *believe* that it was true.

Idealists, we have seen, must assert that whatever is experienced, is *necessarily* so. And this doctrine they commonly express by saying that 'the object of experience is inconceivable apart from the subject.' I have hitherto been concerned with pointing out what meaning this assertion must have, if it is to be an important truth. I now propose to show that it may have an important meaning, which must be false, because it is self-contradictory.

It is a well-known fact in the history of philosophy that *necessary* truths in general, but especially those of which it is said that the opposite is inconceivable, have been commonly supposed to be *analytic*, in the sense that the proposition denying them was self-contradictory. It was in this way, commonly supposed, before Kant, that many truths could be proved by the law of contradiction alone. This is, therefore, a mistake which it is plainly easy for the best philosophers to make. Even since Kant many have continued to assert it; but I am aware that among those Idealists, who most properly deserve the name, it has become more fashionable to assert that truths are *both* analytic and synthetic. Now with many of their reasons for asserting this I am not concerned: it is possible that in some connexions the assertion may bear a useful and true sense. But if we understand 'analytic' in the sense just defined, namely, what is proved by the law of contradiction *alone*, it is plain that, if 'synthetic' means what is *not* proved by this alone, no truth can be both analytic and synthetic. Now it seems to me that those who do maintain truths to be both, do nevertheless maintain that they are so in this as well as in other senses. It is, indeed, extremely unlikely that so essential a part of the historical meaning of 'analytic' and 'synthetic' should have been entirely discarded, especially since we find no express recognition that it is discarded. In that case it is fair to suppose that modern Idealists have been influenced by the view that certain truths can be proved by the law of contradiction alone. I admit they also expressly declare that they can *not*: but this is by no means sufficient to prove that they do not also think they are; since it is very easy to hold two mutually contradictory opinions. What I suggest then is that Idealists hold the particular doctrine in question, concerning the relation of subject and object in experience, because they think it is an analytic truth in this restricted sense that it is proved by the law of contradiction alone.

I am suggesting that the Idealist maintains that object and subject are necessarily connected, mainly because he fails to see that they are *distinct*, that they are *two*, at all. When he thinks of 'yellow' and when he thinks of the 'sensation of yellow,' he fails to see that there is anything whatever in the latter which is not in the former. This being so, to deny that yellow can ever *be* apart from the sensation of yellow is merely to deny that yellow can ever be other than it is; since yellow and the sensation of yellow are absolutely identical. To assert that yellow is necessarily an object of experience is to assert that yellow is necessarily yellow—a purely identical proposition, and therefore proved by the law of contradiction alone. Of course, the proposition also implies that experience is, after all, something distinct from yellow—else there would be no reason for insisting that yellow is a sensation: and that the argument thus both affirms and denies that yellow and sensation of yellow are distinct, is what sufficiently refutes it. But this contradiction can easily be overlooked, because though we are convinced, in other connexions, that 'experience' does mean something and something most important, yet we are never distinctly aware *what* it means, and thus in every particular case we do not notice its presence. The facts present themselves as a kind of antinomy: (1) Experience *is* something unique and different from anything else; (2) Experience of green is entirely indistinguishable from green; two propositions which cannot both be true. Idealists, holding both, can only take refuge in arguing from the one in some connexions and from the other in others.

But I am well aware that there are many Idealists who would repel it as un utterly unfounded charge that they fail to distinguish between a sensation or idea and what I will call its object. And there are, I admit, many who not only imply, as we all do, that green is distinct from the sensation of green, but expressly insist upon the distinction as an important part of their system. They would perhaps only assert that the two form an inseparable unity. But I wish to point out that many, who use this phrase, and who do admit the distinction, are not thereby absolved from the charge that they deny it. For there is a certain doctrine, very prevalent among philosophers nowadays, which by a very simple reduction may be seen to assert that two distinct things both are and are not distinct. A distinction is asserted; but it is *also* asserted that the things distinguished form an 'organic unity.' But, forming such a unity, it is held, each would not be what it is *apart from its relation to the other*. Hence to consider either by itself is to make an *illegitimate abstraction*. The recognition that there are 'organic unities' and 'illegitimate abstractions' in this sense is regarded as one of the chief conquests of modern philosophy. But what is the sense attached to these terms? An abstraction is illegitimate, when and only when we attempt to assert of *a part*—of something abstracted—that which is true only of the *whole* to which it belongs: and it may perhaps be useful to point out that this should not be done. But the application actually made of this principle, and what perhaps would be expressly acknowledged as its meaning, is something much the reverse of useful. The principle is used to assert that certain abstractions are *in all cases* illegitimate; that whenever you try to assert *anything whatever* of that which is *part* of an organic whole, what you assert can only be true of the whole. And this principle, so far from being a useful truth, is necessarily false. For if the whole can, nay *must*, be substituted for the part in all propositions and for all purposes, this can only be because the whole is absolutely identical with the part. When, therefore, we are told that green and the sensation of green are certainly distinct but yet are not separable, or that it is an illegitimate abstraction to consider the one apart from the other, what these provisos are used to assert is, that though the two things are distinct yet you not only can but must treat them as if they were not. Many philosophers, therefore, when they admit a distinction, yet (following the lead of Hegel) boldly assert their right, in a slightly more obscure form of words, *also* to deny it. The principle of organic unities, like that of combined analysis and synthesis, is mainly used to defend the practice of holding *both* of two contradictory propositions, wherever this may seem convenient. In this, as in other matters, Hegel's main service to philosophy has consisted in giving a name to and erecting into a principle, a type of fallacy to which experience had shown philosophers, along with the rest of mankind, to be addicted. No wonder that he has followers and admirers.

I have shown then, so far, that when the Idealist asserts the important principle *'Esse* is *percipi'* he must, if it is to be true, mean by this that: Whatever is experienced also *must* be experienced. And I have also shown that he *may* identify with, or give as a reason for, this proposition, one which must be false, because it is self contradictory. But at this point I propose to make a complete break in my argument. *'Esse* is *percipi,'* we have seen, asserts of two terms, as distinct from one another as 'green' and 'sweet,' that whatever has the one has also the other: it asserts that 'being' and 'being experienced' are necessarily connected: that whatever *is* is *also* experienced. And this, I admit cannot be directly refuted. But I believe it to be false; and I have asserted that anybody who saw that *'esse* and *percipi' were* as distinct as 'green' and 'sweet' would be no more ready to believe that whatever *is* is *also* experienced, than to believe that whatever is green is also sweet. I have asserted that no one would believe that *'esse* is *percipi'* if they saw how different *esse* is from *percipi*: but *this* I shall not try to prove. I have asserted that all who do believe that *'esse* is *percipi'* identity with it or take as a reason for it a self-contradictory proposition: but this I shall not try to prove. I shall only try to show that certain propositions which I assert to be believed, are false. That they are believed, and that without this belief *'esse* is *percipi'* would not be believed either, I must leave without a proof.

I pass, then, from the uninteresting question Is *'esse percipi?'* to the still more uninteresting and apparently irrelevant question 'What is a sensation or idea?'

We all know that the sensation of blue differs from that of green. But it is plain that if both are *sensations* they also have some point in common. What is it that they have in common? And how is this common element related to the points in which they differ?

I will call the common element 'consciousness' without yet attempting to say what the thing I so call *is*. We have then in every sensation two distinct terms, (1) 'consciousness,' in respect of which all sensations are alike; and (2) something else, in respect of which one sensation differs from another. It will be convenient if I may be allowed to call this second term the 'object' of a sensation: this also without yet attempting to say what I mean by the word.

We have then in every sensation two distinct elements, one which I call consciousness, and another which I call the object of consciousness. This must be so if the sensation of blue and the sensation of green, though different in one respect, are alike in another: blue is one object of sensation and green is another, and consciousness, which both sensations have in common, is different from either.

But, further, sometimes the sensation of blue exists in my mind and sometimes it does not; and knowing, as we now do, that the sensation of blue includes two different elements, namely consciousness and blue, the question arises whether, when the sensation of blue exists, it is the consciousness which exists, or the blue which exists, or both. And one point at least is plain: namely that these three alternatives are all different from one another. So that, if any one tells us that to say 'Blue exists' is the *same* thing as to say that 'Both blue and consciousness exist,' he makes a mistake and a self-contradictory mistake.

But another point is also plain, namely, that when the sensation exists, the consciousness, at least, certainly does exist; for when I say that the sensations of blue and of green both exist, I certainly mean that what is common to both and in virtue of which both are called sensations, exists in each case. The only alternative left, then, is that *either* both exist or the consciousness exists alone. If, therefore, any one tell us that the existence of blue is the same thing as the existence of the sensation of blue he makes a mistake and a self-contradictory mistake, for he asserts *either* that blue is the same thing as blue together with consciousness, *or* that it is the same thing as consciousness alone.

Accordingly to identify either "blue" or any other of what I have called "*objects*" of sensation, with the corresponding sensation is in every case, a self-contradictory error. It is to identify a part either with the whole of which it is a part or else with the other part of the same whole. If we are told that the assertion "Blue exists" is *meaningless* unless we mean by it that "The sensation of blue exists," we are told what is certainly false and self-contradictory. If we are told that the existence of blue is inconceivable apart from the existence of the sensation, the speaker *probably* means to convey to us, by this ambiguous expression, what is a self-contradictory error. For we can and must conceive the existence of blue as something quite distinct from the existence of the sensation. We can and must conceive that blue might exist and yet the sensation of blue not exist. For my own part I not only conceive this, but conceive it to be true. Either therefore this terrific assertion of inconceivability means what is false and self-contradictory or else it means only that *as a matter of fact* blue never can exist unless the sensation of it exists also.

And at this point I need not conceal my opinion that no philosopher has ever yet succeeded in avoiding this self-contradictory error: that the most striking results both of Idealism and of Agnosticism are only obtained by identifying blue with the sensation of blue: that *esse* is held to be *percipi*, solely because *what is experienced* is held to be identical with *the experience of it*. That Berkeley and Mill committed this error will, perhaps, be granted: that modern Idealists make it will, I hope, appear more probable later. But that my opinion is plausible, I will now offer two pieces of evidence. The first is that language offers us no means of referring to such objects as "blue" and "green" and "sweet," except by calling them sensations: it is an obvious violation of language to call them "things" or "objects" or "terms." And similarly we have no natural means of referring to such objects as "causality" or "likeness" or "identity," except by calling them "ideas" or "notions" or "conceptions." But it is hardly likely that if philosophers had clearly distinguished in the past between a sensation or idea and what I have called its object, there should have been no separate name for the latter. They have always used the same name for these two different "things" (if I may call them so): and hence there is some probability that they have supposed these "things" *not* to be two and different, but one and the same. And, secondly, there is a very good reason why they should have supposed so, in the fact that when we refer to introspection and try to discover what the sensation of blue is, it is very easy to suppose that we have before us only a single term. The term "blue" is easy enough to distinguish, but the other element which I have called "consciousness"—that which sensation of blue has in common with sensation of green—is extremely difficult to fix. That many people fail to distinguish it at all is sufficiently shown by the fact that there are materialists. And, in general, that which makes the sensation of blue a mental fact seems to escape us: it seems, if I may use a metaphor, to be transparent—we look through it and see nothing but the blue; we may be convinced that there *is something* but *what* it is no philosopher, I think, has yet clearly recognised.

But this was a digression. The point I had established so far was that in every sensation or idea we must distinguish two elements, (1) the "object," or that in which one differs from another; and (2) "consciousness," or that which all have in common—that which makes them sensations or mental facts. This being so, it followed that when a sensation or idea exists, we have to choose between the alternatives that either object alone, or consciousness alone, or both, exist; and I showed that of these alternatives one, namely that the object only exists, is excluded by the fact that what we mean to assert is certainly the existence of a mental fact. There remains the question: Do both exist? Or does the consciousness alone? And to this question one answer has hitherto been given universally: That both exist.

This answer follows from the analysis hitherto accepted of the relation of what I have called "object" to "consciousness" in any sensation or idea. It is held that what I call the object is merely the "content" of a sensation or idea. It is held that in each case we can distinguish two elements and two only, (1) the fact that there is feeling or experience and (2) *what* is felt or experienced; the sensation or idea, it is said forms a whole, in which we must distinguish two "inseparable aspects," "content" and "existence." I shall try to show that this analysis is false; and for that purpose I must ask what may seem an extraordinary question: namely what is meant by saying that one thing is "content" of another? It is not usual to ask this question; the term is used as if everybody must understand it. But since I am going to maintain that "blue" is *not* the content of the sensation of blue, and what is more important, that, even if it were this analysis would leave out the most important element in the sensation of blue, it is necessary that I should try to explain precisely what it is that I shall deny.

What then is meant by saying that one thing is the "content" of another? First of all I wish to point out that "blue" is rightly and properly said to be part of the content of a blue flower. If, therefore we also assert that it is part of the content of the sensation of blue, we assert that it has to the other parts (if any) of this whole the same relation which it has to the other parts of a blue flower—and we assert only this: we cannot mean to assert that it has to the sensation of blue any relation which it does not have to the blue flower. And we have seen that the sensation of blue contains at least one other element beside blue—namely, what I call "consciousness," which makes it a sensation. So far then as we assert that blue is the content of the sensation, we assert that it has to this "consciousness" the same relation which it has to the other parts of a blue flower: we do assert this, and we assert no more than this. Into the question what exactly the relation is between blue and a blue flower in virtue of which we call the former part of its "content" I do not propose to enter. It is sufficient for my purpose to point out that it is the general relation most commonly meant when we talk of a thing and its qualities; and that this relation is such that to say the thing exists implies that the qualities also exist. The *content* of the thing is *what* we assert to exist, when we assert *that* the thing exists.

When, therefore, blue is said to be part of the content of the "sensation of blue," the latter is treated as if it were a whole constituted in exactly the same way as any other "thing." The "sensation of blue," on this view, differs from a blue bead or a blue beard, in exactly the same way in which the two latter differ from one another: the blue bead differs from the blue beard, in that while the former contains glass, the latter contains hair; and the "sensation of blue" differs from both in that, instead of glass or hair, it contains consciousness. The relation of the blue to the consciousness is conceived to be exactly the same as that of the blue to the glass or hair: it is in all three cases the *quality* of a *thing*.

But I said just now that the sensation of blue was analysed into "content" and "existence," and that blue was said to be *the* content of the idea of blue. There is an ambiguity in this and a possible error, which I must note in passing. The term "content" may be used in two senses. If we use "content" as equivalent to what Mr. Bradley calls the *"what"*—if we mean by it the *whole* of what is said to exist, when the thing is said to exist, then blue is certainly not *the* content of the sensation of blue: part of the *content* of the sensation is, in this sense of the term, that other element which I have called consciousness. The analysis of this sensation into the "content" "blue," on the one hand, and mere existence on the other, is therefore certainly false; in it we have again the self-contradictory identification of "Blue exists" with "The sensation of blue exists." But there is another sense in which "blue" might properly be said to be *the* content of the sensation— namely, the sense in which "content," like εἰδος, is opposed to "substance" or "matter." For the element "consciousness," being common to all sensations, may be and certainly is regarded as in some sense their "substance," and by the "content" of each is only meant that in respect of which one differs from another. In this sense then "blue" might be said to be *the* content of the sensation; but, in that case, the analysis into "content" and "existence" is, at least, misleading, since under "existence" must be included *"what* exists" in the sensation other than blue.

We have it, then, as a universally received opinion that blue is related to the sensation or idea of blue, as its *content*, and that this view, if it is to be true, must mean that blue is part of *what* is said to exist when we say that the sensation exists. To say that the sensation exists is to say both that blue exists and that "consciousness," whether we call it the substance of which blue is *the* content or call it another part of the content, exists too. Any sensation or idea is a *"thing,"* and what I have called its object is the quality of this thing. Such a "thing" is what we think of when we think of a *mental image*. A mental image is conceived as if it were related to that of which it is the image (if there be any such thing) in exactly the same way as the image in a looking-glass is related to that of which it is the reflection; in both cases there is identity of content, and the image in the looking-glass differs from that in the mind solely in respect of the fact that in the one case the other constituent of the image is "glass" and in the other case it is consciousness. If the image is of blue, it is not conceived that this "content" has any relation to the consciousness but what it has to the glass: it is conceived *merely* to be its *content*. And owing to the fact that sensations and ideas are all considered to be *wholes* of this description—things in the mind—the question: What do we know? is considered to be identical with the question: What reason have we for supposing that there are things outside the mind *corresponding* to these that are inside it?

What I wish to point out is (1) that we have no reason for supposing that there are such things as mental images at all—for supposing that blue *is* part of the content of the sensation of blue, and (2) that even if there are mental images, no mental image and no sensation or idea is *merely* a thing of this kind: that 'blue,' even if it is part of the content of the image or sensation or idea of blue, is always *also* related to it in quite another way, and that this other relation, omitted in the traditional analysis, is the *only* one which makes the sensation of blue a mental fact at all.

The true analysis of a sensation or idea is as follows. The element that is common to them all, and which I have called 'consciousness,' really *is* consciousness. A sensation is, in reality, a case of 'knowing' or 'being aware of' or 'experiencing' something. When we know that the sensation of blue exists, the fact we know is that there exists an awareness of blue. And this awareness is not merely, as we have hitherto seen it must be, itself something distinct and unique, utterly different from blue: it also has a perfectly distinct and unique relation to blue, a relation which is *not* that of thing or substance to content, nor of one part of content to another part of content. This relation is just that which we mean in every case by 'knowing.' To have in your mind 'knowledge' of blue, is *not* to have in your mind a 'thing' or 'image' of which blue is the content. To be aware of the sensation of blue is *not* to be aware of a mental image—of a 'thing,' of which 'blue' and some other element are constituent parts in the same sense in which blue and glass are constituents of a blue bead. It is to be aware of an awareness of blue; awareness being used, in both cases, in exactly the same sense. This element, we have seen, is certainly neglected by the 'content' theory: that theory entirely fails to express the fact that there is, in the sensation of blue, this unique relation between blue and the other constituent. And what I contend is that this omission is *not* mere negligence of expression, but is due to the fact that though philosophers have recognised that *something* distinct is meant by consciousness, they have never yet had a clear conception of *what* that something is. They have not been able to hold *it* and *blue* before their minds and to compare them, in the same way in which they can compare *blue* and *green*. And this for the reason I gave above: namely that the moment we try to fix our attention upon consciousness and to see *what*, distinctly, it is, it seems to vanish: it seems as if we had before us a mere emptiness. When we try to introspect the sensation of blue, all we can see is the blue: the other element is as if it were diaphanous. Yet it *can* be distinguished if we look attentively enough, and if we know that there is something to look for. My main object in this paragraph has been to try to make the reader *see* it; but I fear I shall have succeeded very ill.

It being the case, then, that the sensation of blue includes in its analysis, beside blue, *both* a unique element 'awareness' *and* a unique relation of this element to blue, I can make plain what I meant by asserting, as two distinct propositions, (1) that blue is probably not part of the content of the sensation at all, and (2) that, even it were, the sensation would nevertheless not be the sensation *of* blue, if blue had only this relation to it. The first hypothesis may now be expressed by saying that, if it were true, then, when the sensation of blue exists, there exists a *blue awareness*: offence may be taken at the expression, but yet it expresses just what should be and is meant by saying that blue is, in this case, a *content* of consciousness or experience. Whether or not, when I have the sensation of blue, my consciousness or awareness is thus blue, my introspection does not enable me to decide with certainty: I only see no reason for thinking that it is. But whether it is or not, the point is unimportant, for introspection *does* enable me to decide that something else is also true: namely that I am aware *of* blue, and by this I mean, that my awareness has to blue a quite different and distinct relation. It is possible, I admit, that my awareness is blue *as well* as being *of* blue: but what I am quite sure of is that it is *of* blue; that it has to blue the simple and unique relation the existence of which alone justifies us in distinguishing knowledge of a thing from the thing known, indeed in distinguishing mind from matter. And this result I may express by saying that what is called the *content* of a sensation is in very truth what I originally called it—the sensation's *object*.

But, if all this be true, what follows?

Idealists admit that some things really exist of which they are not aware: there are some things, they hold, which are not inseparable aspects of *their* experience, even if they be inseparable aspects of some experience. They further hold that some of the things of which they are sometimes aware do really exist, even when they are not aware of them: they hold for instance that they are sometimes aware of other

minds, which continue to exist even when they are not aware of them.
They are, therefore, sometimes aware of something which is *not* an
inseparable aspect of their own experience. They do *know some* things
which are *not* a mere part or content of their experience. And what my
analysis of sensation has been designed to show is, that whenever I
have a mere sensation or idea, the fact is that I am then aware of
something which is equally and in the same sense *not* an inseparable
aspect of my experience. The awareness which I have maintained to be
included in sensation is the very same unique fact which constitutes
every kind of knowledge: "blue" is as much an object, and as little a
mere content, of my experience, when I experience it, as the most
exalted and independent real thing of which I am ever aware. There is,
therefore, no question of how we are to "get outside the circle of our
own ideas and sensations." Merely to have a sensation is already to *be*
outside that circle. It is to know something which is as truly and really
not a part of my experience, as anything which I can ever know.

Now I think I am not mistaken in asserting that the reason why
Idealists suppose that everything which *is* must be an inseparable aspect
of some experience, is that they suppose some things, at least, to be
inseparable aspects of *their* experience. And there is certainly nothing
which they are so firmly convinced to be an inseparable aspect of their
experience as what they call the *content* of their ideas and sensations.
If, therefore, *this* turns out in every case, whether it be also the content or not, to be at least *not* an inseparable aspect of the experience of
it, it will be readily admitted that nothing else which *we* experience
ever is such an inseparable aspect. But if we never experience anything
but what is *not* an inseparable aspect of *that* experience, how can we
infer that anything whatever, let alone *everything*, is an inseparable
aspect of *any* experience? How utterly unfounded is the assumption
that "*esse* is *percipi*" appears in the clearest light.

But further I think it may be seen that if the object of an Idealist's
sensation were, as he supposes, *not* the object but merely the content
of that sensation, if, that is to say, it really were an inseparable aspect
of his experience, each Idealist could never be aware either of himself
or of any other real thing. For the relation of a sensation to its object
is certainly the same as that of any other instance of experience to its
object; and this, I think, is generally admitted even by Idealists: they
state as readily that *what is* judged or thought or perceived is the *content* of that judgment or thought or perception, as that blue is the
content of the sensation of blue. But, if so, then when any Idealist
thinks he is *aware* of himself or of any one else, this cannot really be
the case. The fact is, on his own theory, that himself and that other

person are in reality mere *contents* of an awareness, which is aware *of* nothing whatever. All that can be said is that there is an awareness in him, *with* a certain content: it can never be true that there is in him a consciousness *of* anything. And similarly he is never aware either of the fact that he exists or that reality is spiritual. The real fact, which he describes in those terms, is that his existence and the spirituality of reality are *contents* of an awareness, which is aware of nothing—certainly not, then, of its own content.

And further if everything, of which he thinks he is aware, is in reality merely a content of his own experience he has certainly no *reason* for holding that anything does exist except himself: it will, of course, be possible that other persons do exist; solipsism will not be necessarily true; but he cannot possibly infer from anything he holds that it is not true. That he himself exists will of course follow from his premiss that many things are contents of *his* experience. But since everything, of which he thinks himself aware, is in reality merely an inseparable aspect of that awareness; this premiss allows no inference that any of these contents far less any other consciousness, exists at all except as an inseparable aspect of his awareness, that is, as part of himself.

Such, and not those which he takes to follow from it, are the consequences which *do* follow from the Idealist's supposition that the object of an experience is in reality merely a content or inseparable aspect of that experience. If, on the other hand, we clearly recognise the nature of that peculiar relation which I have called "awareness of anything"; if we see that *this* is involved equally in the analysis of *every* experience—from the merest sensation to the most developed perception or reflexion, and that *this* is in fact the only essential element in an experience—the only thing that is both common and peculiar to all experiences—the only thing which gives us reason to call any fact mental; if, further, we recognise that this awareness is and must be in all cases of such a nature that its object, when we are aware of it, is precisely what it would be, if we were not aware: then it becomes plain that the existence of a table in space is related to my experience of *it* in precisely the same way as the existence of my own experience is related to my experience of *that*. Of both we are merely aware: if we are aware that the one exists, we are aware in precisely the same sense that the other exists; and if it is true that my experience can exist, even when I do not happen to be aware of its existence, we have exactly the same reason for supposing that the table can do so also. When, therefore, Berkeley, supposed that the only thing of which I am directly aware is my own sensations and ideas, he supposed what was false; and when Kant supposed that the objectivity of things in space *consisted* in the fact that they were "Vorstellungen" having to one another different relations from those which the same "Vorstellungen" have to one another in subjective experience, he supposed what was equally false. I am as directly aware of the existence of material things in space as of my own sensations; and *what* I am aware of with regard to each is exactly the same—namely that in one case the material thing, and in the other case my sensation does really exist. The question requiring to be asked about material things is thus not: What reason have we for supposing that anything exists *corresponding* to our sensations? but: What reason have we for supposing that material things do *not* exist, since *their* existence has precisely the same evidence as that of our sensations? That either exist *may* be false; but if it is a reason for doubting the existence of matter, that it is an inseparable aspect of our experience, the same reasoning will prove conclusively that our experience does not exist either, since that must also be an inseparable aspect of our experience of *it*. The only *reasonable* alternative to the admission that matter exists *as well* as spirit, is absolute Scepticism—that, as likely as not *nothing* exists at all. All other suppositions—the Agnostic's, that something, at all events, does exist, as much as the Idealist's, that spirit does—are, if we have no reason for believing in matter, as baseless as the grossest superstitions.

II

BERTRAND RUSSELL

BERTRAND RUSSELL (*b.* 1872) descends from a titled family. His parents were Lord and Lady Amberley and his grandfather, Lord, later Earl, Russell, was prime minister for many years. Orphaned at the age of three, he was reared in the home of his grandparents where he was privately tutored. When he was twelve his grandmother presented him with a Bible in which she wrote on the flyleaf: "Thou shalt not follow a multitude to do evil" and "Be strong, and of a good courage; be not afraid, neither be Thou dismayed; for the Lord Thy God is with thee withersoever thou goest." These two biblical texts, Russell wrote, "have profoundly influenced my life, and still seemed to retain some meaning after I ceased to believe in God."

When Russell was eighteen he went up to Cambridge where, amidst such luminaries as Whitehead, McTaggart, and Moore, he read mostly in mathematics. From 1894 to the present, he has oscillated between the social concerns of the day and the perennial delights of philosophy. Besides lecturing in or visiting all the major countries of the world, and writing many books on history, sociology, and even of fiction, he has contributed some of the most important works in philosophy in the twentieth century (*see* Bibliography). He is a Fellow of the Royal Society and a recipient of the Order of Merit, and in 1950 he was awarded the Nobel Prize for Literature. More recently his central concern has been nuclear disarmament. But probably more than anything else, Russell has been and remains "the passionate sceptic," dogmatically dedicated to absolute truth and transient humanity.

Contemporary philosophical Realism, as initiated by Moore and Russell, is as much characterized by a metaphysical dualism of universals and particulars as it is by its dualism of mind and matter. Motivated mostly by the need to render mathematical truth independent of the mind or the spatio temporal world, Russell resuscitated the Platonic doctrine of the inde pendent subsistence of a realm of universals. His classic statement of his Platonism is in *The Problems of Philosophy* (1912). His most brilliant defence of his dualism of universals and particulars, however, is his essay "On the Relations of Universals and Particulars" (1911). It should be added that Russell subsequently changed his mind on this, as on a great many other philosophical issues.

On the Relations of Universals and Particulars[1,2]

The purpose of the following paper is to consider whether there is a fundamental division of the objects with which metaphysics is concerned into two classes, universals and particulars, or whether there is any method of overcoming this dualism. My own opinion is that the dualism is ultimate; on the other hand, many men with whom, in the main, I am in close agreement, hold that it is not ultimate. I do not feel the grounds in favour of its ultimate nature to be very conclusive, and in what follows I should lay stress rather on the distinctions and considerations introduced during the argument than on the conclusion at which the argument arrives.

It is impossible to begin our discussion with sharp definitions of universals and particulars, though we may hope to reach such definitions in the end. At the beginning, we can only roughly indicate the kind of facts that we wish to analyse and the kind of distinctions that we wish to examine. There are several cognate distinctions which produce confusion by intermingling, and which it is important to disentangle before advancing into the heart of our problem.

The first distinction that concerns us is the distinction between percepts and concepts, i.e., between objects of acts of perception and objects of acts of conception. If there is a distinction between particulars and universals, percepts will be among particulars, while concepts will be among universals. Opponents of universals, such as

1. Presidential Address, Aristotelian Society, 1911; published in *Proceedings of the Aristotelian Society*, 1911-12; reprinted from: R. C. Marsh (ed.), *Logic and Knowledge* (London: George Allen & Unwin, Ltd., 1956), pp. 105-24. Reprinted by permission of George Allen & Unwin, Ltd., London.

2. The thesis of the present paper is closely similar to that of Mr. Moore's paper 'Identity,' read before this Society in 1900-1901. My chief reason for thinking that the question demands a fresh discussion is that the statement of the grounds for the thesis appears to require some examination of the nature of sensible space as opposed to physical space.

37

Berkeley and Hume, will maintain that concepts are derivable from
percepts, as faint copies, or in some other way. Opponents of particulars will maintain that the apparent particularity of percepts is
illusory, and that, though the act of perception may differ from the
act of conception, yet its objects differ only by their greater complexity,
and are really composed of constituents which are, or might be, concepts.

But the distinction of percepts and concepts is too psychological
for an ultimate metaphysical distinction. Percepts and concepts are
respectively the relata of two different relations, perception and conception, and there is nothing in their definitions to show whether, or
how, they differ. Moreover, the distinction of percepts and concepts,
in itself, is incapable of being extended to entities which are not
objects of cognitive acts. Hence we require some other distinction
expressing the intrinsic difference which we seem to feel between
percepts and concepts.

A cognate distinction, which effects part at least of what we want,
is the distinction between things which exist in time and things which
do not. In order to avoid any question as to whether time is relative
or absolute, we may say that an entity x 'exists in time' provided x
is not itself a moment or part of time, and some such proposition
as 'x is before y or simultaneous with y or after y' is true of x. (It
is not to be assumed that *before, simultaneous*, and *after* are mutually
exclusive: if x has duration, they will not be so.) Prima facie, a percept
exists in time, in the above sense, while a concept does not. The
object of perception is simultaneous with the act of perception, while
the object of conception seems indifferent to the time of conceiving
and to all time. Thus, prima facie, we have here the non-psychological
distinction of which we were in search. But the same controversies
will break out as in the case of percepts and concepts. The man who
reduces concepts to percepts will say that nothing is really out of
time, and that the appearance of this in the case of concepts is illusory.
The man who reduces percepts to concepts may either, like most
idealists, deny that anything is in time, or, like some realists, maintain
that concepts can and do exist in time.

In addition to the above distinction as regards time, there is a
distinction as regards space which, as we shall find, is very important
in connexion with our present question. Put as vaguely as possible,
this is a distinction which divides entities into three classes: (a) those
which are not in any place, (b) those which are in one place at one
time, but never in more than one, (c) those which are in many places
at once. To make this threefold division precise, we should have to

discuss what we mean by a place, what we mean by 'in,' and how the different kinds of space—visual, tactile, physical—produce different forms of this threefold division. For the present I will merely illustrate what I mean by examples. Relations, obviously, do not exist anywhere in space. Our bodies, we think, exist in one place at a time, but not in more than one. General qualities, such as whiteness, on the contrary, may be said to be in many places at once: we may say, in a sense, that whiteness is in every place where there is a white thing. This division of entities will be discussed later; for the present I merely wish to indicate that it requires examination.

In addition to the above psychological and metaphysical distinctions, there are two logical distinctions which are relevant in the present enquiry. In the first place, there is the distinction between relations and entities which are not relations. It has been customary for philosophers to ignore or reject relations, and speak as if all entities were either subjects or predicates. But this custom is on the decline, and I shall assume without further argument that there are such entities as relations. Philosophy has, so far as I know, no common name for all entities which are not relations. Among such entities are included not only all the things that would naturally be called particulars, but also all the universals that philosophers are in the habit of considering when they discuss the relation of particulars to universals, for universals are generally conceived as common properties of particulars, in fact, as predicates. For our purpose it is hardly worth while to invent a technical term *ad hoc*; I shall therefore speak of entities which are not relations simply as *non-relations*.

The second logical distinction which we require is one which may or may not be identical in extension with that between relations and non-relations, but is certainly not identical in intention. It may be expressed as the distinction between verbs and substantives, or, more correctly, between the objects denoted by verbs and the objects denoted by substantives.[3] (Since this more correct expression is long and cumbrous, I shall generally use the shorter phrase to mean the same thing. Thus, when I speak of verbs, I mean the objects denoted by verbs, and similarly for substantives.) The nature of this distinction emerges from the analysis of complexes. In most complexes, if not in all, a certain number of different entities are combined into a single entity by means of a relation. '*A*'s hatred for *B*', for example, is a complex in which *hatred* combines *A* and *B* into one whole; '*C*'s belief

3. This is the distinction which I formerly spoke of as the distinction between *things* and *concepts,* but these terms no longer seem to me appropriate. Cf. *Principles of Mathematics,* §48.

that *A hates B'* is a complex in which *belief* combines *A* and *B* and *C* and hatred into one whole, and so on. A relation is distinguished as dual, triple, quadruple, etc., or dyadic, triadic, tetradic, etc., according to the number of terms which it unites in the simplest complexes in which it occurs. Thus in the above examples, hatred is a dual relation and belief is a quadruple relation. The capacity for combining terms into a single complex is the defining characteristic of what I call *verbs*. The question now arises: Are there complexes which consist of a single term and a verb? *'A* exists' might serve as an example of what is possibly such a complex. It is the possibility that there may be complexes of this kind which makes it impossible to decide off-hand that verbs are the same as relations. There may be verbs which are philosophically as well as grammatically intransitive. Such verbs, if they exist, may be called *predicates*, and the propositions in which they are attributed may be called subject-predicate propositions.

If there are no such verbs as those whose possibility we have been considering, i.e., if all verbs are relations, it will follow that subject-predicate propositions, if there are any, will express a *relation* of subject to predicate. Such propositions will then be definable as those that involve a certain relation called *predication*. Even if there are subject-predicate propositions in which the predicate is the verb, there will still be equivalent propositions in which the predicate is related to the subject; thus *'A exists,'* for example, will be equivalent to *'A* has existence.' Hence the question whether predicates are verbs or not becomes unimportant. The more important question is whether there is a specific relation of predication, or whether what are grammatically subject-predicate propositions are really of many different kinds, no one of which has the characteristics one naturally associates with subject-predicate propositions. This question is one to which we shall return at a later stage.

The above logical distinctions are relevant to our enquiry because it is natural to regard particulars as entities which can only be subjects or terms of relations, and cannot be predicates or relations. A particular is naturally conceived as a *this* or something intrinsically analogous to a *this*; and such an entity seems incapable of being a predicate or a relation. A universal, on this view, will be anything that is a predicate or a relation. But if there is no specific relation of predication, so that there is no class of entities which can properly be called predicates, then the above method of distinguishing particulars and universals fails. The question whether philosophy must recognize two ultimately distinct kinds of entities, particulars and universals, turns, as we shall see more fully later on, on the question whether non-relations are of two kinds, subjects and predicates, or rather terms which can only be subjects and terms which may be either subjects or predicates. And this question turns on whether there is an ultimate simple asymmetrical relation which may be called predication, or whether all apparent subject-predicate propositions are to be analysed into propositions of other forms, which do not require a radical difference of nature between the apparent subject and the apparent predicate.

The decision of the question whether there is a simple relation of predication ought perhaps to be possible by inspection, but for my part I am unable to come to any decision in this way. I think, however, that it can be decided in favour of predication by the analysis of *things* and by considerations as to spatio-temporal diversity. This analysis and these considerations will also show the way in which our purely logical question is bound up with the other questions as to particulars and universals which I raised at the beginning of this paper.

The common-sense notion of things and their qualities is, I suppose, the source of the conception of subject and predicate, and the reason why language is so largely based on this conception. But the thing, like other common-sense notions, is a piece of half-hearted metaphysics, which neither gives crude data nor gives a tenable hypothesis as to a reality behind the data. A thing, of the everyday sort, is constituted by a bundle of sensible qualities belonging to various senses, but supposed all to coexist in one continuous portion of space. But the common space which should contain both visual and tactile qualities is not the space of either visual or tactile perception: it is a constructed 'real' space, belief in which has, I suppose, been generated by association. And in crude fact, the visual and tactile qualities of which I am sensible are not in a common space, but each in its own space. Hence if the thing is to be impartial as between sight and touch, it must cease to have the actual qualities of which we are sensible, and become their common cause or origin or whatever vaguer word can be found. Thus the road is opened to the metaphysical theories of science and to the metaphysical theories of philosophy: the thing may be a number of electric charges in rapid motion, or an idea in the mind of God, but it is certainly not what the senses perceive.

The argument against things is trite, and I need not labour it. I introduce it here only in order to illustrate a consequence which is sometimes overlooked. Realists who reject particulars are apt to regard a thing as reducible to a number of qualities coexisting in one place. But, apart from other objections to this view, it is doubtful whether the different qualities in question ever do coexist in one place.

If the qualities are sensible, the place must be in a sensible space; but this makes it necessary that the qualities should belong to only one sense, and it is not clear that genuinely different qualities belonging to one sense ever coexist in a single place in a perceptual space. If, on the other hand, we consider what may be called 'real' space, i.e. the inferred space containing the 'real' objects which we suppose to be the causes of our perceptions, then we no longer know what is the nature of the qualities, if any, which exist in this 'real' space, and it is natural to replace the bundle of. qualities by a collection of pieces of matter having whatever characteristics the science of the moment may prescribe. Thus in any case the bundle of coexisting qualities in the same place is not an admissible substitute for the thing.

For our purposes, the 'real' object by which science or philosophy replaces the thing is not important. We have rather to consider the relations of sensible objects in a single sensible space, say that of sight.

The theory of sensible qualities which dispenses with particulars will say, if the same shade of colour is found in two different places, that what exists is the shade of colour itself, and that what exists in the one place is identical with what exists in the other. The theory which admits particulars will say, on the contrary, that two numerically different *instances* of the shade of colour exist in the two places: in this view, the shade of colour itself is a universal and a predicate of both the instances, but the universal does not exist in space and time. Of the above two views, the first, which does not introduce particulars, dispenses altogether with predication as a fundamental relation: according to this view, when we say 'this thing is white,' the fundamental fact is that whiteness exists here. According to the other view, which admits particulars, what exists here is something of which whiteness is a predicate—not, as for common sense, the thing with many other qualities, but an instance of whiteness, a particular of which whiteness is the only predicate except shape and brightness and whatever else is necessarily connected with whiteness.

Of the above two theories, one admits only what would naturally be called universals, while the other admits both universals and particulars. Before examining them, it may be as well to examine and dismiss the theory which admits only particulars, and dispenses altogether with universals. This is the theory advocated by Berkeley and Hume in their polemic against 'abstract ideas.' Without tying ourselves down to their statements, let us see what can be made of this theory. The general name 'white,' in this view, is defined for a given person at a given moment by a particular patch of white which he sees or imagines; another patch is called white if it has exact likeness in colour to the standard patch. In order to avoid making the colour a universal, we have to suppose that 'exact likeness' is a simple relation, not analysable into community of predicates; moreover, it is not the general relation of likeness that we require, but a more special relation, that of colour-likeness, since two patches might be exactly alike in shape or size but different in colour. Thus, in order to make the theory of Berkeley and Hume workable, we must assume an ultimate relation of colour-likeness, which holds between two patches which would commonly be said to have the same colour. Now, prima facie, this relation of colour-likeness will itself be a universal or an 'abstract idea,' and thus we shall still have failed to avoid universals. But we may apply the same analysis to colour-likeness. We may take a standard particular case of colour-likeness, and say that anything else is to be called a colour-likeness if it is exactly like our standard case. It is obvious, however, that such a process leads to an endless regress: we explain the likeness of two terms as consisting in the likeness which their likeness bears to the likeness of two other terms, and such a regress is plainly vicious. Likeness at least, therefore, must be admitted as a universal, and, having admitted one universal, we have no longer any reason to reject others. Thus the whole complicated theory, which had no motive except to avoid universals, falls to the ground. Whether or not there are particulars, there must be relations which are universals in the sense that (a) they are concepts, not percepts; (b) they do not exist in time; (c) they are verbs, not substantives.

It is true that the above argument does not prove that there are universal qualities as opposed to universal relations. On the contrary, it shows that universal qualities *can*, so far as logic can show, be replaced by exact likeness of various kinds between particulars. This view has, so far as I know, nothing to recommend it beyond its logical possibility. But from the point of view of the problem whether there are particulars, it has no bearing on the argument. It is a view which is only possible if there are particulars, and it demands only an easy re-statement of subject-predicate propositions: instead of saying that an entity has such and such a predicate, we shall have to say that there are entities to which it has such and such a specific likeness. I shall therefore in future ignore this view, which in any case assumes our main thesis, namely, the existence of particulars. To the grounds in favour of this thesis we must now return.

When we endeavoured to state the two theories as to sensible qualities, we had occasion to consider two white patches. On the view which denies particulars, whiteness itself exists in both patches: a numerically single entity, whiteness, exists in all places that are white.

Nevertheless, we speak of *two* white patches, and it is obvious that, in some sense, the patches are two, not one. It is this spatial plurality which makes the difficulty of the theory that denies particulars.

Without attempting, as yet, to introduce all the necessary explanations and distinctions, we may state the argument for particulars roughly as follows. It is logically possible for two exactly similar patches of white, of the same size and shape, to exist simultaneously in different places. Now, whatever may be the exact meaning of 'existing in different places,' it is self-evident that, in such a case, there are two different patches of white. Their diversity might, if we adopted the theory of absolute position, be regarded as belonging. not to the white itself which exists in the two places, but to the complexes 'whiteness in this place' and 'whiteness in that place.' This would derive their diversity from the diversity of this place and that place; and since places cannot be supposed to differ as to qualities, this would require that the places should be particulars. But if we reject absolute position, it will become impossible to distinguish the two patches as two, unless each, instead of being the universal whiteness, is an *instance* of whiteness. It might be thought that the two might be distinguished by means of other qualities in the same place as the one but not in the same place as the other. This, however, presupposes that the two patches are already distinguished as numerically diverse, since otherwise what is in the same place as the one must be in the same place as the other. Thus the fact that it is logically possible for precisely similar things to coexist in two different places, but that things in different places at the same time cannot be numerically identical, forces us to admit that it is particulars, i.e., *instances* of universals, that exist in places, and not universals themselves.

The above is the outline of our argument. But various points in it have to be examined and expanded before it can be considered conclusive. In the first place, it is not necessary to assert that there ever are two exactly similar existents. It is only necessary to perceive that our judgment that this and that are two different existents is not necessarily based on any difference of qualities, but may be based on difference of spatial position alone; and that difference of qualities, whether or not it always in fact accompanies numerical difference, is not logically necessary in order to insure numerical difference where there is difference of spatial position.

Again, it is not easy to state exactly what sort of spatial distribution in perceived space warrants us in asserting plurality. Before we can use space as an argument for particulars, we must be clear on this point. We are accustomed to concede that a thing cannot be in two places at once, but this common-sense maxim, unless very carefully stated, will lead us into inextricable difficulties. Our first business, therefore, is to find out how to state this maxim in an unobjectionable form.

In rational dynamics, where we are concerned with matter and 'real' space, the maxim that nothing can be in two places at once is taken rigidly, and any matter occupying more than a point of space is regarded as at least theoretically divisible. Only what occupies a bare point is simple and single. This view is straightforward, and raises no difficulties as applied to 'real' space.

But as applied to perceived space, such a view is quite inadmissible. The immediate object of (say) visual perception is always of finite extent. If we suppose it to be, like the matter corresponding to it in 'real' space, composed of a collection of entities, one for each point which is not empty, we shall have to suppose two things, both of which seem incredible, namely: (1) that every immediate object of visual (or tactile) perception is infinitely complex; (2) that every such object is always composed of parts which are by their very nature imperceptible. It seems quite impossible that the immediate object of perception should have these properties. Hence we must suppose that an indivisible object of visual perception may occupy a finite extent of visual space. In short, we must, in dividing any complex object of visual perception, reach, after a finite number of steps, a *minimum sensible*, which contains no plurality although it is of finite extent. Visual space may, in a sense, be infinitely *divisible*, for, by attention alone, or by the microscope, the immediate object of perception can be changed in a way which introduces complexity where formerly there was simplicity; and to this process no clear limit can be set. But this is a process which substitutes a new immediate object in place of the old one, and the new object, though more subdivided than the old one, will still consist of only a finite number of parts. We must therefore admit that the space of perception is not infinitely divided, and does not consist of points, but is composed of a finite though constantly varying number of surfaces or volumes, continually breaking up or joining together according to the fluctuations of attention. If there is a 'real' geometrical space corresponding to the space of perception, an infinite number of points in the geometrical space will have to correspond to a single simple entity in the perceived space.

It follows from this that, if we are to apply to the immediate objects of perception the maxim that a thing cannot be in two places at once, a 'place' must not be taken to be a point, but must be taken to be the extent occupied by a single object of perception. A white sheet of paper, for example, may be seen as a single undivided object, or as an object consisting of two parts, an upper and a lower or a right hand and a left hand part, or again as an object consisting of four parts, and so on. If we on this account consider that, even when the sheet appeared as an undivided object, its upper and lower halves were in different places, then we shall have to say that the undivided object was in both these places at once. But it is better to say that, when the sheet appeared as an undivided object, this object occupied only one 'place,' though the place corresponded to what were afterwards two places. Thus a 'place' may be defined as the space occupied by one undivided object of perception.

With this definition, the maxim that a thing cannot be in two places at once might seem to reduce to a tautology. But this maxim, though it may need re-wording, will still have a substantial significance, to be derived from the consideration of spatial relations. It is obvious that perceived spatial relations cannot hold between points, but must hold between the parts of a single complex object of perception. When the sheet of paper is perceived as consisting of two halves, an upper and a lower, these two halves are combined into a complex whole by means of a spatial relation which holds directly between the two halves, not between supposed smaller subdivisions which in fact do not exist in the immediate object of perception. Perceived spatial relations, therefore, must have a certain roughness, not the neat smooth properties of geometrical relations between points. What, for example, shall we say of distance? The distance between two simultaneously perceived objects will have to be defined by the perceived objects between them; in the case of two objects which touch, like the two halves of the sheet of paper, there is no distance between them. What remains definite is a certain order; by means of right and left, up and down, and so on, the parts of a complex object of perception acquire a spatial order, which is definite, though not subject to quite the same laws as geometrical order. The maxim that a thing cannot be in two places at once will then become the maxim that every spatial relation implies diversity of its terms, i.e., that nothing is to the right of itself, or above itself, and so on. In that case, given two white patches, one of which is to the right of the other, it will follow that there is not a single thing, whiteness, which is to the right of itself, but that there are two different things, instances of whiteness, of which one is to the right of the other. In this way our maxim will support the conclusion that there must be particulars as well as universals. But the above outline of an argument needs some amplification before it can be considered conclusive. Let us therefore examine, one by one, the steps of the argument.

Let us suppose, for the sake of definiteness, that within one field of vision we perceive two separated patches of white on a ground of black. It may then be taken as quite certain that the two patches are two and not one. The question is: Can we maintain that there are two if what exists in each is the universal whiteness?

If absolute space is admitted, we can of course say that it is the difference of place that makes the patches two; there is whiteness in this place, and whiteness in that place. From the point of view of our main problem, which is as to the existence of particulars, such a view would prove our thesis, since this place and that place would be or imply particulars constituting absolute space. But from the point of view of our immediate problem, which is concerned with plurality in perceived space, we may reject the above view on the ground that, whatever may be the case with 'real' space, perceived space is certainly not absolute, i.e., absolute positions are not among objects of perception. Thus the whiteness here and the whiteness there cannot be distinguished as complexes of which this place and that place are respectively constituents.

Of course the whitenesses may be of different shapes, say one round and one square, and then they could be distinguished by their shapes. It will be observed that, with the view adopted above as to the nature of perceived space, it is perfectly possible for a simple object of perception to have a shape: the shape will be a quality like another. Since a simple object of perception may be of finite extent, there is no reason to suppose that a shape must imply spatial divisibility in the object of perception. Hence our two patches may be respectively round and square, and yet not be spatially divisible. It is obvious, however, that this method of distinguishing the two patches is altogether inadequate. The two patches are just as easily distinguished if both are square or both are round. So long as we can see both at once, no degree of likeness between them causes the slightest difficulty in perceiving that there are two of them. Thus difference of shape, whether it exists or not, is not what makes the patches two entities instead of one.

It may be said that the two patches are distinguished by the difference in their relations to other things. For example, it may happen that a patch of red is to the right of one and to the left of the other. But this does imply that the patches are two unless we know that one thing cannot be both to the right and to the left of another. This, it might be said, is obviously false. Suppose a surface of black with a small white space in the middle. Then the whole of the black may form only one simple object of perception, and would seem to be both to the right and to the left of the white space which it entirely surrounds.

I think it would be more true to say, in this case, that the black is neither to the right nor to the left of the white. But right and left are complicated relations involving the body of the percipient. Let us take some other simpler relation, say that of surrounding, which the black surface has to the white patch in our example. Suppose we have another white patch, of exactly the same size and shape, entirely surrounded by red. Then, it may be said, the two patches of white are distinguished by difference of relation, since one is surrounded by black and the other by red. But if this ground of distinction is to be valid, we must know that it is impossible for one entity to be both wholly and immediately surrounded by black and wholly and immediately surrounded by red. I do not mean to deny that we do know this. But two things deserve notice—first, that it is not an analytic proposition; second, that it presupposes the numerical diversity of our two patches of white.

We are so accustomed to regarding such relations as 'inside' and 'outside' as incompatible that it is easy to suppose a *logical* incompatibility, although in fact the incompatibility is a characteristic of space, not a result of logic. I do not know what are the unanalysable spatial relations of objects of perception, whether visual or tactile, but whatever they are they must have the kind of characteristics which are required in order to generate an order. They, or some of them, must be asymmetrical, i.e., such that they are incompatible with their converses: for example, supposing 'inside' to be one of them, a thing which is inside another must not also be outside it. They, or some of them, must also be transitive, i.e., such that, for example, if x is inside y and y is inside z, then x is inside z—supposing, for the sake of illustration, 'inside' to be among fundamental spatial relations. Probably some further properties will be required, but these at least are essential, in view of the fact that there is such a thing as spatial order. It follows that some at least of the fundamental spatial relations must be such as no entity can have to itself. It is indeed self-evident that spatial relations fulfil these conditions. But these conditions are not demonstrable by purely logical considerations: they are synthetic properties of perceived spatial relations.

It is in virtue of these self-evident properties that the numerical diversity of the two patches of white is self-evident. They have the relation of being outside each other, and this requires that they should be two, not one. They may or may not have intrinsic differences—of shape, or size, or brightness, or any other quality—but whether they have or not they are two, and it is obviously logically possible that they should have no intrinsic differences whatever. It follows from this that the terms of spatial relations cannot be universals or collections of universals, but must be particulars capable of being exactly alike and yet numerically diverse.

It is very desirable, in such discussions as that on which we are at present engaged, to be able to talk of 'places' and of things or qualities 'occupying' places, without implying absolute position. It must be understood that, on the view which adopts relative position, a 'place' is not a precise notion. But its usefulness arises as follows: Suppose a set of objects, such as the walls and furniture of a room, to retain their spatial relations unchanged for a certain length of time, while a succession of other objects, say people who successively sit in a certain chair, have successively a given set of spatial relations to the relatively fixed objects. Then the people have, one after the other, a given set of properties, consisting in spatial relations to the walls and furniture. Whatever has this given set of properties at a given moment is said to 'occupy' a certain place, the 'place' itself being merely a fixed set of spatial relations to certain objects whose spatial relations to each other do not change appreciably during the time considered. Thus when we say that one thing can only be in one place at one time, we mean that it can only have one set of spatial relations to a given set of objects at one time.

It might be argued that, since we have admitted that a simple object of perception may be of finite extent, we have admitted that it may be in many places at once, and therefore may be outside itself. This, however, would be a misunderstanding. In perceived space, the finite extent occupied by a simple object of perception is not divided into many places. It is a single place occupied by a single thing. There are two different ways in which this place may 'correspond' to many places. First, if there is such a thing as 'real' space with geometrical properties, the one place in perceived space will correspond to an infinite number of points in 'real' space, and the single entity which is the object of perception will correspond to many physical entities in 'real' space. Secondly, there is a more or less partial correspondence between perceived space at one time and perceived space at another. Suppose that we attend closely to our white patch, and meanwhile no other noticeable changes occur in the field of vision. Our white patch may, and often does, change as the result of attention—we may perceive differences of shade or other differentiations, or, without differences of quality, we may merely observe parts in it which make it complex and introduce diversity and spatial relations within it. We consider, naturally, that we are still looking at the same thing as before, and that what we see now was there all along. Thus we conclude that our apparently simple white patch was not really simple. But, in fact, the object of perception is not the same as it was before; what may be the same is the physical object supposed to correspond to the object of perception. This physical object is, of course, complex. And the perception which results from attention will be in one sense more correct than that which perceived a simple object, because, if attention reveals previously unnoticed differences, it may be assumed that there are corresponding differences in the 'real' object which corresponds to the object of perception. Hence the perception resulting from attention gives more information about the 'real' object than the other perception did: but the object of perception itself is no more and no less real in the one case than in the other—that is to say, in both cases it is an object which exists when perceived, but which there is no reason to believe existent except when it is perceived.

In perceived space, the spatial unit is not a point, but a simple object of perception or an ultimate constituent in a complex object of perception. This is the reason why, although two patches of white which are visibly separated from each other must be two, a continuous area of white may not be two. A continuous area, if not too large, may be a single object of perception not consisting of parts, which is impossible for two visibly separated areas. The spatial unit is variable, constantly changing its size, and subject to every fluctuation of attention, but it must occupy a continuous portion of perceived space, since otherwise it would be perceived as plural.

The argument as to numerical diversity which we have derived from perceived space may be reinforced by a similar argument as regards the contents of different minds. If two people are both believing that two and two are four, it is at least theoretically possible that the meanings they attach to the words *two* and *and* and *are* and *four* are the same, and that therefore, so far as the objects of their beliefs are concerned, there is nothing to distinguish the one from the other. Nevertheless, it seems plain that there are two entities, one the belief of the one man and the other the belief of the other. A particular belief is a complex of which something which we may call a subject is a constituent; in our case, it is the diversity of the subjects that produces the diversity of the beliefs. But these subjects cannot be mere bundles of general qualities. Suppose one of our men is characterized by benevolence, stupidity, and love of puns. It would not be correct to say: 'Benevolence, stupidity, and love of puns believe that two and two are four.' Nor would this become correct by the addition of a larger number of general qualities. Moreover, however many qualities we add, it remains possible that the other subject may also have them; hence qualities cannot be what constitutes the diversity of the subjects. The only respect in which two different subjects *must* differ is in their relations to particulars: for example, each will have to the other relations which he does not have to himself. But it is not logically impossible that everything concerning one of the subjects and otherwise only concerning universals might be true of the other subject. Hence, even when differences in regard to such propositions occur, it is not these differences that constitute the diversity of the two subjects. The subjects, therefore, must be regarded as particulars, and as radically different from any collection of those general qualities which may be predicated of them.

It will be observed that, according to the general principles which must govern any correspondence of real things with objects of perception, any principle which introduces diversity among objects of perception must introduce a corresponding diversity among real things. I am not now concerned to argue as to what grounds exist for assuming a correspondence, but, if there is such a correspondence, it must be supposed that diversity in the effects—i.e., the perceived objects—implies diversity in the causes—i.e., the real objects. Hence if I perceive two objects in the field of vision, we must suppose that at least two real objects are concerned in causing my perception.

The essential characteristic of particulars, as they appear in perceived space, is that they cannot be in two places at once. But this is an unsatisfactory way of stating the matter, owing to the doubt as to what a 'place' is. The more correct statement is that certain perceptible spatial relations imply diversity of their terms; for example, if x is above y, x and y must be different entities. So long, however, as it is understood that this is what is meant, no harm is done by the statement that a thing cannot be in two places at once.

We may now return to the question of particulars and universals with a better hope of being able to state precisely the nature of the opposition between them. It will be remembered that we began with three different oppositions: (1) that of percept and concept, (2) that of entities existing in time and entities not existing in time, (3) that of substantives and verbs. But in the course of our discussion a different opposition developed itself, namely, (4) that between entities which can be in one place, but not in more than one, at a given time, and entities which either cannot be anywhere or can be in several places at one time. What makes a particular patch of white particular, whereas whiteness is universal, is the fact that the particular patch cannot be in two places simultaneously, whereas the whiteness, if it exists at all, exists wherever there are white things. This opposition, as stated, might be held not to apply to thoughts. We might reply that a man's thoughts are in his head; but without going into this question, we may observe that there certainly is some relation between a man's thoughts and his head (or some part of it) which there is not between his thoughts and other things in space. We may extend our definition of particulars so as to cover this relation. We may say that a man's thought 'belongs to' the place where his head is. We may then define a particular in our fourth sense as an entity which cannot be in or belong to more than one place at one time, and a universal as an entity which either cannot be in or belong to any place, or can be in or belong to many places at once. This opposition has certain affinities with the three earlier oppositions, which must be examined.

(1) Owing to the admission of particulars in our fourth sense, we can make an absolute division between percepts and concepts. The universal whiteness is a concept, whereas a particular white patch is a percept. If we had not admitted particulars in our fourth sense, percepts would have been identical with certain concepts.

(2) For the same reason, we are able to say that such general qualities as whiteness never exist in time, whereas the things that do exist in time are all particulars in our fourth sense. The converse, that all particulars in our fourth sense exist in time, holds in virtue of their definition. Hence the second and fourth senses of the opposition of particulars and universals are co-extensive.

(3) The third opposition, that of substantives and verbs, presents more difficulties, owing to the doubt whether predicates are verbs or not. In order to evade this doubt, we may substitute another opposition, which will be co-extensive with substantives and verbs if predicates are verbs, but not otherwise. This other opposition puts predicates and relations on one side, and everything else on the other. What is not a predicate or relation is, according to one traditional definition, a substance. It is true that, when substance was in vogue, it was supposed that a substance must be indestructible, and this quality will not belong to our substances. For example, what a man sees when he sees a flash of lightning is a substance in our sense. But the importance of indestructibility was metaphysical, not logical. As far as logical properties are concerned, our substances will be fairly analogous to traditional substances. Thus we have the opposition of substances on the one hand and predicates and relations on the other hand. The theory which rejects particulars allows entities commonly classed as predicates—e.g. white—to exist; thus the distinction between substances and predicates is obliterated by this theory. Our theory, on the contrary, preserves the distinction. In the world we know, substances

are identical with particulars in our fourth sense, and predicates and relations with universals.

It will be seen that, according to the theory which assumes particulars, there is a specific relation of subject to predicate, unless we adopt the view—considered above in connexion with Berkeley and Hume—that common sensible qualities are really derivative from specific kinds of likeness. Assuming this view to be false, ordinary sensible qualities will be predicates of the particulars which are instances of them. The sensible qualities themselves do not exist in time in the same sense in which the instances do. Predication is a relation involving a fundamental logical difference between its two terms. Predicates may themselves have predicates, but the predicates of predicates will be radically different from the predicates of substances. The predicate, on this view, is never part of the subject, and thus no true subject-predicate proposition is analytic. Propositions of the form 'All A is B' are not really subject-predicate propositions, but express relations of predicates; such propositions may be analytic, but the traditional confusion of them with true subject-predicate propositions has been a disgrace to formal logic.

The theory which rejects particulars, and assumes that, e.g., whiteness itself exists wherever (as common sense would say) there are white things, dispenses altogether with predication as a fundamental relation. 'This is white,' which, on the other view, expresses a relation between a particular and whiteness, will, when particulars are rejected, really state that whiteness is one of the qualities in this place, or has certain spatial relations to certain other qualities. Thus the question whether predication is an ultimate simple relation may be taken as distinguishing the two theories; it is ultimate if there are particulars, but not otherwise. And if predication is an ultimate relation, the best definition of particulars is that they are entities which can only be subjects of predicates or terms of relations, i.e., that they are (in the logical sense) substances. This definition is preferable to one introducing space or time, because space and time are accidental characteristics of the world with which we happen to be acquainted, and therefore are destitute of the necessary universality belonging to purely logical categories.

We have thus a division of all entities into two classes: (1) particulars, which enter into complexes only as the subjects of predicates or the terms of relations, and, if they belong to the world of which we have experience, exist in time, and cannot occupy more than one place at one time in the space to which they belong; (2) universals, which can occur as predicates or relations in complexes, do not exist in time, and have no relation to one place which they may not simultaneously have to another. The ground for regarding such a division as unavoidable is the self-evident fact that certain spatial relations imply diversity of their terms, together with the self-evident fact that it is logically possible for entities having such spatial relations to be wholly indistinguishable as to predicates.

The argument in the above article in favour of the existence of particulars no longer seems to me valid for reasons which I have explained in *Human Knowledge: its scope and limits*. The gist of the matter arises out of the last sentence in the above article. I no longer think that there are any spatial or temporal relations which always and necessarily imply diversity. This does not prove that the theory which asserts particulars is wrong, but only that it cannot be proved to be right. The theory which asserts particulars and the theory which denies them would seem equally tenable. If so, the latter has the merit of logical parsimony. [Note added in 1955.]

III

ARTHUR O. LOVEJOY

ARTHUR LOVEJOY (1873-1962) was Professor of Philosophy at The Johns Hopkins University. His book *The Great Chain of Being* (1936) is among the great works of scholarship in the twentieth century and has inspired much further research in the history of ideas, both in philosophy and literary criticism. In philosophy proper, Lovejoy was one of the American Critical Realists who, in their rejection of Idealism, paralleled similar developments in England.

"Natural Dualism" is part of the first lecture of Lovejoy's *The Revolt Against Dualism* (1930), a book which has become a classic in the development of philosophical Realism in the United States. The main burden of this selection is to state and defend epistemological dualism, more particularly a representative as against a direct theory of perception. Such a dualism, unlike the views of Idealism or other forms of Realism, Lovejoy claims, is rooted in our human nature, and can be validated by philosophical reflection upon this nature.

Natural Dualism[1]

The past quarter-century's discussion has shown that it is not easy for the critics of dualism to keep clearly in view its essential outlines in their entirety and in their simplicity, free from extraneous complications and confusions, and to recognize that it, rather than what is called "naïve" or "direct" realism, is the way of thinking natural to man so soon as he becomes even a little reflective about certain facts, of which most are matters of ordinary experience, and all have long been generally accepted. . . .

Specifically, men naturally make at least five assumptions (we need not yet ask whether they are valid assumptions) about the character or status of what may, for short, be called *cognoscenda*—the things-to-be-known-if-possible. (1) Many *cognoscenda*, including most of those to be known, if at all, visually, are assumed to be at places in space external to the body of the percipient. Man may be described biologically as an animal whose habitual and paradoxical employment is the endeavor to reach outside his skin. As a physical organism *homo sapiens*, like other creatures, has a definite spatial boundary of rather irregular outline, formed chiefly of a single material substance. All that, physically or spatially speaking, constitutes the organic functioning of an individual of the species takes place within the narrow room defined by this epidermal surface. What the man as a biological unit is, and what the events that make up his life are, are sought by the biologists wholly within those confines. Yet man is forever attempting, and, as he is wont to believe, with success, to apprehend, to "get at," things which lie beyond this surface. The individual's actual existence as it appears *to him*, can in only very small part be described as a succession of subcuticular events. The stuff of which it *seems* to be mainly composed consists of entities and happenings on the far side of the boundary, some of them so slightly removed from the epidermal

1. From *The Revolt Against Dualism* (Chicago: Open Court Publishing Company, 1930), pp. 10-11, 12-24. Reprinted without footnotes by permission of the publishers.

surface that they are said to be in contact with it, others incalculably remote. The human animal, in short, does not for the most part live where its body is—if an organism's life is made up of what it really experiences; it lives where the things are of which it is aware, upon which its attention and feeling are directed. (How far this may be true of other creatures we cannot judge.) One of the most curious developments in the entire history of thought is the invention in our day of what may best be named the Hypodermic Philosophy—the doctrine, resulting from the application to a cognitive animal of the biological concepts found sufficient in the study of animals assumed to be non-cognitive, that the organic phenomenon of knowing may be exhaustively described in terms of molecular displacements taking place under the skin.

(2) Equally insistent in man, and yet more paradoxical—had most men but the capacity for philosophic wonder which would enable them to see it so—is the demand that he shall have a real traffic with things that are not, because they are by-gone or have not yet come into being. What time and nature have extinguished he makes the matter of his present contemplation, and gains thereby his power to foresee what is still unborn. In memory and in forecast and anticipation he expressly conceives himself to be apprehending entities or events (even though they may be only other experiences of his own) which are not co-existent with the acts or states through which they are apprehended—to be reaching what is nevertheless at that moment in some sense beyond his temporal reach.

(3) An even more exigent desire for knowledge normally arises in man—though some philosophers who profess to have rid themselves of it would have us believe that it is equally wanting in others. Besides his craving to reach that which is spatially and temporally external to himself at the moment of cognition, there is, plainly, in the natural man a wish to attain an acquaintance with entities as they *would be if unknown,* existences not relative to the cognitive situation—in short, with things as they literally are in themselves. He has a persistent, if not easily gratified, curiosity about what M. Meyerson calls the *être intime,* the private life, of things. Tell him that at every moment of his existence he is contemplating nothing but the ghosly offspring of that moment's contemplation itself—even though they be projected into other places—and you contradict one of the most tenacious of his convictions—and, as he will point out to you, if he should be something of a dialectician, you also contradict yourself. He may, under pressure from philosophers, surrender this conviction with regard to one and another limited class of the contents of his experience; surrender it

wholly, neither he nor the most subjectivistic philosopher has ever really done.

And (4) this tenacity in believing that through what goes on within the individual's experience he can know what is other than that experience and as real as it is, is greatest with respect to his knowledge of the experiences of others of his kind. There are a few philosophers among us who profess not only to be satisfied with automatic sweethearts and mindless friends, but also to be unable to attach meaning to the proposition that these automata have any being beyond that which they have in the philosopher's own private and (as some would add) corporeal existence. (It is, of course, evident that if this philosophy is true—supposing the word "true" still to have meaning—there are not several such philosophers, but only one.) But this queer affectation, a hypertrophy of the logic of scientific empiricism, is manifestly belied at every moment by the behavior and speech of the philosophers who assume it; it denies the meaningfulness of a belief which every creature of our kind seems inevitably to hold and from which all the distinctive quality of man's moral consciousness and all the tang and poignancy of his social experience derive the belief that he is surrounded by beings like himself but not himself, having inner lives of their own which are never in the same sense *his* own, but of which, nevertheless, he can attain some knowledge, and to whom, reciprocally, he can convey some understanding of that which is going on within himself. This social realism also, which is manifestly a piece of pure epistemology, seems to be one of the specific characters of *homo sapiens*, as properly a part of his zoölogical definition as his upright posture or his lack of a tail. It is implicit in all his most distinctive modes of feeling and behavior—his elaboration of language and art as means of expression, his craving for affection, the curious and immense potency over the individual's conduct which is possessed by his beliefs about the thoughts and feelings of others about himself, and his occasional ability to recognize the interests of other sentient creatures as ends in themselves. Apply the principle of relativity to men's apprehensions of one another, and you destroy the very idea of a society of the characteristically human type.

(5) Finally, the *cognoscenda* which the individual knower ascribes to places and times in the external world where his body is not, and in which his cognitive act is not occurring, he also conceives to be potentially, if not actually, apprehensible by these other knowers; they must be things capable of verification in experiences other than the one experience in which, at a given moment, they are in some sense before him. Out of his belief in a multiplicity of knowers other than

himself, or a multiplicity of knowings which, though now knowable
by him, are not *his present* knowing, he has framed the category of
publicity, the notion of a world of objects for common knowledge;
and he tends to treat this attribute of common verifiability as the
criterion of that independence of the percipient event or the cognitive
act which he naturally attributes to the *cognoscendum*. In other words,
his character as a social animal has profoundly and permanently infected his very notion of knowing, so that the experience of objects
which he has when in dream or madness, he steps aside into a world
of his own—be it never so vivid and never so coherent—is not, when
seen to be thus private, taken as equivalent to that access to reality
which he seeks.

These, then, are the five articles of the natural and spontaneous
epistemological creed of mankind—a creed which, as I have said, contains its own apparent mysteries, or diverse aspects of the one mystery
of the presence of the absent, the true apprehension, by a being remaining within certain fixed bounds, of things beyond those bounds.
Epistemological dualism arises when reflection, initially accepting these
articles, inquires about their implications and brings them into connection with certain familiar facts of experience. There is, indeed, as
should be evident from what has already been said, a sense in which
all realism is intrinsically dualistic; in all its forms, namely, it asserts
that the thing known may be other in time and place and nature than
the *event or act by means of which* the thing is known. Thus the event
of seeing, as we have remarked, if conceived physiologically as a
neuro-cerebral change, does not appear to occur either where the visual
object is seen or where the real object is assumed to be. A happening
inside of a given body somehow achieves the presentation, in the individual stream of experience connected with that particular body, of
an entity outside the body. And even if the cognitive event be conceived as a purely psychic and non-spatial act of awareness, that act
has at least a date which need not (e.g., in memory) be the date, and
a *quale* which is by hypothesis not the *quale*, of the object known.
But it is not this fundamental sort of dualism necessarily inherent in
any realistic theory of knowledge which we shall here mean by "epistemological dualism"; the term stands for the assertion of quite another
(though not unrelated) duality, that of the content or datum at a
given moment immediately and indubitably presented, and the reality
said to be known thereby. Even the datum, of course, *seems*, in the
case of sight and touch, to be situated outside the body, though whether
it truly is or not must be a matter for subsequent consideration. I
do not actually see the desk inside the head of which I at the same

time can see a small bit—namely, the tip of my nose—and to the rest of which I give in thought a spatial position definitely related to that bit. But epistemological dualism (as here understood) declares that not even the visible desk which is thus directly perceived as spatially external to the perceived body is the same existent as the "real" desk i.e., the *cognoscendum*. And the existential distinctness of datum and *cognoscendum* which is thus held by the dualist to be exemplified in the case of visual perception is also asserted by him, *mutatis mutandis*, in the case of other modes of perception and other forms of cognitive experience; so that, in his view, all knowing is mediated through the presence "before the mind"—as the traditional phrase goes—of entities which must be distinguished from an ulterior reality which is the true objective of knowledge.

Now you obviously cannot discuss whether two particulars—two in the sense that they have been provisionally distinguished in discourse —are identical unless you already know or assume something about both. If you are in a state of blank ignorance about either one, no question concerning the nature of their relations can be raised. It is therefore necessary to know, or postulate, certain propositions about the class *cognoscenda* before we can compare it with the class "data" to ascertain whether the two satisfy our criteria of identity. To assert their non-identity is to ascribe to the one a spatial or a temporal or a spatio-temporal position, or a set of qualities, which is inconsistent with those empirically exhibited by the other. Philosophers, it is true, have often attempted to go about the matter in what seems a different way. They have begun by provisionally assuming that they know nothing whatever except the passing immediate datum, and have then sought to determine, by reflecting upon the nature or implications of this, how much knowledge of existents which are not immediate data they must, or may, suppose themselves to possess. This was, of course, essentially the method of Descartes, though he applied it confusedly and inconsistently. But it is not the natural road to epistemological dualism. That road starts from the position of natural realism—from the assumption that we already have certain information about realities which are not *merely* our immediate, private, and momentary data; and it leads to the discovery, or supposed discovery, that this very assumption forbids us to believe that our acquaintance with these realities is at first hand. The time, place, context, or qualities which we have ascribed to them prove inconsistent with those which belong to the data. Not only is this the natural approach to the dualism of datum and *cognoscendum*, but it is also the only approach which is at all likely to be persuasive to those averse to that theory. The argument starts from the premises of those who would, if possible, avoid its conclusion. We shall, then, in this and the next lecture, not attempt an affectation of universal doubt, but shall tentatively accept—with nearly all of the early and many even of the later insurgents—the broad outlines of the picture of nature familiar to common sense and sanctioned by the older physics. We shall, in particular, not initially question the supposition that there are extended external objects, such as pennies, tables, planets, and distant stars, having at least the primary and possibly also the secondary qualities; having determinable positions in a space like that of visual and tactual perception, whether or not it is identical with it; capable of motion and causal interaction; acting, by means of processes in space, upon our sense-organs; and thereby conditioning the presence in our experience of the data which, whether or not identical with the objects, are our sources of information about them. When these natural assumptions are provisionally adopted, there nevertheless prove to be at least five familiar aspects of experience in which it seems plain that the object of our knowing must be different in the time or place or mode of its existence, or in its character, from the perceptual or other content which is present to us at the moment when we are commonly said to be apprehending that object, and without which we should never apprehend it at all.

(1) Of these, the first is implicit in the second of the above-mentioned articles of man's natural realistic creed. Intertemporal cognition, the knowing at one time of things which exist or events which occur at another time, seems a patent example of a mode of knowledge which we are under the necessity of regarding as potentially genuine and yet as mediate. When I remember, for example, not only is there a present awareness distinct from the past memory-object (that alone would imply only the duality of act and content), but the present awareness manifestly has, and must have, a compresent content. But the past event which we say is *of* cannot be this compresent content. In saying this I am, it is true, including among the natural grounds of epistemological dualism an assumption which some dualistic philosophers—and even some who repudiate the naïvely dualistic theory of memory—regard as unsound. Mr. Broad, for example, has said that there "is no general metaphysical objection to such a theory" on the ground that when an event is past it ceases to exist. "Once an event has happened it exists eternally"; past events, therefore, "are always 'there' waiting to be remembered; and there is no *a priori* reason why they should not from time to time enter unto such a relation with certain present events that they become objects of direct acquaintance." This view, however, implies an inconceivable divorce of the identity of

an event from its date. The things which may be said to subsis
eternally are essences; and the reason why they can so subsist is tha
by definition, they have no dates. They do not "exist" at all, in th
sense in which dated and located things do so; and if "events" eternall
existed after they had "once happened" (and when they were n
longer "happening"), they would likewise exist before they happened
eternalness can hardly be an acquired character. The present image an
the past event may be separate embodiments of the same essence; the
are not identical particulars, because the particularity of each is ur
definable apart from its temporal situation and relations. The dualit
of the memory-image and the bygone existence to which it refers seem
to be inherent in what we *mean* by remembrance; if the two were on
our intertemporal knowing would defeat its own aim of apprehendin
the beyond, by annulling its beyondness. The very wistfulness c
memory implies such duality; the past, in being known, still inexorabl
keeps its distance. Plainest of all is that a man's own experiencin
of yesterday, the event of his then *having* an experience, does no
seem to him, in being remembered, to become to-day's experiencing
Common sense, however much inclined in its more self-confident mc
ments to believe in direct perception, has never, I suppose, believe
in direct memory; it has been well aware that what is present i
retrospection is a duplicate which somehow and in some degree disclose
to us the character, without constituting the existence, of its origina

(2) It is not alone in the case of memory that there is a tempora
sundering, and therefore an existential duality, of the content give
and the reality made known to us through that content. This secon
reason for dualism has not, it is true, like some of the others, alway
been discoverable by the simplest reflection upon everyday experience
But the fact upon which it rests has long been one of the elementar
commonplaces of physical science; and the probability of it had sug
gested itself to acute minds long before its verification. There had a
times occurred to him, wrote Bacon in the *Novum Organum,* "a ver
strange doubt," *a dubitatio plane monstrosa,* "namely, whether the fac
of a clear and starlight sky be seen at the instant at which it reall
exists, and not rather a little later; and whether there be not, as regard
our sight of heavenly bodies, a real time and an apparent time (*tempu
visum*), just as there is a real place and an apparent place taker
account of by astronomers." For it had appeared to him "incredibl
that the images or rays of the heavenly bodies could be conveyed a
once to the sight through such an immense space and did not rathe
take some appreciable time in travelling to us." Unfortunately for hi
reputation Lord Bacon was able to overcome this doubt by invoking

against it several bad reasons, which need not be here recalled; but his subtler medieval namesake had not only propounded but embraced and defended the same conjecture three centuries earlier. Roemer's observation in 1675, through which it became established as one of the fundamental theorems of empirical science, is not usually mentioned in the histories of philosophy; but the omission merely shows how badly the history of philosophy is commonly written, for the discovery was as significant for epistemology as it was for physics and astronomy. It appeared definitely to forbid that naïvely realistic way of taking the content of visual perception to which all men at first naturally incline. The doctrine of the finite velocity of light meant that the sense from which most of our information about the world beyond our epidermal surfaces is derived never discloses anything which (in Francis Bacon's phrase) "really exists" in that world, at the instant at which it indubitably exists in perception. It is with a certain phase in the history of a distant star that the astonomer, gazing through his telescope at a given moment, is supposed to become acquainted; but that phase, and perhaps the star itself, have, ages since, ceased to be; and the astronomer's present sense-data—it has therefore seemed inevitable to say—whatever else they may be, are not identical with the realities they are believed to reveal. They might perhaps be supposed to be identical with the peripheral effect produced by the light-ray on its belated arrival at the eye—in other words, with the retinal images; but two present and inverted retinal images *here* are obviously not the same as one extinct star formerly existing elsewhere, and the duality of datum and object would therefore remain. This particular hypothesis, moreover, is excluded by the now familiar fact established by the physiological psychologists, that there is a further lag—slight, but not theoretically negligible—in the transmission of the neural impulse to the cortical center, and therefore—since the percept does not appear until the impulse reaches the brain—a difference in time between the existence of a given pair of retinal images, or any other excitation of peripheral nerve-endings, and the existence of the corresponding percept. Never, in short, if both the physiologists and the physicists are right, can the datum or character-complex presented in the perception of a given moment be regarded as anything but the report of a messenger, more or less tardy and more or less open to suspicion, from the original object which we are said to know by virtue of that perception.

(3) Another class of empirical facts which are familiar, in their simpler forms, to all men have seemed by the plainest implication to show that perceptual content, even though it appears as external to the physical organs of perception, is not identical with the particular

objects about which it is supposed to convey information. It is commonly assumed that the object, or objective, of a given perception can first of all, be identified, at least roughly, by its position in space and time. What I am "perceiving" at a certain moment is the ink-bottle two feet away from my hand, or the star a hundred light-years distant. Even if the position is defined only vaguely, the thing is at least supposed to be (or have been) "out there" somewhere. This identification of the object referred to is, obviously, possible only by means of the same perception; yet, assuming such identification, experience shows that what I perceive is determined by events or conditions intervening in space and time between that object and my so-called perception of it. The qualities sensibly presented vary with changes which appear to occur, not in the place where *the* object is supposed to exist, but in regions between it and the body itself, and, in particular, in the very organs of perception. The examples are trite: a man puts a lens before his eyes, and the size or shape or number or perceived distance of the objects presented is altered: he puts certain drugs into his stomach, and the colors of all perceived objects external to his body change; he swallows other drugs in sufficient quantity, and sees outside his body objects which no one else can see, and which his own other senses fail to disclose. The discovery of this primary sort of physical relativity, which is really one of the most pregnant of philosophical discoveries, begins in infancy with the earliest experience of the illusions of perspective, or the observation that the objects in the visual field change their spatial relations when looked at with first one eye and then the other. If *homo sapiens* had at the outset been blind, the first seeing man, a paleolithic Einstein, when he reported this astonishing fact—the relativity of position to the motions of eyelids—to his fellow cave-men, would presumably have seemed to them a deviser of intolerable paradoxes, and have been made acquainted with those more effective methods for repressing strange doctrines which cave-men, no doubt, knew how to employ. The evidence of this dependence of the nature of what is perceived upon happenings which, as themselves experienced, do not happen in the right place to permit them to be regarded as changes in the *cognoscendum* itself, has constantly increased with the progress of the sciences of optics, neuro-cerebral physiology, and psychology; the eventual determination of the character of the percept has been removed farther and farther, not only from the external object, but even from the external organ of sense. As Professor Dewey remarked, in the preceding series of these lectures, "it is pure fiction that a 'sensation' or peripheral excitation, or stimulus, travels undisturbed in solitary state in its own coach-and-four to either the brain or consciousness in its purity. A particular excitation is but one of an avalanche of con-temporaneously occurring excitations, peripheral and from propriocep-tors; each has to compete with others, to make terms with them; what happens is an integration of complex forces." And even in the earliest and easiest phases of this discovery, the variability of the percept with conditions extrinsic to the object to be perceived manifestly affects those attributes by which the very identity of the individual object should be defined: it is not colors only but shapes, not shapes only but perceived positions, that prove to be functions of the processes spatially and temporally intervenient between the object and the per-ception, and therefore not attributable to the former. Thus what is actually perceived could be regarded only as the terminal effect of a more or less long and complex causal series of events happening at different places and times, only at the perceptually inaccessible other end of which series the *cognoscendum* was supposed to have—or rather, to have had—its being. Aside from any empirical evidences of the sort mentioned, it has apparently seemed to many minds virtually axiomatic that, if the *cognoscendum* in perception is conceived (as it is in ordinary thought and in most physical theory) as a "causal object" acting upon the bodily organs of perception in the determination of the character of the content experienced, that which is acted *upon* must also have a part—must, indeed, have the last and decisive word—in determining the character of that content. How under these circumstances the exterior causal object could be known at all is an obviously difficult question; this argument for epistemological dualism, and especially the rôle as-signed in it to the organs of perception, gives rise to that "crux of realistic theories" which Mr. C. A. Strong has very precisely expressed: "to explain how a sensation which varies directly only with one physical object, the nervous system, can yet vary with another physical object sufficiently to give knowledge of it." But with these ulterior difficulties we are not for the moment concerned; whatever *their* solution, they obviously do not annul the difficulty, for any realistic philosophy, of identifying the end-term with the initial term of the physico-physi-ological causal series.

(4) This physical and physiological conditionedness of the data manifestly implies that the contents of the experience of percipients having different spatial and physical relations to a postulated external object cannot be wholly identical. But this implication is independently confirmed and extended through that communication and comparison of experiences which is supposed to be possible through language. While the many knowers are, by the fifth article of the natural episte-mological creed, dealing with what is said to be one and the same

object—and if they are not doing so are not achieving what is meant by knowledge—they notoriously are not experiencing the same sensible appearances. There is an assumed identity of the region of space at which the observers are all gazing, and this serves for the requisite antecedent identification of the common *cognoscendum;* but what they severally find occupying this supposedly single locus consists of character-complexes which are not merely diverse but (according to the logic almost universally accepted until recently) contradictory. So long as it is assumed either that there are certain sets of sensible qualities e.g., two or more colors—which are incompatible, i.e., cannot both occupy the same place or the same surface of a material object at the same time, or that there are in nature "things" which at a given moment have a single and harmonious outfit of geometrical and other properties, the conclusion has seemed inevitable that the many discrepant appearances cannot "really" inhabit the one place or be the one thing at that place. So soon as the dimmest notion that there is such a phenomenon as perspective distortion dawned upon men, they began *eo ipso* to be epistemological dualists. It is of course conceivable, so far as the present consideration goes, that *one* of the discordant appearances might be identical with the object-to-be-known or with some part of it; but even so, since all the other observers are also supposed to be apprehending the object, *their* apprehension, at least, must be mediated through data which are *not* identical with it. Nor does it seem a probable hypothesis that, while *almost* all perception is mediate, a few privileged observers now and then attain direct access to the object.

(5) Finally, the experience of error and illusion, however difficult it may be to render philosophically intelligible, seems to have at least one direct and obvious implication: namely, that the thing which at any moment we err about—otherwise than by mere omission—cannot be a thing which is immediately present to us at that moment, since about the latter than can be no error. It, at least, *is* what it is experienced as. In so far as *cognoscendum* and content are identified, error is excluded; in so far as the possibility of error is admitted, *cognoscendum* and content are set apart from one another. It may perhaps seem that this reasoning applies only to the cases in which there *is* error, and that in true judgments (or in veridical perception) the content may still be the same as the *cognoscendum*. And if the term "true judgments" includes the mere awareness of an immediate datum, then in such judgments there is in fact no duality. But these constitute, at best, only a tiny part of the subject-matter of our claims to potential knowledge, the range of our possible judgments at any given time;

and it is, indeed, an obviously inconvenient use of language to call them judgments at all. For the most part we are occupied, when judging, with matters conceived to be so related to us that we are not, from the very nature of that relation, necessarily immune against error; doubt as to the validity of our judgments about them is assumed to be not meaningless. But where error is *conceivable,* the relation between content and *cognoscendum* must be the same as in the case of actual error. The generic nature of judgments-potentially-erroneous must be conceived in such a way as to permit the genus to have both judgments actually true and judgments actually false as its species— and to make it intelligible that the latter are aiming at the same mark as the former without hitting it. But a judgment is about something in particular; it has to do with a specific portion of reality. Since in actually erroneous judgments it is impossible that that portion can be the immediate datum, error must consist in attributing some character now present in perception or imagery, or represented by a verbal symbol, to *another* locus in reality, where it in fact is not present; and the species of actually true judgments will correspondingly be defined as the attribution of some such character to another locus in reality where it in fact *is* present. In all this, once more, I have only been putting explicitly the way of thinking about truth and error which seems to be common to all mankind, barring a few philosophers of more or less recent times. That bit of baldly dualistic epistemology known as the correspondence-theory of truth is one of the most deeply ingrained and persistent of human habits; there is much reason to doubt whether any of the philosophers who repudiate it actually dispense with it; yet *it* is not merely an instinctive faith, but has behind it certain simple and definite logical considerations which it appears absurd to deny. This also, among the five points of natural epistemological dualism, may plausibly be supposed to have been a part of the unformulated working epistemology of our race from an early stage in the progress of intelligence; for there can hardly have been many featherless bipeds so naïve as not to have learned that man is liable to error, and so dull as to be unable to see, at least dimly, that in direct contemplation there is no room for error.

G. E. MOORE

MOORE'S *Principia Ethica* (1903) is a landmark in the history of ethics. Its impact and influence on subsequent ethical theory, at least in Anglo-American philosophy, have been tremendous. Its specific doctrines of the indefinability of good and of the naturalistic fallacy, whether reinforced, amended, or even rejected, by later theorists, have served as the starting points of much of twentieth century philosophy.

Although Moore's contention that *good*—as against *the good*—is a simple, non-natural, indefinable property is consonant with that aspect of Realism that stresses abstract entities or universals, the central importance of *Principia Ethica*, especially its first chapter (reprinted below), is in its use of analysis to establish the main doctrines of the book. Without formulating what he means by analysis—something Moore did not attempt to do until 1942—analysis in this first chapter of *Principia Ethica* seems to function as a technique of direct intellectual inspection for the discovery of the exact nature of concepts as one kind of extralinguistic entity. Analysis, Moore argues, reveals that good is a simple, non-natural, and indefinable property.

The Subject-Matter of Ethics[1]

1. It is very easy to point out some among our every-day judgments, with the truth of which Ethics is undoubtedly concerned.
Whenever we say, 'So and so is a good man,' or 'That fellow is a villain';
whenever we ask, 'What ought I to do?' or 'Is it wrong for me to do
like this?'; whenever we hazard such remarks as 'Temperance is a
virtue and drunkenness a vice'—it is undoubtedly the business of Ethics
to discuss such questions and such statements; to argue what is the
true answer when we ask what it is right to do, and to give reasons
for thinking that our statements about the character of persons or the
morality of actions are true or false. In the vast majority of cases,
where we make statements involving any of the terms 'virtue,' 'vice,'
'duty,' 'right,' 'ought,' 'good,' 'bad,' we are making ethical judgments;
and if we wish to discuss their truth, we shall be discussing a point
of Ethics.

So much as this is not disputed; but it falls very far short of
defining the province of Ethics. That province may indeed be defined
as the whole truth about that which is at the same time common to
all such judgments and peculiar to them. But we have still to ask
the question: What is it that is thus common and peculiar? And this
is a question to which very different answers have been given by
ethical philosophers of acknowledged reputation, and none of them,
perhaps, completely satisfactory.

2. If we take such examples as those given above, we shall not be
far wrong in saying that they are all of them concerned with the question of 'conduct'—with the question, what, in the conduct of us, human
beings, is good, and what is bad, what is right, and what is wrong. For
when we say that a man is good, we commonly mean that he acts
rightly; when we say that drunkenness is a vice, we commonly mean
that to get drunk is a wrong or wicked action. And this discussion of
human conduct is, in fact, that with which the name 'Ethics' is most

---

1. From *Principia Ethica* (Cambridge: Cambridge University Press, 1903),
Chap. 1. Reprinted by permission of the publishers.

intimately associated. It is so associated by derivation; and conduct is
undoubtedly by far the commonest and most generally interesting
object of ethical judgments.

Accordingly, we find that many ethical philosophers are disposed to
accept as an adequate definition of 'Ethics' the statement that it deals
with the question what is good or bad in human conduct. They hold
that its enquiries are properly confined to 'conduct' or to 'practice';
they hold that the name 'practical philosophy' covers all the matter
with which it has to do. Now, without discussing the proper meaning
of the word (for verbal questions are properly left to the writers of
dictionaries and other persons interested in literature; philosophy, as
we shall see, has no concern with them), I may say that I intend to
use 'Ethics' to cover more than this—a usage, for which there is, I
think, quite sufficient authority. I am using it to cover an enquiry for
which, at all events, there is no other word: the general enquiry into
what is good.

Ethics is undoubtedly concerned with the question what good conduct is; but, being concerned with this, it obviously does not start at
the beginning, unless it is prepared to tell us what is good as well as
what is conduct. For 'good conduct' is a complex notion: all conduct
is not good; for some is certainly bad and some may be indifferent.
And on the other hand, other things, beside conduct, may be good;
and if they are so, then, 'good' denotes some property, that is common to them and conduct; and if we examine good conduct alone of all
good things, then we shall be in danger of mistaking for this property,
some property which is not shared by those other things: and thus we
shall have made a mistake about Ethics even in this limited sense;
for we shall not know what good conduct really is. This is a mistake
which many writers have actually made, from limiting their enquiry
to conduct. And hence I shall try to avoid it by considering first what
is good in general; hoping, that if we can arrive at any certainty
about this, it will be much easier to settle the question of good conduct:
for we all know pretty well what 'conduct' is. This, then, is our first
question: What is good? and What is bad? and to the discussion of
this question (or these questions) I give the name of Ethics, since
that science must, at all events, include it.

3. But this is a question which may have many meanings. If, for
example, each of us were to say 'I am doing good now' or 'I had a
good dinner yesterday,' these statements would each of them be some
sort of answer to our question, although perhaps a false one. So, too,
when A asks B what school he ought to send his son to, B's answer
will certainly be an ethical judgment. And similarly all distribution of

praise or blame to any personage or thing that has existed, now exists, or will exist, does give some answer to the question 'What is good?' In all such cases some particular thing is judged to be good or bad: the question 'What?' is answered by 'This.' But this is not the sense in which a scientific Ethics asks the question. Not one, of all the many million answers of this kind, which must be true, can form a part of an ethical system; although that science must contain reasons and principles sufficient for deciding on the truth of all of them. There are far too many persons, things and events in the world, past, present, or to come, for a discussion of their individual merits to be embraced in any science. Ethics, therefore, does not deal at all with facts of this nature, facts that are unique, individual, absolutely particular; facts with which such studies as history, geography, astronomy, are compelled, in part at least, to deal. And, for this reason, it is not the business of the ethical philosopher to give personal advice or exhortation.

4. But there is another meaning which may be given to the question 'What is good?' 'Books are good' would be an answer to it, though an answer obviously false; for some books are very bad indeed. And ethical judgments of this kind do indeed belong to Ethics; though I shall not deal with many of them. Such is the judgment 'Pleasure is good'—a judgment, of which Ethics should discuss the truth, although it is not nearly as important as that other judgment, with which we shall be much occupied presently—'Pleasure *alone* is good.' It is judgments of this sort, which are made in such books on Ethics as contain a list of 'virtues'—in Aristotle's 'Ethics' for example. But it is judgments of precisely the same kind, which form the substance of what is commonly supposed to be a study different from Ethics, and one much less respectable—the study of Casuistry. We may be told that Casuistry differs from Ethics, in that it is much more detailed and particular, Ethics much more general. But it is most important to notice that Casuistry does not deal with anything that is absolutely particular—particular in the only sense in which a perfectly precise line can be drawn between it and what is general. It is not particular in the sense just noticed, the sense in which this book is a particular book, and A's friend's advice particular advice. Casuistry may indeed be *more* particular and Ethics *more* general; but that means that they differ only in degree and not in kind. And this is universally true of 'particular' and 'general,' when used in this common, but inaccurate, sense. So far as Ethics allows itself to give lists of virtues or even to name constituents of the Ideal, it is indistinguishable from Casuistry. Both alike deal with what is general, in the sense in which physics and chemistry deal with what is general. Just as chemistry aims at dis-

covering what are the properties of oxygen, *wherever it occurs,* and not only of this or that particular specimen of oxygen; so Casuistry aims at discovering what actions are good, *wherever they occur.* In this respect Ethics and Casuistry alike are to be classed with such sciences as physics, chemistry and physiology, in their absolute distinction from those of which history and geography are instances. And it is to be noted that, owing to their detailed nature, casuistical investigations are actually nearer to physics and to chemistry than are the investigations usually assigned to Ethics. For just as physics cannot rest content with the discovery that light is propagated by waves of ether, but must go on to discover the particular nature of the ether-waves corresponding to each several colour; so Casuistry, not content with the general law that charity is a virtue must attempt to discover the relative merits of every different form of charity. Casuistry forms, therefore, part of the ideal of ethical science: Ethics cannot be complete without it. The defects of Casuistry are not defects of principle; no objection can be taken to its aim and object. It has failed only because it is far too difficult a subject to be treated adequately in our present state of knowledge. The casuist has been unable to distinguish, in the cases which he treats, those elements upon which their value depends. Hence he often thinks two cases to be alike in respect of value, when in reality they are alike only in some other respect. It is to mistakes of this kind that the pernicious influence of such investigations has been due. For Casuistry is the goal of ethical investigation. It cannot be safely attempted at the beginning of our studies, but only at the end.

5. But our question 'What is good?' may have still another meaning. We may, in the third place, mean to ask, not what thing or things are good, but how 'good' is to be defined. This is an enquiry which belongs only to Ethics, not to Casuistry; and this is the enquiry which will occupy us first.

It is an enquiry to which most special attention should be directed; since this question, how 'good' is to be defined, is the most fundamental question in all Ethics. That which is meant by 'good' is, in fact, except its converse 'bad,' the *only* simple object of thought which is peculiar to Ethics. Its definition is, therefore, the most essential point in the definition of Ethics; and moreover a mistake with regard to it entails a far larger number of erroneous ethical judgments than any other. Unless this first question be fully understood, and its true answer clearly recognised, the rest of Ethics is as good as useless from the point of view of systematic knowledge. True ethical judgments, of the two kinds last dealt with, may indeed be made by those who do not know the answer to this question as well as by those who do; and it goes without saying that the two classes of people may lead equally good lives. But it is extremely unlikely that the *most general* ethical judgments will be equally valid, in the absence of a true answer to this question: I shall presently try to shew that the gravest errors have been largely due to beliefs in a false answer. And, in any case, it is impossible that, till the answer to this question be known, any one should know *what is the evidence* for any ethical judgment whatsoever. But the main object of Ethics, as a systematic science, is to give correct *reasons* for thinking that this or that is good; and, unless this question be answered, such reasons cannot be given. Even, therefore, apart from the fact that a false answer leads to false conclusions, the present enquiry is a most necessary and important part of the science of Ethics.

6. What, then, is good? How is good to be defined? Now, it may be thought that this is a verbal question. A definition does indeed often mean the expressing of one word's meaning in other words. But this is not the sort of definition I am asking for. Such a definition can never be of ultimate importance in any study except lexicography. If I wanted that kind of definition I should have to consider in the first place how people generally used the word 'good'; but my business is not with its proper usage, as established by custom. I should, indeed, be foolish, if I tried to use it for something which it did not usually denote: if, for instance, I were to announce that, whenever I used the word 'good,' I must be understood to be thinking of that object which is usually denoted by the word 'table.' I shall, therefore, use the word in the sense in which I think it is ordinarily used; but at the same time I am not anxious to discuss whether I am right in thinking that it is so used. My business is solely with that object or idea, which I hold, rightly or wrongly, that the word is generally used to stand for. What I want to discover is the nature of that object or idea, and about this I am extremely anxious to arrive at an agreement.

But, if we understand the question in this sense, my answer to it may seem a very disappointing one. If I am asked 'What is good?' my answer is that good is good, and that is the end of the matter. Or if I am asked 'How is good to be defined?' my answer is that it cannot be defined, and that is all I have to say about it. But disappointing as these answers may appear, they are of the very last importance. To readers who are familiar with philosophic terminology, I can express their importance by saying that they amount to this: That propositions about the good are all of them synthetic and never analytic; and that is plainly no trivial matter. And the same thing may be expressed more popularly, by saying that, if I am right, then nobody can foist upon us such an axiom as that 'Pleasure is the only good' or that 'The good is the desired' on the pretence that this is 'the very meaning of the word.'

7. Let us, then, consider this position. My point is that 'good' is a simple notion, just as 'yellow' is a simple notion; that, just as you cannot, by any manner of means, explain to any one who does not already know it, what yellow is, so you cannot explain what good is. Definitions of the kind that I was asking for, definitions which describe the real nature of the object or notion denoted by a word, and which do not merely tell us what the word is used to mean, are only possible when the object or notion in question is something complex. You can give a definition of a horse, because a horse has many different properties and qualities, all of which you can enumerate. But when you have enumerated them all, when you have reduced a horse to his simplest terms, then you can no longer define those terms. They are simply something which you think of or perceive, and to any one who cannot think of or perceive them, you can never, by any definition, make their nature known. It may perhaps be objected to this that we are able to describe to others, objects which they have never seen or thought of. We can, for instance, make a man understand what a chimaera is, although he has never heard of one or seen one. You can tell him that it is an animal with a lioness's head and body, with a goat's head growing from the middle of its back, and with a snake in place of a tail. But here the object which you are describing is a complex object; it is entirely composed of parts, with which we are all perfectly familiar—a snake, a goat, a lioness; and we know, too, the manner in which those parts are to be put together, because we know what is meant by the middle of a lioness's back, and where her tail is wont to grow. And so it is with all objects, not previously known, which we are able to define: they are all complex; all composed of parts, which may themselves, in the first instance, be capable of similar definition, but which must in the end be reducible to simplest parts, which can no longer be defined. But yellow and good, we say, are not complex: they are notions of that simple kind, out of which definitions are composed and with which the power of further defining ceases.

8. When we say, as Webster says, 'The definition of horse is "A hoofed quadruped of the genus Equus,"' we may, in fact, mean three different things. (1) We may mean merely: 'When I say "horse," you are to understand that I am talking about a hoofed quadruped of the genus Equus.' This might be called the arbitrary verbal definition: and I do not mean that good is indefinable in that sense. (2) We may mean,

as Webster ought to mean: 'When most English people say "horse," they mean a hoofed quadruped of the genus Equus.' This may be called the verbal definition proper, and I do not say that good is indefinable in this sense either; for it is certainly possible to discover how people use a word: otherwise, we could never have known that 'good' may be translated by 'gut' in German and by 'bon' in French. But (3) we may, when we define horse, mean something much more important. We may mean that a certain object, which we all of us know, is composed in a certain manner: that it has four legs, a head, a heart, a liver, etc., etc., all of them arranged in definite relations to one another. It is in this sense that I deny good to be definable. I say that it is not composed of any parts, which we can substitute for it in our minds when we are thinking of it. We might think just as clearly and correctly about a horse, if we thought of all its parts and their arrangement intead of thinking of the whole: we could, I say, think how a horse differed from a donkey just as well, just as truly, in this way, as now we do, only not so easily; but there is nothing whatsoever which we could so substitute for good; and that is what I mean, when I say that good is indefinable.

9. But I am afraid I have still not removed the chief difficulty which may prevent acceptance of the proposition that good is indefinable. I do not mean to say that *the* good, that which is good, is thus indefinable; if I did think so, I should not be writing on Ethics, for my main object is to help towards discovering that definition. It is just because I think there will be less risk of error in our serach for a definition of 'the good,' that I am now insisting that *good* is indefinable. I must try to explain the difference between these two. I suppose it may be granted that 'good' is an adjective. Well 'the good,' 'that which is good,' must therefore be the substantive to which the adjective 'good' will apply: it must be the whole of that to which the adjective will apply, and the adjective must *always* truly apply to it. But if it is that to which the adjective will apply, it must be something different from that adjective itself; and the whole of that something different, whatever it is, will be our definition of *the* good. Now it may be that this something will have other adjectives, beside 'good,' that will apply to it. It may be full of pleasure, for example; it may be intelligent: and if these two adjectives are really part of its definition, then it will certainly be true, that pleasure and intelligence are good. And many people appear to think that, if we say 'Pleasure and intelligence are good,' or if we say 'Only pleasure and intelligence are good,' we are defining 'good.' Well, I cannot deny that propositions of this nature may sometimes be called definitions; I do not know well enough how

the word is generally used to decide upon this point. I only wish it to be understood that that is not what I mean when I say there is no possible definition of good, and that I shall not mean this if I use the word again. I do most fully believe that some true proposition of the form 'Intelligence is good and intelligence alone is good' can be found; if none could be found, our definition of *the* good would be impossible. As it is, I believe *the* good to be definable; and yet I still say that good itself is indefinable.

10. 'Good,' then, if we mean by it that quality which we assert to belong to a thing, when we say that the thing is good, is incapable of any definition, in the most important sense of that word. The most important sense of 'definition' is that in which a definition states what are the parts which invariably compose a certain whole; and in this sense 'good' has no definition because it is simple and has no parts. It is one of those innumerable objects of thought which are themselves incapable of definition, because they are the ultimate terms by reference to which whatever *is* capable of definition must be defined. That there must be an indefinite number of such terms is obvious, on reflection; since we cannot define anything except by an analysis, which, when carried as far as it will go, refers us to something, which is simply different from anything else, and which by that ultimate difference explains the peculiarity of the whole which we are defining: for every whole contains some parts which are common to other wholes also. There is, therefore, no intrinsic difficulty in the contention that 'good' denotes a simple and indefinable quality. There are many other instances of such qualities.

Consider yellow, for example. We may try to define it, by describing its physical equivalent; we may state what kind of light-vibrations must stimulate the normal eye, in order that we may perceive it. But a moment's reflection is sufficient to shew that those light-vibrations are not themselves what we mean by yellow. *They* are not what we perceive. Indeed we should never have been able to discover their existence, unless we had first been struck by the patent difference of quality between the different colours. The most we can be entitled to say of those vibrations is that they are what corresponds in space to the yellow which we actually perceive.

Yet a mistake of this simple kind has commonly been made about 'good.' It may be true that all things which are good are *also* something else, just as it is true that all things which are yellow produce a certain kind of vibration in the light. And it is a fact, that Ethics aims at discovering what are those other properties belonging to all things which are good. But far too many philosophers have thought that when they named those other properties they were actually defining good; that these properties, in fact, were simply not 'other,' but absolutely and entirely the same with goodness. This view I propose to call the 'naturalistic fallacy' and of it I shall now endeavour to dispose.

11. Let us consider what it is such philosophers say. And first it is to be noticed that they do not agree among themselves. They not only say that they are right as to what good is, but they endeavour to prove that other people who say that it is something else, are wrong. One, for instance, will affirm that good is pleasure, another, perhaps, that good is that which is desired; and each of these will argue eagerly to prove that the other is wrong. But how is that possible? One of them says that good is nothing but the object of desire, and at the same time tries to prove that it is not pleasure. But from his first assertion, that good just means the object of desire, one of two things must follow as regards his proof:

(1) He may be trying to prove that the object of desire is not pleasure. But, if this be all, where is his Ethics? The position he is maintaining is merely a psychological one. Desire is something which occurs in our minds, and pleasure is something else which so occurs; and our would-be ethical philosopher is merely holding that the latter is not the object of the former. But what has that to do with the question in dispute? His opponent held the ethical proposition that pleasure was the good, and although he should prove a million times over the psychological proposition that pleasure is not the object of desire, he is no nearer proving his opponent to be wrong. The position is like this. One man says a triangle is a circle: another replies 'A triangle is a straight line, and I will prove to you that I am right: *for*' (this is the only argument) 'a straight line is not a circle.' 'That is quite true,' the other may reply; 'but nevertheless a triangle is a circle, and you have said nothing whatever to prove the contrary. What is proved is that one of us is wrong, for we agree that a triangle cannot be both a straight line and a circle: but which is wrong, there can be no earthly means of proving, since you define triangle as straight line and I define it as circle.'—Well, that is one alternative which any naturalistic Ethics has to face; if good is *defined* as something else, it is then impossible either to prove that any other definition is wrong or even to deny such definition.

(2) The other alternative will scarcely be more welcome. It is that the discussion is after all a verbal one. When A says 'Good means pleasant' and B says 'Good means desired,' they may merely wish to assert that most people have used the word for what is pleasant and for what is desired respectively. And this is quite an interesting subject

for discussion: only it is not a whit more an ethical discussion than the last was. Nor do I think that any exponent of naturalistic Ethics would be willing to allow that this was all he meant. They are all so anxious to persuade us that what they call the good is what we really ought to do. 'Do, pray, act so, because the word "good" is generally used to denote actions of this nature': such, on this view, would be the substance of their teaching. And in so far as they tell us how we ought to act, their teaching is truly ethical, as they mean it to be. But how perfectly absurd is the reason they would give for it! 'You are to do this, because most people use a certain word to denote conduct such as this.' 'You are to say the thing which is not, because most people call it lying.' That is an argument just as good!—My dear sirs, what we want to know from you as ethical teachers, is not how people use a word; it is not even, what kind of actions they approve, which the use of this word 'good' may certainly imply: what we want to know is simply what *is* good. We may indeed agree that what most people do think good, is actually so; we shall at all events be glad to know their opinions: but when we say their opinions about what *is* good, we do mean what we say; we do not care whether they call that thing which they mean 'horse' or 'table' or 'chair,' 'gut' or 'bon' or ' $\alpha\gamma\alpha\theta\sigma$ ': we want to know what it is that they so call. When they say 'Pleasure is good,' we cannot believe that they merely mean 'Pleasure is pleasure' and nothing more than that.

12. Suppose a man says 'I am pleased'; and suppose that is not a lie or a mistake but the truth. Well, if it is true, what does that mean? It means that his mind, a certain definite mind, distinguished by certain definite marks from all others, has at this moment a certain definite feeling called pleasure. 'Pleased' *means* nothing but having pleasure, and though we may be more pleased or less pleased, and even, we may admit for the present, have one or another kind of pleasure; yet in so far as it is pleasure we have, whether there be more or less of it, and whether it be of one kind or another, what we have is one definite thing, absolutely indefinable, some one thing that is the same in all the various degrees and in all the various kinds of it that there may be. We may be able to say how it is related to other things: that, for example, it is in the mind, that it causes desire, that we are conscious of it, etc., etc. We can, I say, describe its relations to other things, but define it we can *not*. And if anybody tried to define pleasure for us as being any other natural object; if anybody were to say, for instance, that pleasure *means* the sensation of red, and were to proceed to deduce from that that pleasure is a colour, we should be entitled to laugh at him and to distrust his future statements about pleasure. Well, that would be the

same fallacy which I have called the naturalistic fallacy. That 'pleased' does not mean 'having the sensation of red,' or anything else whatever, does not prevent us from understanding what it does mean. It is enough for us to know that 'pleased' does mean 'having the sensation of pleasure,' and though pleasure is absolutely indefinable, though pleasure is pleasure and nothing else whatever, yet we feel no difficulty in saying that we are pleased. The reason is, of course, that when I say 'I am pleased,' I do *not* mean that 'I' am the same thing as 'having pleasure.' And similarly no difficulty need be found in my saying that 'pleasure is good' and yet not meaning that 'pleasure' is the same thing as 'good,' that pleasure *means* good, and that good *means* pleasure. If I were to imagine that when I said 'I am pleased,' I meant that I was exactly the same thing as 'pleased,' I should not indeed call that a naturalistic fallacy, although it would be the same fallacy as I have called naturalistic with reference to Ethics. The reason of this is obvious enough. When a man confuses two natural objects with one another, defining the one by the other, if for instance, he confuses himself, who is one natural object, with 'pleased' or with 'pleasure' which are others, then there is no reason to call the fallacy naturalistic. But if he confuses 'good,' which is not in the same sense a natural object, with any natural object whatever, then there is a reason for calling that a naturalistic fallacy; its being made with regard to 'good' marks it as something quite specific, and this specific mistake deserves a name because it is so common. As for the reasons why good is not to be considered a natural object, they may be reserved for discussion in another place. But, for the present, it is sufficient to notice this: Even if it were a natural object, that would not alter the nature of the fallacy nor diminish its importance one whit. All that I have said about it would remain quite equally true: only the name which I have called it would not be so appropriate as I think it is. And I do not care about the name: what I do care about is the fallacy. It does not matter what we call it, provided we recognise it when we meet with it. It is to be met with in almost every book on Ethics; and yet it is not recognised: and that is why it is necessary to multiply illustrations of it, and convenient to give it a name. It is a very simple fallacy indeed. When we say that an orange is yellow, we do not think our statement binds us to hold that 'orange' means nothing else than 'yellow,' or that nothing can be yellow but an orange. Supposing the orange is also sweet! Does that bind us to say that 'sweet' is exactly the same thing as 'yellow,' that 'sweet' must be defined as 'yellow'? And supposing it be recognised that 'yellow' just means 'yellow' and nothing else whatever, does that make it any more difficult to hold that oranges are yellow? Most certainly it does not: on the contrary, it would be absolutely meaningless to say that oranges were yellow, unless yellow did in the end mean just 'yellow' and nothing else whatever—unless it was absolutely indefinable. We should not get any very clear notion about things, which are yellow—we should not get very far with our science, if we were bound to hold that everything which was yellow, *meant* exactly the same thing as yellow. We should find we had to hold that an orange was exactly the same thing as a stool, a piece of paper, a lemon, anything you like. We could prove any number of absurdities; but should we be the nearer to the truth? Why, then, should it be different with 'good'? Why, if good is good and indefinable, should I be held to deny that pleasure is good? Is there any difficulty in holding both to be true at once? On the contrary, there is no meaning in saying that pleasure is good, unless good is something different from pleasure. It is absolutely useless, so far as Ethics is concerned, to prove, as Mr. Spencer tries to do, that increase of pleasure coincides with increase of life, unless good *means* something different from either life or pleasure. He might just as well try to prove that an orange is yellow by shewing that it always is wrapped up in paper.

13. In fact, if it is not the case that 'good' denotes something simple and indefinable, only two alternatives are possible: either it is a complex, a given whole, about the correct analysis of which there may be disagreement; or else it means nothing at all, and there is no such subject as Ethics. In general, however, ethical philosophers have attempted to define good, without recognising what such an attempt must mean. They actually use arguments which involve one or both of the absurdities considered in §11. We are, therefore, justified in concluding that the attempt to define good is chiefly due to want of clearness as to the possible nature of definition. There are, in fact, only two serious alternatives to be considered, in order to establish the conclusion that 'good' does denote a simple and indefinable notion. It might possibly denote a complex, as 'horse' does; or it might have no meaning at all. Neither of these possibilities has, however, been clearly conceived and seriously maintained, as such, by those who presume to define good; and both may be dismissed by a simple appeal to facts.

(1) The hypothesis that disagreement about the meaning of good is disagreement with regard to the correct analysis of a given whole, may be most plainly seen to be incorrect by consideration of the fact that, whatever definition be offered, it may be always asked, with significance, of the complex so defined, whether it is itself good. To take, for instance, one of the more plausible, because one of the more complicated, of such proposed definitions, it may easily be thought, at first

sight, that to be good may mean to be that which we desire to desire. Thus if we apply this definition to a particular instance and say 'When we think that A is good, we are thinking that A is one of the things which we desire to desire,' our proposition may seem quite plausible. But, if we carry the investigation further, and ask ourselves 'Is it good to desire to desire A?' it is apparent, on a little reflection, that this question is itself as intelligible, as the original question 'Is A good?'—that we are, in fact, now asking for exactly the same information about the desire to desire A, for which we formerly asked with regard to A itself. But it is also apparent that the meaning of this second question cannot be correctly analysed into 'Is the desire to desire A one of the things which we desire to desire?': we have not before our minds anything so complicated as the question 'Do we desire to desire to desire to desire A?' Moreover any one can easily convince himself by inspection that the predicate of this proposition—'good'—is positively different from the notion of 'desiring to desire' which enters into its subject: 'That we should desire to desire A is good' is *not* merely equivalent to 'That A should be good is good.' It may indeed be true that what we desire to desire is always also good; perhaps, even the converse may be true: but it is very doubtful whether this is the case, and the mere fact that we understand very well what is meant by doubting it, shews clearly that we have two different notions before our minds.

(2) And the same consideration is sufficient to dismiss the hypothesis that 'good' has no meaning whatsoever. It is very natural to make the mistake of supposing that what is universally true is of such a nature that its negation would be self-contradictory: the importance which has been assigned to analytic propositions in the history of philosophy shews how easy such a mistake is. And thus it is very easy to conclude that what seems to be a universal ethical principle is in fact an identical proposition; that if, for example, whatever is called 'good' seems to be pleasant, the proposition 'Pleasure is the good' does not assert a connection beween two different notions, but involves only one, that of pleasure, which is easily recognised as a distinct entity. But whoever will attentively consider with himself what is actually before his mind when he asks the question 'Is pleasure (or whatever it may be) after all good?' can easily satisfy himself that he is not merely wondering whether pleasure is pleasant. And if he will try this experiment with each suggested definition in succession, he may become expert enough to recognise that in every case he has before his mind a unique object, with regard to the connection of which with any other object, a distinct question may be asked. Every one does in fact understand the question 'Is this good?' When he thinks of it, his state of mind is different from

what it would be, were he asked 'Is this pleasant, or desired, or approved?' It has a distinct meaning for him, even though he may not recognise in what respect it is distinct. Whenever he thinks of 'intrinsic value,' or 'instrinsic worth,' or says that a thing 'ought to exist,' he has before his mind the unique object—the unique property of things—which I mean by 'good.' Everybody is constantly aware of this notion, although he may never become aware at all that it is different from other notions of which he is also aware. But, for correct ethical reasoning, it is extremely important that he should become aware of this fact; and, as soon as the nature of the problem is clearly understood, there should be little difficulty in advancing so far in analysis.

14. 'Good,' then, is indefinable; and yet, so far as I know, there is only one ethical writer, Prof. Henry Sidgwick, who has clearly recognised and stated this fact. We shall see, indeed, how far many of the most reputed ethical systems fall short of drawing the conclusions which follow from such recognition. As present I will only quote one instance, which will serve to illustrate the meaning and importance of this principle that 'good' is indefinable, or, as Prof. Sidgwick says, an 'unanalysable notion.' It is an instance to which Prof. Sidgwick himself refers in a note on the passage, in which he argues that 'ought' is unanalysable.[2]

'Bentham,' says Sidgwick, 'explains that his fundamental principle "states the greatest happiness of all those whose interest is in question as being the right and proper end of human action" '; and yet 'his language in other passages of the same chapter would seem to imply' that he *means* by the word "right" "conducive to the general happiness."' Prof. Sidgwick sees that, if you take these two statements together, you get the absurd result that 'greatest happiness is the end of human action, which is conducive to the general happiness'; and so absurd does it seem to him to call this result, as Bentham calls it, 'the fundamental principle of a moral system,' that he suggests that Bentham cannot have meant it. Yet Prof. Sidgwick himself states elsewhere[3] that Psychological Hedonism is 'not seldom confounded with Egoistic Hedonism'; and that confusion, as we shall see, rests chiefly on that same fallacy, the naturalistic fallacy, which is implied in Bentham's statements. Prof. Sidgwick admits therefore that this fallacy is sometimes committed, absurd as it is; and I am inclined to think that Bentham may really have been one of those who committed it. Mill, as we shall see, certainly did commit it. In any case, whether Bentham committed it or not, his doctrine, as above quoted, will serve as a very good illustration of this

2. *Methods of Ethics,* Bk. i, Chap. iii, § 1 (6th edition).
3. *Methods of Ethics,* Bk. i, Chap. iv, § 1.

fallacy, and of the importance of the contrary proposition that good is indefinable.

Let us consider this doctrine. Bentham seems to imply, so Prof. Sidgwick says, that the word 'right' *means* 'conducive to general happiness.' Now this, by itself, need not necesssarily involve the naturalistic fallacy. For the word 'right' is very commonly appropriated to actions which lead to the attainment of what is good; which are regarded as *means* to the ideal and not as ends-in-themselves. This use of 'right,' as denoting what is good as a means, whether or not it be also good as an end, is indeed the use to which I shall confine the word. Had Bentham been using 'right' in this sense, it might be perfectly coinsistent for him to *define* right as 'conducive to the general happiness,' *provided only* (and notice this proviso) he had already proved, or laid down as an axiom, that general happiness was *the* good, or (what is equivalent to this) that general happiness alone was good. For in that case he would have already defined *the* good as general happiness (a position prefectly consistent, as we have seen, with the contention that 'good' is indefinable), and, since right was to be defined as 'conducive to *the* good,' it would actually *mean* 'conducive to general happiness.' But this method of escape from the charge of having committed the naturalistic fallacy has been closed by Bentham himself. For his fundamental principle is, we see, that the greatest happiness of all concerned is the *right* and proper *end* of human action. He applies the word 'right,' therefore, to the end, as such, not only to the means which are conducive to it; and, that being so, right can no longer be defined as 'conducive to the general happiness,' without involving the fallacy in question. For now it is obvious that the definition of right as conducive to general happiness can be used by him in support of the fundamental principle that general happiness is the right end; instead of being itself derived from that principle. If right, by definition, means conducive to general happiness, then it is obvious that general happiness is the right end. It is not necessary now first to prove or assert that general happiness is the right end, before right is defined as conducive to general happiness—a prefectly valid procedure; but on the contrary the definition of right as conducive to general happiness proves general happiness to be the right end—a perfectly invalid procedure, since in the case the statement that 'general happiness is the right end of human action' is not an ethical principle at all, but either, as we have seen, a proposition about the meaning of words, or else a proposition about the *nature* of general happiness, not about its righteousness or goodness.

Now, I do not wish the importance I assign to this fallacy to be misunderstood. The discovery of it does not at all refute Bentham's contention that greatest happiness is the proper end of human action, if that be understood as an ethical proposition, as he undoubtely in-tended it. That principle may be true all the same; we shall consider whether it is so in succeeding chapters. Bentham might have main-tained it, as Prof. Sidgwick does, even if the fallacy had been pointed out to him. What I am maintaining is that the *reasons* which he actually gives for his ethical proposition are fallacious ones so far as they con-sist in a definition of right. What I suggest is that he did not perceive them to be fallacious; that, if he had done so, he would have been led to seek for other reasons in support of his Utilitarianism; and that, had he sought for other reasons, he *might* have found none which he thought to be sufficient. In that case he would have changed his whole system—a most important consequence. It is undoubtedly also possible that he would have thought other reasons to be sufficient, and in that case his ethical system, in its main results, would still have stood. But, even in this latter case, his use of the fallacy would be a serious objection to him as an ethical philosopher. For it is the business of Ethics, I must insist, not only to obtain true results, but also to find valid reasons for them. The direct object of Ethics is knowledge and not practice; and any one who uses the naturalistic fallacy has certainly not fulfilled this first object, however correct his practical principles may be.

My objections to Naturalism are then, in the first place, that it offers no reason at all, far less any valid reason, for any ethical principle whatever; and in this it already fails to satisfy the requirements of Ethics, as a scientific study. But in the second place I contend that, though it gives a reason for no ethical principle, it is a *cause* of the ac-ceptance of false principles—it deludes the mind into accepting ethical principles, which are false; and in this it is contrary to every aim of Ethics. It is easy to see that if we start with a definition or right con-duct as conduct conducive to general happiness; then, knowing that right conduct is universally conduct conducive to the good, we very easily arrive at the result that the good is general happiness. If, on the other hand, we once recognise that we must start our Ethics without a definition, we shall be much more apt to look about us, before we adopt any ethical principle whatever; and the more we look about us, the less likely are we to adopt a false one. It may be replied to this: Yes, but we shall look about us just as much, before we settle on our definition, and are therefore just as likely to be right. But I will try to shew that this is not the case. If we start with the conviction that a definition of good can be found, we start with the conviction that good *can mean* nothing else than some one property of things; and our only business will then be to discover what that property is. But if we recognise that, so far as the meaning of good goes, anything whatever may be good, we start with a much more open mind. Moreover, apart from the fact that, when we think we have a definition, we cannot logically defend our ethical principles in any way whatever, we shall also be much less apt to defend them well, even if illogically. For we shall start with the conviction that good must mean so and so, and shall therefore be inclined either to misunderstand our opponent's arguments or to cut them short with the reply, 'This is not an open question: the very meaning of the word decides it; no one can think otherwise except through confusion.'

15. Our first conclusion as to the subject-matter of Ethics is, then, that there is a simple, indefinable, unanalysable object of thought by reference to which it must be defined. By what name we call this unique object is a matter of indifference, so long as we clearly recognise what it is and that it does differ from other objects. The words which are commonly taken as the signs of ethical judgments all do refer to it; and they are expressions of ethical judgments solely because they do so refer. But they may refer to it in two different ways, which it is very important to distinguish, if we are to have a complete definition of the range of ethical judgments. Before I proceeded to argue that there was such an indefinable notion involved in ethical notions, I stated (§4) that it was necessary for Ethics to enumerate all true universal judgments, asserting that such and such a thing was good, whenever it occurred. But, although all such judgments do refer to that unique notion which I have called 'good,' they do not all refer to it in the same way. They may either assert that this unique property *does* always attach to the thing in question, or else they may assert only that the thing in question is *a cause or necessary condition* for the existence of other things to which this unique property does attach. The nature of these two species of universal ethical judgments is extremely different; and a great part of the difficulties, which are met with in ordinary ethical speculation, are due to the failure to distinguish them clearly. Their difference has, indeed, received expression in ordinary language by the contrast between the terms 'good as means' and 'good in itself,' 'value as a means' and 'intrinsic value.' But these terms are apt to be applied correctly only in the more obvious instances; and this seems to be due to the fact that the distinction between the conceptions which they denote has not been made a separate object of investigation. This distinction may be briefly pointed out as follows.

16. Whenever we judge that a thing is 'good as a means,' we are making a judgment with regard to its causal relations: we judge *both* that it will have a particular kind of effect, *and* that that effect will be

good in itself. But to find causal judgments that are universally true is notoriously a matter of extreme difficulty. The late date at which most of the physical sciences became exact, and the comparative fewness of the laws which they have succeeded in establishing even now, are sufficient proofs of this difficulty. With regard, then, to what are the most frequent objects of ethical judgments, namely actions, it is obvious that we cannot be satisfied that any of our universal causal judgments are true, even in the sense in which scientific laws are so. We cannot even discover hypothetical laws of the form 'Exactly this action will always, under these conditions, produce exactly that effect.' But for a correct ethical judgment with regard to the effect of certain actions we require more than this in two respects. (1) We require to know that a given action will produce a certain effect, *under whatever circumstances it occurs*. But this is certainly impossible. It is certain that in different circumstances the same action may produce effects which are utterly different in all respects upon which the value of the effects depends. Hence we can never be entitled to more than a *generalisation*—to a proposition of the form 'This result *generally* follows this kind of action'; and even this generalisation will only be true, if the circumstances under which the action occurs are generally the same. This is in fact the case, to a great extent, within any one particular age and state of society. But, when we take other ages into account, in many most important cases the normal circumstances of a given kind of action will be so different, that the generalisation which is true for one will not be true for another. With regard then to ethical judgments which assert that a certain kind of action is good as a means to a certain kind of effect, none will be *universally* true; and many, though *generally* true at one period, will be generally false at others. But (2) we require to know not only that *one* good effect will be produced, but that, among all subsequent events affected by the action in question, the balance of good will be greater than if any other possible action had been performed. In other words, to judge that an action is generally a means to good is to judge not only that it generally does *some* good, but that it generally does the greatest good of which the circumstances admit. In this respect ethical judgments about the effects of action involve a difficulty and a complication far greater than that involved in the establishment of scientific laws. For the latter we need only consider a single effect; for the former it is essential to consider not only this, but the effects of that effect, and so on as far as our view into the future can reach. It is, indeed, obvious that our view can never reach far enough for us to be certain that any action will produce the best possible effects. We must be content, if the greatest possible balance of good seems to be produced within a limited period. But it is important to notice that the whole series of effects within a period of considerable length is actually taken account of in our common judgments that an action is good as a means; and that hence this additional complication, which makes ethical generalisations so far more difficult to establish than scientific laws, is one which is involved in actual eithical discussions, and is of practical importance. The commonest rules of conduct involve such considerations as the balancing of future bad health against immediate gains; and even if we can never settle with any certainty how we shall secure the greatest possible total of good, we try at least to assure ourselves that probable future evils will not be greater than the immediate good.

17. There are, then, judgments which state that certain kinds of things have good effects; and such judgments, for the reasons just given, have the important characteristics (1) that they are unlikely to be true, if they state that the kind of thing in question *always* has good effects, and (2) that, even if they only state that it *generally* has good effects, many of them will only be true of certain periods in the world's history. On the other hand there are judgments which state that certain kinds of things are themselves good; and these differ from the last in that, if true at all, they are all of them universally true. It is, therefore, extremely important to distinguish these two kinds of possible judgments. Both may be expressed in the same language: in both cases we commonly say 'Such and such a thing is good.' But in the one case 'good' will mean 'good as means,' *i.e.* merely that the thing is a means to good— will have good effects: in the other case it will mean 'good as end'—we shall be judging that the thing itself has the property which, in the first case, was asserted only to belong to its effects. It is plain that these are very different assertions to make about a thing; it is plain that either or both of them may be made, both truly and falsely, about all manner of things; and it is certain that unless we are clear as to which of the two we mean to assert, we shall have a very poor chance of deciding rightly whether our assertion is true or false. It is precisely this clearness as to the meaning of the question asked which has hitherto been almost entirely lacking in ethical speculation. Ethics has always been predominantly concerned with the investigation of a limited class of actions. With regard to these we may ask *both* how far they are good in themselves *and* how far they have a general tendency to produce good results. And the arguments brought forward in ethical discussion have always been of both classes—both such as would prove the conduct in question to be good in itself and such as would prove it to be good as a means. But that these are the only questions which any ethical discussion can have to settle, and that to settle the one is *not* the same thing

as to settle the other—these two fundamenal facts have in general es
caped the notice of ethical philosophers. Ethical questions are com
monly asked in an ambiguous form. It is asked 'What is a man's duty
under these circumstances?' or 'Is it right to act in this way?' or 'What
ought we to aim at securing?' But all these questions are capable of fur
ther analysis; a correct answer to any of them involves both judgments
of what is good in itself and causal judgments. This is implied even by
those who maintain that we have a direct and immediate judgment of
absolute rights and duties. Such a judgment can only mean that the
course of action in question is *the* best thing to do; that, by acting so
every good that *can* be secured will have been secured. Now we are not
concerned with the question whether such a judgment will ever be true
The question is: What does it imply, if it is true? And the only possible
answer is that, whether true or false, it implies both a proposition as to
the degree of goodness of the action in question, as compared with
other things, and a number of causal propositions. For it cannot be
denied that the action will have consequences: and to deny that the
consequences matter is to make a judgment of their intrinsic value, as
compared with the action itself. In asserting that the action is *the* best
thing to do, we assert that it together with its consequences presents
a greater sum of intrinsic value than any possible alternative. And this
condition may be realised by any of the three cases:—*(a)* If the action
itself has greater instrinsic value than any alternative, whereas both its
consequences and those of the alternatives are absolutely devoid either
of intrinsic merit or intrinsic demerit; or *(b)* if, though, its consequences are intrinsically bad, the balance of intrinsic value is greater
than would be produced by any alternative; or *(c)* if, its consequences
being intrinsically good, the degree of value belonging to them and it
conjointly is greater than that of any alternative series. In short, to
assert that a certain line of conduct is, at a given time, absolutely right
or obligatory, is obviously to assert that more good or less evil will exist
in the world, if it be adopted than if anything else be done instead. But
this implies a judgment as to the value both of its own consequences and
of those of any possible alternative. And that an action will have such
and such consequences involves a number of causal judgments.

Similarly, in answering the question 'What ought we to aim at securing?' causal judgments are again involved, but in a somewhat different
way. We are liable to forget, because it is so obvious, that this question
can never be answered correctly except by naming something which
can be secured. Not everything can be secured; and, even if we judge
that nothing which cannot be obtained would be of equal value with
that which can, the possibility of the latter, as well as its value, is es-

ential to its being a proper end of action. Accordingly neither our
udgments as to what actions we ought to perform, nor even our judgments as to the ends which they ought to produce, are pure judgments
of instrinsic value. With regard to the former, an action which is absolutely obligatory *may* have no intrinsic value whatsoever; that it is
perfectly virtuous may mean merely that it causes the best possible
effects. And with regard to the latter, these best possible results which
justify our action can, in any case, have only so much of intrinsic value
as the laws of nature allow us to secure; and they in their turn *may*
have no intrinsic value whatsoever, but may merely be a means to the
attainment (in a still further future) of something that has such value.
Whenever, therefore, we ask 'What ought we to do?' or 'What ought
we to try to get?' we are asking questions which involve a correct answer to two others, completely different in kind from one another. We
must know *both* what degree of intrinsic value different things have,
and how these different things may be obtained. But the vast majority
of questions which have actually been discussed in Ethics—*all* practical questions, indeed—involve this double knowledge; and they have
been discussed without any clear separation of the two distinct questions involved. A great part of the vast disagreements prevalent in
Ethics is to be attributed to this failure in analysis. By the use of conceptions which involve both that of intrinsic value and that of causal
relation, as if they involved instrinsic value only, two different errors
have been rendered almost universal. Either it is assumed that nothing has intrinsic value which it not possible, or else it is assumed that
what is necessary must have intrinsic value. Hence the primary and
peculiar business of Ethics, the determination what things have intrinsic value and in what degrees, has received no adequate treatment
at all. And on the other hand a *thorough* discussion of means has been
also largely neglected, owing to an obscure perception of the truth that
it is perfectly irrelevant to the question of intrinsic values. But however
this may be, and however strongly any particular reader may be convinced that some one of the mutually contradictory systems which
hold the field has given a correct answer either to the question what
has intrinsic value, or to the question what we ought to do, or to both,
it must at least be admitted that the questions what is best in itself and
what will bring about the best possible, are utterly distinct; that both
belong to the actual subject-matter of Ethics; and that the more clearly
distinct questions are distinguished, the better is our chance of answering both correctly.

18. There remains one point which must not be omitted in a complete description of the kind of questions which Ethics has to answer.

The main division of those questions is, as I have said, into two; the question what things are good in themselves, and the question to what other things these are related as effects. The first of these, which is the primary ethical question and is presupposed by the other, includes a correct comparison of the various things which have intrinsic value (if there are many such) in respect of the degree of value which they have; and such comparison involves a difficulty of principle which has greatly aided the confusion of intrinsic value with mere 'goodness as a means.' It has been pointed out that one difference between a judgment which asserts that a thing is good in itself, and a judgment which asserts that it is a means to good, consists in the fact that the first, if true of one instance of the thing in question, is necessarily true of all; whereas a thing which has good effects under some circumstances may have bad ones under others. Now it is certainly true that all judgments of intrinsic value are in this sense universal; but the principle which I have now to enunciate may easily make it appear as if they were not so but resembled the judgment of means in being merely general. There is, as will presently be maintained, a vast number of different things, each of which has intrinsic value; there are also very many which are positively bad; and there is a still larger class of things, which appear to be indifferent. But a thing belonging to any of these three classes may occur as part of a whole, which includes among its other parts other things belonging both to the same and to the other two classes; and these wholes, as such, may also have intrinsic value. The paradox, to which it is necessary to call attention, is that *the value of such a whole bears no regular proportion to the sum of the values of its parts*. It is certain that a good thing may exist in such a relation to another good thing that the value of the whole thus formed is immensely greater than the sum of the values of the two good things. It is certain that a whole formed of a good thing and an indifferent thing may have immensely greater value than that good thing itself possesses. It is certain that two bad things or a bad thing and an indifferent thing may form a whole much worse than the sum of badness of its parts. And it seems as if indifferent things may also be the sole constituents of a whole which has great value, either positive or negative. Whether the addition of a bad thing to a good whole may increase the positive value of the whole, or the addition of a bad thing to a bad may produce a whole having positive value, may seem more doubtful; but it is, at least possible, and this possibility must be taken into account in our ethical investigations. However we may decide particular questions, the principle is clear. *The value of a whole must not be assumed to be the same as the sum of the values of its parts*.

A single instance will suffice to illustrate the kind of relation in question. It seems to be true that to be conscious of a beautiful object is a thing of great intrinsic value; whereas the same object, if no one be conscious of it has certainly comparatively little value, and is commonly held to have none at all. But the consciousness of a beautiful object is certainly a whole of some sort in which we can distinguish as parts the object on the one hand and the being conscious on the other. Now this latter factor occurs as part of a different whole, whenever we are conscious of anything; and it would seem that some of these wholes have at all events very little value, and may even be indifferent or positively bad. Yet we cannot always attribute the slightness of their value to any positive demerit in the object which differentiates them from the consciousness of beauty; the object itself may approach as near as possible to absolute neutrality. Since, therefore, mere consciousness does not always confer great value upon the whole of which its forms a part, even though its object may have no great demerit, we cannot attribute the great superiority of the consciousness of a beautiful thing over the beautiful thing itself to the mere addition of the value of consciousness to that of the beautiful thing. Whatever the intrinsic value of consciousness may be, it does not give to the whole of which it forms a part a value proportioned to the sum of its value and that of its object. If this be so, we have here an instance of a whole possessing a different intrinsic value from the sum of that of its parts; and whether it be so or not, what is meant by such a difference is illustrated by this case.

19. There are, then, wholes which possess the property that their value is different from the sum of the values of their parts; and the relations which subsist between such parts and the whole of which they form a part have not hitherto been distinctly recognised or received a separate name. Two points are especially worthy of notice. (1) It is plain that the existence of any such part is a necessary condition for the existence of that good which is constituted by the whole. And exactly the same language will also express the relation between a means and the good thing which is its effect. But yet there is a most important difference between the two cases, constituted by the fact that the part is, whereas the means is not, a part of the good thing for the existence of which its existence is a necessary condition. The necessity by which, if the good in question is to exist, the means to it must exist is merely a natural or causal necessity. If the laws of nature were different, exactly the same good might exist, although what is now a necessary condition of its existence did not exist. The existence of the means has no intrinsic value; and its utter annihilation would leave the value

of that which it is now necessary to secure entirely unchanged. But in the case of a part of such a whole as we are now considering, it is otherwise. In this case the good in question cannot conceivably exist unless the part exist also. The necessity which connects the two is quite independent of natural law. What is asserted to have intrinsic value is the existence of the whole; and the existence of the whole includes the existence of its part. Suppose the part removed, and what remains is *not* what was asserted to have intrinsic value; but if we suppose a means removed, what remains is just what *was* asserted to have intrinsic value. And yet (2) the existence of the part may *itself* have no more intrinsic value than that of the means. It is this fact which constitutes the paradox of the relation which we are discussing. It has just been said that what has intrinsic value is the existence of the whole, and that this includes the existence of the part; and from this it would seem a natural inference that the existence of the part has intrinsic value. But the inference would be as false as if we were to conclude that, because the number of two stones was two, each of the stones was also two. The part of a valuable whole retains exactly the same value when it is, as when it is not, a part of that whole. If it had value under other circumstances, its value is not any greater, when it is part of a far more valuable whole; and if it had no value by itself, it has none still, however great be that of the whole of which it now forms a part. We are not then justified in asserting that one and the same thing is under some circumstances intrinsically good, and under others not so; as we are justified in asserting of a means that it sometimes does and sometimes does not produce good results. And yet we are justified in asserting that it is far more desirable that a certain thing should exist under some circumstances than under others; namely when other things will exist in such relations to it as to form a more valuable whole. *It* will not have more intrinsic value under these circumstances than under others; *it* will not necessarily even be a mean to the existence of things having more intrinsic value: but it will, like a means, be a necessary condition for the existence of that which *has* greater intrinsic value, although, unlike a means, it will itself form a part of of this more valuable existent.

20. I have said that the peculiar relation between part and whole which I have just been trying to define is one which has received no separate name. It would, however, be useful that it should have one; and there is a name, which might well be appropriated to it, if only it could be divorced from its present unfortunate usage. Philosophers, especially those who profess to have derived great benefit from the writings of Hegel, have latterly made much use of the terms 'organic

whole', 'organic unity', 'organic relation.' The reason why these terms might well be appropriated to the use suggested is that the peculiar relation of parts to whole, just defined, is one of the properties which distinguishes the wholes to which they are actually applied with the greatest frequency. And the reason why it is desirable that they should be divorced from their present usage is that, as at present used, they have no distinct sense and, on the contrary, both imply and propagate errors of confusion.

To say that a thing is an 'organic whole' is generally understood to imply that its parts are related to one another and to itself as means to end; it is also understood to imply that they have a property described in some such phrase as that they have 'no meaning or significance apart from the whole'; and finally such a whole is also treated as if it had the property to which I am proposing that the name should be confined. But those who use the term give us, in general, no hint as to how they suppose these three properties to be related to one another. It seems generally to be assumed that they are identical; and always, at least, that they are necessarily connected with one another. That they are not identical I have already tried to shew; to suppose them so is to neglect the very distinctions pointed out in the last paragraph; and the usage might well be discontinued merely because it encourages such neglect. But a still more cogent reason for its discontinuance is that, so far from being necessarily connected, the second is a property which can attach to nothing, being a self-contradictory conception; whereas the first, if we insist on its most important sense, applies to many cases, to which we have no reason to think that the third applies also, and the third certainly applies to many to which the first does not apply.

21. These relations between the three properties just distinguished may be illustrated by reference to a whole of the kind from which the name 'organic' was derived—a whole which is an organism in the scientific sense—namely the human body.

(1) There exists between many parts of our body (though not between all) a relation which has been familiarised by the fable, attributed to Menenius Agrippa, concerning the belly and its members. We can find in it parts such that the continued existence of the one is a necessary condition for the continued existence of the other; while the continued existence of this latter is also a necessary condition for the continued existence of the former. This amounts to no more than saying that in the body we have instances of two things, both enduring for some time, which have a relation of mutual causal dependence on one another—a relation of 'reciprocity.' Frequently no more than this is meant by saying that the parts of the body form an 'organic unity', or

that they are mutually means and ends to one another. And we ce tainly have here a striking characteristic of living things. But it woul be extremely rash to assert that this relation of mutual causal depend ence was only exhibited by living things and hence was sufficient t define their peculiarity. And it is obvious that of two things which hav this relation of mutual dependence, neither may have intrinsic value, one may have it and the other lack it. They are not necessarily 'ends' t one another in any sense except that in which 'end' means 'effect.' An moreover it is plain that in this sense the whole cannot be an end t any of its parts. We are apt to talk of 'the whole' in contrast to one its parts, when in fact we mean only *the rest* of the parts. But strictl the whole must include all its parts and no part can be a cause of th whole, because it cannot be a cause of itself. It is plain, therefore, tha this relation of mutual causal dependence implies nothing with regar to the value of either of the objects which have it; and that, even both of them happen also to have value, this relation between them one which cannot hold between part and whole.

But (2) it may also be the case that our body as a whole has a valu greater than the sum of values of its parts; and this may be what meant when it is said that the parts are means to the whole. It obvious that if we ask the question 'Why *should* the parts be such they are?' a proper answer may be 'Because the whole they form ha so much value.' But it is equally obvious that the relation which we th assert to exist between part and whole is quite different from that whic we assert to exist between part and part when we say 'This part exist because that one could not exist without it.' In the latter case we asse the two parts to be causally connected; but, in the former, part an whole cannot be causally connected, and the relation which we assert t exist between them may exist even though the parts are not causall connected either. All the parts of a picture do not have that relation mutual causal dependence, which certain parts of the body have, an yet the existence of those which do not have it may be absolutely es sential to the value of the whole. The two relations are quite distinct i kind, and we cannot infer the existence of the one from that of th other. It can, therefore, serve no useful purpose to include them bot under the same name; and if we are to say that a whole is organic be cause its parts are (in this sense) 'means' to the whole, we must n say that it is organic because its parts are causally dependent on on another.

22. But finally (3) the sense which has been most prominent i recent uses of the term 'organic whole' is one whereby it asserts th parts of such a whole to have a property which the parts of no whol

an possibly have. It is supposed that just as the whole would not be what it is but for the existence of the parts, so the parts would not be what they are but for the existence of the whole; and this is understood to mean not merely that any particular part could not exist unless the others existed too (which is the case where relation (1) exists between the parts), but actually that the part is no distinct object of thought—that the whole, of which it is a part, is in its turn a part of it. That this supposition is self-contradictory a very little reflection should be sufficient to shew. We may admit, indeed, that when a particular thing is a part of a whole, it does possess a predicate which it would not otherwise possess—namely that it is a part of that whole. But what cannot be admitted is that this predicate alters the nature or enters into the definition of the thing which has it. When we think of the part *itself*, we mean just *that which* we assert, in this case, to *have* the predicate that it is part of the whole; and the mere assertion that *it* is a part of the whole involves that it should itself be distinct from that which we assert of it. Otherwise we contradict ourselves since we assert that, not *it*, but something else—namely it together with that which we assert of it—has the predicate which we assert of it. In short, it is obvious that no part contains analytically the whole to which it belongs, or any other parts of that whole. The relation of part to whole is *not* the same as that of whole to part; and the very definition of the latter is that it does contain analytically that which is said to be its part. And yet this very self-contradictory doctrine is the chief mark which shews the influence of Hegel upon modern philosophy—an influence which pervades almost the whole of orthodox philosophy. This is what is generally implied by the cry against falsification by abstraction: that a whole is always a part of its part! 'If you want to know the truth about a part,' we are told, 'you must consider *not* that part, but something else—namely the whole: *nothing* is true of the part, but only of the whole.' Yet plainly it must be true of the part at least that it is a part of the whole; and it is obvious that when we say it is, we do *not* mean merely that the whole is a part of itself. This doctrine, therefore that a part can have 'no meaning or significance apart from its whole' must be utterly rejected. It implies itself that the statement 'This is a part of that whole' has a meaning; and in order that this may have one, both subject and predicate must have a distinct meaning. And it is easy to see how this false doctrine has arisen by confusion with the two relations (1) and (2) which may really be properties of wholes.

(*a*) The *existence* of a part may be connected by a natural or causal necessity with the existence of the other parts of its whole; and further what is a part of a whole and what has ceased to be such a part, although differing intrinsically from one another, may be called by one and the same name. Thus, to take a typical example, if an arm be cut off from the human body, we still call it an arm. Yet an arm, when it is a part of the body, undoubtedly differs from a dead arm: and hence we may easily be led to say 'The arm which is a part of the body would not be what it is, if it were not such a part,' and to think that the contradiction thus expressed is in reality a characteristic of things. But, in fact, the dead arm never was a part of the body; it is only *partially* identical with the living arm. Those parts of it which are identical with parts of the living arm are exactly the same, whether they belong to the body or not; and in them we have an undeniable instance of one and the same thing at one time forming a part, and at another not forming a part of the presumed 'organic whole.' On the other hand those properties which *are* possessed by the living, and *not* by the dead, arm, do not exist in a changed form in the latter: they simply do not exist there *at all*. By a causal necessity their existence depends on their having that relation to the other parts of the body which we express by saying that they form part of it. Yet, most certainly, *if* they ever did not form part of the body, they *would* be exactly what they are when they do. That they differ intrinsically from the properties of the dead arm and that they form part of the body are propositions not analytically related to one another. There is no contradiction in supposing them to retain such intrinsic differences and yet not to form part of the body.

But *(b)* when we are told that a living arm has no *meaning* or *significance* apart from the body to which it belongs, a different fallacy is also suggested. 'To have meaning or significance' is commonly used in the sense of 'to have importance'; and this again means 'to have value either as a means or as an end.' Now it is quite possible that even a living arm, apart from its body, would have no intrinsic value whatever; although the whole of which it is a part has great intrinsic value owing to its presence. Thus we may easily come to say that, *as* a part of the body, it has great value, whereas *by itself* it would have none; and thus that its whole 'meaning' lies in its relation to the body. But in fact the value in question obviously does not belong to *it* at all. To have value merely as a part is equivalent to having no value at all, but merely being a part of that which has it. Owing, however, to neglect of this distinction, the assertion that a part has value, *as a part*, which it would not otherwise have, easily leads to the assumption that it is also different, as a part, from what it would otherwise be; for it is, in fact, true that two things which have a different value must also differ in other respects. Hence the assumption that one and the same thing, because it is a part of a more valuable whole at one time than at another, therefore has more intrinsic value at one time than at another, has encouraged the self-contradictory belief that one and the same thing may be two different things, and that only in one of its forms is it truly what it is.

For these reasons, I shall, where it seems convenient, take the liberty to use the term 'organic' with a special sense. I shall use it to denote the fact that a whole has an intrinsic value different in amount from the sum of the values of its parts. I shall use it to denote this and only this. The term will not imply any causal relation whatever between the parts of the whole in question. And it will not imply either, that the parts are inconceivable except as parts of that whole, or that, when they form parts of such a whole, they have a value different from that which they would have if they did not. Understood in this special and perfectly definite sense the relation of an organic whole to its parts is one of the most important which Ethics has to recognise. A chief part of that science should be occupied in comparing the relative values of various goods; and the grossest errors will be committed in such comparison if it be assumed that wherever two things form a whole, the value of that whole is merely the sum of the values of those two things. With this question of 'organic wholes,' then, we complete the enumeration of the kind of problems, with which it is the business of Ethics to deal.

23. In this chapter I have endeavoured to enforce the following conclusions. (1) The peculiarity of Ethics is not that it investigates assertions about human conduct, but that it investigates assertions about that property of things which is denoted by the term 'good,' and the converse property denoted by the term 'bad.' It must, in order to establish its conclusions, investigate the truth of *all* such assertions, *except* those which assert the relation of this property only to a single existent (1—4). (2) This property, by reference to which the subject-matter of Ethics much be defined, is itself simple and indefinable (5—14). And (3) all assertions about its relation to other things are of two, and only two, kinds: they either assert in what degree things themselves possess this property, or else they assert causal relations between other things and those which possess it (15—17). Finally, (4) in considering the different degrees in which things themselves possess this property, we have to take account of the fact that a whole may possess it in a degree different from that which is obtained by summing the degrees in which its parts possess it (18—22).

G. E. MOORE

RUSSELL AND MOORE, the two leading exponents of Realism, divided sharply after Russell's *Problems of Philosophy*. Russell more and more emphasized the implicit dubiety of common-sense beliefs about the world, deriving these doubts from rigorous analyses of the nature of the mental and the physical. Moore, on the other hand, stressed the absolute certainty of the truth of common-sense beliefs, contending that Russell's (and others') scepticism regarding these beliefs rested upon a confusion of knowledge of their truth with correct analyses of this knowledge. His essay, "A Defence of Common Sense" (1925), recapitulates his own set of common-sense beliefs which, he claims, he and everyone else, their counterclaims notwithstanding, know with absolute certainty to be true. This essay, along with "Proof of an External World" (1939), has given rise to much vehement debate over the role of ordinary language in Moore's philosophy as well as in philosophy in general.

A Defence of Common Sense[1]

In what follows I have merely tried to state, one by one, some of the most important points in which my philosophical position differs from positions which have been taken up by *some* other philosophers. It may be that the points which I have had room to mention are not really the most important, and possibly some of them may be points as to which no philosopher has ever really differed from me. But, to the best of my belief, each is a point as to which many have really differed; although (in most cases, at all events) each is also a point as to which many have agreed with me.

I. The first point is a point which embraces a great many other points. And it is one which I cannot state as clearly as I wish to state it, except at some length. The method I am going to use for stating it is this. I am going to begin by enunciating, under the heading (1), a whole long list of propositions, which may seem, at first sight, such obvious truisms as not to be worth stating: they are, in fact, a set of propositions, every one of which (in my own opinion) I *know*, with certainty, to be true. I shall, next, under the heading (2), state a single proposition which makes an assertion about a whole set of *classes* of propositions—each class being defined, as the class consisting of all propositions which resemble *one* of the propositions in (1) in a certain respect. (2), therefore, is a proposition which could not be stated, until the list of propositions in (1), or some similar list, had already been given. (2) is itself a proposition which may seem such an obvious truism as not to be worth stating: and it is also a proposition which (in my own opinion) I *know*, with certainty, to be true. But, nevertheless, it is, to the best of my belief, a proposition with regard to which many philosophers have, for different reasons, differed from me; even if they have not directly denied (2) itself, they have held views incompatible with it. My first point, then, may be said to be that

1. From J. H. Muirhead (ed.), *Contemporary British Philosophy* (Second Series, London: The Macmillan Company, 1925), pp. 193-223. Reprinted by permission of The Macmillan Company, New York, and George Allen & Unwin, Ltd., London.

(2), together with all its implications, some of which I shall expressly mention, is true.

(1) I begin, then, with my list of truisms, every one of which (in my own opinion) I *know*, with certainty, to be true. The propositions to be included in this list are the following:—

There exists at present a living human body, which is *my* body. This body was born at a certain time in the past, and has existed continuously ever since, though not without undergoing changes; it was, for instance, much smaller when it was born, and for some time afterwards, than it is now. Ever since it was born, it has been either in contact with or not far from the surface of the earth; and, at every moment since it was born, there have also existed many other things, having shape and size in three dimensions (in the same familiar sense in which it has), from which it has been *at various distances* (in the familiar sense in which it is now at a distance both from that mantel-piece and from that book-case, and at a greater distance from the book-case than it is from the mantel-piece); also there have (very often, at all events) existed some other things of this kind with which it was *in contact* (in the familiar sense in which it is now in contact with the pen I am holding in my right hand and with some of the clothes I am wearing). Among the things which have, in this sense, formed part of its environment (i.e. have been either in contact with it, or at *some* distance from it, however *great*) there have, at every moment since its birth, been large numbers of other living human bodies, each of which has, like it, (*a*) at some time been born, (*b*) continued to exist for some time after birth, (*c*) been, at every moment of its life after birth, either in contact with or not far from the surface of the earth; and many of these bodies have already died and ceased to exist. But the earth had existed also for many years before my body was born; and for many of these years, also, large numbers of human bodies had, at every moment, been alive upon it; and many of these bodies had died and ceased to exist before it was born. Finally (to come to a different class of propositions), I am a human being, and I have, at different times since my body was born, had many different experiences, of each of many different kinds: e.g. I have often perceived both my own body and other things which formed part of its environment, including other human bodies; I have not only perceived things of this kind, but have also observed facts about them, such as, for instance, the fact which I am now observing, that that mantel-piece is at present nearer to my body than that book-case; I have been aware of other facts, which I was not at the time observing, such as, for instance, the fact, of which I am now aware, that my body existed yesterday and was then also for some time nearer to that mantel-piece than to that book-case; I have had expectations with regard to the future, and many beliefs of other kinds, both true and false; I have thought of imaginary things, and persons and incidents, in the reality of which I did not believe; I have had dreams; and I have had feelings of many different kinds. And, just as my body has been the body of a human being, namely myself, who has, during its life-time, had many experiences of each of these (and other) different kinds; so, in the case of very many of the other human bodies which have lived upon the earth, each has been the body of a different human being, who has, during the life-time of that body, had many different experiences of each of these (and other) different kinds.

(2) I now come to the single truism which, as will be seen, could not be stated except by reference to the whole list of truisms, just given in (1). This truism also (in my own opinion) I *know*, with certainty, to be true; and it is as follows:—

In the case of *very many* (I do not say *all*) of the human beings belonging to the class (which includes myself) defined in the following way, i.e. as human beings who have had human bodies, that were born and lived for some time upon the earth, and who have, during the life-time of those bodies, had many different experiences of each of the kinds mentioned in (1), it is true that each has frequently, during the life of his body, known, with regard to *himself* or *his* body, and with regard to some time earlier than any of the times at which I wrote down the propositions in (1), a proposition *corresponding* to each of the propositions in (1), in the sense that it asserts with regard to *him*self or *his* body and the earlier time in question (namely, in each case, the time at which he knew it), just what the corresponding proposition in (1) asserts with regard to *me* or *my* body and the time at which I wrote that proposition down.

In other words what (2) asserts is only (what seems an obvious enough truism) that each of *us* (meaning by "us," very many human beings of the class defined) has frequently *known*, with regard to *him*self or *his* body and the time at which he knew it, everything which, in writing down my list of propositions in (1), I was claiming to know about *my*self or *my* body and the time at which I wrote that proposition down. I.e. just as *I* knew (when I wrote it down) "There exists at present a living human body which is my body," so each of us has frequently known with regard to himself and some other time the different but corresponding proposition, which *he* could *then* have properly expressed by, "There exists *at present* a human body which is *my* body"; just as *I* know "Many human bodies other than mine have before now lived on the earth," so each of us has frequently known the different but corresponding proposition "Many human bodies other than *mine* have before *now* lived on the earth"; just as *I* know "Many human human beings other than myself have before now perceived and dreamed, and felt," so each of *us* has frequently known the different but corresponding proposition "Many human beings other than *myself* have before *now* perceived, and dreamed, and felt"; and so on, in the case of *each* of the propositions enumerated in (1).

I hope there is no difficulty in understanding, so far, what this proposition (2) asserts. I have tried to make clear by examples what I mean by "propositions *corresponding* to each of the propositions in (1)." And what (2) asserts is merely that each of us has frequently known to be true a proposition *corresponding* (in that sense) to each of the propositions in (1)—a *different* corresponding proposition, of course, at each of the times at which he knew such a proposition to be true.

But there remain two points, which, in view of the way in which some philosophers have used the English language, ought, I think, to be expressly mentioned, if I am to make quite clear exactly how much I am asserting in asserting (2).

The first point is this. Some philosophers seem to have thought it legitimate to use the word "true" in such a sense, that a proposition which is partially false may nevertheless also be true; and some of these, therefore, would perhaps *say* that propositions like those enumerated in (1) are, in their view, true, when all the time they believe that every such proposition is partially false. I wish, therefore, to make it quite plain that I am not using "true" in any such sense. I am using it in such a sense (and I think this is the ordinary usage) that if a proposition is partially false, it follows that it is *not* true, though, of course, it may be *partially* true. I am maintaining, in short, that all the propositions in (1), and also many propositions corresponding to each of these, are *wholly* true; I am asserting this in asserting (2). And hence any philosopher, who does in fact believe, with regard to any or all of these classes of propositions, that every proposition of the class in question is partially false, is, in fact, disagreeing with me and holding a view incompatible with (2), even though he may think himself justified in *saying* that he believes some propositions belonging to all of these classes to be "true."

And the second point is this. Some philosophers seem to have thought it legitimate to use such expressions as, e.g., "The earth has existed for many years past," as if they expressed something which they really believed, when in fact they believe that every proposition which such an expression would *ordinarily* be understood to express, is at least partially, false; and all they really believe is that there is some *other* set of propositions, related in a certain way to those which such expressions do actually express, which, unlike these, really are true. That is to say, they use the expression "The earth has existed for many years past" to express, not what it would ordinarily be understood to express, but the proposition that some proposition, related to this in a certain way, is true; when all the time they believe that the proposition, which this expression would ordinarily be understood to express is, at least partially, false. I wish, therefore, to make it quite plain that I was not using the expressions I used in (1) in any such subtle sense. I meant by each of them precisely what every reader, in reading them, will have understood me to mean. And any philosopher, therefore, who holds that any of these expressions, if understood in this popular manner, expresses a proposition which embodies some popular error, is disagreeing with me and holding a view incompatible with (2), even though he may hold that there is some *other,* true, proposition which the expression in question might be legitimately used to express.

In what I have just said, I have assumed that there is some meaning which is *the* ordinary or popular meaning of such expressions as "The earth has existed for many years past." And this, I am afraid, is an assumption which some philosophers are capable of disputing. They seem to think that the question "Do you believe that the earth has existed for many years past?" is not a plain question, such as should be met either by a plain "Yes" or "No," or by a plain "I can't make up my mind," but is the sort of question which can be properly met by: "It all depends on what you mean by 'the earth' and 'exists' and 'years': if you mean so and so, and so and so, and so and so, then I do; but if you mean so and so, and so and so, and so and so, or so and so, and so and so, and so and so, or so and so, and so and so, and so and so, then I don't, or at least I think it is extremely doubtful." It seems to me that such a view is as profoundly mistaken as any view can be. Such an expression as "The earth has existed for many years past" is the very type of an unambiguous expression, the meaning of which we all understand. Any one who takes a contrary view must, I suppose, be confusing the question whether we understand its meaning (which we all certanily do) with the entirely different question whether we *know what it means,* in the sense that we are able to *give a correct analysis* of its meaning. The question what is the correct analysis of *the* proposition meant *on any occasion* (for, of course, as I insisted in defining (2), a different proposition is meant at every different time at which the expression is used) by "The earth has existed for many years past" is, it seems to me, a profoundly difficult question, and one to which, as I shall presently urge, no one knows the answer. But to hold that we do not know what, in certain respects, is the analysis of what we understand by such an expression, is an entirely different thing from holding that we do not understand the expression. It is obvious that we cannot even raise the question how what we do understand by it is to be analysed, unless we do understand it. So soon, therefore, as we know that a person who uses such an expression, is using it in its ordinary sense, we understand his meaning. So that in explaining that I was using the expressions used in (1) in their ordinary sense (those of them which have an ordinary sense, which is not the case with quite all of them), I have done all that is required to make my meaning clear.

But now, assuming that the expressions which I have used to express (2) are understood, I think, as I have said, that many philosophers have really held views incompatible with (2). And the philosophers who have done so may, I think, be divided into two main groups. A. What (2) asserts is, with regard to a whole set of *classes* of propositions, that we have, each of us, frequently *known* to be true propositions belonging to *each* of these classes. And one way of holding a view incompatible with this proposition is, of course, to hold, with regard to one or more of the classes in question, that *no* propositions of that class *are* true—that all of them are, at least partially, false; since if, in the case of any one of these classes, *no* propositions of that class *are* true, it is obvious that nobody can have *known* any propositions of that class to be true, and therefore that *we* cannot have known to be true propositions belonging to *each* of these classes. And my first group of philosophers consists of philosophers who have held views incompatible with (2) for this reason. They have held, with regard to one or more of the classes in question, simply that no propositions of that class *are* true. Some of them have held this with regard to *all* the classes in question; some only with regard to *some* of them. But, of course, whichever of these two views they have held, they have been holding a view inconsistent with (2). B. Some philosophers, on the other hand, have not ventured to assert, with regard to *any* of the classes in (2), that no propositions of that class *are* true, but what they have asserted is that, in the case of some of these classes, no human being has ever *known*, with certainty, that any propositions of the class in question are true. That is to say, they differ profoundly from philosophers of group A, in that they hold that propositions of *all* these classes *may* be true; but nevertheless they hold a view incompatible with (2) since they hold, with regard to some of these classes, that none of us has ever *known* a proposition of the class in question to be true.

A. I said that some philosophers, belonging to this group, have held that no propositions belonging to *any* of the classes in (2) are wholly true, while others have only held this with regard to *some* of the classes in (2). And I think the chief division of this kind has been the following. Some of the propositions in (1) (and, therefore, of course, all propositions belonging to the corresponding classes in (2) are propositions which cannot be true, unless some *material things* have existed and have stood *in spatial relations* to one another: that is to say, they are propositions which, *in a certain sense,* imply *the reality of material things,* and *the reality of Space.* E.g. the proposition that my body has existed for many years past, and has, at every moment during that time been either in contact with or not far from the earth, is a proposition which implies both the *reality of material things* (provided you use "material things" in such a sense that to deny the reality of material things implies that no proposition which asserts that human bodies have existed, or that the earth has existed, is wholly true) and also the *reality of Space* (provided, again, that you use "Space" in such a sense that to deny the reality of Space implies that no proposition which asserts that anything has ever been in contact with or at a distance from another, in the familiar senses pointed out in (1), is wholly true). But others among the propositions in (1) (and, therefore, propositions belonging to the corresponding classes in (2)), do not (at least obviously) imply either the reality of material things or the reality of Space: e.g. the propositions that I have often had dreams, and have had many different feelings at different times. It is true that propositions of this second class do imply one thing which is also implied by all propositions of the first, namely that (*in a certain sense*) *Time is real,* and imply also one thing not implied by propositions of the first class, namely that (*in a certain sense*) *at least one Self is real.* But I think there are some philosophers, who, while denying that (in the senses in question) either material things or Space are real, have been willing to admit that Selves and Time are real, in the sense required. Other philosophers, on the other hand, have used the expression "Time is not real," to express some view that they held; and some, at least, of these have, I think, meant by this expression something which is incompatible with the truth of *any* of the propositions in (1) —they have meant, namely, that *every* proposition of the sort that is expressed by the use of "now" or "at present," e.g. "I am now both seeing and hearing" or "There exists at present a living human body," or by the use of a *past* tense, e.g. "I *have* had many experiences in the past," or "The earth *has* existed for many years," are, at least partially, false.

All the four expressions I have just introduced, namely "Material things are not real," "Space is not real," "Time is not real," "The Self is not real," are, I think, unlike the expressions I used in (1), really ambiguous. And it may be that, in the case of each of them, some philosopher has used the expression in question to express some view he held which was not incompatible with (2). With such philosophers, if there are any, I am not, of course, at present concerned. But it seems to me that the most natural and proper usage of each of these expressions is a usage in which it *does* express a view incompatible with (2); and, in the case of each of them, some philosophers have, I think, really used the expression in question to express such a view. All such philosophers have, therefore, been holding a view incompatible with (2).

All such views, whether incompatible with *all* of the propositions in (1), or only with *some* of them, seem to me to be quite certainly false; and I think the following points are specially deserving of notice with regard to them:—

(*a*) If *any* of the classes of propositions in (2) is such that no proposition of that class is true, then no philosopher has ever existed, and therefore none can ever have held with regard to any such class, that no proposition belonging to it is true. In other words, the proposition that some propositions belonging to each of these classes are true is a proposition which has the peculiarity, that, if any philosopher has ever denied it, it follows from the fact that he has denied it, that he must have been wrong in denying it. For when I speak of "philosophers" I mean, of course (as we all do), exclusively philosophers who have been human beings, with human bodies that have lived upon the earth, and who have at different times had many different experiences. If, therefore, there have been any philosophers, there have been human beings of this class; and if there have been human beings of this class, all the rest of what is asserted in (1) is certainly true too. Any view, therefore, incompatible with the proposition that many propositions corresponding to each of the propositions in (1) are true, can only be true, on the hypothesis that no philosopher has ever held any such view. It follows, therefore, that, in considering whether this proposition is true, I cannot consistently regard the fact that many philosophers, whom I respect, have, to the best of my belief, held views incompatible with it, as having any weight at all against it. Since, if I know that they have held such views, I am, *ipso facto,* knowing that they were mistaken; and, if I have no reason to believe that the proposition in question is true, I have still less reason to believe that they held views incompatible with it; since I am more certain that they have existed and held *some* views, i.e. that the proposition in question is true, than that they have held any views incompatible with it.

(b) It is, of course, the case that all philosophers who have held such views have repeatedly, even in their philosophical works, expressed other views inconsistent with them: i.e. no philosopher has ever been able to hold such views consistently. One way in which they have betrayed this inconsistency, is by alluding to the existence of other philosophers. Another way is by alluding to the existence of the human race, and in particular by using "we" in the sense in which I have already constantly used it, in which any philosopher who asserts that "we" do so and so, e.g. that *"we* sometimes believe propositions that are not true,"* is asserting not only that he himself has done the thing in question, but that *very many other human beings, who have had bodies and lived upon the earth,* have done the same. The fact is, of course, that all philosophers have belonged to the class of human beings, which exists only if (2) be true: that is to say, to the class of human beings, who have frequently *known* propositions corresponding to each of the propositions in (1). In holding views incompatible with the proposition that propositions of all these classes are true, they have, therefore, been holding views inconsistent with propositions which they themselves *knew* to be true; and it was, therefore, only to be expected that they should sometimes betray their knowledge of such propositions. The strange thing is that philosophers should have been able to hold sincerely, as part of their philosophical creed, propositions inconsistent with what they themselves *knew* to be true; and yet, so far as I can make out, this has really frequently happened. My position, therefore, on the first point, differs from that of philosophers belonging to this group A, not in that I hold anything which they don't hold, but only in that I don't hold, as part of my philosophical creed, things which they do hold as part of theirs—that is to say propositions inconsistent with some which they and I both hold in common. But this difference seems to me to be an important one.

(c) Some of these philosophers have brought forward, in favour of their position, arguments designed to show, in the case of some or all of the propositions in (1), that no proposition of that type can possibly be wholly true, because every such proposition entails both of two incompatible propositions. And I admit, of course, that if any of the propositions in (1) did entail both of two incompatible propositions it could not be true. But it seems to me I have an absolutely conclusive argument to show that none of them does entail both of two incompatible propositions. Namely this: All of the propositions in (1) are true; no true proposition entails both of two incompatible propositions; therefore, none of the propositions in (1) entails both of two incompatible propositions.

(d) Although, as I have urged, no philosopher who has held with regard to any of these types of proposition, that no propositions of that type are true, has failed to hold also other views inconsistent with his view in this respect, yet I do not think that the view, with regard to any or all of these types, that no proposition belonging to them is true, is *in itself* a self-contradictory view, i.e. entails both of two incompatible propositions. On the contrary, it seems to me quite clear that it *might* have been the case that Time was not real, material things not real, Space not real, selves not real. And in favour of my view that none of these things, which might have been the case, *is* in fact the case, I have, I think, no better argument than simply this—namely, that all the propositions in (1) are, in fact, true.

B. This view, which is usually considered a much more modest view than A, has, I think, the defect that, unlike A, it really is self-contradictory, i.e. entails both of two mutually incompatible propositions.

Most philosophers who have held this view, have held, I think, that though each of us knows propositions corresponding to *some* of the propositions in (1), namely to those which merely assert that *I* myself have had in the past experiences of certain kinds at many different times, yet none of us knows *for certain* any propositions either of the type (*a*) which assert the existence of material things or of the type (*b*) which assert the existence of *other* selves, beside myself, and that *they* also have had experiences. They admit that we do in fact *believe* propositions of both these types, and that they *may* be true: some would even say that we know them to be highly probable; but they deny that we ever know them, *for certain, to be true*. Some of them have spoken of such beliefs as "beliefs of Common Sense," expressing thereby their conviction that beliefs of this kind are very commonly entertained by mankind: but they are convinced that these things are, in all cases, only *believed*, not known for certain; and some have expressed this by saying that they are matters of Faith, not of Knowledge.

Now the remarkable thing, which those who take this view have not, I think, in general duly appreciated, is that, in each case, the philosopher who takes it is making an assertion about "us"—that is to say, not merely about himself, but about *many other human beings as well*. When he says "No human being has ever *known* of the existence of other human beings," he is saying: "There have been many other human beings beside myself, and none of them (including myself) has ever known of the existence of other human beings." If he says: "These beliefs are beliefs of Common Sense, but they are not matters of *knowledge*," he is saying: "There have been many other human beings, besides myself, who have shared these beliefs, but neither I nor any of the rest has ever known them to be true." In other words, he asserts with confidence that these beliefs *are* beliefs of Common Sense, and seems often to fail to notice that, *if* they are, they must be true; since the proposition that they are beliefs of Common Sense, is one which logically entails propositions both of type (*a*) and of type (*b*); it logically entails the proposition that many human beings, beside the philosopher himself, have had human bodies, which lived upon the earth, and have had various experiences, including beliefs of this kind. This is why this position, as contrasted with positions of group A, seems to me to be self-contradictory. Its difference from A consists in the fact that it is making a proposition about *human knowledge* in general, and therefore is actually asserting the existence of many human beings, whereas philosophers of group A in stating their position are not doing this: they are only contradicting *other* things which they hold. It is true that a philosopher who says "There have existed many human beings beside myself and none of us has ever known of the existence of any human beings beside himself," is only contradicting himself, if what he holds is "There have *certainly* existed many human beings beside myself" or, in other words, *"I* know that there have existed other human beings beside myself." But this, it seems to me, is what such philosophers have in fact been generally doing. They seem to me constantly to betray the fact that they regard the proposition that those beliefs *are* beliefs of Common Sense, or the proposition that they themselves are not the only members of the human race, as not merely true, but *certainly* true; and *certainly* true it cannot be, unless one member, at least, of the human race, namely themselves, has *known* the very things which that member is declaring that no human being has ever known.

Nevertheless, my position that I *know,* with certainty, to be true all of the propositions in (1), is certainly not a position, the denial of which entails both of two incompatible propositions. If I do *know* all these propositions to be true, then, I think, it is quite certain that other human beings also have known corresponding propositions: that is to say (2) also *is* true, and *I* know it to be true. But do I really *know* all the propositions in (1) to be true? Isn't it possible that I merely believe them? Or I know them to be highly probable? In answer to this question, I think I have nothing better to say than that it seems to me that I *do* know them, with certainty. It is, indeed, obvious that, in the case of most of them, I do not know them *directly:* that is to say, I only know them because, in the past, I have known to be true *other* propositions which were evidence for them. If, for instance, I do know that the earth had existed for many years before I was born, I certainly only know this because I have known other things in the past which were evidence for it. And I certainly do not know exactly what the evidence was. Yet all this seems to me to be no good reason for doubting that I do know it. We are all, I think, in this strange position that we do *know* many things, with regard to which we *know* further that we must have had evidence for them, and yet we do not know *how* we know them, i.e. we do not know what the evidence was. If there is any "we," and if we know that there is, this must be so: for, that there is a "we," is one of the things in question. And that I do know that there is a "we," that is to say, that many other human beings, with human bodies, have lived upon the earth, it seems to me that I do know, for certain.

If this first point in my philosophical position, namely my belief in (2), is to be given any name, which has actually been used by philosophers in classifying the positions of other philosophers, it would have, I think, to be expressed by saying that I am one of those philosophers who have held that the "Common Sense view of the world" is, in certain fundamental features, *wholly* true. But it must be remembered that, according to me, *all* philosophers, without exception, have agreed with me in holding this: and that the real difference, which is commonly expressed in this way, is only a difference between those philosophers, who have *also* held views inconsistent with these features in "the Common Sense view of the world," and those who have not.

The features in question (namely, propositions of any of the classes defined in defining (2)) are all of them features, which have this peculiar property—namely, that *if we know that they are features in the "Common Sense view of the world," it follows that they are true:* it is self-contradictory to maintain that *we* know them to be features in the Common Sense view, and that yet they are not true; since to say that *we* know this, is to say that they are true. And many of them also have the further peculiar property that, *if they are features in the Common Sense view of the world (whether "we" know this or not), it follows that they are true,* since to say that there is a "Common Sense view of the world," is to say that they are true. The phrases "Common Sense view of the world" or "Common Sense beliefs" (as used by philosophers) are, of course, extraordinarily vague; and, for all I know, there may be many propositions which may be properly called features in "the Common Sense view of the world" or "Common Sense beliefs," which are not true, and which deserve to be mentioned with the contempt with which some philosophers speak of "Common Sense beliefs." But to speak with contempt of those "Common Sense beliefs" which I have mentioned is quite certainly the height of absurdity. And there are, of course, enormous numbers of other features in "the Common Sense view of the world" which, if these are true, are quite certainly true too: e.g. that there have lived upon the surface of the earth not only human beings, but also many different species of plants and animals, etc., etc.

II. What seems to me the next in importance of the points in which my philosophical position differs from positions held by *some* other philosophers, is one which I will express in the following way. I hold, namely, that there is no good reason to suppose either (A) that *every* physical fact is *logically* dependent upon some mental fact or (B) that *every* physical fact is *causally* dependent upon some mental fact. In saying this, I am not, of course, saying that there *are* any physical facts which are wholly independent (i.e. both logically and causally) of mental facts: I do, in fact, believe that there are; but that is not what I am asserting. I am only asserting that there is *no good reason* to suppose the contrary; by which I mean, of course, that none of the human beings, who have had human bodies that lived upon the earth, have, during the life-time of their bodies, had any good reason to suppose the contrary. Many philosophers have, I think, not only believed either that *every* physical fact is *logically* dependent upon some mental fact ("physical fact" and "mental fact" being understood in the sense in which I am using these terms) or that *every* physical fact is *causally* dependent upon some mental fact, or both, but also that they themselves had good reason for these beliefs. In this respect, therefore, I differ from them.

In the case of the term "physical fact," I can only explain how I am using it by giving examples. I mean by "physical facts," facts *like* the following: "That mantel-piece it at present nearer to this body than that book-case is," "The earth has existed for many years past," "The moon has at every moment for many years past been nearer to the earth than to the sun," "That mantel-piece is of a light colour." But, when I say "facts *like* these," I mean, of course, facts like them *in a certain respect;* and what this respect is, I cannot define. The term "physical fact" is, however, in common use; and I think that I am using it in its ordinary sense. Moreover, there is no need for a definition to make my point clear; since among the examples I have given, there are some with regard to which I hold that there is no reason to suppose *them* (i.e. these particular physical facts) either logically or causally dependent upon any mental fact.

"Mental fact," on the other hand, is a much more unusual expression, and I am using it in a specially limited sense, which, though I think it is a natural one, does need to be explained. There may be many other senses in which the term can be properly used. But I am only concerned with this one; and hence it is essential that I should explain what it is.

There may, possibly, I hold, be "mental facts" of three different kinds. It is only with regard to the first kind that I am sure that there are facts of that kind; but if there were any facts of either of the other two kinds, they would be "mental facts" in my limited sense, and therefore I must explain what is meant by the hypothesis that there are facts of those two kinds.

(*a*) My first kind is this. I am conscious now; and also I am seeing something now. These two facts are both of them mental facts of my first kind; and my first kind consists exclusively of facts which resemble one or other of the two in a certain respect.

(*α*) The fact that I am conscious now is obviously, in a certain sense, a fact, with regard to a particular individual and a particular time, to the effect that that individual is conscious at that time. And every fact which resembles this one in that respect is to be included in my first kind of mental fact. Thus the fact that I was also conscious at many different times yesterday is not itself a fact of this kind: but it entails that there *are* (or, as we should commonly say, because the times in question are past times, "were") many other facts of this kind, namely each of the facts, which, at each of the times in question, I could have properly expressed by "I am conscious *now*." *Any* fact which is, in this sense, a fact with regard to an individual and a time (whether the individual be myself or another, and whether the time be past or present), to the effect that that individual *is* conscious at that time, is to be included in my first kind of mental fact: and I call such facts, facts of class (*α*).

(*β*) The second example I gave, namely the fact that I am seeing something now, is obviously related to the fact that I am conscious now in a peculiar manner. It not only *entails* the fact that I am conscious now (for from the fact that I am seeing something it *follows* that I am conscious: I *could* not have been seeing anything, unless I had been conscious, though I might quite well have been conscious without seeing anything) but it also is a fact, with regard to a *specific way* (or mode) of being conscious, to the effect that I am conscious in that way: in the same sense in which the proposition (with regard to any particular thing) "This is red" both entails the proposition (with regard to the same thing) "This is coloured," and is also a proposition, with regard to a *specific way* of being coloured, to the effect that that thing is coloured in that way. And any fact which is related in this peculiar manner to any fact of class (a), is also to be included in my first kind of mental fact, and is to be called a fact of class (β). Thus the fact that I am hearing now, is, like the fact that I am seeing now, a fact of class (β); and so is any fact, with regard to myself and a past time, which could at that time have been properly expressed by "I am dreaming now," "I am imagining now," "I am at present aware of the fact that . . ." etc., etc. In short, any fact, which is a fact with regard to a particular individual (myself or another), a particular time (past or present), and *any particular kind of experience,* to the effect that that individual is having at that time an experience of that particular kind, is a fact of class (β): and only such facts are facts of class (β).

My first kind of mental facts consists exclusively of facts of classes (a) and (β), and consists of *all* facts of either of these kinds.

(b) That there are many facts of classes (a) and (β) seems to me perfectly certain. But many philosophers seem to me to have held a certain view with regard to the *analysis* of facts of class (a), which is such that, if it were true, there would be facts of another kind, which I should wish also to call "mental facts." I don't feel at all sure that this analysis is true; but it seems to me that it *may* be true; and since we can understand what is meant by the supposition that it is true, we can also understand what is meant by the supposition that there are "mental facts" of this second kind.

Many philosophers have, I think, held the following view as to the analysis of what each of us knows, when he knows (at any time) "I am conscious now." They have held, namely, that there is a certain intrinsic property (with which we are all of us familiar and which might be called that of "being an experience") which is such that, at any time at which any man knows "I am conscious now," he is knowing, with regard to that property and himself and the time in question, "There is occurring now an event which has this property (i.e. 'is an experience') and which is an experience of *mine,*" and such that this fact is what he expresses by "I am conscious now." And if this view is true, there must be many facts of each of three kinds, each of which I should wish to call "mental facts"; viz. (1) facts with regard to some event, which has this supposed intrinsic property, and to some time, to the effect that that event is occurring at that time, (2) facts with regard to this supposed intrinsic property and some time, to the effect that *some* event which has that property is occurring at that time, and (3) facts with regard to some property, which is a *specific way* of having the supposed intrinsic property (in the sense above explained in which "being red" is a specific way of "being coloured") and some time, to the effect that some event which has that specific property is occurring at that time. Of course, there not only are not but *cannot* be, facts of any of these kinds, unless there is an intrinsic property related to what each of us (on any occasion) expresses by "I am conscious now," in the manner defined above; and I feel very doubtful whether there is any such property; in other words, although I know for certain both that I have had many experiences, and that I have had experiences of many different kinds, I feel very doubtful whether to say the first is the same thing as to say that there have been many events, each of which was an experience and an experience of mine, and whether to say the second is the same thing as to say that there have been many events, each of which was an experience of mine, and each of which also had a different property, which was a specific way of being an experience. The proposition that I have had experiences does not necessarily entail the proposition that there have been any events which were experiences; and I cannot satisfy myself that I am acquainted with any events of the supposed kind. But yet it seems to me possible that the proposed analysis of "I am conscious now" is correct: that I am really acquainted with events of the supposed kind, though I cannot see that I am. And *if* I am, then I should wish to call the three kinds of facts defined above, "mental facts." Of course, if there are "experiences" in the sense defined, it would be possible (as many have held) that there *can* be no experiences which are not *some individual's experiences;* and in that case any fact of any of these three kinds would be logically dependent on, though not necessarily identical with, some fact of class (α) or class (β). But it seems to me also a possibility that, if there are "experiences," there might be experiences which did not belong to any individual; and, in that case, there would be "mental facts" which were neither identical with nor logically dependent on any fact of class (α) or class (β).

(*c*) Finally some philosophers have, so far as I can make out, held that there are or may be facts, which are facts with regard to some individual, to the effect that he is conscious, or is conscious in some specific way, which differ from facts of classes (α) and (β), in the important respect that they are not facts *with regard to any time:* they have conceived the possibility that there may be one or more individuals, who are *timelessly* conscious, and timelessly conscious in specific modes. And others, again, have, I think, conceived the hypothesis that the intrinsic property defined in (*b*) may be one which does not belong only to *events,* but may also belong to one or more wholes which do *not* occur at any time: in other words, that there may be one or more *timeless* experiences, which might or might not be the experiences of some individual. It seems to me very doubtful whether any of these hypotheses are even possibly true; but I cannot see for certain that they are not possible: and, if they are possible, then I should wish to give the name "mental fact" to any fact (if there were any) of any of the five following kinds, viz. (1) to any fact which is the fact, with regard to any individual, that he is *timelessly* conscious, (2) to any fact which is the fact, with regard to any individual, that he is *timelessly* conscious in any specific way, (3) to any fact which is the fact with regard to a *timeless* experience that it exists, (4) to any fact which is the fact with regard to the supposed intrinsic property "being an experience," which is the fact that something timelessly exists which has that property, and (5) to any fact which is the fact, with regard to any property, which is a specific mode of this supposed intrinsic property, that something timelessly exists which has that property.

I have then defined three different kinds of facts, each of which is such that, if there *were* any facts of that kind (as there certainly *are*, in the case of the first kind), the facts in question *would be* "mental facts" in my sense; and to complete the definition of the limited sense in which I am using "mental facts," I have only to add that I wish also to apply the name to one *fourth* class of facts: namely to any fact, which is the fact, with regard to any of these three kinds of facts, or any kinds included in them, *that there are facts of the kind in question;* i.e. not only will each individual fact of class (α) be, in my sense, a "mental fact," but also the general fact "that there are facts of class (α)," will itself be a "mental fact"; and similarly in all other cases: e.g. not only will the fact that I am now perceiving (which is a fact of class (β)) be a "mental fact," but also the general fact that *there are* facts, with regard to individuals and times, to the effect that the individual in question is perceiving at the time in question, will be a "mental fact."

A. Understanding "physical fact" and "mental fact" in the senses *just* explained, I hold, then, that there is no good reason to suppose that *every* physical fact is *logically* dependent upon some mental fact. And I use the phrase, with regard to two facts, F_1 and F_2, "F_1 is *logically dependent* on F_2," wherever and only where F_1 *entails* F_2, either in the sense in which the proposition "I am seeing now" *entails* the proposition "I am conscious now," or the proposition (with regard to any particular thing) "This is red" entails the proposition (with regard to the same thing) "This is coloured," or else in the more strictly logical sense in which (for instance) the conjunctive proposition "All men are mortal, and Mr. Baldwin is a man" entails the proposition "Mr. Baldwin is mortal." To say, then, of two facts, F_1 and F_2, that F_1 is *not* logically dependent upon F_2, is only to say that F_1 *might* have been a fact, even if there had been no such fact as F_2; or that the conjunctive proposition "F_1 is a fact, but there is no such fact as F_2" is a proposition which is not self-contradictory, i.e. does not entail both of two mutually incompatible propositions.

I hold, then, that, in the case of *some* physical facts, there is no good reason to suppose that there is some mental fact, such that the physical fact in question could not have been a fact unless the mental fact in question had also been one. And my position is perfectly definite, since I hold that this is the case with all the four physical facts, which I have given as examples of physical facts. E.g. there is no good reason to suppose that there is any mental fact whatever, such that the fact that that mantel-piece is at present nearer to my body than that book-case could not have been a fact, unless the mental fact in question had also been a fact; and, similarly, in all the other three cases.

In holding this I am certainly differing from some philosophers. I am, for instance, differing from Berkeley, who held that that mantel-piece, that book-case, and my body are, all of them, either "ideas" or "constituted by ideas," and that no "idea" can possibly exist without being perceived. He held, that is, that this physical fact is logically dependent upon a mental fact of my fourth class: namely a fact which is the fact that there is at least one fact, which is a fact with regard to an individual and the present time, to the effect that that individual is now perceiving something. He does not say that this physical fact is logically dependent upon any fact which is a fact of any of my first three classes, e.g. on any fact which is the fact, with regard to a particular individual and the present time, that *that* individual is now perceiving something: what he does say is that the physical fact couldn't have been a fact, unless it had been a fact that there was *some* mental fact of this sort. And it seems to me that many philosophers, who would perhaps disagree either with Berkeley's assumption that my body is an "idea" or "constituted by ideas," or with his assumption that "ideas" cannot exist without being perceived, or with both, nevertheless would agree with him in thinking that this physical fact is logically dependent upon *some* "mental fact": e.g. they might say, that it could not have been a fact, unless there had been, at some time or other, or, were timelessly, *some* "experience." Many, indeed, so far as I can make out, have held that *every* fact is logically dependent on every other fact. And, of course, they have held in the case of their opinions, as Berkeley did in the case of his, that they had good reasons for them.

B. I also hold that there is no good reason to suppose that *every* physical fact is *causally* dependent upon some mental fact. By saying that F_1 is *causally* dependent on F_2, I mean only that F_1 *wouldn't* have been a fact unless F_2 had been; *not* (which is what "logically dependent" asserts) that F_1 *couldn't conceivably* have been a fact, unless F_2 had been. And I can illustrate my meaning by reference to the example which I have just given. The fact that that mantel-piece is at present nearer to my body than that book-case, is (as I have just explained) so far as I can see, not *logically* dependent upon any mental fact; it *might* have been a fact, even if there has been no mental facts. But it certainly is *causally* dependent on many mental facts: my body *would* not have been here unless I had been conscious in various ways in the past; and the mantel-piece and the book-case certainly *would* not have existed, unless other men had been conscious too.

But with regard to two of the facts, which I gave as instances of physical facts, namely the fact that the earth has existed for many years past, and the fact that the moon has for many years past been nearer to the earth than to the sun, I hold that there is no good reason to suppose that these are *causally* dependent upon any mental fact. So far as I can see, there is no reason to suppose that there is any mental fact of which it could be truly said: unless this fact had been a fact, the earth would not have existed for many years past. And in holding this, again, I think I differ from some philosophers. I differ, for instance, from those who have held that all material things were created by God, and that they had good reasons for supposing this.

III. I have just explained that I differ from those philosophers who have held that there is good reason to suppose that all material things were created by God. And it is, I think, an important point in my position, which should be mentioned, that I differ also from all philosophers who have held that there is good reason to suppose that there is a God at all, whether or not they have held it likely that he created all material things.

And similarly, where as some philosophers have held that there is good reason to suppose that we, human beings, shall continue to exist and to be conscious after the death of our bodies, I hold that there is no good reason to suppose this.

IV. I now come to a point of a very different order.
As I have explained under I., I am not at all sceptical as to the

truth of such propositions as "The earth has existed for many years past," "Many human bodies have each lived for many years upon it," i.e. propositions which assert the existence of material things: on the contrary, I hold that we all know, with certainty, many such propositions to be true. But I am very sceptical as to what, in certain respects, the correct *analysis* of such propositions is. And this is a matter as to which I think I differ from many philosophers. Many seem to hold that there is no doubt at all as to their *analysis,* nor, therefore, as to the analysis of the proposition "Material things have existed," in certain respects in which I hold that the analysis of the propositions in question is extremely doubtful; and some of them, as we have seen, while holding that there is no doubt as to their *analysis,* seem to have doubted whether any such propositions are *true.* I, on the other hand, while holding that there is no doubt whatever that many such propositions are wholly true, hold also that no philosopher, hitherto, has succeeded in suggesting an analysis of them, as regards certain important points, which comes anywhere near to being certainly true.

It seems to me quite evident that the question how propositions of the type I have just given are to be analysed, depends on the question how propositions of another and simpler type are to be analysed. I know, at present, that I am perceiving a human hand, a pen, a sheet of paper, etc.; and it seems to me that I cannot know how the proposition "Material things exist" is to be analysed, until I know how, in certain respects, these simpler propositions are to be analysed. But even these are not simple enough. It seems to me quite evident that my knowledge that I am now perceiving a human hand is a deduction from a pair of propositions simpler still—propositions which I can only express in the form "I am perceiving *this*" and *"This* is a human hand." It is the analysis of propositions of the latter kind, which seems to me to present such great difficulties; while neverthless the whole question as to the *nature* of material things obviously depends upon their analysis. It seems to me a surprising thing that so few philosophers, while saying a great deal as to what material things *are* and as to what it is to perceive them, have attempted to give a clear account as to what precisely they suppose themselves to *know* (or to *judge,* in case they have held that we don't *know* any such propositions to be true, or even that no such propositions *are* true) when they know or judge such things as "This is a hand," "That is the sun," "This is a dog," etc. etc. etc.

Two things only seem to me to be quite certain about the analysis of such propositions (and even with regard to these I am afraid some philosophers would differ from me) namely that whenever I know, or judge, such a proposition to be true, (1) there is always some *sense-datum* about which the proposition in question is a proposition—some sense-datum which is *a* subject (and, in a certain sense, the principal or ultimate subject) of the proposition in question, and (2) that, nevertheless, *what* I am knowing or judging to be true about this sense-datum is not (in general) that it is *itself* a hand, or a dog, or the sun, etc. etc., as the case may be.

Some philosophers have I think doubted whether there are any such things as other philosophers have meant by "sense-data" or "sensa." And I think it is quite possible that some philosophers (including myself, in the past) have used these terms in senses, such that it is really doubtful whether there are any such things. But there is no doubt at all that there are sense-data, in the sense in which I am now using that term. I am at present seeing a great number of them, and feeling others. And, in order to point out to the reader what sort of things I mean by sense-data, I need only ask him to look at his own right hand. If he does this he will be able to pick out something (and, unless he is seeing double, *only* one thing) with regard to which he will see that it is, at first sight, a natural view to take that that thing is identical, not, indeed, with his whole right hand, but with that part of its surface which he is actually seeing, but will also (on a little reflection) be able to see that it is doubtful whether it can be identical with the part of the surface of his hand in question. Things of *the sort* (in a certain respect) of which this thing is, which he sees in looking at his hand, and with regard to which he can understand how some philosophers should have supposed it to *be* the part of the surface of his hand which he is seeing, while others have supposed that it can't be, are what I mean by "sense-data." I therefore define the term in such a way that it is an open question whether the sense-datum which I now see in looking at my hand and which is a sense-datum of my hand is or is not identical with that part of its surface which I am now actually seeing.

That what I know, with regard to this sense-datum, when I know "This is a human hand," is not that it is *itself* a human hand, seems to me certain because I know that my hand has many parts (e.g. its other side, and the bones inside it), which are quite certainly *not* parts of this sense-datum.

I think it certain, therefore, that the analysis of the proposition "This a human hand" is, roughly at least, of the form "There is a thing, and only one thing, of which it is true both that it is a human hand and that *this surface* is a part of its surface." In other words, to put my view in terms of the phrase "theory of representative perception," I hold it to be quite certain that I do not *directly* perceive *my hand;* and that when I am said (as I may be correctly said) to "perceive" it, that I "perceive" it means that I perceive (in a different and more fundamental sense) something which is (in a suitable sense) *representative* of it, namely, a certain part of its surface.

This is all that I hold to be *certain* about the analysis of the proposition "This is a human hand." We have seen that it includes in its analysis a proposition of the form "This is part of the surface of a human hand" (where "This," of course, has a different meaning from that which it has in the original propositon which has now been analysed). But this proposition also is undoubtedly a proposition about the sense-datum, which I am seeing, which is a sense-datum *of* my hand. And hence the further question arises: *What,* when I know *"This is part of the surface of* a human hand," am I knowing about the sense-datum in question? Am I, in this case, really knowing, about the sense-datum in question that it *itself* is part of the surface of a human hand? Or, just as we found in the case of "This is a human hand," that what I was knowing about the sense-datum was certainly not that it *itself* was a human hand, so, is it perhaps the case, with this new proposition, that even here I am not knowing, with regard to the sense-datum, that it is *itself* part of the surface of a hand? and, if so, what is it that I am knowing about the sense-datum itself?

This is the question to which, as it seems to me, no philosopher has hitherto suggested an answer which comes anywhere near to being *certainly* true.

There seem to me to be three, and only three, alternative types of answer possible; and to any answer yet suggested, of any of these types, there seem to me to be very grave objections.

(1) Of the first type, there is but one answer: namely, that in this case what I am knowing really is that the sense-datum *itself* is part of the surface of a human hand. In other words that, though I don't perceive *my hand* directly, I do *directly* perceive part of its surface; that the sense-datum itself *is* this part of its surface and not merely something which (in a sense yet to be determined) "represents" this part of its surface; and that hence the sense in which I "perceive" this part of the surface of my hand, is not in its turn a sense which needs to be defined by reference to yet a third more ultimate sense of "perceive," which is the only one in which perception is direct, namely that in which I perceive the sense-datum.

If this view is true (as I think it may just possibly be), it seems to me certain that we must abandon a view which has been held to be certainly true by most philosophers, namely the view that our sense-data always really have the qualities which they sensibly appear to us to have. For I know that if another man were looking through a microscope at the same surface which I am seeing with the naked eye, the sense-datum which he saw would sensibly appear to him to have qualities very different from and incompatible with those which my sense-datum sensibly appears to me to have: and yet, if my sense-datum is identical with the surface we are both of us seeing, his must be identical with it also. My sense-datum can, therefore, be identical with this surface only on condition that it is identical with his sense-datum; and, since his sense-datum sensibly appears to him to have qualities incompatible with those which mine sensibly appears to me to have, his sense-datum can be identical with mine, only on condition that the sense-datum in question either has not got the qualities which it sensibly appears to me to have, or has not got those which it sensibly appears to him to have.

I do not, however, think that this is a fatal objection to this first type of view. A far more serious objection seems to me to be that, when we see a thing double (have what is called "a double image" of it), we certainly have *two* sense-data each of which is *of* the surface seen, and which cannot therefore both be identical with it; and that yet it seems as if, if any sense-datum is ever identical with the surface *of* which it is a sense-datum, each of these so-called "images" must be so. It looks, therefore, as if every sense-datum is, after all, only "representative" of the surface, *of* which it is a sense-datum.

(2) But, if so, what relation has it to the surface in question?

This second type of view is one which holds that when I know "This is part of the surface of a human hand," what I am knowing with regard to the sense-datum which is *of* that surface, is, *not* that it is *itself* part of the surface of a human hand, but something of the following kind. There is, it says, *some* relation, R, such that what I am knowing with regard to the sense-datum is either "There is one thing and only one thing, of which it is true both that it is a part of the surface of a human hand, and that it has R to this sense-datum," or else "There are a set of things, of which it is true both that that set, taken collectively, *are* part of the surface of a human hand, and also that each member of the set has R to this sense-datum, and that nothing which is not a member of the set has R to it."

Obviously, in the case of this second type, many different views are possible, differing according to the view they take as to what the relation R is. But there is only one of them, which seems to me to have any plausibility; namely that which holds that R is an ultimate and unanalysable relation, which might be expressed by saying that "xRy" means the same as "y is an appearance or manifestation of x." I.e. the analysis which this answer would give of "This is part of the surface of a human hand" would be "There is one and only one thing of which it is true both that it is part of the surface of a human hand, and that this sense-datum is an appearance or manifestation of it."

To this view also there seem to me to be very grave objections, chiefly drawn from a consideration of the questions how we can possibly *know* with regard to any of our sense-data that there is one thing and one thing only which has to them such a supposed ultimate relation; and how, if we do, we can possibly *know* anything further about such things, e.g. of what size or shape they are.

(3) The third type of answer, which seems to me to be the only possible alternative if (1) and (2) are rejected, is the type of answer which J. S. Mill seems to have been implying to be the true one when he said that material things are "permanent possibilities of sensation." He seems to have thought that when I know such a fact as "This is part of the surface of a human hand," what I am knowing with regard to the sense-datum which is the principal subject of that fact, is not that it is itself part of the surface of a human hand, nor yet, with regard to any relation, that *the* thing which has to it that relation is part of the surface of a human hand, but a whole set of hypothetical facts each of which is a fact of the form "If *these* conditions had been fulfilled, I should have been perceiving a sense-datum intrinsically related to *this* sense-datum in *this* way," "If *these* (other) conditions had been fulfilled, I should have been perceiving a sense-datum intrinsically related to *this* sense-datum in *this* (other) way," etc. etc.

With regard to this third type of view as to the analysis of propositions of the kind we are considering, it seems to me, again, just *possible* that it is a true one; but to hold (as Mill himself and others seem to have held) that it is *certainly,* or nearly certainly, true, seems to me as great a mistake, as to hold with regard either to (1) or to (2) that they are *certainly,* or nearly certainly, true. There seem to me to be very grave objections to it; in particular the three, (*a*) that though in general, when I know such a fact as "This is a hand," I certainly do know some hypothetical facts of the form "If *these* conditions had been fulfilled, I should have been perceiving a sense-datum of *this* kind, which would have been a sense-datum of the same surface of which *this* is a sense-datum," it seems doubtful whether any conditions with regard to which I know this are not themselves conditions of the form "If this and that *material thing* had been in those positions and conditions . . ." (*b*) that it seems again very doubtful whether there is

any intrinsic relation, such that my knowledge that (under *these* conditions) I should have been perceiving a sense-datum of *this* kind, which
would have been a sense-datum of the same surface of which *this* is a
sense-datum is equivalent to a knowledge, with regard to that relation,
that I should, under those conditions, have been perceiving a sense-
datum related by it to *this* sense-datum and (*c*) that, if it were true, the
sense in which a material surface is "round" or "square," would necessarily be utterly different from that in which our sense-data sensibly
appear to us to be "round" or "square."

V. Just as I hold that the proposition "There are and have been
material things" is quite certainly true, but that the question how
this proposition is to be analysed is one to which no answer that has
been hitherto given is anywhere near certainly true; so I hold that
the proposition "There are and have been many Selves" is quite certainly true, but that here again all the analyses of this proposition
that have been suggested by philosophers are highly doubtful.

That I am now perceiving many different sense-data, and that I have
at many times in the past perceived many different sense-data, I know
or certain—that is to say, I know that there are mental facts of
class (β), connected in a way which it is proper to express by saying
that they are all of them facts about *me;* but how this kind of connection is to be analysed, I do not know for certain, nor do I think
that any other philosopher knows with any approach to certainty. Just
as in the case of the proposition "This is part of the surface of a
human hand," there are several extremely different views as to its
analysis, each of which seems to me *possible,* but none nearly certain, so also in the case of the proposition "This, that and that sense-
datum are all at present being perceived by *me,*" and still more so
in the case of the proposition "*I* am now perceiving this sense-datum,
and *I* have in the past perceived sense-data of these other kinds."
Of the *truth* of these propositions there seems to me to be no doubt,
but as to what is the correct analysis of them there seems to me
to be the gravest doubt—the true analysis may, for instance, *possibly*
be quite as paradoxical as is the third view given above under IV as to
the analysis of "This is part of the surface of a human hand"; but
whether it *is* as paradoxical as this seems to me to be quite as doubtful as in that case. Many philosophers, on the other hand, seem to me
to have assumed that there is little or no doubt as to the correct analysis of such propositions; and many of these, just reversing my position, have also held that the propositions themselves are not true.

LOGICAL ANALYSIS

BERTRAND RUSSELL

In *Principia Mathematica* (1910-13), written with A. N. Whitehead, Russell brought to a grand climax his inquiries into the philosophy of mathematics. In effect, he established the foundations of mathematics by reducing mathematics to logic. This was accomplished by his method of analysis (or translation or "contextual definition") of mathematical concepts, in their appropriate contexts, into their logical equivalents.

Upon the completion of *Principia Mathematica*, Russell expanded his "logistic" program, as he called it, for the philosophy of mathematics, into the "logical-analytic" method for the solution of other traditional philosophical problems, especially in those relating to the basic concepts of physics and psychology. The Lowell Lectures, *Our Knowledge of the External World* (1914), are among the first of these attempts "to show, by means of examples, the nature, capacity, and limitations of the logical-analytic method in philosophy."

The second lecture, "Logic as the Essence of Philosophy" (reprinted below), is a succinct statement of the nature of logic and the role Russell assigns to it in philosophical analysis. Parts of the lecture, such as the refutation of the adequacy of traditional subject-predicate logic, Russell articulated as far back as 1900. But the major doctrine of the twofold nature of logic, and especially of the importance of the analysis of forms, is not only new, it also anticipates Russell's own version of logical atomism—the ontological thesis that the ultimate elements of the world are not things (such as minds or physical objects) but logical particulars and their qualities in their external relations—that he develops fully in "The Philosophy of Logical Atomism" (1918-19).

Logic as the Essence of Philosophy[1]

The topics we discussed in our first lecture, and the topics we shall discuss later, all reduce themselves, in so far as they are genuinely philosophical, to problems of logic. This is not due to any accident, but to the fact that every philosophical problem, when it is subjected to the necessary analysis and purification, is found either to be not really philosophical at all, or else to be, in the sense in which we are using the word, logical. But as the word "logic" is never used in the same sense by two different philosophers, some explanation of what I mean by the word is indispensable at the outset.

Logic, in the Middle Ages, and down to the present day in teaching, meant no more than a scholastic collection of technical terms and rules of syllogistic inference. Aristotle had spoken, and it was the part of humbler men merely to repeat the lesson after him. The trivial nonsense embodied in this tradition is still set in examinations, and defended by eminent authorities as an excellent "propaedeutic," *i.e.* a training in those habits of solemn humbug which are so great a help in later life. But it is not this that I mean to praise in saying that all philosophy is logic. Ever since the beginning of the seventeenth century, all vigorous minds that have concerned themselves with inference have abandoned the mediaeval tradition, and in one way or other have widened the scope of logic.

The first extension was the introduction of the inductive method by Bacon and Galileo—by the former in a theoretical and largely mistaken form, by the latter in actual use in establishing the foundations of modern physics and astronomy. This is probably the only extension of the old logic which has become familiar to the general educated public. But induction, important as it is when regarded as a method of investigation, does not seem to remain when its work is done: in the final form of a perfected science, it would seem that everything ought to be

1. From *Our Knowledge of the External World* (London: George Allen & Unwin, Ltd., 1914), Lecture II. Reprinted by permission of the publishers.

deductive. If induction remains at all, which is a difficult question, i
will remain merely as one of the principles according to which deduc
tions are effected. Thus the ultimate result of the introduction of the ir
ductive method seems not the creation of a new kind of non-deductiv
reasoning, but rather the widening of the scope of deduction by point
ing out a way of deducing which is certainly not syllogistic, and does no
fit into the mediaeval scheme.

The question of the scope and validity of induction is of great diffi
culty, and of great importance to our knowledge. Take such a question
as, "Will the sun rise tomorrow?" Our first instinctive feeling is that w
have abundant reason for saying that it will, because it has risen on s
many previous mornings. Now, I do not myself know whether this doe
afford a ground or not, but I am willing to suppose that it does. Th
question which then arises is: What is the principle of inference b
which we pass from past sunrises to future ones? The answer given b
Mill is that the inference depends upon the law of causation. Let us sup
pose this to be true; then what is the reason for believing in the law o
causation? There are broadly three possible answers: (1) that it is it
self known *a priori;* (2) that it is a postulate; (3) that it is an empirica
generalisation from past instances in which it has been found to hold
The theory that causation is known *a priori* cannot be definitely refuted
but it can be rendered very unplausible by the mere process of formu
lating the law exactly, and thereby showing that it is immensely mor
complicated and less obvious than is generally supposed. The theor
that causation is a postulate, *i.e.* that it is something which we choose t
assert although we know that it is very likely false, is also incapable o
refutation; but it is plainly also incapable of justifying any use of th
law in inference. We are thus brought to the theory that the law is a
empirical generalisation, which is the view held by Mill.

But if so, how are empirical generalisations to be justified? The evi
dence in their favour cannot be empirical, since we wish to argue from
what has been observed to what has not been observed, which can only
be done by means of some known relation of the observed and the un
observed; but the unobserved, by definition, is not known empirically
and therefore its relation to the observed, if known at all, must be
known independently of empirical evidence. Let us see what Mill say
on this subject.

According to Mill, the law of causation is proved by an admittedly
fallible process called "induction by simple enumeration." This process
he says, "consists in ascribing the nature of general truths to all proposi
tions which are true in every instance that we happen to know of."[2] A

---

2. *Logic,* book iii, chapter iii., § 2.

egards its fallibility, he asserts that "the precariousness of the method
of simple enumeration is in an inverse ratio to the largeness of the gen-
ralisation. The process is delusive and insufficient, exactly in propor-
ion as the subject-matter of the observation is special and limited in ex-
ent. As the sphere widens, this unscientific method becomes less and
ess liable to mislead; and the most universal class of truths, the laws of
ausation for instance, and the principles of number and of geometry,
re duly and satisfactorily proved by that method alone, nor are they
usceptible of any other proof."[3]

In the above statement, there are two obvious lacunae: (1) How is
he method of simple enumeration itself justified? (2) What logical
rinciple, if any, covers the same ground as this method, without being
iable to its failures? Let us take the second question first.

A method of proof which, when used as directed, gives sometimes
ruth and sometimes falsehood—as the method of simple enumeration
loes—is obviously not a valid method, for validity demands invariable
ruth. Thus, if simple enumeration is to be rendered valid, it must not
e stated as Mill states it. We shall have to say, at most, that the data
ender the result *probable*. Causation holds, we shall say, in every in-
tance we have been able to test; therefore it *probably* holds in untested
nstances. There are terrible difficulties in the notion of probability, but
ve may ignore them at present. We thus have what at least *may* be a
ogical principle, since it is without exception. If a proposition is true in
very instance that we happen to know of, and if the instances are very
umerous, then, we shall say, it becomes very probable, on the data,
hat it will be true in any further instance. This is not refuted by the
act that what we declare to be probable does not always happen, for an
vent may be probable on the data and yet not occur. It is, however,
bviously capable of further analysis, and of more exact statement. We
hall have to say something like this: that every instance of a proposi-
ion[4] being true increases the probability of its being true in a fresh in-
tance, and that a sufficient number of favourable instances will, in the
bsence of instances to the contrary, make the probability of the truth
f a fresh instance approach indefinitely near to certainty. Some such
rinciple as this is required if the method of simple enumeration is to
e valid.

But this brings us to our other question, namely, how is our principle
nown to be true? Obviously, since it is required to justify induction, it
annot be proved by induction; since it goes beyond the empirical data,
t cannot be proved by them alone; since it is required to justify all in-

3. Book iii, Chapter xxi., § 3.
4. Or rather a propositional function.

ferences from empirical data to what goes beyond them, it cannot itself be even rendered in any degree probable by such data. Hence, *if* it is known, it is not known by experience, but independently of experience. I do not say that any such principle is known: I only say that it is required to justify the inferences from experience which empiricists allow, and that it cannot itself be justified empirically.[5]

A similar conclusion can be proved by similar arguments concerning any other logical principle. Thus logical knowledge is not derivable from experience alone, and the empiricist's philosophy can therefore not be accepted in its entirety, in spite of its excellence in many matters which lie outside logic.

Hegel and his followers widened the scope of logic in quite a different way—a way which I believe to be fallacious, but which requires discussion if only to show how their conception of logic differs from the conception which I wish to advocate. In their writings, logic is practically identical with metaphysics. In broad outline, the way this came about is as follows. Hegel believed that, by means of *a priori* reasoning, it could be shown that the world *must* have various important and interesting characteristics, since any world without these characteristics would be impossible and self-contradictory. Thus what he calls "logic" is an investigation of the nature of the universe, in so far as this can be inferred merely from the principle that the universe must be logically self-consistent. I do not myself believe that from this principle alone anything of importance can be inferred as regards the existing universe. But, however that may be, I should not regard Hegel's reasoning, even if it were valid, as properly belonging to logic: it would rather be an application of logic to the actual world. Logic itself would be concerned rather with such questions as what self-consistency is, which Hegel, so far as I know, does not discuss. And though he criticises the traditional logic, and professes to replace it by an improved logic of his own, there is some sense in which the traditional logic, with all its faults, is uncritically and unconsciously assumed throughout his reasoning. It is not in the direction advocated by him, it seems to me, that the reform of logic is to be sought, but by a more fundamental, more patient, and less ambitious investigation into the presuppositions which his system shares with those of most other philosophers.

The way in which, as it seems to me, Hegel's system assumes the ordinary logic which it subsequently criticises, is exemplified by the general conception of "categories" with which he operates throughout. This conception is, I think, essentially a product of logical confusion, but it

5. The subject of causality and induction will be discussed again in Lecture VIII [*Our Knowledge of the External World*].

seems in some way to stand for the conception of "qualities of Reality as a whole." Mr. Bradley has worked out a theory according to which, in all judgment, we are ascribing a predicate to Reality as a whole; and this theory is derived from Hegel. Now the traditional logic holds that every proposition ascribes a predicate to a subject, and from this it easily follows that there can be only one subject, the Absolute, for if there were two, the proposition that there were two would not ascribe a predicate to either. Thus Hegel's doctrine, that philosophical propositions must be of the form, "the Absolute is such-and-such," depends upon the traditional belief in the universality of the subject-predicate form. This belief, being traditional, scarcely self-conscious, and not supposed to be important, operates underground, and is assumed in arguments which, like the refutation of relations, appear at first sight such as to establish its truth. This is the most important respect in which Hegel uncritically assumes the traditional logic. Other less important respects —though important enough to be the source of such essentially Hegelian conceptions as the "concrete universal" and the "union of identity in difference"—will be found where he explicitly deals with formal logic.[6]

There is quite another direction in which a large technical development of logic has taken place: I mean the direction of what is called logistic or mathematical logic. This kind of logic is mathematical in two different senses: it is itself a branch of mathematics, and it is the logic which is specially applicable to other more traditional branches of mathematics. Historically, it began as *merely* a branch of mathematics: its special applicability to other branches is a more recent development. In both respects, it is the fulfilment of a hope which Leibniz cherished throughout his life, and pursued with all the ardour of his amazing intellectual energy. Much of his work on this subject has been published recently, after his discoveries had been remade by others; but

---

6. See the translation by H. S. Macran, *Hegel's Doctrine of Formal Logic,* Oxford, 1912. Hegel's argument in this portion of his "Logic" depends throughout upon confusing the "is" of predication, as in "Socrates is mortal" with the "is" of identity, as in "Socrates is the philosopher who drank the hemlock." Owing to this confusion, he thinks that "Socrates" and "mortal" must be identical. Seeing that they are different, he does not infer, as others would, that there is a mistake somewhere, but that they exhibit "identity in difference." Again, Socrates is particular, "mortal" is universal. Therefore, he says, since Socrates is mortal, it follows that the particular is the universal—taking the "is" to be throughout expressive of identity. But to say "the particular is the universal" is self-contradictory. Again Hegel does not suspect a mistake, but proceeds to synthesise particular and universal in the individual, or concrete universal. This is an example of how, for want of care at the start, vast and imposing systems of philosophy are built upon stupid and trivial confusions, which, but for the almost incredible fact that they are unintentional, one would be tempted to characterise as puns.

none was published by him, because his results persisted in contradicting certain points in the traditional doctrine of the syllogism. We now
know that on these points the traditional doctrine is wrong, but respect
for Aristotle prevented Leibniz from realising that this was possible.[7]

The modern development of mathematical logic dates from Boole's
Laws of Thought (1854). But in him and his successors, before Peano
and Frege, the only thing really achieved, apart from certain details,
was the invention of a mathematical symbolism for deducing consequences from the premisses which the newer methods shared with those
of Aristotle. This subject has considerable interest as an independent
branch of mathematics, but it has very little to do with real logic. The
first serious advance in real logic since the time of the Greeks was made
independently by Peano and Frege—both mathematicians. They both
arrived at their logical results by an analysis of mathematics. Traditional logic regarded the two propositions, "Socrates is mortal" and "All
men are mortal," as being of the same form;[8] Peano and Frege showed
that they are utterly different in form. The philosophical importance of
logic may be illustrated by the fact that this confusion—which is still
committed by most writers—obscured not only the whole study of the
forms of judgment and inference, but also the relations of things to their
qualities, of concrete existence to abstract concepts, and of the world
of sense to the world of Platonic ideas. Peano and Frege, who pointed
out the error, did so for technical reasons, and applied their logic mainly
to technical developments; but the philosophical importance of the
advance which they made is impossible to exaggerate.

Mathematical logic, even in its most modern form, is not *directly* of
philosophical importance except in its beginnings. After the beginnings,
it belongs rather to mathematics than to philosophy. Of its beginnings,
which are the only part of it that can properly be called *philosophical*
logic, I shall speak shortly. But even the later developments, though not
directly philosophical, will be found of great indirect use in philosophising. They enable us to deal easily with more abstract conceptions than
merely verbal reasoning can enumerate; they suggest fruitful hypotheses
which otherwise could hardly be thought of; and they enable us to see
quickly what is the smallest store of materials with which a given logical
or scientific edifice can be constructed. Not only Frege's theory of
number, which we shall deal with in Lecture VII., but the whole theory
of physical concepts which will be outlined in our next two lectures, is
inspired by mathematical logic, and could never have been imagined
without it.

7. *Cf.* Couturat, *La Logique de Leibniz*, pp. 361, 386.
8. It was often recognised that there was *some* difference between them, but it was
not recognised that the difference is fundamental, and of very great importance.

In both these cases, and in many others, we shall appeal to a certain principle called "the principle of abstraction." This principle, which might equally well be called "the principle which dispenses with abstraction," and is one which clears away incredible accumulations of metaphysical lumber, was directly suggested by mathematical logic, and could hardly have been proved or practically used without its help. The principle will be explained in our fourth lecture, but its use may be briefly indicated in advance. When a group of objects have that kind of similarity which we are inclined to attribute to possession of a common quality, the principle in question shows that membership of the group will serve all the purposes of the supposed common quality, and that therefore, unless some common quality is actually known, the group or class of similar objects may be used to replace the common quality, which need not be assumed to exist. In this and other ways, the indirect uses of even the later parts of mathematical logic are very great; but it is now time to turn our attention to its philosophical foundations.

In every proposition and in every inference there is, besides the particular subject-matter concerned, a certain *form*, a way in which the constituents of the proposition or inference are put together. If I say, "Socrates is mortal," "Jones is angry," "The sun is hot," there is something in common in these three cases, something indicated by the word "is." What is in common is the *form* of the proposition, not an actual constituent. If I say a number of things about Socrates—that he was an Athenian, that he married Xantippe, that he drank the hemlock —there is a common constituent, namely Socrates, in all the propositions I enunciate, but they have diverse forms. If, on the other hand, I take any one of these propositions and replace its constituents, one at a time, by other constituents, the form remains constant, but no constituent remains. Take (say) the series of propositions, "Socrates drank the hemlock," "Coleridge drank the hemlock," "Coleridge drank opium," "Coleridge ate opium." The form remains unchanged throughout this series, but all the constituents are altered. Thus form is not another constituent, but is the way the constituents are put together. It is forms, in this sense, that are the proper object of philosophical logic.

It is obvious that the knowledge of logical forms is something quite different from knowledge of existing things. The form of "Socrates drank the hemlock" is not an existing thing like Socrates or the hemlock, nor does it even have that close relation to existing things that drinking has. It is something altogether more abstract and remote. We might understand all the separate words of a sentence without understanding the sentence: if a sentence is long and complicated, this is apt to happen. In such a case we have knowledge of the constituents, but not of the form. We may also have knowledge of the form without having knowledge of the constituents. If I say, "Rorarius drank the hemlock," those among you who have never heard of Rorarius (supposing there are any) will understand the form, without having knowledge of all the constituents. In order to understand a sentence, it is necessary to have knowledge both of the constituents and of the particular instance of the form. It is in this way that a sentence conveys information, since it tells us that certain known objects are related according to a certain known form. Thus some kind of knowledge of logical forms, though with most people it is not explicit, is involved in all understanding of discourse. It is the business of philosophical logic to extract this knowledge from its concrete integuments, and to render it explicit and pure.

In all inference, form alone is essential: the particular subject-matter is irrelevant except as securing the truth of the premisses. This is one reason for the great importance of logical form. When I say, "Socrates was a man, all men are mortal, therefore Socrates was mortal," the connection of premisses and conclusion does not in any way depend upon its being Socrates and man and mortality that I am mentioning. The general form of the inference may be expressed in some such words as, "If a thing has a certain property, and whatever has this property has a certain other property, then the thing in question also has that other property." Here no particular things or properties are mentioned: the proposition is absolutely general. All inferences, when stated fully, are instances of propositions having this kind of generality. If they seem to depend upon the subject-matter otherwise than as regards the truth of the premisses, that is because the premisses have not been all explicitly stated. In logic, it is a waste of time to deal with inferences concerning particular cases: we deal throughout with completely general and purely formal implications, leaving it to other sciences to discover when the hypotheses are verified and when they are not.

But the forms of propositions giving rise to inferences are not the simplest forms: they are always hypothetical, stating that if one proposition is true, then so is another. Before considering inference, therefore, logic must consider those simpler forms which inference presupposes. Here the traditional logic failed completely: it believed that there was only one form of simple proposition (*i.e.* of proposition not stating a relation between two or more other propositions), namely, the form which ascribes a predicate to a subject. This is the appropriate form in assigning the qualities of a given thing—we may say "This thing is round, and red, and so on." Grammar favours this form, but philosophically it is so far from universal that it is not even very common. If we say "this thing is bigger than that," we are not assigning a mere quality of "this," but a relation of "this" and "that." We might express the same fact by saying "that thing is smaller than this," where grammatically the subject is changed. Thus propositions stating that two things have a certain relation have a different form from subject-predicate propositions, and the failure to perceive this difference or to allow for it has been the source of many errors in traditional metaphysics.

The belief or unconscious conviction that all propositions are of the subject-predicate form—in other words, that every fact consists in some thing having some quality—has rendered most philosophers incapable of giving any account of the world of science and daily life. If they had been honestly anxious to give such an account, they would probably have discovered their error very quickly; but most of them were less anxious to understand the world of science and daily life, than to convict it of unreality in the interests of a super-sensible "real" world. Belief in the unreality of the world of sense arises with irresistible force in certain moods—moods which, I imagine, have some simple physiological basis, but are none the less powerfully persuasive. The conviction born of these moods is the source of most mysticism and of most metaphysics. When the emotional intensity of such a mood subsides, a man who is in the habit of reasoning will search for logical reasons in favour of the belief which he finds in himself. But since the belief already exists, he will be very hospitable to any reason that suggests itself. The paradoxes apparently proved by his logic are really the paradoxes of mysticism, and are the goal which he feels his logic must reach if it is to be in accordance with insight. It is in this way that logic has been pursued by those of the great philosophers who were mystics—notably Plato, Spinoza, and Hegel. But since they usually took for granted the supposed insight of the mystic emotion, their logical doctrines were presented with a certain dryness, and were believed by their disciples to be quite independent of the sudden illumination from which they sprang. Nevertheless their origin clung to them, and they remained—to borrow a useful word from Mr. Santayana—"malicious" in regard to the world of science and common sense. It is only so that we can account for the complacency with which philosophers have accepted the inconsistency of their doctrines with all the common and scientific facts which seem best established and most worthy of belief.

The logic of mysticism shows, as is natural, the defects which are inherent in anything malicious. While the mystic mood is dominant, the need of logic is not felt; as the mood fades, the impulse to logic reasserts itself, but with a desire to retain the vanishing insight, or at least to prove that it *was* insight, and that what seems to contradict it is illusion. The logic which thus arises is not quite disinterested or candid, and is inspired by a certain hatred of the daily world to which it is to be applied. Such an attitude naturally does not tend to the best results. Everyone knows that to read an author's books simply in order to refute him is not the way to understand him; and to read the book of Natrue with a conviction that it is all illusion is just as unlikely to lead to understanding. If our logic is to find the common world intelligible, it must not be hostile, but must be inspired by a genuine acceptance such as is not usually to be found among metaphysicians.

Traditional logic, since it holds that all propositions have the subject-predicate form, is unable to admit the reality of relations: all relations, it maintains, must be reduced to properties of the apparently related terms. There are many ways of refuting this opinion; one of the easiest is derived from the consideration of what are called "asymmetrical" relations. In order to explain this, I will first explain two independent ways of classifying relations.

Some relations, when they hold between A and B, also hold between B and A. Such, for example, is the relation "brother or sister." If A is a brother or sister of B, then B is a brother or sister of A. Such again is any kind of similarity, say similarity of colour. Any kind of dissimilarity is also of this kind: if the colour of A is unlike the colour of B, then the colour of B is unlike the color of A. Relations of this sort are called *symmetrical*. Thus a relation is symmetrical if, whenever it holds between A and B, it also holds between B and A.

All relations that are not symmetrical are called *non-symmetrical*. Thus "brother" is non-symmetrical, because if A is a brother of B, it may happen that B is a *sister* of A.

A relation is called *asymmetrical* when, if it holds between A and B, it *never* holds between B and A. Thus husband, father, grandfather, etc., are asymmetrical relations. So are *before, after, greater, above, to the right of,* etc. All the relations that give rise to series are of this kind.

Classification into symmetrical, asymmetrical, and merely non-symmetrical relations is the first of the two classifications we had to consider. The second is into transitive, intransitive, and merely non-transitive relations, which are defined as follows.

A relation is said to be *transitive,* if, whenever it holds between A and B and also between B and C, it holds between A and C. Thus *before, after, greater, above* are transitive. All relations giving rise to series are transitive, but so are many others. The transitive relations just mentioned were asymmetrical, but many transitive relations are symmetrical—for instance, equality in any respect, exact identity of colour, being equally numerous (as applied to collections), and so on.

A relation is said to be *non-transitive* whenever it is not transitive. Thus "brother" is non-transitive, because a brother of one's brother may be oneself. All kinds of dissimilarity are non-transitive.

A relation is said to be *intransitive* when, if A has the relation to B, and B to C, A never has it to C. Thus "father" is intransitive. So is such a relation as "one inch taller" or "one year later."

Let us now, in the light of this classification, return to the question whether all relations can be reduced to predications.

In the case of symmetrical relations—*i.e.* relations which, if they hold between A and B, also hold between B and A—some kind of plausibility can be given to this doctrine. A symmetrical relation which is transitive, such as equality, can be regarded as expressing possession of some common property, while one which is not transitive, such as inequality, can be regarded as expressing possession of different properties. But when we come to asymmetrical relations, such as before and after, greater and less, etc., the attempt to reduce them to properties becomes obviously impossible. When for example, two things are merely known to be unequal, without our knowing which is greater, we may say that the inequality results from their having different magnitudes, because inequality is a symmetrical relation; but to say that when one thing is *greater* than another, and not merely unequal to it, that means that they have different magnitudes, is formally incapable of explaining the facts. For if the other thing had been greater than the one, the magnitudes would also have been different, though the fact to be explained would not have been the same. Thus mere *difference* of magnitude is not *all* that is involved, since, if it were, there would be no difference between one thing being greater than other, and the other being greater than the one. We shall have to say that the one magnitude is *greater* than the other, and thus we shall have failed to get rid of the relation "greater." In short, both possession of the same property and possession of different properties are *symmetrical* relations, and therefore cannot account for the existence of *asymmetrical* relations.

Asymmetrical relations are involved in all series—in space and time, greater and less, whole and part, and many others of the most important characteristics of the actual world. All these aspects, therefore, the logic which reduces everything to subjects and predicates is compelled to condemn as error and mere appearance. To those whose logic is not malicious, such a wholesale condemnation appears impossible. And in fact there is no reason except prejudice, so far as I can discover, for denying the reality of relations. When once their reality is admitted, all *logical* grounds for supposing the world of sense to be illusory disappear. If this is to be supposed, it must be frankly and simply on the ground of mystic insight unsupported by argument. It is impossible to argue against what professes to be insight, so long as it does not argue in its own favour. As logicians, therefore, we may admit the possibility of the mystic's world, while yet, so long as we do not have his insight, we must continue to study the everyday world with which we are familiar. But when he contends that our world is impossible, then our logic is ready to repel his attack. And the first step in creating the logic which is to perform this service is the recognition of the reality of relations.

Relations which have two terms are only one kind of relations. A relation may have three terms, or four, or any number. Relations of two terms, being the simplest, have received more attention than the others, and have generally been alone considered by philosophers, both those who accepted and those who denied the reality of relations. But other relations have their importance, and are indispensable in the solution of certain problems. Jealousy, for example, is a relation between three people. Professor Royce mentions the relation "giving": when A gives B to C, that is a relation of three terms.[9] When a man says to his wife: "My dear, I wish you could induce Angelina to accept Edwin," his wish constitutes a relation between four people, himself, his wife, Angelina, and Edwin. Thus such relations are by no means recondite or rare. But in order to explain exactly how they differ from relations of two terms, we must embark upon a classification of the logical forms of facts, which is the first business of logic, and the business in which the traditional logic has been most deficient.

The existing world consists of many things with many qualities and relations. A complete description of the existing world would require not only a catalogue of the things, but also a mention of all their qualities and relations. We should have to know not only this, that, and the other thing, but also which was red, which yellow, which was earlier than which, which was between which two others, and so on. When I speak of a "fact," I do not mean one of the simple things in the world; I mean that a certain thing has a certain quality, or that certain things have a certain relation. Thus, for example, I should not call Napoleon a fact, but I should call it a fact that he was ambitious, or that he married Josephine. Now a fact, in this sense, is never simple, but always has two or more constituents. When it simply assigns a quality to a thing, it has only two constituents, the thing and the quality. When it consists of a relation between two things, it has three constituents, the things and the relation. When it consists of a relation between three things, it has four constitutents, and so on. The constituents of facts, in the

9. *Encyclopaedia of the Philosophical Sciences,* vol. i., p. 97.

sense in which we are using the word "fact," are not other facts, but are things and qualities or relations. When we say that there are relations of more than two terms, we mean that there are single facts consisting of a single relation and more than two things. I do not mean that one relation of two terms may hold between A and B, and also between A and C, as, for example, a man is the son of his father and also the son of his mother. This constitutes two distinct facts: if we choose to treat it as one fact, it is a fact which has facts for its constituents. But the facts I am speaking of have no facts among their constituents, but only things and relations. For example, when A is jealous of B on account of C, there is only one fact, involving three people; there are not two instances of jealousy, but only one. It is in such cases that I speak of a relation of three terms, where the simplest possible fact in which the relation occurs is one involving three things in addition to the relation. And the same applies to relations of four terms or five or any other number. All such relations must be admitted in our inventory of the logical forms of facts: two facts involving the same number of things have the same form, and two which involve different numbers of things have different forms.

Given any fact, there is an assertion which expresses the fact. The fact itself is objective, and independent of our thought or opinion about it; but the assertion is something which involves thought, and may be either true or false. An assertion may be positive or negative: we may assert that Charles I. was executed, or that he did *not* die in his bed. A negative assertion may be said to be a *denial*. Given a form of words which must be either true or false, such as "Charles I. died in his bed," we may either assert or deny this form of words: in the one case we have a positive assertion, in the other a negative one. A form of words which must be either true or false I shall call a *proposition*. Thus a proposition is the same as what may be significantly asserted or denied. A proposition which expresses what we have called a fact, *i.e.* which, when asserted, asserts that a certain thing has a certain quality, or that certain things have a certain relation, will be called an atomic proposition, because, as we shall see immediately, there are other propositions into which atomic propositions enter in a way analogous to that in which atoms enter into molecules. Atomic propositions, although, like facts, they may have any one of an infinite number of forms, are only one kind of propositions. All other kinds are more complicated. In order to preserve the parallelism in language as regards facts and propositions, we shall give the name "atomic facts" to the facts we have hitherto been considering. Thus atomic facts are what determine whether atomic propositions are to be asserted or denied.

Whether an atomic proposition, such as "this is red," or "this is before that," is to be asserted or denied can only be known empirically. Perhaps one atomic fact may sometimes be capable of being inferred from another, though I do not believe this to be the case; but in any case it cannot be inferred from premises no one of which is an atomic fact. It follows that, if atomic facts are to be known at all, some at least must be known without inference. The atomic facts which we come to know in this way are the facts of sense-perception; at any rate, the facts of sense-perception are those which we most obviously and certainly come to know in this way. If we knew all atomic facts, and also knew that there were none except those we knew, we should, theoretically, be able to infer all truths of whatever form.[10] Thus logic would then supply us with the whole of the apparatus required. But in the first acquisition of knowledge concerning atomic facts, logic is useless. In pure logic, no atomic fact is ever mentioned: we confine ourselves wholly to forms, without asking ourselves what objects can fill the forms. Thus pure logic is independent of atomic facts; but conversely, they are, in a sense, independent of logic. Pure logic and atomic facts are the two poles, the wholly *a priori* and the wholly empirical. But between the two lies a vast intermediate region, which we must now briefly explore.

"Molecular" propositions are such as contain conjunctions—*if, or, and, unless,* etc.—and such words are the marks of a molecular proposition. Consider such an assertion as, "If it rains, I shall bring my umbrella." This assertion is just as capable of truth or falsehood as the assertion of an atomic proposition, but it is obvious that either the corresponding fact, or the nature of the correspondence with fact, must be quite different from what it is in the case of an atomic proposition. Whether it rains, and whether I bring my umbrella, are each severally matters of atomic fact, ascertainable by observation. But the connection of the two involved in saying that *if* the one happens, *then* the other will happen, is something radically different from either of the two separately. It does not require for its truth that it should actually rain, or that I should actually bring my umbrella; even if the weather is cloudless, it may still be true that I should have brought my umbrella if the weather had been different. Thus we have here a connection of two propositions, which does not depend upon whether they are to be asserted or denied, but only upon the second being

---

10. This perhaps requires modification in order to include such facts as beliefs and wishes, since such facts apparently contain propositions as components. Such facts, though not strictly atomic, must be supposed included if the statement in the text is to be true.

inferable from the first. Such propositions, therefore, have a form which is different from that of any atomic proposition.

Such propositions are important to logic, because all inference depends upon them. If I have told you that if it rains I shall bring my umbrella, and if you see that there is a steady downpour, you can infer that I shall bring my umbrella. There can be no inference except where propositions are connected in some such way, so that from the truth or falsehood of the one something follows as to the truth or falsehood of the other. It seems to be the case we can sometimes know molecular propositions, as in the above instance of the umbrella, when we do not know whether the component atomic propositions are true or false. The *practical* utility of inference rests upon this fact.

The next kind of propositions we have to consider are *general* propositions, such as "all men are mortal," "all equilateral triangles are equiangular." And with these belong propositions in which the word "some" occurs, such as "some men are philosophers" or "some philosophers are not wise." These are the denials of general propositions, namely (in the above instances), of "all men are non-philosophers" and "all philosophers are wise." We will call propositions containing the word "some" *negative* general propositions, and those containing the word "all" *positive* general propositions. These propositions, it will be seen, begin to have the appearance of the propositions in logical text-books. But their peculiarity and complexity are not known to the text-books, and the problems which they raise are only discussed in the most superficial manner.

When we were discussing atomic facts, we saw that we should be able, theoretically, to infer all other truths by logic if we knew all atomic facts and also knew that there were no other atomic facts besides those we knew. The knowledge that there are no other atomic facts is positive general knowledge; it is the knowledge that "all atomic facts are known to me," or at least "all atomic facts are in this collection"—however the collection may be given. It is easy to see that general propositions, such as "all men are mortal," cannot be known by inference from atomic facts alone. If we could know each individual man, and know that he was mortal, that would not enable us to know that all men are mortal, unless we *knew* that those were all the men there are, which is a general proposition. If we knew every other existing thing throughout the universe, and knew that each separate thing was not an immortal man, that would not give us our result unless we *knew* that we had explored the whole universe, *i.e.* unless we knew "all things belong to this collection of things I have examined." Thus general truths cannot be inferred from particular truths alone, but must, if they are to be known, be either self-evident, or inferred from prem-isses of which at least one is a general truth. But all *empirical* evidence is of *particular* truths. Hence, if there is any knowledge of general truths at all, there must be *some* knowledge of general truths which is independent of empirical evidence, *i.e.* does not depend upon the data of sense.

The above conclusion, of which we had an instance in the case of the inductive principle, is important, since it affords a refutation of the older empiricists. They believed that all our knowldege is derived from the senses and dependent upon them. We see that, if this view is to be maintained, we must refuse to admit that we know any general propositions. It is perfectly possible logically that this should be the case, but it does not appear to be so in fact, and indeed no one would dream of maintaining such a view except a theorist at the last extremity. We must therefore admit that there is general knowledge not derived from sense, and that some of this knowledge is not obtained by in-ference but is primitive.

Such general knowledge is to be found in logic. Whether there is any such knowledge not derived from logic, I do not know; but in logic, at any rate, we have such knowledge. It will be remembered that we ex-cluded from pure logic such propositions as, "Socrates is a man, all men are mortal, therefore Socrates is mortal," because *Socrates* and *man* and *mortal* are empirical terms, only to be understood through particular experience. The corresponding proposition in pure logic is: "If anything has a certain property, and whatever has this property has a certain other property, then the thing in question has the other prop-erty." This propositon is absolutely general: it applies to all things and all properties. And it is quite self-evident. Thus in such proposi-tions of pure logic we have the self-evident general propositions of which we were in search.

A proposition such as "If Socrates is a man, and all men are mortal, then Socrates is mortal," is true in virtue of its *form* alone. Its truth, in this hypothetical form, does not depend upon whether Socrates actually is a man, nor upon whether in fact all men are mortal; thus it is equally true when we substitute other terms for *Socrates* and *man* and *mortal*. The general truth of which it is an instance is purely formal, and belongs to logic. Since it does not mention any particular thing, or even any particular quality or relation, it is wholly independent of the accidental facts of the existent world, and can be known, theoretically, without any experience of particular things or their qualities and rela-tions.

Logic, we may say, consists of two parts. The first part investigates what propositions are and what forms they may have; this part enumerates the different kinds of atomic propositions, of molecular propositions, of general propositions, and so on. The second part consists of certain supremely general propositions, which assert the truth of all propositions of certain forms. This second part merges into pure mathematics, whose propositions all turn out, on analysis, to be such general formal truths. The first part, which merely enumerates forms, is the more difficult, and philosophically the more important; and it is the recent progress in this first part, more than anything else, that has rendered a truly scientific discussion of many philosophical problems possible.

The problem of the nature of judgment or belief may be taken as an example of a problem whose solution depends upon an adequate inventory of logical forms. We have already seen how the supposed universality of the subject-predicate form made it impossible to give a right analysis of serial order, and therefore made space and time unintelligible. But in this case it was only necessary to admit relations of two terms. The case of judgment demands the admission of more complicated forms. If all judgments were true, we might suppose that a judgment consisted in apprehension of a *fact,* and that the apprehension was a relation of a mind to the fact. From poverty in the logical inventory, this view has often been held. But it leads to absolutely insoluble difficulties in the case of error. Suppose I believe that Charles I. died in his bed. There is no objective fact "Charles I.'s death in his bed" to which I can have a relation of apprehension. Charles I. and death and his bed are objective, but they are not, except in my thought, put together as my false belief supposes. It is therefore necessary, in analysing a belief, to look for some other logical form than a two-term relation. Failure to realise this necessity has, in my opinion, vitiated almost everything that has hitherto been written on the theory of knowledge, making the problem of error insoluble and the difference between belief and perception inexplicable.

Modern logic, as I hope is now evident, has the effect of enlarging our abstract imagination, and providing an infinite number of possible hypotheses to be applied in the analysis of any complex fact. In this respect it is the exact opposite of the logic practised by the classical tradition. In that logic, hypotheses which seem *prima facie* possible are professedly proved impossible, and it is decreed in advance that reality must have a certain special character. In modern logic, on the contrary, while the *prima facie* hypotheses as a rule remain admissible, others, which only logic would have suggested, are added to our stock, and are very often found to be indispensable if a right analysis of the facts is to be obtained. The old logic put thought in fetters, while the new logic gives it wings. It has, in my opinion, introduced the same kind of advance into philosophy as Galileo introduced into physics, making it possible at last to see what kinds of problems may be capable of solution, and what kinds must be abandoned as beyond human powers. And where a solution appears possible, the new logic provides a method which enables us to obtain results that do not merely embody personal idiosyncrasies, but must comand the assent of all who are competent to form an opinion.

VII

BERTRAND RUSSELL

RUSSELL'S "THEORY OF DESCRIPTIONS" is justly regarded as one of the great contributions in the history of philosophy. Praised by many as a paradigm of philosophy and by others as identical with proper philosophical method, it has profoundly influenced the whole of contemporary philosophical analysis from the inception of the theory to P. F. Strawson's brilliant critique of it in "On Referring" (*Mind*, 1950). First stated in "On Denoting" (1905), rigorously formulated in *Principia Mathematica* (1910-13), and informally expounded in "Philosophy of Logical Atomism" (1918-19), the clearest exposition of the theory is in Russell's *Introduction to Mathematical Philosophy* (1919). It is the latter, written while Russell was in prison because of his pacifist activities, that is reprinted here.

How can we render intelligible our talk about unreal or self-contradictory objects without assuming their existence in order to talk about them? This is the problem the theory of descriptions was designed to solve. Basic to the theory is a fundamental distinction between proper names, e.g., "Scott," and descriptions, e.g., "the author of *Waverley*." A proper name is a simple symbol; it denotes an individual directly; that individual is its meaning; and it has this meaning independently of all other symbols. A description is a complex symbol and, because it does not designate an individual directly, is an "incomplete symbol," i.e., a symbol that has no meaning in isolation but that can be given a meaning in a context with other symbols. Descriptions, such as "the author of *Waverly*," can be resolved by putting them into certain propositional contexts, such as "The author of *Waverley* was Scotch," and analyzing (or translating or contextually defining) the whole context in such a manner that the grammatical subject disappears, to be replaced by other symbols. Propositions about the author of *Waverley*, the round square, or the present King of France, therefore, can all be rendered intelligible by being construed as discourse that involves propositional functions and variables, and not as discourse about real objects.

Descriptions[1]

We dealt in the preceding chapter with the words *all* and *some;* in this chapter we shall consider the word *the* in the singular, and in the next chapter we shall consider the word *the* in the plural. It may be thought excessive to devote two chapters to one word, but to the philosophical mathematician it is a word of very great importance: like Browning's Grammarian with the enclitic $\delta\epsilon$, I would give the doctrine of this word if I were "dead from the waist down" and not merely in a prison.

We have already had occasion to mention "descriptive functions," *i.e.* such expressions as "the father of x" or "the sine of x." These are to be defined by first defining "descriptions."

A "description" may be of two sorts, definite and indefinite (or ambiguous). An indefinite description is a phrase of the form "a so-and-so," and a definite description is a phrase of the form "the so-and-so" (in the singular). Let us begin with the former.

"Who did you meet?" "I met a man." "That is a very indefinite description." We are therefore not departing from usage in our terminology. Our question is: What do I really assert when I assert "I met a man"? Let us assume, for the moment, that my assertion in true, and that in fact I met Jones. It is clear that what I assert is *not* "I met Jones." I may say "I met a man, but it was not Jones"; in that case, though I lie, I do not contradict myself, as I should do if when I say I met a man I really mean that I met Jones. It is clear also that the person to whom I am speaking can understand what I say, even if he is a foreigner and has never heard of Jones.

But we may go further: not only Jones, but no actual man, enters into my statement. This becomes obvious when the statement is false, since then there is no more reason why Jones should be supposed to enter into the proposition than why anyone else should. Indeed the statement would remain significant, though it could not possibly be true, even if there were no man at all. "I met a unicorn" or "I met a

1. From *Introduction to Mathematical Philosophy* (London: George Allen & Unwin, Ltd., 1919), Chap. 16. Reprinted by permission of the publishers.

sea-serpent" is a perfectly significant assertion, if we know what it would be to be a unicorn or a sea-serpent, *i.e.* what is the definition of these fabulous monsters. Thus it is only what we may call the *concept* that enters into the proposition. In the case of "unicorn," for example, there is only the concept: there is not also, somewhere among the shades, something unreal which may be called "a unicorn." Therefore, since it is significant (though false) to say "I met a unicorn," it is clear that this proposition, rightly analysed, does not contain a constituent "a unicorn," though it does contain the concept "unicorn."

The question of "unreality," which confronts us at this point, is a very important one. Misled by grammar, the great majority of those logicians who have dealt with this question have dealt with it on mistaken lines. They have regarded grammatical form as a surer guide in analysis than, in fact, it is. And they have not known what differences in grammatical form are important. "I met Jones" and "I met a man" would count traditionally as propositions of the same form, but in actual fact they are of quite different forms: the first names an actual person, Jones; while the second involves a propositional function, and becomes, when made explicit: "The function 'I met x and x is human' is sometimes true." (It will be remembered that we adopted the convention of using "sometimes" as not implying more than once.) This proposition is obviously not of the form "I met x," which accounts for the existence of the proposition "I met a unicorn" in spite of the fact that there is no such thing as "a unicorn."

For want of the apparatus of propositional functions, many logicians have been driven to the conclusion that there are unreal objects. It is argued, *e.g.* by Meinong,[2] that we can speak about "the golden mountain," "the round square," and so on; we can make true propositions of which these are the subjects; hence they must have some kind of logical being, since otherwise the propositions in which they occur would be meaningless. In such theories, it seems to me, there is a failure of that feeling for reality which ought to be preserved even in the most abstract studies. Logic, I should maintain, must no more admit a unicorn than zoology can; for logic is concerned with the real world just as truly as zoology, though with its more abstract and general features. To say that unicorns have an existence in heraldry, or in literature, or in imagination, is a most pitiful and paltry evasion. What exists in heraldry is not an animal, made of flesh and blood, moving and breathing of its own initiative. What exists is a picture, or a description in words. Similarly, to maintain that Hamlet, for example, exists in his own world, namely, in the world of Shakespeare's imagination, just as

2. *Untersuchungen zur Gegenstandstheorie und Psychologie*, 1904.

truly as (say) Napoleon existed in the ordinary world, is to say something deliberately confusing, or else confused to a degree which is scarcely credible. There is only one world, the "real" world: Shakespeare's imagination is part of it, and the thoughts that he had in writing Hamlet are real. So are the thoughts that we have in reading the play. But it is of the very essence of fiction that only the thoughts, feelings, etc., in Shakespeare and his readers are real, and that there is not, in addition to them, an objective Hamlet. When you have taken account of all the feelings roused by Napoleon in writers and readers of history, you have not touched the actual man; but in the case of Hamlet you have come to the end of him. If no one thought about Hamlet, there would be nothing left of him; if no one had thought about Napoleon, he would have soon seen to it that some one did. The sense of reality is vital in logic, and whoever juggles with it by pretending that Hamlet has another kind of reality is doing a disservice to thought. A robust sense of reality is very necessary in framing a correct analysis of propositions about unicorns, golden mountains, round squares, and other such pseudo-objects.

In obedience to the feeling of reality, we shall insist that, in the analysis of propositions, nothing "unreal" is to be admitted. But, after all, if there *is* nothing unreal, how, it may be asked, *could* we admit anything unreal? The reply is that, in dealing with propositions, we are dealing in the first instance with symbols, and if we attribute significance to groups of symbols which have no significance, we shall fall into the error of admitting unrealities, in the only sense in which this is possible, namely, as objects described. In the proposition "I met a unicorn," the whole four words together make a significant proposition, and the word "unicorn" by itself is significant, in just the same sense as the word "man." But the *two* words "a unicorn" do not form a subordinate group having a meaning of its own. Thus if we falsely attribute meaning to these two words, we find ourselves saddled with "a unicorn," and with the problem how there can be such a thing in a world where there are no unicorns. "A unicorn" is an indefinite description which describes nothing. It is not an indefinite description which describes something unreal. Such a proposition as "x is unreal" only has meaning when "x" is a description, definite or indefinite; in that case the proposition will be true if "x" is a description which describes nothing. But whether the description "x" describes something or describes nothing, it is in any case not a constituent of the proposition in which it occurs; like "a unicorn" just now, it is not a subordinate group having a meaning of its own. All this results from the fact that, when "x" is a description, "x is unreal" or "x does not exist" is not nonsense, but is always significant and sometimes true.

We may now proceed to define generally the meaning of propositions which contain ambiguous descriptions. Suppose we wish to make some statement about "a so-and-so," where "so-and-so's" are those objects that have a certain property ϕ, *i.e.* those objects x for which the propositional function ϕx is true. (*E.g.* if we take "a man" as our instance of "a so-and-so," ϕx will be "x is human.") Let us now wish to assert the property Ψ of "a so-and-so," *i.e.*, we wish to assert that "a so-and-so" has that property which x has when Ψx is true. (*E.g.* in the case of "I met a man," Ψx will be "I met x.") Now the proposition that "a so-and-so" has the property Ψ is *not* a proposition of the form "Ψx." If it were, "a so-and-so" would have to be identical with x for a suitable x; and although (in a sense) this may be true in some cases, it is certainly not true in such a case as "a unicorn." It is just this fact, that the statement that a so-and-so has the propery Ψ is not of the form Ψx, which makes it possible for "a so-and-so" to be, in a certain clearly definable sense, "unreal." The definition is as follows:—

The statement that "an object having the property ϕ has the property Ψ"

means:

"The joint assertion of ϕx and Ψx is not always false."

So far as logic goes, this is the same proposition as might be expressed by "some ϕ's are Ψ's"; but rhetorically there is a difference, because in the one case there is a suggestion of singularity, and in the other case of plurality. This, however, is not the important point. The important point is that, when rightly analysed, propositions verbally about "a so-and-so" are found to contain no constituent represented by this phrase. And that is why such propositions can be significant even when there is no such thing as a so-and-so.

The definition of *existence*, as applied to ambiguous descriptions, results from what was said at the end of the preceding chapter. We say that "men exist" or "a man exists" if the propositional function "x is human" is sometimes true; and generally "a so-and-so" exists if "x is so-and-so" is sometimes true. We may put this in other language. The proposition "Socrates is a man" is no doubt *equivalent* to "Socrates is human," but it is not the very same proposition. The *is* of "Socrates is human" expresses the relation of subject and predicate; the *is* of "Socrates is a man" expresses identity. It is a disgrace to the human race that it has chosen to employ the same word "is" for these two entirely different ideas—a disgrace which a symbolic logical language of course remedies. The identity in "Socrates is a man" is identity between an object named (accepting "Socrates" as a name, subject to qualifications explained later) and an object ambiguously described. An object ambiguously described will "exist" when at least one such proposition is true, *i.e.* when there is at least one true proposition of the form "*x* is a so-and-so," where "*x*" is a name. It is characteristic of ambiguous (as opposed to definite) descriptions that there may be any number of true propositions of the above form—Socrates is a man, Plato is a man, etc. Thus "a man exists" follows from Socrates, or Plato, or anyone else. With definite descriptions, on the other hand, the corresponding form of proposition, namely, "*x* is the so-and-so" (where "*x*" is a name), can only be true for one value of *x* at most. This brings us to the subject of definite descriptions, which are to be defined in a way analogous to that employed for ambiguous descriptions, but rather more complicated.

We come now to the main subject of the present chapter, namely, the definition of the word *the* (in the singular). One very important point about the definition of "a so-and-so" applies equally to "the so-and-so"; the definition to be sought is a definition of propositions in which this phrase occurs, not a definition of the phrase itself in isolation. In the case of "a so-and-so," this is fairly obvious: no one could suppose that "a man" was a definite object, which could be defined by itself. Socrates is a man, Plato is a man, Aristotle is a man, but we cannot infer that "a man" means the same as "Socrates" means and also the same as "Plato" means and also the same as "Aristotle" means, since these three names have different meanings. Nevertheless, when we have enumerated all the men in the world, there is nothing left of which we can say, "This is a man, and not only so, but it is *the* 'a man,' the quintessential entity that is just an indefinite man without being anybody in particular." It is of course quite clear that whatever there is in the world is definite: if it is a man it is one definite man and not any other. Thus there cannot be such an entity as "a man" to be found in the world, as opposed to specific men. And accordingly it is natural that we do not define "a man" itself, but only the propositions in which it occurs.

In the case of "the so-and-so" this is equally true, though at first sight less obvious. We may demonstrate that this must be the case, by a consideration of the difference between a *name* and a *definite description*. Take the proposition, "Scott is the author of *Waverley*." We have here a name, "Scott," and a description, "the author of *Waverly*," which are asserted to apply to the same person. The distinction between a name and all other symbols may be explained as follows:—

A name is a simple symbol whose meaning is something that can only occur as subject, *i.e.* something of the kind that, in Chapter XIII., we defined as an "indiivdual" or a "particular." And a "simple" symbol is one which has no parts that are symbols. Thus "Scott" is a simple symbol, because, though it has parts (namely, separate letters), these parts are not symbols. On the other hand, "the author of *Waverley*" is not a simple symbol, because the separate words that compose the phrase are parts which are symbols. If, as may be the case, whatever *seems* to be an "individual" is really capable of further analysis, we shall have to content ourselves with what may be called "relative individuals," which will be terms that, throughout the context in question, are never analysed and never occur otherwise than as subjects. And in that case we shall have correspondingly to content ourselves with "relative names." From the standpoint of our present problem, namely, the definition of descriptions, this problem, whether these are absolute names or only relative names, may be ignored, since it concerns different stages in the hierarchy of "types," whereas we have to compare such couples as "Scott" and "the author of *Waverley*," which both apply to the same object, and do not raise the problem of types. We may, therefore, for the moment, treat names as capable of being absolute; nothing that we shall have to say will depend upon this assumption, but the wording may be a little shortened by it.

We have, then, two things to compare: (1) a *name*, which is a simple symbol, directly designating an individual which is its meaning, and having this meaning in its own right, independently of the meanings of all other words; (2) a *description*, which consists of several words, whose meanings are already fixed, and from which results whatever is to be taken as the "meaning" of the description.

A proposition containing a description is not identical with what that proposition becomes when a name is substituted, even if the name names the same object as the description describes. "Scott is the author of *Waverley*" is obviously a different proposition from "Scott is Scott": the first is a fact in literary history, the second a trivial truism. And if we put anyone other than Scott in place of "the author of *Waverley*," our proposition would become false, and would therefore certainly no longer be the same proposition. But, it may be said, our proposition is essentially of the same form as (say) "Scott is Sir Walter," in which two names are said to apply to the same person. The reply is that, if "Scott is Sir Walter" really means "the person named 'Scott' is the person named 'Sir Walter,'" then the names are being used as descriptions: *i.e.* the individual, instead of being named, is being described as the person having that name. This is a way in which names are frequently used in practice, and there will, as a rule, be nothing in the phraseology to show whether they are being used in this way or *as* names. When a name is used directly, merely to indicate what we are speaking about, it is no part of the *fact* asserted, or of the falsehood if our assertion happens to be false: it is merely part of the symbolism by which we express our thought. What we want to express is something which might (for example) be translated into a foreign language; it is something for which the actual words are a vehicle, but of which they are no part. On the other hand, when we make a proposition about "the person called 'Scott,'" the actual name "Scott" enters into what we are asserting, and not merely into the language used in making the assertion. Our proposition will now be a different one if we substitute "the person called 'Sir Walter.'" But so long as we are using names *as* names, whether we say "Scott" or whether we say "Sir Walter" is as irrelevant to what we are asserting as whether we speak English or French. Thus so long as names are used *as* names, "Scott is Sir Walter" is the same trivial proposition as "Scott is Scott." This completes the proof that "Scott is the author of *Waverley*" is not the same proposition as results from substituting a name for "the author of *Waverley*," no matter what name may be substituted.

When we use a variable, and speak of a propositional function, ϕx say, the process of applying general statements about x to particular cases will consist in substituting a name for the letter "x," assuming that ϕ is a function which has individuals for its arguments. Suppose, for example, that ϕx is "always true"; let it be, say, the "law of identity," $x = x$. Then we may substitute for "x" any name we choose, and we shall obtain a true proposition. Assuming for the moment that "Socrates," "Plato," and "Aristotle" are names (a very rash assumption), we can infer from the law of identity that Socrates is Socrates, Plato is Plato, and Aristotle is Aristotle. But we shall commit a fallacy if we attempt to infer, without further premisses, that the author of *Waverley* is the author of *Waverley*. This results from what we have just proved, that, if we substitute a name for "the author of *Waverley*" in a proposition, the proposition we obtain is a different one. That is to say, applying the result to our present case: If "x" is a name, "$x = x$" is not the same proposition as "the author of *Waverley* is the author of *Waverley*," no matter what name "x" may be. Thus from the fact that all propositions of the form "$x = x$" are true we cannot infer, without more ado, that the author of *Waverley* is the author of *Waverley*. In fact, propositoins of the form "the so-and-so is the so-and-so" are not always true: it is necessary that the so-and-so should *exist* (a term which will be explained shortly). It is false that the present King of France is the present King of France, or that the round square is the round square. When we substitute a description for a name, propositional functions which are "always true" may become false, if the description describes nothing. There is no mystery in this as soon as we realise (what was proved in the preceding paragraph) that when we substitute a description the result is not a value of the propositional function in question.

We are now in a position to define propositions in which a definite description occurs. The only thing that distinguishes "the so-and-so" from "a so-and-so" is the implication of uniqueness. We cannot speak of "*the* inhabitant of London," because inhabiting London is an attribute which is not unique. We cannot speak about "the present King of France," because there is none; but we can speak about "the present King of England." Thus propositions about "the so-and-so" always imply the corresponding propositions about "a so-and-so," with the addendum that there is not more than one so-and-so. Such a proposition as "Scott is the author of *Waverley*" could not be true if *Waverley* had never been written, or if several people had written it; and no more could any other proposition resulting from a propositional function x by the substitution of "the author of *Waverley*" for "x." We may say that "the author of *Waverley*" means "the value of x for which 'x wrote *Waverley*' is true." Thus the proposition "the author of *Waverley* was Scotch," for example, involves:

(1) "x wrote *Waverley*" is not always false;
(2) "if x and y wrote *Waverley*, x and y are identical" is always true;
(3) "if x wrote *Waverley*, x was Scotch" is always true.

These three propositions, translated into ordinary language, state:

(1) at least one person wrote *Waverley*;
(2) at most one person wrote *Waverley*;
(3) whoever wrote *Waverley* was Scotch.

All these three are implied by "the author of *Waverley* was Scotch." Conversely, the three together (but no two of them) imply that the author of *Waverley* was Scotch. Hence the three together may be taken as defining what is meant by the proposition "the author of *Waverley* was Scotch."

We may somewhat simplify these three propositions. The first and second together are equivalent to: "There is a term c such that 'x wrote *Waverley*' is true when x is c and is false when x is not c." In other words, "There is a term c such that 'x wrote *Waverley*' is always equivalent to 'x is c.'" (Two propositions are "equivalent" when both are true or both are false.) We have here, to begin with, two functions of

x, "x wrote *Waverley*" and "x is c," and we form a function of c by considering the equivalence of these two functions of x for all values of x; we then proceed to assert that the resulting function of c is "sometimes true," *i.e.* that it is true for at least one value of c. (It obviously cannot be true for more than one value of c.) These two conditions together are defined as giving the meaning of "the author of *Waverley* exists."

We may now define "the term satisfying the function ϕx exists." This is the general form of which the above is a particular case. "The author of *Waverley*" is "the term satisfying the function 'x wrote *Waverley*.'" And "the so-and-so" will always involve reference to some propositional function, namely, that which defines the property that makes a thing a so-and-so. Our definition is as follows:—

"The term satisfying the function ϕx exists" means:

"There is a term c such that ϕx is always equivalent to 'x is c.'"

In order to define "the author of *Waverley* was Scotch," we have still to take account of the third of our three propositions, namely, "Whoever wrote *Waverley* was Scotch." This will be satisfied by merely adding that the c in question is to be Scotch. Thus "the author of *Waverley* was Scotch" is:

"There is a term c such that (1) 'x wrote *Waverley*' is always equivalent to 'x is c,' (2) c is Scotch."

And generally: "the term satisfying ϕx satisfies Ψx" is defined as meaning:

"There is a term c such that (1) ϕx is always equivalent to 'x is c,' (2) Ψc is true."

This is the definition of propositions in which descriptions occur.

It is possible to have much knowledge concerning a term described, *i.e.* to know many propositions concerning "the so-and-so," without actually knowing what the so-and-so is, *i.e.* without knowing any proposition of the form "x is the so-and-so," where "x" is a name. In a detective story propositions about "the man who did the deed" are accumulated, in the hope that ultimately they will suffice to demonstrate that it was A who did the deed. We may even go so far as to say that, in all such knowledge as can be expressed in words—with the exception of "this" and "that" and a few other words of which the meaning varies on different occasions—no names, in the strict sense, occur, but what seem like names are really descriptions. We may inquire significantly whether Homer existed, which we could not do if "Homer" were a name. The proposition "the so-and-so exists" is significant, whether true or false; but if a is the so-and-so (where "a" is a name), the words "*a* exists" are meaningless. It is only of descriptions—definite or indefinite—that existence can be significantly asserted; for, if "*a*" is a name, it *must* name something: what does not name anything is not a name, and therefore, if intended to be a name, is a symbol devoid of meaning, whereas a description, like "the present King of France," does not become incapable of occurring significantly merely on the ground that it describes nothing, the reason being that it is a *complex* symbol, of which the meaning is derived from that of its constituent symbols. And so, when we ask whether Homer existed, we are using the word "Homer" as an abbreviated description: we may replace it by (say) "the author of the *Iliad* and the *Odyssey*." The same considerations apply to almost all uses of what look like proper names.

When descriptions occur in propositions, it is necessary to distinguish what may be called "primary" and "secondary" occurrences. The abstract distinction is as follows. A description has a "primary" occurrence when the proposition in which it occurs results from substituting the description for "x" in some propositional function ϕx; a description has a "secondary" occurrence when the result of substituting the description for x in ϕx gives only *part* of the proposition concerned. An instance will make this clearer. Consider "the present King of France is bald." Here "the present King of France" has a primary occurrence, and the proposition is false. Every proposition in which a description which describes nothing has a primary occurrence is false. But now consider "the present King of France is not bald." This is ambiguous. If we are first to take "x is bald," then substitute "the present King of France" for "x," and then deny the result, the occurrence of "the present King of France" is secondary and our proposition is true; but if we are to take "x is not bald" and substitute "the present King of France" for "x," then "the present King of France" has a primary occurrence and the proposition is false. Confusion of primary and secondary occurrences is a ready source of fallacies where descriptions are concerned.

Descriptions occur in mathematics chiefly in the form of *descriptive functions*, *i.e.* "the term having the relation R to y," or "the R of y" as we may say, on the analogy of "the father of y" and similar phrases. To say "the father of y is rich," for example, is to say that the following propositional function of c: "c is rich, and 'x begat y' is always equivalent to 'x is c,'" is "sometimes true," *i.e.* is true for at least one value of c. It obviously cannot be true for more than one value.

The theory of descriptions, briefly outlined in the present chapter, is of the utmost importance both in logic and in theory of knowledge. But for purposes of mathematics, the more philosophical parts of the theory are not essential, and have therefore been omitted in the above account, which has confined itself to the barest mathematical requisites.

VIII

BERTRAND RUSSELL

"THE RELATION OF SENSE-DATA TO PHYSICS" (1914) is a superb example of the logical-analytic method in philosophy. In the essay, Russell joins his theory of descriptions—the resolution of one kind of symbol—with his new principle: "Wherever possible, logical constructions are to be substituted for inferred entities." The symbols for certain inferred entities, such as the symbols of physics, e.g., "points," "instants," and "particles," are also construed as incomplete; they too can be resolved (or analyzed or translated) in their propositional contexts, into logically equivalent statements about uninferred or empirical entities along the lines suggested by the theory of descriptions. Statements about unempirical material particles, for example are resolved into statements about classes of empirical sensible entities.

The Relation of Sense-data to Physics[1]

¶ I. The Problem Stated

Physics is said to be an empirical science, based upon observation and experiment.

It is supposed to be verifiable, i.e. capable of calculating beforehand results subsequently confirmed by observation and experiment.

What can we learn by observation and experiment?

Nothing, so far as physics is concerned, except immediate data of sense: certain patches of colour, sounds, tastes, smells, etc., with certain spatio-temporal relations.

The supposed contents of the physical world are *prima facie* very different from these: molecules have no colour, atoms make no noise, electrons have no taste, and corpuscles do not even smell.

If such objects are to be verified, it must be solely through their relation to sense-data: they must have some kind of correlation with sense-data, and must be verifiable through their correlation *alone*.

But how is the correlation itself ascertained? A correlation can only be ascertained empirically by the correlated objects being constantly *found* together. But in our case, only one term of the correlation, namely, the sensible term, is ever *found:* the other term seems essentially incapable of being found. Therefore, it would seem, the correlation with objects of sense, by which physics was to be verified, is itself utterly and for ever unverifiable.

There are two ways of avoiding this result.

(1) We may say that we know some principle *a priori,* without the need of empirical verification, e.g. that our sense-data have *causes* other than themselves, and that something can be known about these causes by inference from their effects. This way has been often adopted by philosophers. It may be necessary to adopt this way to some extent, but in so far as it is adopted physics ceases to be empirical or based upon

---

1. From *Mysticism and Logic* (London: Longmans, Green Co., 1918), Chap. 8. Reprinted by permission of George Allen & Unwin, Ltd., London.

experiment and observation alone. Therefore this way is to be avoided as much as possible.

(2) We may succeed in actually defining the objects of physics as functions of sense-data. Just in so far as physics leads to expectations, this *must* be possible, since we can only *expect* what can be experienced. And in so far as the physical state of affairs is inferred from sense-data, it must be capable of expression as a function of sense-data. The problem of accomplishing this expression leads to much interesting logico-mathematical work.

In physics as commonly set forth, sense-data appear as functions of physical objects: when such-and-such waves impinge upon the eye we see such-and-such colours, and so on. But the waves are in fact inferred from the colours, not vice versa. Physics cannot be regarded as validly based upon empirical data until the waves have been expressed as functions of the colours and other sense-data.

Thus if physics is to be verifiable we are faced with the following problem: Physics exhibits sense-data as functions of physical objects, but verification is only possible if physical objects can be exhibited as functions of sense-data. We have therefore to solve the equations giving sense-data in terms of physical objects, so as to make them instead give physical objects in terms of sense-data.

¶ II. CHARACTERISTICS OF SENSE-DATA

When I speak of a "sense-datum," I do not mean the whole of what is given in sense at one time. I mean rather such a part of the whole as might be singled out by attention: particular patches of colour, particular noises, and so on. There is some difficulty in deciding what is to be considered *one* sense-datum: often attention causes divisions to appear where, so far as can be discovered, there were no divisions before. An observed complex fact, such as that this patch of red is to the left of that patch of blue, is also to be regarded as a datum from our present point of view: epistemologically, it does not differ greatly from a simple sense-datum as regards its function in giving knowledge. Its *logical* structure is very different, however, from that of sense: *sense* gives acquaintance with particulars, and is thus a two-term relation in which the object can be *named* but not asserted, and is inherently incapable of truth or falsehood, whereas the observation of a complex fact, which may be suitably called perception, is not a two-term relation, but involves the propositional form on the object-side, and gives knowledge of a truth, not mere acquaintance with a particular. This logical difference, important as it is, is not very relevant to our present problem; and it will be convenient to regard data of perception as included among sense-data for the purposes of this paper. It is to be observed that the particulars which are constituents of a datum of perception are always sense-data in the strict sense.

Concerning sense-data, we know that they are there while they are data, and this is the epistemological basis of all our knowledge of external particulars. (The meaning of the word "external" of course raises problems which will concern us later.) We do not know, except by means of more or less precarious inferences, whether the objects which are at one time sense-data continue to exist at times when they are not data. Sense-data at the times when they are data are all that we directly and primitively know of the external world; hence in epistemology the fact that they are *data* is all-important. But the fact that they are all that we directly know gives, of course, no presumption that they are all that there is. If we could construct an impersonal metaphysic, independent of the accidents of our knowledge and ignorance, the privileged position of the actual data would probably disappear, and they would probably appear as a rather haphazard selection from a mass of objects more or less like them. In saying this, I assume only that it is probable that there are particulars with which we are not acquainted. Thus the special importance of sense-data is in relation to epistemology, not to metaphysics. In this respect, physics is to be reckoned as metaphysics: it is impersonal, and nominally pays no special attention to sense-data. It is only when we ask how physics can be *known* that the importance of sense-data re-emerges.

¶ III. Sensibilia

I shall give the name *sensibilia* to those objects which have the same metaphysical and physical status as sense-data, without necessarily being data to any mind. Thus the relation of a *sensibile* to a sense-datum is like that of a man to a husband: a man becomes a husband by entering into the relation of marriage, and similarly a *sensibile* becomes a sense-datum by entering into the relation of acquaintance. It is important to have both terms; for we wish to discuss whether an object which is at one time a sense-datum can still exist at a time when it is not a sense-datum. We cannot ask "Can sense-data exist without being given?" for that is like asking "Can husbands exist without being married?" We must ask "Can *sensibilia* exist without being given?" and also "Can a particular *sensibile* be at one time a sense-datum, and at another not?" Unless we have the word *sensibile* as well as the word "sense-datum," such questions are apt to entangle us in trivial logical puzzles.

It will be seen that all sense-data are *sensibilia*. It is a metaphysical

question whether all *sensibilia* are sense-data, and an epistemologica[l]
question whether there exist means of inferring *sensibilia* which are no[t]
data from those that are.

A few preliminary remarks, to be amplified as we proceed, will serv[e]
to elucidate the use which I propose to make of *sensibilia*.

I regard sense-data as not mental, and as being, in fact, part o[f]
the actual subject-matter of physics. There are arguments, shortly t[o]
be examined, for their subjectivity, but these arguments seem to me onl[y]
to prove *physiological* subjectivity, i.e. causal dependence on th[e]
sense-organs, nerves, and brain. The appearance which a thing present[s]
to us is causally dependent upon these, in exactly the same way as it i[s]
dependent upon intervening fog or smoke or coloured glass. Bot[h]
dependences are contained in the statement that the appearance whic[h]
a piece of matter presents when viewed from a given place is a functio[n]
not only of the piece of matter, but also of the intervening medium[.]
(The terms used in this statement—"matter," "view from a give[n]
place," "appearance," "intervening medium"—will all be defined in th[e]
course of the present paper.) We have not the means of ascertaining ho[w]
things appear from places not surrounded by brain and nerves an[d]
sense-organs, because we cannot leave the body; but continuity make[s]
it not unreasonable to suppose that they present *some* appearance a[t]
such places. Any such appearance would be included among *sensibilia*. I[f]
—*per impossibile*—there were a complete human body with no min[d]
inside it, all those *sensibilia* would exist, in relation to that body[,]
which would be sense-data if there were a mind in the body. What th[e]
mind adds to *sensibilia*, in fact, is *merely* awareness: everything els[e]
is physical or physiological.

¶ IV. SENSE-DATA ARE PHYSICAL

Before discussing this question it will be well to define the sens[e]
in which the terms "mental" and "physical" are to be used. The wor[d]
"physical," in all preliminary discussions, is to be understood as meaning "what is dealt with by physics." Physics, it is plain, tells us something about some of the constituents of the actual world; what thes[e]
constituents are may be doubtful, but it is they that are to be calle[d]
physical, whatever their nature may prove to be.

The definition of the term "mental" is more difficult, and can onl[y]
be satisfactorily given after many difficult controversies have been discussed and decided. For present purposes therefore I must conten[t]
myself with assuming a dogmatic answer to these controversies. I shal[l]
call a particular "mental" when it is aware of something, and I shal[l]

call a fact "mental" when it contains a mental particular as a constituent.

It will be seen that the mental and the physical are not necessarily mutually exclusive, although I know of no reason to suppose that they overlap.

The doubt as to the correctness of our definition of the "mental" is of little importance in our present discussion. For what I am concerned to maintain is that sense-data are physical, and this being granted it is a matter of indifference in our present inquiry whether or not they are also mental. Although I do not hold, with Mach and James and the "new realists," that the difference between the mental and the physical is *merely* one of arrangement, yet what I have to say in the present paper is compatible with their doctrine and might have been reached from their standpoint.

In discussions on sense-data, two questions are commonly confused, namely:

(1) Do sensible objects persist when we are not sensible of them? In other words, do *sensibilia* which are data at a certain time sometimes continue to exist at times when they are not data? And (2) are sense-data mental or physical?

I propose to assert that sense-data are physical, while yet maintaining that they probably never persist unchanged after ceasing to be data. The view that they do not persist is often thought, quite erroneously in my opinion, to imply that they are mental; and this has, I believe, been a potent source of confusion in regard to our present problem. If there were, as some have held, a *logical impossibility* in sense-data persisting after ceasing to be data, that certainly would tend to show that they were mental; but if, as I contend, their non-persistence is merely a probable inference from empirically ascertained causal laws, then it carries no such implication with it, and we are quite free to treat them as part of the subject-matter of physics.

Logically a sense-datum is an object, a particular of which the subject is aware. It does not contain the subject as a part, as for example beliefs and volitions do. The existence of the sense-datum is therefore not logically dependent upon that of the subject; for the only way, so far as I know, in which the existence of A can be *logically* dependent upon the existence of B is when B is part of A. There is therefore no *a priori* reason why a particular which is a sense-datum should not persist after it has ceased to be a datum, nor why other similar particulars should not exist without ever being data. The view that sense-data are mental is derived, no doubt, in part from their physiological subjectivity, but in part also from a failure to distinguish between sense-data and "sensations." By a sensation I mean the fact consisting in the subject's awareness of the sense-datum. Thus a sensation is a complex of which the subject is a constituent and which therefore is mental. The sense-datum, on the other hand, stands over against the subject as that external object of which in sensation the subject is aware. It is true that the sense-datum is in many cases in the subject's body, but the subject's body is as distinct from the subject as tables and chairs are, and is in fact merely a part of the material world. So soon, therefore, as sense-data are clearly distinguished from sensations, and as their subjectivity is recognised to be physiological not psychical, the chief obstacles in the way of regarding them as physical are removed.

¶ V. "SENSIBILIA" AND "THINGS"

But if "sensibilia" are to be recognised as the ultimate constituents of the physical world, a long and difficult journey is to be performed before we can arrive either at the "thing" of common sense or at the "matter" of physics. The supposed impossibility of combining the different sense-data which are regarded as appearances of the same "thing" to different people has made it seem as though these "sensibilia" must be regarded as mere subjective phantasms. A given table will present to one man a rectangular appearance, while to another it appears to have two acute angles and two obtuse angles; to one man it appears brown, while to another, towards whom it reflects the light, it appears white and shiny. It is said, not wholly without plausibility, that these different shapes and different colours cannot co-exist simultaneously in the same place, and cannot therefore both be constituents of the physical world. This argument I must confess appeared to me until recently to be irrefutable. The contrary opinion has, however, been ably maintained by Dr. T. P. Nunn in an article entitled: "Are Secondary Qualities Independent of Perception?"[2] The supposed impossibility derives its apparent force from the phrase: *"in the same place,"* and it is precisely in this phrase that its weakness lies. The conception of space is too often treated in philosophy—even by those who on reflection would not defend such treatment—as though it were as given, simple, and unambiguous as Kant, in his psychological innocence, supposed. It is the unperceived ambiguity of the world "place" which, as we shall shortly see, has caused the difficulties to realists and given an undeserved advantage to their opponents. Two "places" of different kinds are involved in every sense-datum, namely the place *at*

2. *Proc. Arist. Soc.*, 1909-10, pp. 191-218.

which it appears and the place *from* which it appears. These belong to different spaces, although, as we shall see, it is possible, with certain limitations, to establish a correlation between them. What we call the different appearances of the same thing to different observers are each in a space private to the observer concerned. No place in the private world of one observer is identical with a place in the private world of another observer. There is therefore no question of combining the different appearances in the one place; and the fact that they cannot all exist in one place affords accordingly no ground whatever for questioning their physical reality. The "thing" of common sense may in fact be identified with the whole class of its appearances—where, however, we must include among appearances not only those which are actual sense-data, but also those "sensibilia," if any, which, on grounds of continuity and resemblance, are to be regarded as belonging to the same system of appearances, although there happen to be no observers to whom they are data.

An example may make this clearer. Suppose there are a number of people in a room, all seeing, as they say, the same tables and chairs, walls and pictures. No two of these people have exactly the same sense-data, yet there is sufficient similarity among their data to enable them to group together certain of these data as appearances of one "thing" to the several spectators, and others as appearances of another "thing." Besides the appearances which a given thing in the room presents to the actual spectators, there are, we may suppose, other appearances which it would present to other possible spectators. If a man were to sit down between two others, the appearance which the room would present to him would be intermediate between the appearances which it presents to the two others: and although this appearance would not exist as it is without the sense-organs, nerves and brain, of the newly arrived spectator, still it is not unnatural to suppose that, from the position which he now occupies, *some* appearance of the room existed before his arrival. This supposition, however, need merely be noticed and not insisted upon.

Since the "thing" cannot, without indefensible partiality, be identified with any single one of its appearances, it came to be thought of as something distinct from all of them and underlying them. But by the principle of Occam's razor, if the class of appearances will fulfill the purposes for the sake of which the thing was invented by the prehistoric metaphysicians to whom common sense is due, economy demands that we should identify the thing with the class of its appearances. It is not necessary to *deny* a substance or substratum underlying these appearances; it is merely expedient to abstain from asserting this unnecessary entity. Our procedure here is precisely analogous to that which has swept away from the philosophy of mathematics the useless menagerie of metaphysical monsters with which it used to be infested.

¶ VI. Constructions versus Inferences

Before proceeding to analyse and explain the ambiguities of the word "place," a few general remarks on method are desirable. The supreme maxim in scientific philosophising is this:

Wherever possible, logical constructions are to be substituted for inferred entities.

Some examples of the substitution of construction for inference in the realm of mathematical philosophy may serve to elucidate the uses of this maxim. Take first the case of irrationals. In old days, irrationals were inferred as the supposed limits of series of rationals which had no rational limit; but the objection to this procedure was that it left the existence of irrationals merely optative, and for this reason the stricter methods of the present day no longer tolerate such a definition. We now define an irrational number as a certain class of ratios, thus constructing it logically by means of ratios, instead of arriving at it by a doubtful inference from them. Take again the case of cardinal numbers. Two equally numerous collections appear to have something in common: this something is supposed to be their cardinal number. But so long as the cardinal number is inferred from the collections, not constructed in terms of them, its existence must remain in doubt, unless in virtue of a metaphysical postulate *ad hoc*. By defining the cardinal number of a given collection as the class of all equally numerous collections, we avoid the necessity of this metaphysical postulate, and thereby remove a needless element of doubt from the philosophy of arithmetic. A similar method, as I have shown elsewhere, can be applied to classes themselves, which need not be supposed to have any metaphysical reality, but can be regarded as symbolically constructed fictions.

The method by which the construction proceeds is closely analogous in these and all similar cases. Given a set of propositions nominally dealing with the supposed inferred entities, we observe the properties which are required of the supposed entities in order to make these propositions true. By dint of a little logical ingenuity, we then construct some logical function of less hypothetical entities which has the requisite properties. This constructed function we substitute for the supposed inferred entities, and thereby obtain a new and less doubtful interpretation of the body of propositions in question. This method, so fruitful in the philosophy of mathematics, will be found equally applicable in the philosophy of physics, where, I do not doubt, it would have been applied long ago but for the fact that all who have studied this subject hitherto have been completely ignorant of mathematical logic. I myself cannot claim originality in the application of this method to physics, since I owe the suggestion and the stimulus for its application entirely to my friend and collaborator Dr. Whitehead, who is engaged in applying it to the more mathematical portions of the region intermediate between sense-data and the points, instants and particles of physics.

A complete application of the method which substitutes constructions for inferences would exhibit matter wholly in terms of sense-data, and even, we may add, of the sense-data of a single person, since the sense-data of others cannot be known without some element of inference. This, however, must remain for the present an ideal, to be approached as nearly as possible, but to be reached, if at all, only after a long preliminary labour of which as yet we can only see the very beginning. The inferences which are unavoidable can, however, he subjected to certain guiding principles. In the first place they should always be made perfectly explicit, and should be formulated in the most general manner possible. In the second place the inferred entities should, whenever this can be done, be similar to those whose existence is given, rather than, like the Kantian *Ding an sich,* something wholly remote from the data which nominally support the inference. The inferred entities which I shall allow myself are of two kinds: (*a*) the sense-data of other people, in favour of which there is the evidence of testimony, resting ultimately upon the analogical argument in favour of minds other than my own; (*b*) the "sensibilia" which would appear from places where there happen to be no minds, and which I suppose to be real although they are no one's data. Of these two classes of inferred entities, the first will probably be allowed to pass unchallenged. It would give me the greatest satisfaction to be able to dispense with it, and thus establish physics upon a solipsistic basis; but those—and I fear they are the majority—in whom the human affections are stronger than the desire for logical economy, will, no doubt, not share my desire to render solipsism scientifically satisfactory. The second class of inferred entities raises much more serious questions. It may be thought monstrous to maintain that a thing can present any appearance at all in a place where no sense-organs and nervous structure exist through which it could appear. I do not myself feel the monstrosity; nevertheless I should regard these supposed appearances only in the light of a hypothetical scaffolding, to be used while the edifice of physics is being raised, though possibly capable of being removed as soon as the edifice is completed. These "sensibilia" which are not data to anyone are therefore to be taken rather as an illustrative hypothesis and as an aid in preliminary statement than as a dogmatic part of the philosophy of physics in its final form.

¶ VII. PRIVATE SPACE AND THE SPACE OF PERSPECTIVES

We have now to explain the ambiguity in the word "place," and how it comes that two places of different sorts are associated with every sense-datum, namely the place *at* which it is and the place *from* which it is perceived. The theory to be advocated is closely analogous to Leibniz's monadology, from which it differs chiefly in being less smooth and tidy.

The first fact to notice is that, so far as can be discovered, no sensibile is ever a datum to two people at once. The things seen by two different people are often closely similar, so similar that the same *words* can be used to denote them, without which communication with others concerning sensible objects would be impossible. But, in spite of this similarity, it would seem that some difference always arises from difference in the point of view. Thus each person, so far as his sense-data are concerned, lives in a private world. This private world contains its own space, or rather spaces, for it would seem that only experience teaches us to correlate the space of sight with the space of touch and with the various other spaces of other senses. This multiplicity of private spaces, however, though interesting to the psychologist, is of no great importance in regard to our present problem, since a merely solipsistic experience enables us to correlate them into the one private space which embraces all our own sense-data. The place *at* which a sense-datum is, is a place in private space. This place therefore is different from any place in the private space of another percipient. For if we assume, as logical economy demands, that all position is relative, a place is only definable by the things in or around it, and therefore the same place cannot occur in two private worlds which have no common constituent. The question, therefore, of combining what we call different appearances of the same thing in the same place does not arise, and the fact that a given object appears to different spectators to have different shapes and colours affords no argument against the physical reality of all these shapes and colours.

In addition to the private spaces belonging to the private worlds of different percipients, there is, however, another space, in which one whole private world counts as a point, or at least as a spatial unit. This might be described as the space of points of view, since each private world may be regarded as the appearance which the universe presents from a certain point of view. I prefer, however, to speak of it as the space of *perspectives,* in order to obviate the suggestion that a private world is only real when someone views it. And for the same reason, when I wish to speak of a private world without assuming a percipient, I shall call it a "perspective."

We have now to explain how the different perspectives are ordered in one space. This is effected by means of the correlated "sensibilia" which are regarded as the appearances, in different perspectives, of one and the same thing. By moving, and by testimony, we discover that two different perspectives, though they cannot both contain the same "sensibilia," may nevertheless contain very similar ones; and the spatial order of a certain group of "sensibilia" in private space of one perspective is found to be identical with, or very similar to, the spatial order of the correlated "sensibilia" in the private space of another perspective. In this way one "sensibile" in one perspective is correlated with one "sensibile" in another. Such correlated "sensibilia" will be called "appearances of one thing." In Leibniz's monadology, since each monad mirrored the whole universe, there was in each perspective a "sensibile" which was an appearance of each thing. In our system of perspectives, we make no such assumption of completeness. A given thing will have appearances in some perspectives, but presumably not in certain others. The "thing" being defined as the class of its appearances, if κ is the class of perspectives in which a certain thing θ appears, then θ is a member of the multiplicative class of κ, κ being a class of mutually exclusive classes of "sensibilia." And similarly a perspective is a member of the multiplicative class of the things which appear in it.

The arrangement of perspectives in a space is effected by means of the differences between the appearances of a given thing in the various perspectives. Suppose, say, that a certain penny appears in a number of different perspectives; in some it looks larger and in some smaller, in some it looks circular, in others it presents the appearance of an ellipse of varying eccentricity. We may collect together all those perspectives in which the appearance of the penny is circular. These we will place on one straight line, ordering them in a series by the variations in the apparent size of the penny. Those perspectives in which the penny appears as a straight line of a certain thickness will similarly be placed upon a plane (though in this case there will be many different perspectives in which the penny is of the same size; when one arrangement is completed these will form a circle concentric with the penny), and ordered as before by the apparent size of the penny. By such means, all those perspectives in which the penny presents a visual appearance can be arranged in a three-dimensional spatial order. Experience shows that the same spatial order of perspectives would have resulted if, instead of the penny, we had chosen any other thing which appeared in all the perspectives in question, or any other method of utilising the differences between the appearances of the same things in different perspectives. It is this empirical fact which has made it possible to construct the one all-embracing space of physics.

The space whose construction has just been explained, and whose elements are whole perspectives, will be called "perspective-space."

¶ VIII. The Placing of "Things" and "Sensibilia" in Perspective Space

The world which we have so far constructed is a world of six dimensions, since it is a three-dimensional series of perspectives, each of which is itself three-dimensional. We have now to explain the correlation between the perspective space and the various private spaces contained within the various perspectives severally. It is by means of this correlation that the one three-dimensional space of physics is constructed; and it is because of the unconscious performance of this correlation that the distinction between perspective space and the percipient's private space has been blurred, with disastrous results for the philosophy of physics. Let us revert to our penny: the perspectives in which the penny appears larger are regarded as being nearer to the penny than those in which it appears smaller, but as far as experience goes the apparent size of the penny will not grow beyond a certain limit, namely, that where (as we say) the penny is so near the eye that if it were any nearer it could not be seen. By touch we may prolong the series until the penny touches the eye, but no further. If we have been travelling along a line of perspectives in the previously defined sense, we may, however, by imagining the penny removed, prolong the line of perspectives by means, say, of another penny; and the same may be done with any other line of perspectives defined by means of the penny. All these lines meet in a certain place, that is, in a certain perspective. This perspective will be defined as "the place where the penny is."

It is now evident in what sense two places in constructed physical space are associated with a given "sensibile." There is first the place which is the perspective of which the "sensibile" is a member. This is the place *from* which the "sensibile" appears. Secondly there is the place where the thing is of which the "sensibile" is a member, in other words an appearance; this is the place *at* which the "sensibile" appears. The "sensibile" which is a member of one perspective is correlated with another perspective, namely, that which is the place where the thing is of which the "sensibile" is an appearance. To the psychologist the "place from which" is the more interesting, and the "sensibile" accordingly appears to him subjective and where the percipient is. To the physicist the "place at which" is the more interesting, and the "sensibile" accordingly appears to him physical and external. The causes, limits and partial justification of each of these two apparently incompatible views are evident from the above duplicity of places associated with a given "sensibile."

We have seen that we can assign to a physical thing a place in the perspective space. In this way different parts of our body acquire positions in perspective space, and therefore there is a meaning (whether true or false need not much concern us) in saying that the perspective to which our sense-data belong is inside our head. Since our mind is correlated with the perspective to which our sense-data belong, we may regard this perspective as being the position of our mind in perspective space. If, therefore, this perspective is, in the above defined sense, inside our head, there is a good meaning for the statement that the mind is in the head. We can now say of the various appearances of a given thing that some of them are nearer to the thing than others; those are nearer which belong to perspectives that are nearer to "the place where the thing is." We can thus find a meaning, true or false, for the statement that more is to be learnt about a thing by examining it close to than by viewing it from a distance. We can also find a meaning for the phase "the things which intervene between the subject and a thing of which an appearance is a datum to him." One reason often alleged for the subjectivity of sense-data is that the appearance of a thing may change when we find it hard to suppose that the thing itself has changed—for example, when the change is due to our shutting our eyes, or to our screwing them up so as to make the thing look double. If the thing is defined as the class of its appearances (which is the definition adopted above), there is of course necessarily *some* change in the thing whenever any one of its appearances changes. Nevertheless there is a very important distinction between two different ways in which the appearances may change.

If after looking at a thing I shut my eyes, the appearance of my eyes changes in every perspective in which there is such an appearance, whereas most of the appearances of the thing will remain unchanged. We may say, as a matter of definition, that a thing changes when, however near to the thing an appearance of it may be, there are changes in appearances as near as, or still nearer to, the thing. On the other hand we shall say that the change is in some other thing if all appearances of the thing which are at not more than a certain distance from the thing remain unchanged, while only comparatively distant appearances of the thing are altered. From this consideration we are naturally led to the consideration of *matter*, which must be our next topic.

¶ IX. THE DEFINITION OF MATTER

We defined the "physical thing" as the class of its appearances, but this can hardly be taken as a definition of matter. We want to be able to express the fact that the appearance of a thing in a given perspective is causally affected by the matter between the thing and the perspective. We have found a meaning for "between a thing and a perspective." But we want matter to be something other than the whole class of appearances of a thing, in order to state the influence of matter on appearances.

We commonly assume that the information we get about a thing is more accurate when the thing is nearer. Far off, we see it is a man, then we see it is Jones; then we see he is smiling. Complete accuracy would only be attainable as a limit: if the appearances of Jones as we approach him tend towards a limit, that limit may be taken to be what Jones really is. It is obvious that from the point of view of physics the appearances of a thing close to "count" more than the appearances far off. We may therefore set up the following tentative definition:

The *matter* of a given thing is the limit of its appearances as their distance from the thing diminishes.

It seems probable that there is something in this definition, but it is not quite satisfactory, because empirically there is no such limit to be obtained from sense-data. The definition will have to be eked out by constructions and definitions. But probably it suggests the right direction in which to look.

We are now in a position to understand in outline the reverse journey from matter to sense-data which is performed by physics. The appearance of a thing in a given perspective is a function of the matter composing the thing and of the intervening matter. The appearance of a thing is altered by intervening smoke or mist, by blue spectacles or by alterations in the sense-organs or nerves of the percipient (which also must be reckoned as part of the intervening medium). The nearer we approach to the thing, the less its appearance is affected by the intervening matter. As we travel further and further from the thing, its appearances diverge more and more from their initial character; and the causal laws of their divergence are to be stated in terms of the matter which lies between them and the thing. Since the appearances at very small distances are less affected by causes other than the thing itself, we come to think that the limit towards which these appearances tend as the distance diminishes is what the thing "really is," as opposed to what it merely seems to be. This, together with its necessity for the statement of causal laws, seems to be the source of the entirely erroneous feeling that matter is more "real" than sense-data.

Consider for example the infinite divisibility of matter. In looking at a given thing and approaching it, one sense-datum will become several, and each of these will again divide. Thus *one* appearance may represent *many* things, and to this process there seems no end. Hence in the limit, when we approach indefinitely near to the thing, there will be an indefinite number of units of matter coresponding to what, at a finite distance, is only one appearance. This is how infinite divisibility arises.

The whole causal efficacy of a thing resides in its matter. This is in some sense an empirical fact, but it would be hard to state it precisely, because "causal efficacy" is difficult to define.

What can be known empirically about the matter of a thing is only approximate, because we cannot get to know the appearances of the thing from very small distances, and cannot accurately infer the limit of these appearances. But it *is* inferred *approximately* by means of the appearances we can observe. It then turns out that these appearances can be exhibited by physics as a function of the matter in our immediate neighbourhood; e.g. the visual appearance of a distant object is a function of the light-waves that reach the eyes. This leads to confusions of thought, but offers no real difficulty.

One appearance, of a visible object for example, is not sufficient to determine its other simultaneous appearances, although it goes a certain distance towards determining them. The determination of the hidden structure of a thing, so far as it is possible at all, can only be effected by means of elaborate dynamical inferences.

¶ X. TIME[3]

It seems that the one all-embracing time is a construction, like the one all-embracing space. Physics itself has become conscious of this fact through the discussions connected with relativity.

Between two perspectives which both belong to one person's experience, there will be a direct time-relation of before and after. This suggests a way of dividing history in the same sort of way as it is divided by different experiences, but without introducing experience or any thing mental: we may define a "biography" as everything that is (directly) earlier or later than, or simultaneous with, a given "sensibile." This will give a series of perspectives, which *might* all form parts of one person's experience, though it is not necessary that all or any of them should actually do so. By this means, the history of the world is divided into a number of mutually exclusive biographies.

We have now to correlate the times in the different biographies. The natural thing would be to say that the appearances of a given (momentary) thing in two different perspectives belonging to different biographies are to be taken as simultaneous; but this is not convenient. Suppose *A* shouts to *B,* and *B* replies as soon as he hears *A's* shout. Then between *A's* hearing of his own shout and his hearing of *B's* there is an interval; thus if we made *A's* and *B's* hearing of the same shout exactly simultaneous with each other, we should have events exactly simultaneous with given event but not with each other. To obviate this, we assume a "velocity of sound." That is, we assume that the time when *B* hears *A's* shout is half-way between the time when *A* hears his own shout and the time when he hears *B's*. In this way the correlation is effected.

What has been said about sound applies of course equally to light. The general principle is that the appearances, in different perspectives, which are to be grouped together as constituting what a certain thing is at a certain moment, are not to be all regarded as being at that moment. On the contrary they spread outward from the thing with various velocities according to the nature of the appearances. Since no *direct* means exist of correlating the time in one biography with the time in another, this temporal grouping of the appearances belonging to a given thing at a given moment is in part conventional. Its motive is partly to secure the verification of such maxims as that events which

3. On this subject, compare *A Theory of Time and Space,* by Mr. A. A. Robb (Camb. Univ. Press), which first suggested to me the views advocated here, though I have, for present purposes, omitted what is most interesting and novel in his theory. Mr. Robb has given a sketch of his theory in a pamphlet with the same title (Heffer and Sons, Cambridge, 1913).

are exactly simultaneous with the same event are exactly simultaneous with one another, partly to secure convenience in the formulation of causal laws.

¶ XI. The Persistence of Things and Matter

Apart from any of the fluctuating hypotheses of physics, three main problems arise in connecting the world of physics with the world of sense, namely:

1. the construction of a single space;
2. the construction of a single time;
3. the construction of permanent things or matter.

We have already considered the first and second of these problems; it remains to consider the third.

We have seen how correlated appearances in different perspectives are combined to form one "thing" at one moment in the all-embracing time of physics. We have now to consider how appearances at different times are combined as belonging to one "thing," and how we arrive at the persistent "matter" of physics. The assumption of permanent substance, which technically underlies the procedure of physics, cannot of course be regarded as metaphysically legitimate: just as the one thing simultaneously seen by many people is a construction, so the one thing seen at different times by the same or different people must be a construction, being in fact nothing but a certain grouping of certain "sensibilia."

We have seen that the momentary state of a "thing" is an assemblage of "sensibilia," in different perspectives, not all simultaneous in the one constructed time, but spreading out from "the place where the thing is" with velocities depending upon the nature of the "sensibilia." The time *at* which the "thing" is in this state is the lower limit of the times at which these appearances occur. We have now to consider what leads us to speak of another set of appearances as belonging to the same "thing" at a different time.

For this purpose, we may, at least to begin with, confine ourselves within a single biography. If we can always say when two "sensibilia" in a given biography are appearances of one thing, then, since we have seen how to connect "sensibilia" in different biographies as appearances of the same momentary state of a thing, we shall have all that is necessary for the complete construction of the history of a thing.

It is to be observed, to begin with, that the identity of a thing for common sense is not always correlated with the identity of matter for physics. A human body is one persisting thing for common sense, but for physics its matter is constantly changing. We may say, broadly, that the common-sense conception is based upon continuity in appearances at the ordinary distances of sense-data, while the physical conception is based upon the continuity of appearances at very small distances from the thing. It is probable that the common-sense conception is not capable of complete precision. Let us therefore concentrate our attention upon the conception of the persistence of matter in physics.

The first characteristic of two appearances of the same piece of matter at different times is *continuity*. The two appearances must be connected by a series of intermediaries, which, if time and space form compact series, must themselves form a compact series. The colour of the leaves is different in autumn from what it is in summer; but we believe that the change occurs gradually, and that, if the colours are different at two given times, there are intermediate times at which the colours are intermediate between those at the given times.

But there are two considerations that are important as regards continuity.

First, it is largely hypothetical. We do not observe any one thing continuously, and it is merely a hypothesis to assume that, while we are not observing it, it passes through conditions intermediate between those in which it is perceived. During uninterrupted observation, it is true, continuity is nearly verified, but even here, when motions are very rapid, as in the case of explosions, the continuity is not actually capable of direct verification. Thus we can only say that the sense-data are found to *permit* a hypothetical complement of "sensibilia" such as will preserve continuity, and that therefore there *may* be such a complement. Since, however, we have already made such use of hypothetical "sensibilia," we will let this point pass, and admit such "sensibilia," as are required to preserve continuity.

Secondly, continuity is not a sufficient criterion of material identity. It is true that in many cases, such as rocks, mountains, tables, chairs, etc., where the appearances change slowly, continuity is sufficient, but in other cases, such as the parts of an approximately homogeneous fluid, it fails us utterly. We can travel by sensibly continuous gradations from any one drop of the sea at any one time to any other drop at any other time. We infer the motions of sea-water from the effects of the current, but they cannot be inferred from direct sensible observation together with the assumption of continuity.

The characteristic required in addition to continuity is conformity with the laws of dynamics. Starting from what common sense regards as persistent things, and making only such modifications as from time to time seem reasonable, we arrive at assemblages of "sensibilia" which are found to obey certain simple laws, namely those of dynamics. By regarding "sensibilia" at different times as belonging to the same piece of matter, we are able to define *motion*, which presupposes the assumption or construction of something persisting throughout the time of the motion. The motions which are regarded as occurring, during a period in which all the "sensibilia" and the times of their appearance are given, will be different according to the manner in which we combine "sensibilia" at different times as belonging to the same piece of matter. Thus even when the whole history of the world is given in every particular, the question what motions take place is still to a certain extent arbitrary even after the assumption of continuity. Experience shows that it is possible to determine motions in such a way as to satisfy the laws of dynamics, and that this determination, roughly and on the whole, is fairly in agreement with the common-sense opinions about persistent things. This determination, therefore, is adopted, and leads to a criterion by which we can determine, sometimes practically, sometimes only theoretically, whether two appearances at different times are to be regarded as belonging to the same piece of matter. The persistence of all matter throughout all time can, I imagine, be secured by definition.

To recommend this conclusion, we must consider what it is that is proved by the empirical success of physics. What is proved is that its hypotheses, though unverifiable where they go beyond sense-data, are at no point in contradiction with sense-data, but, on the contrary, are ideally such as to render all sense-data calculable when a sufficient collection of "sensibilia" is given. Now physics has found it empirically possible to collect sense-data into series, each series being regarded as belonging to one "thing" and behaving, with regard to the laws of physics, in a way in which series not belonging to one thing would in general not behave. If it is to be unambiguous whether two appearances belong to the same thing or not, there must be only one way of grouping appearances so that the resulting things obey the laws of physics. It would be very difficult to prove that this is the case, but for our present purposes we may let this point pass, and assume that there is only one way. Thus we may lay down the following definition: *Physical things are those series of appearances whose matter obeys the laws of physics.* That such series exist is an empirical fact, which constitutes the verifiability of physics.

¶ XII. Illusions, Hallucinations, and Dreams

It remains to ask how, in our system, we are to find a place for sense-data which apparently fail to have the usual connection with the world of physics. Such sense-data are of various kinds, requiring somewhat different treatment. But all are of the sort that would be called "unreal," and therefore, before embarking upon the discussion, certain logical remarks must be made upon the conceptions of reality and unreality.

Mr. A. Wolf[4] says:

The conception of mind as a system of transparent activities is, I think, also untenable because of its failure to account for the very possibility of dreams and hallucinations. It seems impossible to realise how a bare, transparent activity can be directed to what is not there, to apprehend what is not given.

This statement is one which, probably, most people would endorse. But it is open to two objections. First, it is difficult to see how an activity, however un- "transparent," can be directed towards a nothing: a term of a relation cannot be a mere non-entity. Secondly, no reason is given, and I am convinced that none can be given, for the assertion that dream-objects are not "there" and not "given." Let us take the second point first.

(1) The belief that dream-objects are not given comes, I think, from failure to distinguish, as regards waking life, between the sense-datum and the corresponding "thing." In dreams, there is no such corresponding "thing" as the dreamer supposes; if, therefore, the "thing" were given in waking life, as *e.g.* Meinong maintains,[5] then there would be a difference in respect of givenness between dreams and waking life. But if, as we have maintained, what is given is never the thing, but merely one of the "sensibilia" which compose the thing, then what we apprehend in a dream is just as much given as what we apprehend in waking life.

Exactly the same argument applies as to the dream-objects being "there." They have their position in the private space of the perspective of the dreamer; where they fail is in their correlation with other private spaces and therefore with perspective space. But in the only sense in which "there" can be a datum, they are "there" just as truly as any of the sense-data of waking life.

(2) The conception of "illusion" or "unreality," and the correlative

---

4. "Natural Realism and Present Tendencies in Philosophy," *Proc. Arist. Soc.,* 1908-9, p. 165.

5. *Die Erfahrungsgrundlagen unseres Wissens,* p. 28.

conception of "reality," are generally used in a way which embodies profound logical confusions. Words that go in pairs, such as "real" and "unreal," "existent" and "non-existent," "valid" and "invalid," etc., are all derived from the one fundamental pair, "true" and "false." Now "true" and "false" are applicable only—except in derivative significations—to *propositions*. Thus wherever the above pairs can be significantly applied, we must be dealing either with propositions or with such incomplete phrases as only acquire meaning when put into a context which, with them, forms a proposition. Thus such pairs of words can be applied to *descriptions*,[6] but not to proper names: in other words, they have no application whatever to data, but only to entities or non-entities described in terms of data.

Let us illustrate by the terms "existence" and "non-existence." Given any datum x, it is meaningless either to assert or to deny that x "exists." We might be tempted to say: "Of course x exists, for otherwise it could not be a datum." But such a statement is really meaningless, although it is significant and true to say "My present sense-datum exists," and it may also be true that "x is my present sense-datum." The inference from these two propositions to "x exists" is one which seems irresistible to people unaccustomed to logic; yet the apparent proposition inferred is not merely false, but strictly meaningless. To say "My present sense-datum exists" is to say (roughly): "There is an object of which 'my present sense-datum' is a description." But we cannot say: "There is an object of which 'x' is a description," because 'x' is (in the case we are supposing) a name, not a description. Dr. Whitehead and I have explained this point fully elsewhere (*loc. cit.*) with the help of symbols, without which it is hard to understand; I shall not therefore here repeat the demonstration of the above propositions, but shall proceed with their application to our present problem.

The fact that "existence" is only applicable to descriptions is concealed by the use of what are grammatically proper names in a way which really transforms them into descriptions. It is, for example, a legitimate question whether Homer existed; but here "Homer" means "the author of the Homeric poems," and is a description. Similarly we may ask whether God exists; but then "God" means "the Supreme Being" or "the *ens realissimum*" or whatever other description we may prefer. If "God" were a proper name, God would have to be a datum; and then no question could arise as to His existence. The distinction between existence and other predicates, which Kant obscurely felt, is

6. Cf. *Principia Mathematica*, Vol. I, * 14, and Introduction, Chap. III. For the definition of *existence*, cf. * 14. 02.

brought to light by the theory of descriptions, and is seen to remove "existence" altogether from the fundamental notions of metaphysics.

What has been said about "existence" applies equally to "reality," which may, in fact, be taken as synonymous with "existence." Concerning the immediate objects in illusions, hallucinations, and dreams, it is meaningless to ask whether they "exist" or are "real." There they are, and that ends the matter. But we may legitimately inquire as to the existence or reality of "things" or other "sensibilia" inferred from such objects. It is the unreality of these "things" and other "sensibilia," together with a failure to notice that they are not data, which has led to the view that the objects of dreams are unreal.

We may now apply these considerations in detail to the stock arguments against realism, though what is to be said will be mainly a repetition of what others have said before.

(1) We have first the variety of normal appearances, supposed to be incompatible. This is the case of the different shapes and colours which a given thing presents to different spectators. Locke's water which seems both hot and cold belongs to this class of cases. Our system of different perspectives fully accounts for these cases, and shows that they afford no argument against realism.

(2) We have cases where the correlation between different senses is unusual. The bent stick in water belongs here. People say it looks bent but is straight: this only means that it is straight to the touch, though bent to sight. There is no "illusion," but only a false inference, if we think that the stick would feel bent to the touch. The stick would look just as bent in a photograph, and, as Mr. Gladstone used to say, "the photograph cannot lie."[7] The case of seeing double also belongs here, though in this case the cause of the unusual correlation is physiological, and would therefore not operate in a photograph. It is a mistake to ask whether the "thing" is duplicated when we see it double. The "thing" is a whole system of "sensibilia," and it is only those visual "sensibilia" which are data to the percipient that are duplicated. The phenomenon has a purely physiological explanation; indeed, in view of our having two eyes, it is in less need of explanation than the single visual sense-datum which we normally obtain from the things on which we focus.

(3) We come now to cases like dreams, which may, at the moment of dreaming, contain nothing to arouse suspicion, but are condemned on the ground of their supposed incompatibility with earlier and later data. Of course it often happens that dream-objects fail to behave

7. Cf. Edwin B. Holt, *The Place of Illusory Experience in a Realistic World,* "The New Realism," p. 305, both on this point and as regards *seeing double.*

in the accustomed manner: heavy objects fly, solid objects melt, babies turn into pigs or undergo even greater changes. But none of these unusual occurrences *need* happen in a dream, and it is not on account of such occurrences that dream-objects are called "unreal." It is their lack of continuity with the dreamer's past and future that makes him, when he wakes, condemn them; and it is their lack of correlation with other private worlds that makes others condemn them. Omitting the latter ground, our reason for condemning them is that the "things" which we infer from them cannot be combined according to the laws of physics with the "things" inferred from waking sense-data. This might be used to condemn the "things" inferred from the data of dreams. Dream-data are no doubt appearances of "things," but not of such "things" as the dreamer supposes. I have no wish to combat psychological theories of dreams, such as those of the psycho-analysts. But there certainly are cases where (whatever psychological causes may contribute) the presence of physical causes also is very evident. For instance, a door banging may produce a dream of a naval engagement, with images of battleships and sea and smoke. The whole dream will be an appearance of the door banging, but owing to the peculiar condition of the body (especially the brain) during sleep, this appearance is not that expected to be produced by a door banging, and thus the dreamer is led to entertain false beliefs. But his sense-data are still physical, and are such as a completed physics would include and calculate.

(4) The last class of illusions are those which cannot be discovered within one person's experience, except through the discovery of discrepancies with the experiences of others. Dreams might conceivably belong to this class, if they were jointed sufficiently neatly into waking life; but the chief instances are recurrent sensory hallucinations of the kind that lead to insanity. What makes the paaient, in such cases, become what others call insane is the fact that, within his own experience, there is nothing to show that the hallucinatory sense-data do not have the usual kind of connection wtih "sensibilia" in other perspectives. Of course he may learn this through testimony, but he probably finds it simpler to suppose that the testimony is untrue and that he is being wilfully deceived. There is, so far as I can see, no theoretical criterion by which the patient can decide, in such a case, between the two equally satisfactory hypotheses of his madness and of his friends' mendacity.

From the above instances it would appear that abnormal sense-data, of the kind which we regard as deceptive, have intrinsically just the same status as any others, but differ as regards their correlations or causal connections with other "sensibilia" and with "things." Since the usual correlations and connections become part of our unreflective expectations, and even seem, except to the psychologist, to form part of our data, it comes to be thought, mistakenly, that in such cases the data are unreal, whereas they are merely the causes of false inferences. The fact that correlations and connections of unusual kinds occur adds to the difficulty of inferring things from sense and of expressing physics in terms of sense-data. But the unusualness would seem to be always physically or physiologically explicable, and therefore raises only a complication, not a philosophical objection.

I conclude, therefore, that no valid objection exists to the view which regards sense-data as part of the actual substance of the physical world, and that, on the other hand, this view is the only one which accounts for the empirical verifiability of physics. In the present paper, I have given only a rough preliminary sketch. In particular, the part played by *time* in the construction of the physical world is, I think, more fundamental than would appear from the above account. I should hope that, with further elaboration, the part played by unperceived "sensibilia" could be indefinitely diminished, probably by invoking the history of a "thing" to eke out the inferences derivable from its momentary appearance.

IX

GILBERT RYLE

GILBERT RYLE (b. 1900) was educated at Brighton College and The Queen's College, Oxford, where he was a Classical Scholar. In 1924 he became a Lecturer in Philosophy and later a Student and Tutor in Philosophy at Christ Church. In 1945 he was elected Waynflete Professor of Metaphysical Philosophy at the University of Oxford. In 1947 he became Editor of *Mind*. His two important books are *The Concept of Mind* (1949) and the Tarner Lectures at Cambridge, *Dilemmas* (1954).

Ryle's "Systematically Misleading Expressions" (1931-32) is one among a number of important essays published during the 1930s that show the influence of Russell's theory of descriptions and the conception of analysis embodied in that theory. Ryle classifies and analyzes a number of expressions that mislead philosophers into thinking that these expressions record one kind of fact when actually they record another; and whose logical form, as opposed to their grammatical form, can be elicited only by correct logical paraphrases of these original expressions.

From his examination of systematically misleading expressions, Ryle suggests that the primary—perhaps the whole—task of philosophy should be analysis conceived as correct logical paraphrase. The major result of philosophical analysis, however, is not to clarify the structure of reality or even of language, but to reveal as the sources of traditional philosophical theories and disputes the persistent confusions of grammatical with logical form. Philosophy, thus, shifts from logical clarifications of expressions to exposures of philosophical absurdities that rest on inadequate conceptions of language.

Systematically Misleading Expressions[1]

Philosophical arguments have always largely, if not entirely, consisted in attempts to thrash out 'what it means to say so and so.' It is observed that men in their ordinary discourse, the discourse, that is, that they employ when they are not philosophizing, use certain expressions, and philosophers fasten on to certain more or less radical types or classes of such expressions and raise their question about all expressions of a certain type and ask what they really mean.

Sometimes philosophers say that they are analysing or clarifying the 'concepts' which are embodied in the 'judgements' of the plain man or of the scientist, historian, artist, or who-not. But this seems to be only a gaseous way of saying that they are trying to discover what is meant by the general terms contained in the sentences which they pronounce or write. For, as we shall see, 'x is a concept' and 'y is a judgement' are themselves systematically misleading expressions.

But the whole procedure is very odd. For, if the expressions under consideration are intelligently used, their employers must already know what they mean and do not need the aid or admonition of philosophers before they can understand what they are saying. And if their hearers understand what they are being told, they too are in no such perplexity that they need to have this meaning philosophically 'analysed' or 'clarified' for them. And, at least, the philosopher himself must know what the expressions mean, since otherwise he could not know what it was that he was analysing.

Certainly it is often the case that expressions are not being intelligently used and to that extent their authors are just gabbling parrot-wise. But then it is obviously fruitless to ask what the expressions really mean. For there is no reason to suppose that they mean anything. It would not be mere gabbling if there was any such reason. And if the philosopher cares to ask what these expressions *would* mean *if* a rational man were using them, the only answer would be that they would mean what they would then mean. Understanding them would be enough, and that could be done by any reasonable listener. Philosophizing could not help him, and, in fact, the philosopher

1. From *Proceedings of the Aristotelian Society*, 1931-32. Reprinted by permission of the Editor.

himself would not be able to begin unless he simply understood them in the ordinary way.

It seems, then, that if an expression can be understood, then it is already known in that understanding what the expression means. So there is no darkness present and no illumination required or possible.

And if it is suggested that the non-philosophical author of an expression (be he plain man, scientist, preacher, or artist) does know but only knows dimly or foggily or confusedly what his expression means, but that the philosopher at the end of his exploration knows clearly, distinctly, and definitely what it means, a two-fold answer seems inevitable. First, that if a speaker only knows confusedly what his expression means, then he is in that respect and to that extent just gabbling. And it is not the rôle—nor the achievement—of the philosopher to provide a medicine against that form of flux. And next, the philosopher is not *ex officio* concerned with ravings and ramblings: he studies expressions for what they mean when intelligently and intelligibly employed, and not as noises emitted by this idiot or that parrot.

Certainly expressions do occur for which better substitutes could be found and should be or should have been employed. (1) An expression may be a breach of, e.g., English or Latin grammar. (2) A word may be a foreign word, or a rare word or a technical or trade term for which there exists a familiar synonym. (3) A phrase or sentence may be clumsy or unfamiliar in its structure. (4) A word or phrase may be equivocal and so be an instrument of possible puns. (5) A word or phrase may be ill-chosen as being general where it should be specific, or allusive where the allusion is not known or not obvious. (6) Or a word may be a malapropism or a misnomer. But the search for paraphrases which shall be more swiftly intelligible to a given audience or more idiomatic or stylish or more grammatically or etymologically correct is merely applied lexicography or philology—it is not philosophy.

We ought then to face the question: Is there such a thing as analysing or clarifying the meaning of the expressions which people use, except in the sense of substituting philologically better expressions for philologically worse ones? (We might have put the problem in the more misleading terminology of 'concepts' and asked: How can philosophizing so operate by analysis and clarification, upon the concepts used by the plain man, the scientist, or the artist, that after this operation the concepts are illumined where before they were dark? The same difficulties arise. For there can be no such thing as a confused concept, since either a man is conceiving, i.e. knowing the nature of his subject-matter, or he is failing to do so. If he is succeeding, no clarification is required or possible; and if he is failing, he must find out more or think more about the subject-matter, the apprehension of the nature of which we call his 'concept.' But this will not be philosophizing about the concept, but exploring further the nature of the thing, and so will be economics, perhaps, or astronomy or history. But as I think that it can be shown that it is not true in any natural sense that 'there are concepts,' I shall adhere to the other method of stating the problem.)

The object of this paper is not to show what philosophy in general is investigating, but to show that there remains an important sense in which philosophers can and must discover and state what is really meant by expressions of this or that radical type, and none the less that these discoveries do not in the least imply that the naïve users of such expressions are in any doubt or confusion about what their expressions mean or in any way need the results of the philosophical analysis for them to continue to use intelligently their ordinary modes of expression or to use them so that they are intelligible to others.

The gist of what I want to establish is this. There are many expressions which occur in non-philosophical discourse which, though they are perfectly clearly understood by those who use them and those who hear or read them, are nevertheless couched in grammatical or syntactical forms which are in a demonstrable way *improper* to the states of affairs which they record (or the alleged states of affairs which they profess to record). Such expressions can be reformulated and for philosophy but *not* for non-philosophical discourse must be reformulated into expressions of which the syntactical form is proper to the facts recorded (or the alleged facts alleged to be recorded).

I use 'expression' to cover single words, phrases, and sentences. By 'statement' I mean a sentence in the indicative. When a statement is true, I say it 'records' a fact or state of affairs. False statements do not record. To know that a statement is true is to know that something is the case and that the statement records it. When I barely understand a statement I do not know that it records a fact, nor need I know the fact that it records, if it records one. But I know what state of affairs *would* obtain, if the statement recorded a state of affairs.

Every significant statement is a quasi-record, for it has both the requisite structure and constituents to be a record. But knowing these, we don't yet know that it is a record of a fact. False statements are pseudo-records and are no more records than pseudo-antiquities are antiquities. So the question, What do false statements state? is meaningless if 'state' means 'record.' If it means, What *would* they record if they recorded something being the case? the question contains its own answer.

When an expression is of such a syntactical form that it is improper to the fact recorded, it is systematically misleading in that it naturally suggests to some people—though not to 'ordinary' people—that the state of affairs recorded is quite a different sort of state of affairs from that which it in fact is.

I shall try to show what I am driving at by examples. I shall begin by considering a whole class of expressions of one type which occur and occur perfectly satisfactorily in ordinary discourse, but which are, I argue, *systematically misleading,* that is to say, that they are couched in a syntactical form improper to the facts recorded and proper to facts of quite another logical form than the facts recorded. (For simplicity's sake, I shall speak as if all the statements adduced as examples are true. For false statements are not formally different from true ones. Otherwise grammarians could become omniscient. And when I call a statement 'systematically misleading' I shall not mean that it is false, and certainly not that it is senseless. By 'systematically' I mean that all expressions of that grammatical form would be misleading in the same way and for the same reason.)

¶ I. Quasi-ontological Statements

Since Kant, we have, most of us, paid lip service to the doctrine that 'existence is not a quality' and so we have rejected the pseudo-implication of the ontological argument; 'God is perfect, being perfect entails being existent, . . . God exists.' For if existence is not a quality, it is not the sort of thing that can be entailed by a quality.

But until fairly recently it was not noticed that if in 'God exists' 'exists' is not a predicate (save in grammar), then in the same statement 'God' cannot be (save in grammar) the subject of predication. The realization of this came from examining negative existential propositions like 'Satan does not exist' or 'unicorns are non-existent.' If there is no Satan, then the statement 'Satan does not exist' cannot be about Satan in the way in which 'I am sleepy' is about me. Despite appearances the word 'Satan' cannot be signifying a subject of attributes.

Philosophers have toyed with theories which would enable them to continue to say that 'Satan does not exist' is none the less still somehow about Satan, and that 'exists' still signifies some sort of attribute or character, although not a quality.

So some argued that the statement was about something described as 'the idea of Satan,' others that it was about a subsistent but non-actual entity called 'Satan.' Both theories in effect try to show that something may *be* (whether as being 'merely mental' or as being in 'the realm of subsistents'), but not be in existence. But as we can say 'round squares do not exist,' and 'real nonentities do not exist,' this sort of interpretation of negative existentials is bound to fill either the realm of subsistents or the realm of ideas with walking self-contradictions. So the theories had to be dropped and a new analysis of existential propositions had to begin.

Suppose I assert of (apparently) the general subject 'carnivorous cows' that they 'do not exist,' and my assertion is true, I cannot really be talking about carnivorous cows, for there are none. So it follows that the expression 'carnivorous cows' is not really being used, though the grammatical appearances are to the contrary, to denote the thing or things of which the predicate is being asserted. And in the same way as the verb 'exists' is not signifying the character asserted, although grammatically it looks as if it was, the real predicate must be looked for elsewhere.

So the clue of the grammar has to be rejected and the analysis has been suggested that 'carnivorous cows do not exist' means what is meant by 'no cows are carnivorous' or 'no carnivorous beasts are cows.' But a further improvement seems to be required.

'Unicorns do not exist' seems to mean what is meant by 'nothing is *both* a quadruped *and* herbivorous *and* the wearer of one horn' (or whatever the marks of being an unicorn are). And this does not seem to imply that there are some quadrupeds or herbivorous animals.

So 'carnivorous cows do not exist' ought to be rendered 'nothing is both a cow and carnivorous,' which does not as it stands imply that anything is either.

Take now an apparently singular subject as in 'God exists' or 'Satan does not exist.' If the former analysis was right, then here too 'God' and 'Satan' are in fact, despite grammatical appearance, predicative expressions. That is to say, they are that element in the assertion that something has a specified character, which signifies the character by which the subject is being asserted to be characterized. 'God exists' must mean what is meant by 'Something, and one thing only, is omniscient, omnipotent, and infinitely good' (or whatever else are the characters summed in the compound character of being a god and the only god). And 'Satan does not exist' must mean what is meant by 'nothing is both devilish and alone in being devilish,' or perhaps 'nothing is both devilish and called "Satan,"' or even ' "Satan" is not the proper name of anything.' To put it roughly, 'x exists' and 'x does not exist' do not assert or deny that a given subject of attributes x has the attribute of existing, but assert or deny the attribute of being x-ish or being an x of something not named in the statement.

Now I can show my hand. I say that expressions such as 'carnivorous cows do not exist' are systematically misleading and that the expressions by which we paraphrased them are not or are not in the same way or to the same extent systematically misleading. But they are not false, nor are they senseless. They are true, and they really do mean what their less systematically misleading papaphrases mean. Nor (save in a special class of cases) is the non-philosophical author of such expressions ignorant or doubtful of the nature of the state of affairs which his expression records. He is not a whit misled. There is a trap, however, in the form of his expression, but a trap which only threatens the man who has begun to generalize about sorts or types of states of affairs and assumes that every statement gives in its syntax a clue to the logical form of the fact that it records. I refer here not merely nor even primarily to the philosopher, but to any man who embarks on abstraction.

But before developing this theme I want to generalize the results of our examination of what we must now describe as 'so-called existential statements.' It is the more necessary in that, while most philosophers are now forewarned by Kant against the systematic misleadingness of 'God exists,' few of them have observed that the same taint infects a whole host of other expressions.

If 'God exists' means what we have said it means, then patently 'God is an existent,' 'God is an entity,' 'God has being,' or 'existence' require the same analysis. So '. . . is an existent,' '. . . is an entity' are only bogus predicates, and that of which (in grammar) they are asserted is only a bogus subject.

And the same will be true of all the items in the following pair of lists.

Mr. Baldwin—	Mr. Pickwick—
is a being.	is a nonentity.
is real, or a reality.	is unreal or an unreality, or an appearance.
is a genuine entity.	is a bogus or sham entity.
is a substance.	is not a substance.
is an actual object or entity.	is an unreal object or entity.
is objective.	is not objective or is subjective.
is a concrete reality.	is a fiction or figment.
is an object.	is an imaginary object.
is.	is not.
	is a mere idea.
	is an abstraction.
	is a logical construction.

None of these statements is really about Mr. Pickwick. For if the
are true, there is no such person for them to be about. Nor is an
of them about Mr. Baldwin. For if they were false, there would be n
one for them to be about. Nor in any of them is the grammatica
predicate that element in the statement which signifies the characte
that is being asserted to be characterizing or not to be characterizin
something.

I formulate the conclusion in this rather clumsy way. There is
class of statements of which the grammatical predicate *appears* t
signify not the having of a specified character but the having (or n
having) of a specified *status*. But in all such statements the appearanc
is a purely grammatical one, and what the statements really recor
can be stated in statements embodying no such quasi-ontological pred
icates.

And, again, in all such quasi-ontological statements the gram
matical subject-word or phrase *appears* to denote or refer to somethin
as that of which the quasi-ontological predicate is being predicated
but in fact the apparent subject term is a concealed predicative ex
pression, and what is really recorded in such statements can be re-state
in statements no part of which even appears to refer to any suc
subject.

In a word, all quasi-ontological statements are systematically mis
leading. (If I am right in this, then the conclusion follows, whic
I accept, that those metaphysical philosophers are the greatest sinner
who, as if they were saying something of importance, make 'Reality
or 'Being' the subject of their propositions, or 'real' the predicate. Fo
at best what they say is systematically misleading, which is the on
thing which a philosopher's propositions have no right to be; and a
worst it is meaningless.)

I must give warning again, that the naïve employer of such quasi
ontological expressions is not necessarily and not even probably misled
He has said what he wanted to say, and anyone who knew Englisl
would understand what he was saying. Moreover, I would add, i
the cases that I have listed, the statements are not merely significan
but true. Each of them records a real state of affairs. Nor *need* the
mislead the philosopher. We, for instance, I hope are not misled. Bu
the point is that anyone, the philosopher included, who abstracts an
generalizes and so tries to consider what different facts of the sam
type (i.e. facts of the same type about different things) have in com
mon, is compelled to use the common grammatical form of the state
ments of those facts as handles with which to grasp the common logica
form of the facts themselves. For (what we shall see later) as the wa

n which a fact *ought* to be recorded in expressions *would* be a clue to the form of that fact, we jump to the assumption that the way in which a fact *is* recorded *is* such a clue. And very often the clue is misleading and suggests that the fact is of a different form from what really is its form. 'Satan is not a reality' from its grammatical form looks as if it recorded the same sort of fact as 'Capone is not a philosopher,' and so was just as much denying a character of a somebody called 'Satan' as the latter does deny a character of a somebody called 'Capone.' But it turns out that the suggestion is a fraud; for the fact recorded would have been properly or less improperly recorded in the statement ' "Satan" is not a proper name' or 'No one is called "Satan" ' or 'No one is both called "Satan" and is infinitely malevolent, etc.', or perhaps 'Some people believe that someone is both called "Satan" and infinitely malevolent, but their belief is false.' And none of these statements even pretend to be 'about Satan.' Instead, they are and are patently about the noise 'Satan' or else about people who misuse it.

In the same way, while it is significant, true, and directly intelligible to say 'Mr. Pickwick is a fiction,' it is a systematically misleading expression (i.e. an expression misleading in virtue of a formal property which it does or might share with other expressions); for it does not really record, as it appears to record, a fact of the same sort as is recorded in 'Mr. Baldwin is a statesman.' The world does not contain fictions in the way in which it contains statesmen. There is no subject of attributes of which we can say *'there* is a fiction.' What we can do is to say of Dickens *'there* is a story-teller,' or of Pickwick Papers *'there* is a pack of lies'; or of a sentence in that novel, which contains the pseudo-name 'Mr. Pickwick' *'there* is a fable.' And when we say things of this sort we are recording just what we recorded when we said 'Mr. Pickwick is a fiction,' only our new expressions do not suggest what our old one did that some subject of attributes has the two attributes of being called 'Mr. Pickwick' and of being a fiction, but instead that some subject of attributes has the attributes of being called Dickens and being a coiner of false propositions and pseudo-proper names, or, on the other analysis, of being a book or a sentence which could only be true or false *if* someone was called 'Mr. Pickwick.' The proposition 'Mr. Pickwick is a fiction' is really, despite its *prima facies*, about Dickens or else about Pickwick Papers. But the fact that it is so is concealed and not exhibited by the form of the expression in which it is said.

It must be noted that the sense in which such quasi-ontological statements are misleading is not that they are false and not even that any word in them is equivocal or vague, but only that they are formally improper to facts of the logical form which they are employed to record and proper to facts of quite another logical form. What the implications are of these notions of formal propriety or formal impropriety we shall see later on.

¶ II. Statements Seemingly about Universals, or Quasi-Platonic Statements

We often and with great convenience use expressions such as 'Unpunctuality is reprehensible' and 'Virtue is its own reward.' And at first sight these seem to be on all fours with 'Jones merits reproof' and 'Smith has given himself the prize.' So philosophers, taking it that what is meant by such statements as the former is precisely analogous to what is meant by such statements as the latter, have accepted the consequence that the world contains at least two sorts of objects, namely, particulars like Jones and Smith, and 'universals' like Unpunctuality and Virtue.

But absurdities soon crop up. It is obviously silly to speak of a universal meriting reproof. You can no more praise or blame an 'universal' than you can make holes in the Equator.

Nor when we say 'unpunctuality is reprehensible' do we really suppose that unpunctuality ought to be ashamed of itself.

What we do mean is what is also meant but better expressed by 'Whoever is unpunctual deserves that other people should reprove him for being unpunctual.' For it is unpunctual men and not unpunctuality who can and should be blamed, since they are, what it is not, moral agents. Now in the new expression 'whoever is unpunctual merits reproof' the word 'unpunctuality' has vanished in favour of the predicative expression '. . . is unpunctual.' So that while in the original expression 'unpunctuality' seemed to denote the subject of which an attribute was being asserted, it now turns out to signify the having of an attribute. And we are really saying that anyone who has that attribute, has the other.

Again, it is not literally true that Virtue is a recipient of rewards. What is true is that anyone who is virtuous is benefited thereby. Whoever is good, gains something by being good. So the original statement was not 'about Virtue' but about good men, and the grammatical subject word 'Virtue' meant what is meant by '. . . is virtuous' and so was, what it pretended not to be, a predicative expression.

I need not amplify this much. It is not literally true that 'honesty compels me to state so and so,' for 'honesty' is not the name of a coercive agency. What is true is more properly put 'because I am honest, or wish to be honest, I am bound to state so and so.' 'Colour involves extension' means what is meant by 'Whatever is coloured is extended'; 'hope deferred maketh the heart sick' means what is meant by 'whoever for a long time hopes for something without getting it becomes sick at heart.'

It is my own view that all statements which seem to be 'about universals' are analysable in the same way, and consequently that general terms are never really the names of subjects of attributes. So 'universals' are not objects in the way in which Mt. Everest is one, and therefore the age-old question what *sort* of objects they are is a bogus question. For general nouns, adjectives, etc., are not proper names, so we cannot speak of 'the objects called "equality," "justice," and "progress." '

Platonic and anti-Platonic assertions, such as that 'equality is, or is not, a real entity,' are, accordingly, alike misleading, and misleading in two ways at once; for they are both quasi-ontological statements and quasi-Platonic ones.

However, I do not wish to defend this general position here, but only to show that in *some* cases statements which from their grammatical form seem to be saying that 'honesty does so and so' or 'equality is such and such,' are really saying in a formally improper way (though one which is readily understandable and idiomatically correct) 'anything which is equal to x is such and such' or 'whoever is honest, is so and so.' These statements state overtly, what the others stated covertly, that something's having one attribute necessitates its having the other.

Of course, the plain man who uses such quasi-Platonic expressions is not making a philosophical mistake. He is not philosophizing at all. He is not misled by and does not even notice the fraudulent pretence contained in such propositions that they are 'about Honesty' or 'about Progress.' He knows what he means and will, very likely, accept our more formally proper restatement of what he means as a fair paraphrase, but he will not have any motive for desiring the more proper form of expression, nor even any grounds for holding that it is more proper. For he is not attending to the form of the fact in abstraction from the special subject-matter that the fact is about. So for him the best way of expressing something is the way which is the most brief, the most elegant, or the most emphatic, whereas those who, like philosophers, must generalize about the *sorts* of statements that have to be made of *sorts* of facts about *sorts* of topics, cannot help treating as clues to the logical structures for which they are looking the grammatical forms of the common types of expressions in which these structures are recorded. And these clues are often misleading.

¶ III. Descriptive Expressions and Quasi-descriptions

We all constantly use expressions of the form 'the so and so,' as 'the Vice-Chancellor of Oxford University.' Very often we refer by means of such expressions to some one uniquely described individual. The phrases 'the present Vice-Chancellor of Oxford University' and 'the highest mountain in the world' have such a reference in such propositions as 'the present Vice-Chancellor of Oxford University is a tall man' and 'I have not seen the highest mountain in the world.'

There is nothing intrinsically misleading in the use of 'the'-phrases as unique descriptions, though there is a sense in which they are highly condensed or abbreviated. And philosophers can and do make mistakes in the accounts they give of what such descriptive phrases mean. What are misleading are, as we shall see, 'the'-phrases which behave grammatically as if they were unique descriptions referring to individuals when in fact they are not referential phrases at all. But this class of systematically misleading expressions cannot be examined until we have considered how genuine unique descriptions do refer.

A descriptive phrase is not a proper name, and the way in which the subject of attributes which it denotes is denoted by it is not in that subject's being *called* 'the so and so,' but in its possessing and being *ipso facto* the sole possessor of the idiosyncratic attribute which is what the descriptive phrase signifies. If Tommy is the eldest son of Jones, then 'the eldest son of Jones' denotes Tommy, not because someone or other *calls* him 'the eldest son of Jones,' but because he is and no one else can be both a son of Jones and older than all the other sons of Jones. The descriptive phrase, that is, is not a proper name but a predicative expression signifying the joint characters of being a son of Jones and older than the other sons of Jones. And it refers to Tommy only in the sense that Tommy and Tommy alone has those characters.

The phrase does not in any sense *mean* Tommy. Such a view would be, as we shall see, nonsensical. It means what is meant by the predicative expression, '. . . is both a son of Jones and older than his other sons,' and so it is itself only a predicative expression. By a 'predicative expression' I mean that fragment of a statement in virtue of which the having of a certain character or characters is expressed. And the having a certain character is not a subject of attributes but, so to speak, the tail end of the facts that some subject of attributes has it and some others lack it. By itself it neither names the subject which has the character nor records the fact that any subject has it. It cannot indeed occur by itself, but only as an element, namely, a predicative element in a full statement.

So the full statement 'the eldest son of Jones was married to-day' means what is meant by 'someone (namely, Tommy) (1) is a son of Jones, (2) is older than the other sons of Jones [this could be unpacked further] and (3) was married to-day.'

The whole statement could not be true unless the three or more component statements were true. But *that* there is someone of whom both (1) and (2) are true is not guaranteed by their being stated. (No statement can guarantee its own truth.) Consequently the characterizing expression '. . . is the eldest son of Jones' does not *mean* Tommy either in the sense of being his proper name or in the sense of being an expression the understanding of which involves the knowledge that Tommy has this idiosyncratic character. It only *refers* to Tommy in the sense that well-informed listeners will know already, that Tommy and Tommy only has in fact this idiosyncratic character. But this knowledge is not part of what must be known in order to understand the statement, 'Jones' eldest son was married to-day.' For we could know what it meant without knowing that Tommy was that eldest son or was married to-day. All we must know is that someone or other must be so characterized for the whole statement to be true.

For understanding a statement or apprehending what a statement means is not knowing that this statement records this fact, but knowing what *would* be the case if the statement *were* a record of fact.

There is no understanding or apprehending the meaning of an isolated proper name or of an isolated unique description. For *either* we know that someone in particular is called by that name by certain persons or else has the idiosyncratic characters signified by the descriptive phrase, which requires that we are acquainted both with the name or description and with the person named or described. *Or* we do not know these things, in which case we don't know that the quasi-name is a name at all or that the quasi-unique description describes anyone. But we can understand statements in which quasi-names or quasi-unique descriptions occur; for we can know what would be the case if someone were so called or so describable, and also had the other characters predicated in the predicates of the statements.

We see, then, that descriptive phrases are condensed predicative expressions, and so that their function is to be that element or (more often) one of those elements in statements (which as a whole record that something has a certain character or characters) in which the having of this or that character is expressed.

And this can easily be seen by another approach.

Take any 'the'-phrase which is naturally used referentially as the grammatical subject of a sentence, as 'The Vice-Chancellor of Oxford University' in 'The Vice-Chancellor of Oxford University is busy.' We can now take the descriptive phrase, lock, stock, and barrel, and use it non-referentially as the grammatical predicate in a series of statements and expressions, 'Who is the present Vice-Chancellor of Oxford University?' 'Mr. So-and-So is the present Vice-Chancellor of Oxford University,' 'Georges Carpentier is not the present Vice-Chancellor of Oxford University,' 'Mr. Such-and-Such is either the Vice-Chancellor of Oxford University or Senior Proctor,' 'Whoever is Vice-Chancellor of Oxford University is overworked,' etc. It is clear, anyhow, in the cases of the negative, hypothetical, and disjunctive statements containing this common predicative expression that it is not implied or even suggested that anyone does hold the office of Vice-Chancellor. So the 'the'-phrase is here quite non-referential, and does not even pretend to denote someone. It signifies an idiosyncratic character, but does not involve that anyone has it. This leads us back to our original conclusion that a descriptive phrase does not in any sense *mean* this person or that thing; or, to put it in another way, that we can understand a statement containing a descriptive phrase and still not know of this subject of attributes or of that one that the description fits it. (Indeed, we hardly need to argue the position. For no one with a respect for sense would dream of pointing to someone or something and saying 'that is the meaning of such and such an expression' or 'the meaning of yonder phrase is suffering from influenza.' 'Socrates is a meaning' is a nonsensical sentence. The whole pother about denoting seems to arise from the supposition that we could significantly describe an object as 'the meaning of the expression "*x*"' or 'what the expression "*x*" means.' Certainly a descriptive phrase can be said to *refer* to or *fit* this man or that mountain, and this man or that mountain can be described as that to which the expression '*x*' refers. But this is only to say that this man or that mountain has and is alone in having the characters the having of which is expressed in the predicative sentence-fragment '. . . is the so-and-so.')

All this is only leading up to another class of systematically misleading expressions. But the 'the'-phrases which we have been studying, whether occurring as grammatical subjects or as predicates in statements, were not formally fraudulent. There was nothing in the grammatical form of the sentences adduced to suggest that the facts recorded were of a different logical form from that which they really had.

The previous argument was intended to be critical of certain actual or possible philosophical errors, but they were errors about descriptive expressions and not errors *due* to a trickiness in descriptive expressions as such. Roughly, the errors that I have been trying to dispel are the views (1) that descriptive phrases are proper names and (2) that the thing which a description describes is what the description means. I want now to come to my long-delayed muttons and discuss a farther class of systematically misleading expressions.

¶ Systematically Misleading Quasi-referential 'The'-phrases

1. There frequently occur in ordinary discourse expressions which, though 'the'-phrases, are not unique descriptions at all, although from their grammatical form they look as if they are. The man who does not go in for abstraction and generalization uses them without peril or perplexity and knows quite well what he means by the sentences containing them. But the philosopher has to re-state them in a different and formally more proper arrangement of words if he is not to be trapped.

When a descriptive phrase is used as the grammatical subject of a sentence in a formally non-misleading way, as in 'the King went shooting to-day,' we know that if the statement as a whole is true (or even false) then there must be in the world someone in particular to whom the description 'the King' refers or applies. And we could significantly ask 'Who is the King?' and 'Are the father of the Prince of Wales and the King one and the same person?'

But we shall see that there are in common use quasi-descriptive phrases of the form 'the so-and-so,' in the cases of which there is in the world no one and nothing that could be described as that to which the phrase refers or applies, and thus that there is nothing and no-body about which or whom we could even ask 'Is it the so-and-so?' or 'Are he and the so-and-so one and the same person?'

It can happen in several ways. Take first the statement, which is true and clearly intelligible, 'Poincaré is not the King of France.' This at first sight looks formally analogous to 'Tommy Jones is not (i.e. is not identical with) the King of England.' But the difference soon shows itself. For whereas if the latter is true then its converse 'the King of England is not Tommy Jones' is true, it is neither true nor false to say 'The King of France is not Poincaré.' For there is no King of France and the phrase 'the King of France' does not fit any-body—nor did the plain man who said 'Poincaré is not the King of France' suppose the contrary. So 'the King of France' in this state-ment is not analogous to 'the King of England' in the others. It is not really being used referentially or as a unique description of some-body at all.

We can now redraft the contrasted propositions in forms of words

196 GILBERT RYLE

which shall advertise the difference which the original propositions concealed between the forms of the facts recorded.

'Tommy Jones is not the same person as the King of England' means what is meant by '(1) Somebody and—of an unspecified circle —one person only is called Tommy Jones; (2) Somebody, and one person only has royal power in England; and (3) No one both is called Tommy Jones and is King of England.' The original statement could not be true unless (1) and (2) were true.

Take now 'Poincaré is not the King of France.' This means what is meant by '(1) Someone is called "Poincaré" and (2) Poincaré has not got the rank, being King of France.' And this does not imply that anyone has that rank.

Sometimes this twofold use, namely the referential and the non-referential use of 'the'-phrases, troubles us in the mere practice of ordinary discourse. 'Smith is not the only man who has ever climbed Mont Blanc' might easily be taken by some people to mean what is meant by 'One man and one man only has climbed Mont Blanc, but Smith is not he,' and by others, 'Smith has climbed Mont Blanc but at least one other man has done so too.' But I am not interested in the occasional ambiguity of such expressions, but in the fact that an expression of this sort which is really being used in the non-referential way is apt to be construed as if it *must* be referentially used, or as if any 'the'-phrase was referentially used. Philosophers and others who have to abstract and generalize tend to be misled by the verbal similarity of 'the'-phrases of the one sort with 'the'-phrases of the other into 'coining entities' in order to be able to show to what a given 'the'-phrase refers.

Let us first consider the phrase 'the top of that tree' or 'the centre of that bush' as they occur in such statements as 'an owl is perched on the top of that tree,' 'my arrow flew through the centre of the bush.' These statements are quite unambiguous, and convey clearly and correctly what they are intended to convey.

But as they are in syntax analogous to 'a man is sitting next to the Vice-Chancellor' and 'my arrow flew through the curtain,' and as further an indefinite list could be drawn up of different statements having in common the 'the'-phrases, 'the top of that tree' and 'the centre of that bush,' it is hard for people who generalize to escape the temptation of supposing or even believing that these 'the'-phrases refer to objects in the way in which 'the Vice-Chancellor' and 'the curtain' refer to objects. And this is to suppose or believe that the top of that tree is a genuine subject of attributes in just the same way as the Vice-Chancellor is.

But (save in the case where the expression is being misused for the expression 'the topmost branch' or 'the topmost leaf of the tree') 'the top of the tree' at once turns out not to be referring to any object. There is nothing in the world of which it is true (or even false) to say 'That is the top of such and such a tree.' It does not, for instance, refer to a bit of the tree, or it could be cut down and burned or put in a vase. 'The top of the tree' does not refer to anything, but it signifies an attribute, namely, the having of a relative position, when it occurs in statements of the form 'x is at or near or above or below the top of the tree.' To put it crudely, it does not refer to a thing but signifies a thing's being in a certain place, or else signifies not a thing but the site or locus of a thing such as of the bough or leaf which is higher than any of the other boughs or leaves on the tree. Accordingly it makes sense to say that now one bough and now another is at the top of the tree. But 'at the top of the tree' means no more than what is meant by 'higher than any other part of the tree,' which latter phrase no one could take for a referential phrase like 'the present Vice-Chancellor.'

The place of a thing, or the whereabouts of a thing is not a thing but the tail end of the fact that something is there. 'Where the bee sucks, there suck I,' but it is the clover flower that is there which holds the honey, and not the whereabouts of the flower. All that this amounts to is that though we can use quasi-descriptive phrases to enable us to state where something is, that the thing is there is a relational character of the thing and not itself a subject of characters.

I suspect that a lot of Cartesian and perhaps Newtonian blunders about Space and Time originate from the systematically misleading character of the 'the'-phrases which we use to date and locate things, such as 'the region occupied by x', 'the path followed by y', 'the moment or date at which z happened.' It was not seen that these are but hamstrung predicative expressions and are not and are not even ordinarily taken to be referentially used descriptive expressions, any more than 'the King of France' in 'Poincaré is not the King of France' is ordinarily treated as if it was a referentially used 'the'-phrase.

Take another case. 'Jones hates the thought of going to hospital,' 'the idea of having a holiday has just occurred to me.' These quasi-descriptive phrases suggest that there is one object in the world which is what is referred to by the phrase 'the thought of going to hospital' and another which is what is referred to by 'the idea of having a holiday.' And anyhow partly through accepting the grammatical *prima facies* of such expressions, philosophers have believed as devoutly in the existence of 'ideas,' 'conceptions' and 'thoughts' or 'judgements' as their predecessors did (from similar causes) in that of substantial forms or as children do (from similar causes) in that of the Equator, the sky, and the North Pole.

But if we re-state them, the expressions turn out to be no evidence whatsoever in favour of the Lockean demonology. For 'Jones hates the thought of going to hospital' only means what is meant by 'Jones feels distressed when he thinks of what he will undergo if he goes to hospital.' The phrase 'the thought of . . .' is transmuted into 'whenever he thinks of . . .', which does not even seem to contain a reference to any other entity than Jones and, perhaps, the hospital. For it to be true, the world must contain a Jones who is sometimes thinking and sometimes, say, sleeping; but it need no more contain both Jones and 'the thought or idea of so and so' than it need contain both someone called 'Jones' and something called 'Sleep.'

Similarly, the statement 'the idea of taking a holiday has just occurred to me' seems grammatically to be analogous to 'that dog has just bitten me.' And as, if the latter is true, the world must contain both me and the dog, so it would seem, if the former is true, the world must contain both me and the idea of taking a holiday. But the appearance is a delusion. For while I could not re-state my complaint against the dog in any sentence not containing a descriptive phrase referring to it, I can easily do so with the statement about 'the idea of taking a holiday,' e.g. in the statement 'I have just been thinking that I might take a holiday.'

A host of errors of the same sort has been generated in logic itself and epistemology by the omission to analyse the quasi-descriptive phrase 'the meaning of the expression "x."' I suspect that all the mistaken doctrines of concepts, ideas, terms, judgements, objective propositions, contents, objectives and the like derive from the same fallacy, namely, that there must be *something* referred to by such expressions as 'the meaning of the word (phrase or sentence) "x,"' on all fours with the policeman who really is referred to by the descriptive phrase in 'our village policeman is fond of football.' And the way out of the confusion is to see that some 'the'-phrases are only similar in grammar and not similar in function to referentially-used descriptive phrases, e.g. in the case in point, 'the meaning of "x"' is like 'the King of France' in 'Poincaré is not the King of France,' a predicative expression used non-referentially.

And, of course, the ordinary man does not pretend to himself or anyone else that when he makes statements containing such expressions as 'the meaning of "x,"' he is referring to a queer new object: it does not cross his mind that his phrase might be misconstrued as a referentially used descriptive phrase. So he is not guilty of philosophical error or clumsiness. None the less, his form of words is systematically misleading. For an important difference of logical form is disguised by the complete similarity of grammatical form between 'the village policeman is reliable' and 'the meaning of "x" is doubtful' or again between 'I have just met the village policeman' and 'I have just grasped the meaning of "x."'

(Consequently, as there is no object describable as that which is referred to by the expression 'the meaning of "x,"' questions about the status of such objects are meaningless. It is as pointless to discuss whether word-meanings (i.e. 'concepts' or 'universals') are subjective or objective, or whether sentence-meanings (i.e. 'judgements' or 'objectives') are subjective or objective, as it would be to discuss whether the Equator or the sky is subjective or objective. For the questions themselves are not about anything.)

All this does not, of course, in the least prevent us from using intelligently and intelligibly sentences containing the expression 'the meaning of "x"' where this can be re-drafted as 'what "x" means'. For here the 'the'-phrase is being predicatively used and not as an unique description. 'The meaning of "x" is the same as the meaning of "y"' is equivalent to '"x" means what "y" means', and that can be understood without any temptation to multiply entities.

But this argument is, after all, only about a very special case of the systematic misleadingness of quasi-descriptions.

2. There is another class of uses of 'the'-phrases which is also liable to engender philosophical misconstructions, though I am not sure that I can recall any good instances of actual mistakes which have occurred from this source.

Suppose I say, 'the defeat of the Labour Party has surprised me', what I say could be correctly paraphrased by 'the fact that the Labour Party was defeated, was a surprise to me' or 'the Labour Party has been defeated and I am surprised that it has been defeated'. Here the 'the'-phrase does not refer to a thing but is a condensed record of something's being the case. And this is a common and handy idiom. We can always say instead of 'because A is B, therefore C is D' 'the D-ness of C is due to the B-ness of A'. 'The severity of the winter is responsible for the high price of cabbages' means what is meant by 'Cabbages are expensive because the winter was severe.'

But if I say 'the defeat of the Labour Party occurred in 1931', my 'the'-phrase is referentially used to describe an event and not as a condensed record of a fact. For events have dates, but facts do not. So the facts recorded in the grammatically similar statements 'the defeat of the Labour Party has surprised me' and 'the defeat of the Labour Party occurred in 1931' are in logical form quite different. And both sorts of facts are formally quite different from this third fact which is recorded in 'the victory of the Labour Party would have surprised me'. For this neither refers to an event, nor records the fact that the Labour Party was victorious, but says 'if the Labour Party had won, I should have been surprised'. So here the 'the'-phrase is a protasis. And, once more, all these three uses of 'the'-phrases are different in their sort of significance from 'the defeat of the Conservative Party at the next election is probable', or 'possible', or 'impossible'. For these mean 'the available relevant data are in favour of' or 'not incompatible with' or 'incompatible with the Conservative Party being defeated at the next election'.

So there are at least these four different types of facts which can be and, in ordinary discourse, are conveniently and intelligibly recorded in statements containing grammatically indistinguishable 'the'-phrases. But they can be re-stated in forms of words which do exhibit in virtue of their special grammatical forms the several logical structures of the different sorts of facts recorded.

3. Lastly, I must just mention one further class of sytematically misleading 'the-'phrase. 'The whale is not a fish but a mammal' and 'the true Englishman detests foul play' record facts, we may take it. But they are not about this whale or that Englishman, and they might be true even if there were no whales or no true Englishmen. These are, probably, disguised hypothetical statements. But all I wish to point out is that they are obviously disguised.

I have chosen these three main types of systematically misleading expressions because all alike are misleading in a certain direction. They all suggest the existence of new sorts of objects, or, to put it in another way, they are all temptations to us to 'multiply entities'. In each of them, the quasi-ontological, the quasi-Platonic and the quasi-descriptive expressions, an expression is misconstrued as a denoting expression which in fact does not denote, but only looks grammatically like expressions which are used to denote. Occam's prescription was, therefore, in my view, 'Do not treat all expressions which are grammatically like proper names or referentially used "the"-phrases, as if they were therefore proper names or referentially used "the"-phrases'.

But there are other types of systematically misleading expressions, of which I shall just mention a few that occur to me.

'Jones is an alleged murderer', or 'a suspected murderer', 'Smith is a possible or probable Lord Mayor', 'Robinson is an ostensible, or seeming or mock or sham or bogus hero', 'Brown is a future or a past

Member of Parliament', etc. These suggest what they do not mean, that the subjects named are of a special kind of murderer, or Lord Mayor, or hero, or Member of Parliament. But being an alleged murderer does not entail being a murderer, nor does being a likely Lord Mayor entail being a Lord Mayor.

'Jones is popular' suggests that being popular is like being wise, a quality; but in fact it is a relational character, and one which does not directly characterize Jones, but the people who are fond of Jones, and so 'Jones is popular' means what is meant by 'Many people like Jones, and many more like him than either dislike him or are indifferent to him', or something of the sort.

But I have, I think, given enough instances to show in what sense expressions may seem to mean something quite different from what they are in fact used to mean; and therefore I have shown in what sense some expressions are systematically misleading.

So I am taking it as established (1) that what is expressed in one expression can often be expressed in expressions of quite different grammatical forms, and (2) that of two expressions, each meaning what the other means, which are of different grammatical forms, one is often more systematically misleading than the other.

And this means that while a fact or state of affairs *can* be recorded in an indefinite number of statements of widely differing grammatical forms, it is stated better in some than in others. The ideal, which may never be realized, is that it should be stated in a completely non-misleading form of words.

Now, when we call one form of expression better than another, we do not mean that it is more elegant or brief or familiar or more swiftly intelligible to the ordinary listener, but that in virtue of its grammatical form it exhibits, in a way in which the others fail to exhibit, the logical form of the state of affairs or fact that is being recorded. But this interest in the best way of exhibiting the logical form of facts is not for every man, but only for the philosopher.

I wish now to raise, but not to solve, some consequential problems which arise.

1. Given that an expression of a certain grammatical form is proper (or anyhow approximates to being proper) to facts of a certain logical form and to those facts only, is this relation of propriety of grammatical to logical form *natural* or *conventional?*

I cannot myself credit what seems to be the doctrine of Wittgenstein and the school of logical grammarians who owe allegiance to him, that what makes an expression formally proper to a fact is some real and non-conventional one-one picturing relation between the composition of the expression and that of the fact. For I do not see how, save in a small class of specially-chosen cases, a fact or state of affairs can be deemed like or even unlike in structure a sentence, gesture or diagram. For a fact is not a collection—even an arranged collection—of bits in the way in which a sentence is an arranged collection of noises or a map an arranged collection of scratches. A fact is not a thing and so is not even an arranged thing. Certainly a map may be like a country or a railway system, and in a more general, or looser, sense a sentence, as an ordered series of noises, might be a similar sort of series to a series of vehicles in a stream of traffic or the series of days in the week.

But in Socrates being angry or in the fact that either Socrates was wise or Plato was dishonest, I can see no concatenation of bits such that a concatenation of parts of speech could be held to be of the same general architectural plan as it. But this difficulty may be just denseness on my part.

On the other hand, it is not easy to accept what seems to be the alternative that it is just by convention that a given grammatical form is specially dedicated to facts of a given logical form. For, in fact, customary usage is perfectly tolerant of systematically misleading expressions. And, moreover, it is hard to explain how in the genesis of languages our presumably non-philosophical forbears could have decided on or happened on the dedication of a given grammatical form to facts of a given logical form. For presumably the study of abstract logical form is later than the entry into common use of syntactical idioms.

It is, however, my present view that the propriety of grammatical to logical forms is more nearly conventional than natural: though I do not suppose it to be the effect of whim or of deliberate plan.

2. The next question is: How are we to discover in particular cases whether an expression is systematically misleading or not? I suspect that the answer to this will be of this sort. We meet with and understand and even believe a certain expression such as 'Mr. Pickwick is a fictitious person' and 'the Equator encircles the globe'. And we know that if these expressions are saying what they seem to be saying, certain other propositions will follow. But it turns out that the naturally consequential propositions 'Mr. Pickwick was born in such and such a year' and 'the Equator is of such and such a thickness' are not merely false but, on analysis, in contradiction with something in that from which they seemed to be logical consequences. The only solution is to see that being a fictitious person is not to be a person of a certain sort, and that the sense in which the Equator girdles the earth is not that of being any sort of a ring or ribbon enveloping the earth. And this

is to see that the original propositions were not saying what they seemed on first analysis to be saying. Paralogisms and antinomies are the evidence that an expression is systematically misleading.

None the less, the systematically misleading expressions as intended and as understood contain no contradictions. People do not really talk philosophical nonsense—unless they are philosophizing or, what is quite a different thing, unless they are being sententious. What they do is to use expressions which, from whatever cause—generally the desire for brevity and simplicity of discourse—disguise instead of exhibiting the forms of the facts recorded. And it is to reveal these forms that we abstract and generalize. These processes of abstraction and generalization occur before philosophical analysis begins. It seems indeed that their results are the subject matter of philosophy. Pre-philosophical abstract thinking is always misled by systematically misleading expressions, and even philosophical abstract thinking, the proper function of which is to cure this disease, is actually one of its worst victims.

3. I do not know any way of classifying or giving an exhaustive list of the possible types of systematically misleading expressions. I fancy that the number is in principle unlimited, but that the number of prevalent and obsessing types is fairly small.

4. I do not know any way of proving that an expression contains no systematic misleadingness at all. The fact that antinomies have not yet been shown to arise is no proof that they never will arise. We can know that of two expressions 'x' and 'y' which record the same fact, 'x' is less misleading than 'y'; but not that 'x' cannot itself be improved upon.

5. Philosophy must then involve the exercise of systematic restatement. But this does not mean that it is a department of philology or literary criticism.

Its restatement is not the substitution of one noun for another or one verb for another. That is what lexicographers and translators excel in. Its restatements are transmutations of syntax, and transmutations of syntax controlled not by desire for elegance or stylistic correctness but by desire to exhibit the forms of the facts into which philosophy is the inquiry.

I conclude, then, that there is, after all, a sense in which we can properly inquire and even say 'what it really means to say so and so'. For we can ask what is the real form of the fact recorded when this is concealed or disguised and not duly exhibited by the expression in question. And we can often succeed in stating this fact in a new form of words which does exhibit what the other failed to exhibit. And I am for the present inclined to believe that this is what philosophical analysis is, and that this is the sole and whole function of philosophy. But I do not want to argue this point now.

But, as confession is good for the soul, I must admit that I do not very much relish the conclusions towards which these conclusions point. I would rather allot to philosophy a sublimer task than the detection of the sources in linguistic idioms of recurrent misconstructions and absurd theories. But that it is at least this I cannot feel any serious doubt.

LOGICAL POSITIVISM

X

RUDOLF CARNAP

RUDOLF CARNAP (*b*. 1891) was educated in Germany. From 1926 to 1935, he taught at the universities of Vienna and Prague where, with others, he contributed much to the formation and development of the Vienna Circle. In 1936 he came to the University of Chicago where he remained as Professor of Philosophy until 1954. Since that time he has been at the University of California at Los Angeles. He has published voluminously in logic, philosophy of physics, and geometry, and, most recently, in probability theory. Among his important works are *Der Logische Aufbau der Welt* (1928), *The Logical Syntax of Language* (1934), and *Logical Foundations of Probability* (1950).

Carnap's *Philosophy and Logical Syntax* (1935) contains the text of three lectures he delivered at the University of London. The lectures expound, in a popular form, the main ideas of the Vienna Circle. Part I (reprinted below), concentrates on the central doctrine of the logical positivist movement, that a proposition is cognitively meaningful if and only if it is verifiable. From this principle, certain well-known implications for metaphysics and ethics are drawn.

The Rejection of Metaphysics[1]

¶ 1. Verifiability

The problems of philosophy as usually dealt with are of very different kinds. From the point of view which I am here taking we may distinguish mainly three kinds of problems and doctrines in traditional philosophy. For the sake of simplicity we shall call these parts *Metaphysics, Psychology,* and *Logic.* Or, rather, there are not three distinct regions, but three sorts of components which in most theses and questions are combined: a metaphysical, a psychological, and a logical component.

The considerations that follow belong to the third region: we are here carrying out *Logical Analysis.* The function of logical analysis is to analyse all knowledge, all assertions of science and of everyday life, in order to make clear the sense of each such assertion and the connections between them. One of the principal tasks of the logical analysis of a given statement is to find out the method of verification for that statement. The question is: What reasons can there be to assert this statement; or: How can we become certain as to its truth or falsehood? This question is called by the philosophers the epistemological question; epistemology or the philosophical theory of knowledge is nothing other than a special part of logical analysis, usually combined with some psychological questions concerning the process of knowing.

What, then, is the method of verification of a statement? Here we have to distinguish between two kinds of verification: direct and indirect. If the question is about a statement which asserts something about a present perception, e.g. "Now I see a red square on a blue ground," then the statement can be tested directly by my present perception. If at present I do see a red square on a blue ground, the statement

1. From *Philosophy and Logical Syntax* (London: Kegan Paul, Trench, Trubner & Co., 1935), Part I. Reprinted by kind permission of Professor Carnap, who has offered certain terminological changes incorporated in the present version, and by kind permission of the Executors of the estate of the late C. K. Ogden.

is directly verified by this seeing; if I do not see that, it is disproved. To be sure, there are still some serious problems in connection with direct verification. We will however not touch on them here, but give our attention to the question of indirect verification, which is more important for our purposes. A statement P which is not directly verifiable can only be verified by direct verification of statements deduced from P together with other already verified statements.

Let us take the statement P_1: "This key is made of iron." There are many ways of verifying this statement: e.g.: I place the key near a magnet; then I perceive that the key is attracted. Here the deduction is made in this way:

Premises: P_1: "This key is made of iron"; the statement to be examined.
P_2: "If an iron thing is placed near a magnet, it is attracted"; this is a physical law, already verified.
P_3: "This object—a bar—is a magnet"; statement already verified.
P_4: "The key is placed near the bar"; this is now directly verified by our observation.

From these four premises we can deduce the conclusion:

P_5: "The key will now be attracted by the bar."

This statement is a prediction which can be examined by observation. If we look, we either observe the attraction or we do not. In the first case we have found a positive instance, an instance of verification of the statement P_1 under consideration; in the second case we have a negative instance, an instance of disproof of P_1.

In the first case the examination of the statement P_1 is not finished. We may repeat the examination by means of a magnet, i.e. we may deduce other statements similar to P_5 by the help of the same or similar premises as before. After that, or instead of that, we may make an examination by electrical tests, or by the mechanical, chemical, or optical tests, etc. If in these further investigations all instances turn out to be positive, the certainty of the statement P_1 gradually grows. We may soon come to a degree of certainty sufficient for all practical purposes, but *absolute* certainty we can never attain. The number of instances deducible from P_1 by the help of other statements already verified or directly verifiable is infinite. Therefore there is always a possibility of finding in the future a negative instance, however small its probability may be. Thus the statement P_1 *can never be completely verified*. For this reason it is called an hypothesis.

So far we have considered a similar statement concerning one single thing. If we take a universal statement concerning all things or events at whatever time and place, a so-called natural *law*, it is still clearer that the number of examinable instances is infinite and so the statement is an hypothesis.

Every assertion P in the wide field of science has this character, that it either asserts something about present perceptions or other experiences, and therefore is verifiable by them, or that statements about future perceptions are deducible from P together with some other statements already verified. If a scientist should venture to make an assertion from which no perceptual statements could be deduced, what should we say to that? Suppose, e.g., he asserts that there is not only a gravitational field having an effect on bodies according to the known laws of gravitation, but also a levitational field, and on being asked what sort of effect this levitational field has, according to his theory, he answers that there is no observable effect; in other words, he confesses his inability to give rules according to which we could deduce perceptual statements from his assertion. In that case our reply is: your assertion is no assertion at all; it does not speak about any thing; it is nothing but a series of empty words; it is simply without sense.

It is true that he may have images and even feelings connected with his words. This fact may be of psychological importance; logically, it is irrelevant. What gives theoretical meaning to a statement is not the attendant images and thoughts, but the possibility of deducing from it perceptual statements, in other words, the possibility of verification. To give sense to a statement the presence of images is not sufficient; it is not even necessary. We have no actual image of the electromagnetic field, nor even, I should say, of the gravitational field. Nevertheless the statements which physicists assert about these fields have a perfect sense, because perceptual statements are deducible from them. I by no means object to the statement just mentioned about a levitational field that we do not know how to imagine or conceive such a field. My only objection to that statement is that we are not told how to verify it.

¶ 2. METAPHYSICS

What we have been doing so far is *logical analysis*. Now we are going to apply these considerations not to statements of physics as before, but to statements of *metaphysics*. Thus our investigation belongs to *logic*, to the third of the three parts of philosophy spoken about before, but the *objects* of this investigation belong to the first part.

I will call *metaphysical* all those statements which claim to represent knowledge about something which is over or beyond all experience, e.g. about the real Essence of things, about Things in themselves, the Absolute, and such like. I do not include in metaphysics those theories—sometimes called metaphysical—whose object is to arrange the most general statements of the various regions of scientific knowledge in a well-ordered system; such theories belong actually to the field of empirical science, not of philosophy, however daring they may be. The sort of statements I wish to denote as metaphysical may most easily be made clear by some examples: "The Essence and Principle of the world is Water," said Thales; "Fire," said Heraclitus; "the Infinite," said Anaximander; "Number," said Pythagoras. "All things are nothing but shadows of eternal ideas which themselves are in a spaceless and timeless sphere," is a doctrine of Plato. From the monists we learn: "There is only one principle on which all that is, is founded"; but the dualists tell us: "There are two principles." The materialists say: "All that is, is in its essence material," but the spiritualists say: "All that is, is spiritual." To metaphysics (in our sense of the word) belong the principal doctrines of Spinoza, Schelling, Hegel, and—to give at least one name of the present time—Bergson.

Now let us examine this kind of statement from the point of view of *verifiability*. It is easy to realize that such statements are not verifiable. From the statement: "The Principle of the world is Water" we are not able to deduce any statement asserting any perceptions or feelings or experiences whatever which may be expected for the future. Therefore the statement, "The Principle of the world is Water," asserts nothing at all. It is perfectly analogous to the statement in the fictitious example above about the levitational field and therefore it has no more sense than that statement. The water-metaphysician—as we may call him—has no doubt many images connected with his doctrine; but they cannot give sense to the statement any more than they could in the case of the levitational field. Metaphysicians cannot avoid making their statements nonverifiable, because if they made them verifiable, the decision about the truth or falsehood of their doctrines would depend upon experience and therefore belong to the region of empirical science. This consequence they wish to avoid, because they pretend to teach knowledge which is of a higher level than that of empirical science. Thus they are compelled to cut all connection between their statements and experience; and precisely by this procedure they deprive them of any sense.

¶ 3. PROBLEMS OF REALITY

So far I have considered only examples of such statements as are usually called metaphysical. The judgment I have passed on these statements, namely, that they have no empirical sense, may perhaps appear not very astonishing, and even trivial. But it is to be feared that the reader will find it somewhat more difficult to agree when I now proceed to apply that judgment also to philosophical doctrines of the type usually called epistemological. I prefer to call them also metaphysical because of their similarity, in the point under consideration, to the statements usually so called. What I have in mind are the doctrines of realism, idealism, solipsism, positivism and the like, taken in their traditional form as asserting or denying the reality of something. The realist asserts the reality of the external world, the idealist denies it. The realist—usually at least—asserts also the reality of other minds, the solipsist—an especially radical idealist—denies it, and asserts that only his own mind or consciousness is real. Have these assertions sense?

Perhaps it may be said that assertions about the reality or unreality or something occur also in empirical science, where they are examined in an empirical way, and that therefore they must have sense. This is quite true. But we have to distinguish between two concepts of reality, one occurring in empirical statements and the other occurring in the philosophical statements just mentioned. When a zoologist asserts the reality of kangaroos, his assertion means that there are things of a certain sort which can be found and perceived at certain times and places; in other words that there are objects of a certain sort which are elements of the space-time-system of the physical world. This assertion is of course verifiable; by empirical investigation every zoologist arrives at a positive verification, independent of whether he is a realist or an idealist. Between the realist and the idealist there is full agreement as to the question of the reality of things of a specified sort, i.e., of the possibility of locating elements of that sort in the system of the physical world. The disagreement begins only when the question about the reality of the physical world as a whole is raised. But this question has no sense, because the reality of anything is nothing else than the possibility of its being placed in a certain system, in this case, in the space-time-system of the physical world, and such a question has sense only if it concerns elements or parts, not if it concerns the system itself.

The same result is obtained by applying the criterion explained before: the possibility of deducing perceptual statements. While from the assertion of the reality or the existence of kangaroos we *can* deduce perceptual statements, from the assertion of the reality of the physical world this is not possible; neither it is possible from the opposite assertion of the unreality of the physical world. Therefore both assertions have no empirical content—no sense at all. It is to be emphasized that this criticism of having no sense applies equally to the assertion of unreality. Sometimes the views of the *Vienna Circle* have been mistaken for a denial of the reality of the physical world, but we make no such denial. It is true that we reject the thesis of the reality of the physical world; but we do not reject it as false, but as having no sense, and its idealistic *anti-* thesis is subject to exactly the same rejection. We neither assert nor deny these theses, we reject the whole question.

All the considerations which apply to the question of the reality of the physical world apply also to the other philosophical questions of reality, e.g. the reality of other minds, the reality of the given, the reality of universals, the reality of qualities, the reality of relations, the reality of numbers, etc. If any philosophical thesis answering any of these questions positively or negatively is added to the system of scientific hypotheses, this system will not in the least become more effective; we shall not be able to make any further prediction as to future experiences. Thus all these philosophical theses are deprived of empirical content, of theoretical sense; they are pseudo-theses.

If I am right in this assertion, the philosophical problems of reality —as distinguished from the empirical problems of reality—have the same logical character as the problems (or rather, pseudo-problems) of transcendental metaphysics earlier referred to. For this reason I call those problems of reality not epistemological problems—as they usually are called—but metaphysical.

Among the metaphysical doctrines that have no theoretical sense I have also mentioned positivism, although the Vienna Circle is sometimes designated as positivistic. It is doubtful whether this designation is quite suitable for us. In any case we do not assert the thesis that only the given is real, which is one of the principal theses of traditional positivism. The name "logical positivism" seems more suitable, but this also can be misunderstood. At any rate it is important to realize that our doctrine is a logical one and has nothing to do with metaphysical theses of the reality or unreality of anything whatever. What the character of a *logical* thesis is, will be made clear in the following chapters.

¶ 4. ETHICS

One division of philosophy, which by some philosophers is considered the most important, has not been mentioned at all so far, namely, the philosophy of values, with its main branch, moral philosophy or *Ethics*. The word "Ethics" is used in two different senses. Sometimes a certain empirical investigation is called "Ethics," viz. psychological and sociological investigations about the actions of human beings, especially regarding the origin of these actions from feelings and volitions and their effects upon other people. Ethics in this sense is an empirical, scientific investigation; it belongs to empirical science rather than to philosophy. Fundamentally different from this is ethics in the second sense, as the philosophy of moral values or moral norms, which one can designate normative ethics. This is not an investigation of facts, but a pretended investigation of what is good and what is evil, what it is right to do and what it is wrong to do. Thus the purpose of this philosophical, or normative, ethics is to state norms for human action or judgments about moral values.

It is easy to see that it is merely a difference of formulation, whether we state a norm or a value judgment. A norm or rule has an imperative form, for instance: "Do not kill!" The corresponding value judgment would be: "Killing is evil." This difference of formulation has become practically very important, especially for the development of philosophical thinking. The rule, "Do not kill," has grammatically the imperative form and will therefore not be regarded as an assertion. But the value statement, "Killing is evil," although, like the rule it is merely an expression of a certain wish, has the grammatical form of a declarative sentence. Most philosophers have been deceived by this form into thinking that a value statement is really an assertive statement, and must be either true or false. Therefore they give reasons for their own value statements and try to disprove those of their opponents. But actually a value statement is nothing but a command in a misleading grammatical form. It may have effects upon the actions of men, and these effects may either be in accordance with our wishes or not; but it is neither true nor false. It does not assert anything and can neither be proved nor disproved.

This is revealed as soon as we apply to such statements our method of logical analysis. From the statement "Killing is evil" we cannot deduce any statement about future experiences. Thus this statement is not verifiable and has no theoretical sense, and the same thing is true of all other value statements.

Perhaps somebody will contend in opposition that the following statement is deducible: "If a person kills anybody he will have feelings of remorse." But this statement is in no way deducible from the statement "Killing is evil." It is deducible only from psychological statements about the character and the emotional reactions of the person. These statements are indeed verifiable and not without sense. They belong to psychology, not to philosophy; to psychological ethics (if one wishes to use this word), not to philosophical or normative ethics. The statements of normative ethics, whether they have the form of rules or the form of value statements, have no theoretical sense, are not scientific statements (taking the word scientific to mean any assertive statement).

To avoid misunderstanding it must be said that we do not at all deny the possibility of importance of a scientific investigation of value statements as well as of acts of valuation. Both of these are acts of individuals and are, like all other kinds of acts, possible objects of empirical investigation. Historians, psychologists, and sociologists may give analyses and causal explanations of them, and such historical and psychological statements about acts of valuation and about value statements are indeed meaningful scientific statements which belong to ethics in the first sense of this word. But the value statements themselves are here only objects of investigation; they are not statements in these theories, and have, here as elsewhere, no theoretical sense. Therefore we assign them to the realm of metaphysics.

¶ 5. METAPHYSICS AS EXPRESSION

Now we have analysed the statements of metaphysics in a wide sense of this word, including not only transcendental metaphysics, but also the problems of philosophical reality and lastly normative ethics. Perhaps many will agree that the statements of all these kinds of metaphysics are not verifiable, i.e., that their truth cannot be examined by experience. And perhaps many will even grant that for this reason they have not the character of scientific statements. But when I say that they are without sense, assent will probably seem more difficult. Someone may object: these statements in the metaphysical books obviously have an effect upon the reader, and sometimes a very strong effect; therefore, they certainly *express* something, but nevertheless they have no sense, no theoretical content.

We have here to distinguish two functions of language, which we may call the expressive function and the representative or cognitive function. Almost all the conscious and unconscious movements of a person, including his linguistic utterances, express something of his feelings, his present mood, his temporary or permanent dispositions to reaction, and the like. Therefore, we may take almost all his movements and words as symptoms from which we can infer something about his feelings or his character. That is the expressive function of movements and words. But besides that, a certain portion of linguistic utterances (e.g. "this book is black"), as distinguished from other linguistic utterances and movements, has a second function: these utterances represent a certain state of affairs; they tell us that something is the case; they assert something, they predicate something, they judge something.

In special cases, this asserted state may be the same as that which is inferred from a certain expressive utterance; but even in such cases we must sharply distinguish between the assertion and the expression. If, for instance, somebody is laughing we may take this as a symptom of his merry mood; if, on the other hand, he tells us without laughing: "Now I am merry," we can learn from his words the same thing which we inferred in the first case from his laughing. Nevertheless, there is a fundamental difference between the laughter and the words: "I am merry now." This linguistic utterance *asserts* the merry mood, and therefore it is either true or false. The laughter does not assert merry mood but *expresses* it. It is neither true nor false, because it does not assert anything, although it may be either genuine or deceptive.

Now many linguistic utterances are analogous to laughing in that they have only an expressive function, no representative function. Examples of this are cries like "Oh, Oh" or, on a higher level, lyrical verses. The aim of a lyrical poem in which occur the words "sunshine" and "clouds," is not to inform us of certain meteorological facts, but to express certain feelings of the poet and to excite similar feelings in us. A lyrical poem has no assertive sense, no theoretical sense, it does not contain knowledge.

The meaning of our anti-metaphysical thesis may now be more clearly explained. This thesis asserts that metaphysical statements—like lyrical verses—have only an expressive function, but no representative function. Metaphysical statements are neither true nor false, because they assert nothing, they contain neither knowledge nor error, they lie completely outside the field of knowledge, of theory, outside the discussion of truth or falsehood. But they are, like laughing, lyrics, and music, expressive. They express not so much temporary feelings as permanent emotional or volitional dispositions. Thus, for instance, a metaphysical system of monism may be an expression of an even and harmonious mode of life, a dualistic system may be an expression of the emotional state of someone who takes life as an eternal struggle; an ethical system of rigorism may be expressive of a strong sense of duty or perhaps of a desire to rule severely. Realism is often a symptom of the type of constitution called by psychologists extroverted, which is characterized by easily forming connections with men and things; idealism, of an opposite constitution, the so-called introverted type, which has a tendency to withdraw from the unfriendly world and to live within its own thoughts and fancies.

Thus we find a great similarity between metaphysics and lyrics. But there is one decisive difference between them. Both have no representative function, no theoretical content. A metaphysical statement, however —as distinguished from a lyrical verse—seems to have such a content, and by this not only is the reader deceived, but the metaphysician himself. He believes that in his metaphysical treatise he has asserted something, and is led by this into argument and polemics against the statements of some other metaphysician. A poet, however, does not assert that the verses of another are wrong or erroneous; he usually contents himself with calling them bad.

The non-theoretical character of metaphysics would not be in itself a defect; all arts have this non-theoretical character without thereby losing their high value for personal as well as for social life. The danger lies in the *deceptive* character of metaphysics; it gives the illusion of knowledge without actually giving any knowledge. This is the reason why we reject it.

¶ 6. PSYCHOLOGY

When we have eliminated metaphysical problems and doctrines from the region of knowledge or theory, there remain still two kinds of philosophical questions: psychological and logical. Now we shall eliminate the psychological questions also, not from the region of knowledge, but from philosophy. Then, finally, philosophy will be reduced to logic alone (in a wide sense of this word).

Psychological questions and statements are certainly not without sense. From such statements we can deduce other statements about future experiences and by their help we can verify the psychological statements. But the statements of psychology belong to the region of empirical science in just the same way as do the statements of chemistry, biology, history and the like. The character of psychology is by no means more philosophical than that of the other sciences mentioned. When we look at the historical development of the sciences we see that philosophy has been the mother of them all. One science after another has been detached from philosophy and has become an independent science. Only in our time has the umbilical cord between psychology and philosophy been cut. Many philosophers have not yet realized quite clearly that psychology is no longer an embryo, but an independent organism, and that psychological questions have to be left to empirical research.

Of course, we have no objection to connecting psychological and logical investigations, any more than to connecting investigations of any scientific kind. We reject only the confusion of the two kinds of questions. We demand that they should be clearly distinguished even where in practice they are combined. The confusion sometimes consists in dealing with a logical question as if it were a psychological one. This mistake—called psychologism—leads to the opinion that logic is a science concerning thinking, that is, either concerning the actual operation of thinking or the rules according to which thinking should proceed. But, as a matter of fact, the investigation of operations of thinking as they really occur is a task for psychology and has nothing to do with logic. And learning how to think aright is what we do in every other science as well as in logic. In astronomy we learn how to think aright about stars; in logic we learn how to think aright about the special objects of logic. What these special objects of logic are, will be seen in the next chapter. In any case, thinking is not an object of logic, but of psychology.

Psychological questions concern all kinds of so-called mental events, all kinds of sensations, feelings, thoughts, images, etc., whether they are conscious or unconscious. These questions of psychology can be answered only by experience, not by philosophising.

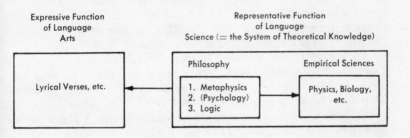

¶ 7. LOGICAL ANALYSIS

The only proper task of *philosophy* is *logical analysis*. And now the principal question to be answered here will be: *"What is logical analysis?"* In our considerations so far we have already practised logical analysis: we have tried to determine the character of physical hypotheses, of metaphysical statements (or rather, pseudo-statements), of psychological statements. And now we have to apply logical analysis to logical analysis itself; we have to determine the character of the statements of logic, of those statements which are the results of logical analysis.

The opinion that metaphysical statements have no sense because they do not concern any facts, has already been expressed by *Hume*. He writes in the last chapter of his "Enquiry Concerning Human Understanding" (published in the year 1748) as follows: "It seems to me, that the only objects of the abstract sciences or of demonstration, are quantity and number. . . . All other enquiries of men regard only matter of fact and existence; and these are evidently incapable of demonstration. . . . When we run over libraries, persuaded of these principles, what havoc must we make? If we take in our hand any volume, of divinity or school metaphysics, for instance; let us ask, Does it contain any abstract reasoning concerning quantity or number? No. Does it contain any experimental reasoning concerning matter of fact and existence? No. Commit it then to the flames: for it can contain nothing but sophistry and illusion." We agree with this view of Hume, which says —translated into our terminology—that only the statements of mathematics and empirical science have sense, and that all other statements are without sense.

But now it may perhaps be objected: "How about your own statements? In consequence of your view your own writings, including this book, would be without sense, for they are neither mathematical nor empirical, that is, verifiable by experience." What answer can be given to this objection? What is the character of my statements and in general of the statements of logical analysis? This question is decisive for the consistency of the view which has been explained here.

An answer to the objection is given by Wittgenstein in his book *Tractatus Logico-Philosophicus*. This author has developed most radically the view that the statements of metaphysics are shown by logical analysis to be without sense. How does he reply to the criticism that in that case his own statements are also without sense? He replies by agreeing with it. He writes: *"The result of philosophy is not a number* of 'philosophical statements,' but to make statements clear" (p. 77). "My statements are elucidatory in this way: he who understands me finally recognizes them as senseless, when he has climbed out through them, on them, over them. (He must so to speak throw away the ladder after he has climbed up on it.) He must surmount these statements; then he sees the world rightly. Whereof one cannot speak, thereof one must be silent" (p. 189).

I, as well as my friends in the Vienna Circle, owe much to Wittgenstein, especially as to the analysis of metaphysics. But on the point just mentioned I cannot agree with him. In the first place, he seems to me to be inconsistent in what he does. He tells us that one cannot make philosophical statements and that whereof one cannot speak, thereof one must be silent; and then instead of keeping silent, he writes a whole philosophical book. Secondly, I do not agree with his assertion that all his statements are quite as much without sense as metaphysical statements are. My opinion is that a great number of his statements (unfortunately not all of them) have in fact sense; and that the same is true for all statements of logical analysis.

It will be the purpose of the following chapters to give reasons for this positive answer to the question about the character of philosophical statements, to show a way of formulating the results of logical analysis, a way not exposed to the objection mentioned, and thus to exhibit an *exact method of philosophy*.

XI

HANS HAHN

Hans Hahn (1879-1934) was one of the founders of the Vienna Circle. Influenced by Mach and later by Russell and Whitehead, especially by their *Principia Mathematica,* he lectured on mathematics at the University of Vienna. He also introduced Wittgenstein's *Tractatus Logico-Philosophicus* to the members of the Vienna Circle.

Hahn's essay, "Logic, Mathematics and Knowledge of Nature" (1933) centers on the problem of the status of logical and mathematical truth. Traditional rationalism explains knowledge in this area as *a priori* intuition of certain universal features of reality, for example, that nothing can both be what it is and not what it is at the same time in the same respect. Traditional empiricism construes this knowledge as highly validated generalizations about the world. For Hahn, as well as for all the logical positivists, neither explanation will do. The alternative solution, which reconciles the positivist commitment to empiricism with the belief in the universally valid character of logic and mathematics, is that logic and mathematics are tautologies, and hence say nothing about the world. As Hahn sums it up in his essay:

"We must distinguish two kinds of statements: those which say something about facts and those which merely express the way in which the rules which govern the application of words to facts depend upon each other. Let us call statements of the latter kind *tautologies:* they say nothing about objects and are for this very reason certain, universally valid, irrefutable by observation; whereas the statements of the former kind are not certain and are refutable by observation. The logical laws of contradiction and of the excluded middle are tautologies, likewise, e.g., the statement 'nothing is both red and blue.'"

220

Hahn's solution, derived as it was from Wittgenstein's doctrine of logical truths as truth-value tautologies, in one variant or another, was commonly adopted by analytic philosophers until very recent years.

Since Quine's "Two Dogmas of Empiricism" (1951), this view has been less popular among philosophers who are otherwise in sympathy with the basic aims of the logical positivists.

Logic, Mathematics and Knowledge of Nature[1]

I

Even a cursory glance at the statements of physics shows that they are obviously of a very diverse character. There are statements like "if a stretched string is plucked, a tone is heard" or "if a ray of sunlight is passed through a glass prism, then a colored band, interspersed with dark lines, is visible on a screen placed behind the prism," which can be tested at any time by observation. We also find statements like "the sun contains hydrogen," "the satellite of Sirius has a density of about 60,000," "a hydrogen atom consists of a positively charged nucleus around which a negatively charged electron revolves," which cannot by any means be tested by immediate observation but which are made only on the basis of theoretical considerations and likewise are testable only with the help of theoretical considerations. And thus we are confronted by the urgent question: what is the relationship between *observation* and *theory* in physics—and not just in physics, but in science generally. For there is but one science, and wherever there is scientific investigation it proceeds ultimately according to the same methods; only we see everything with the greatest clarity in the case of physics, because it is the most advanced, neatest, most scientific of all the sciences. And in physics, indeed, the interaction of observation and theory is especially pronounced, even officially recognized by the institution of special professorships for experimental physics and for theoretical physics.

Now, presumably the usual conception is roughly speaking the following: we have two sources of knowledge, by means of which

1. From *Logik, Mathematik und Naturerkennen* (Vienna: Gerold & Co., 1933), Sections 1-4, second volume of the series entitled *"Einheitswissenschaft."* Translated by Arthur Pap. Reprinted by permission of Van Stockum and Zoon, 'S-Gravenhage, Netherlands.

we comprehend "the world," "the reality" in which we are "placed": *experience,* or *observation* on the one hand, and *thinking* on the other. For example, one is engaged in experimental physics or in theoretical physics according to one's using the one or the other of these sources of knowledge in physics.

Now, in philosophy we find a time-honored controversy about these two sources of knowledge, which parts of our knowledge derive from observation, are "a posteriori," and which derive from thinking, are "a priori"? Is one of these sources of knowledge superior to the others, and if so, which?

From the very beginning philosophy has raised doubts about the reliability of *observation* (indeed, these doubts are perhaps the source of all philosophy). It is quite understandable that such doubts arose: they spring from the belief that sense-perception is frequently deceptive. At sunrise or at sunset the snow on distant mountains appears red, but "in reality" it is surely white! A stick which is immersed in water appears crooked, but "in reality" it is surely straight! If a man recedes from me, he appears smaller and smaller to me, but surely he does not change size "in reality"!

Now, although all the phenomena to which we have been referring have long since been accounted for by physical theories, so that nobody any longer regards them as deceptions caused by sense-perception, the consequences which flow from this primitive, long discarded conception still exert a powerful influence. One says: if observation is sometimes deceptive, perhaps it is always so! Perhaps everything disclosed by the senses is mere illusion! Everybody knows the phenomenon of dreams, and everybody knows how difficult it is at times to decide whether a given experience was "real life" or "a mere dream." Perhaps, then, whatever we observe is merely a dream object! Everybody knows that hallucinations occur, and that they can be so vivid that the subject cannot be dissuaded from taking his hallucination for reality. Perhaps then, whatever we observe is only a hallucination! If we look through appropriately polished lenses, everything appears distorted; who knows whether perhaps we do not always, unknowingly, look at the world as it were through distorting glasses, and therefore see everything distorted, different from what it really is! This is one of the basic themes of the philosophy of Kant.

But let us return to antiquity. As we said, the ancients believed that they were frequently deceived by observation. But nothing of this kind ever happened in the case of thought: there were plenty of *delusions of sense,* but no *delusions of thought!* And thus, as confidence in observation got shaken, the belief may have arisen that *thinking* is a method of knowledge which is absolutely superior to observation, indeed the only reliable method of knowledge: observation discloses mere appearance, thought alone grasps true being.

This, "rationalistic," doctrine that thinking is a source of knowledge which surpasses observation, that it is indeed the only reliable source of knowledge, has remained dominant from the climax of Greek philosophy until modern times. I cannot even intimate what peculiar fruits matured on the tree of such knowledge. At any rate, they proved to have extraordinarily little nourishing value; and thus the "empiricist" reaction, originating in England, slowly gained the upper hand, supported by the tremendous success of modern natural science—the philosophy which teaches that observation is superior to thought, indeed is the only source of knowledge: *nihil est in intellectu, quot non prius fuerit in sensu;* in English: "nothing is in the intellect which was not previously in the senses."

But at once this empiricism faces an apparently insuperable difficulty: how is it to account for the real validity of logical and mathematical statements? Observation discloses to me only the transient, it does not reach beyond the observed; there is no bond that would lead from one observed fact to another, that would compel future observations to have the same result as those already made. The laws of logic and mathematics, however, claim *absolutely universal* validity: that the door of my room is now closed, I know by observation; next time I observe it it may be open. That heated bodies expand, I know by observation; yet the very next observation may show that some heated body does not expand; but that two and two make four, holds not only for the case in which I verify it by counting I know with certainty that it holds always and everywhere. Whatever I know by observation could be otherwise: the door of my room might have been open now, I can easily imagine it; and I can easily imagine that a body does not expand on being heated; but two and two could not occasionally make five, I cannot imagine in any way what it would be like for twice two to equal five.

The conclusion seems inevitable: since the propositions of logic and mathematics have absolutely universal validity, are apodeictically certain, since it must be as they say and cannot be otherwise, these propositions cannot be derived from experience. In view of the tremendous importance of logic and mathematics in the system of our knowledge, empiricism, therefore, seems to be irrevocably refuted. To be sure, in spite of all this the older empiricists have attempted to found logic and mathematics upon experience. According to them we

LOGIC, MATHEMATICS AND KNOWLEDGE OF NATURE

now believe that something must be this way and cannot be otherwise simply because the relevant experience is so old and the relevant observations have been repeated innumerable times. On this view, therefore, it is entirely conceivable that, just as an observation might show that a heated body does not expand, two and two might sometimes make five. This is alleged to have escaped our notice so far because it happens with such extraordinary rarity, like finding a piece of four-leaved clover which for superstitious people is a sign of good luck, an occurrence which is not so very rare—how much more promise of fortune would there be in the discovery of a case where two and two make five! One can safely say that on closer sight these attempts to derive logic and mathematics from experience are fundamentally unsatisfactory, and it is doubtful whether anybody seriously holds this view today.

Rationalism and empiricism having thus, as it were, suffered shipwreck—rationalism, because its fruits lacked nourishing value, empiricism, because it could not do justice to logic and mathematics—*dualistic* conceptions gained the upper hand, with the view that thinking and observation are equally legitimate sources of knowledge which are both indispensable to our comprehension of the world and play a distinctive role in the system of our knowledge. *Thought* grasps the most general laws of all being, as formulated perhaps in logic and mathematics; *observation* provides the detailed filling of this framework. As regards the limits set to the two sources of knowledge, opinions diverge.

Thus it is, for instance, disputed whether geometry is *a priori* or *a posteriori*, whether it is based on pure thinking or on experience. And the same dispute is encountered in connection with the most fundamental physical laws, e.g. the law of inertia, the laws of the conservation of mass and energy, the law of attraction of masses: all of them have already been acclaimed as *a priori*, as necessities of thought, by various philosophers—but always after they had been established and well confirmed as empirical laws in physics. This was bound to lead to a skeptical attitude, and as a matter of fact there is probably a prevalent tendency among physicists to regard the framework which can be grasped by pure thinking as being as wide and general as possible, and to acknowledge experience as the source of our knowledge of everything that is somehow concrete.

The usual conception, then, may be described roughly as follows: from experience we learn certain facts, which we formulate as "laws of nature"; but since we grasp by means of thought the most general lawful connections (of a logical and mathematical character) that pervade reality, we can control nature on the basis of facts disclosed by observation to a much larger extent than it has actually been observed. For we know in addition that anything which can be deduced from observed facts by application of logic and mathematics must be found to exist. According to this view, the experimental physicist provides knowledge of laws of nature by direct observation. The theoretical physicist thereafter enlarges this knowledge tremendously by thinking, in such a way that we are in a position also to assert propositions about processes that occur far from us in space and time and about processes which, on account of their magnitude or minuteness, are not directly observable but which are connected with what is directly observed by the most general laws of being, grasped by thought, the laws of logic and mathematics. This view seems to be strongly supported by numerous discoveries that have been made with the help of theory, like—to mention just some of the best known—the calculation of the position of the planet Neptune by Leverrier, the calculation of electric waves by Maxwell, the calculation of the bending of light rays in the gravitational field of the sun by Einstein and the calculation of the redshift in the solar spectrum, also by Einstein.

Nevertheless we are of the opinion that this view is entirely untenable. For on closer analysis it appears that the function of thought is immeasurably more modest than the one ascribed to it by this theory. The idea that thinking is an instrument for learning more about the world than has been observed, for acquiring knowledge of something that has absolute validity always and everywhere in the world, an instrument for grasping general laws of all being, seems to us wholly mystical. Just how should it come to pass that we could predict the necessary outcome of an observation before having made it? Whence should our thinking derive an executive power, by which it could compel an observation to have this rather than that result? Why should that which compels our thoughts also compel the course of nature? One would have to believe in some miraculous pre-established harmony between the course of our thinking and the course of nature, an idea which is highly mystical and ultimately theological.

There is no way out of this situation except a return to a purely *empiricist* standpoint, to the view that observation is the only source of knowledge of facts: there is no *a priori* knowledge about matters of fact, *there is no "material" a priori*. However, we shall have to avoid the error committed by earlier empiricists, that of interpreting the propositions of logic and mathematics as mere facts of experience. We must look out for a different interpretation of logic and mathematics.

II

Let us begin with logic. The old conception of logic is approximately as follows: logic is the account of the most universal properties of things, the account of those properties which are common to all things; just as ornithology is the science of birds, zoology the science of all animals, biology the science of all living beings, so logic is the science of *all* things, the science of being as such. If this were the case, it would remain wholly unintelligible whence logic derives its certainty. For we surely do not know all things. We have not observed everything and hence we cannot know how everything behaves.

Our thesis, on the contrary, asserts: logic does not by any means treat of the totality of things, it does not treat of objects at all but *only of our way of speaking about objects;* logic is first generated by language. The certainty and universal validity, or better, the irrefutability of a proposition of logic derives just from the fact that it says nothing about objects of any kind.

Let us clarify the point by an example. I talk about a well-known plant: I describe it, as is done in botanical reference books, in terms of the number, color and form of its blossom leaves, its calyx leaves, its stamina, the shape of its leaves, its stem, its root, etc., and I make the stipulation: let us call any plant of this kind "snow rose," but let us also call it "helleborus niger." Thereupon I can pronounce with absolute certainty the universally valid proposition: "every snow rose is a helleborus niger." It is certainly valid, always and everywhere; it is not refutable by any sort of observation; but it says nothing at all about facts. I learn nothing from it about the plant in question, when it is in bloom, where it may be found, whether it is common or rare. It tells me nothing about the plant; it cannot be disconfirmed by any observation. This is the basis of its certainty and universal validity. The statement merely expresses a convention concerning the way we wish to talk about the plant in question.

Similar considerations apply to the principles of logic. Let us make the point with reference to the two most famous laws of logic: the law of contradiction and the law of the excluded middle. Take, for example, colored objects. We learn, by training as I am tempted to say, to apply the designation "red" to some of these objects, and we stipulate that the designation "not red" be applied to all other objects. On the basis of this stipulation we now can assert with absolute certainty the proposition that there is no object to which both the designation "red" and the designation "not red" is applied. It is customary to formulate this briefly by saying that nothing is both red and not red. This is the law of contradiction. And since we have stipulated that the designation "red" is to be applied to some objects and the designation "not red" to *all* other objects, we can likewise pronounce with absolute certainty the proposition: everything is either designated as "red" or as "not red," which it is customary to formulate briefly by saying that everything is either red or not red. This is the law of the excluded middle. These two propositions, the law of contradiction and the law of the excluded middle, say nothing at all about objects of any kind. They do not tell me of any of them whether they are red or not red, which color they have, or anything else. They merely stipulate a method for applying the designations "red" and "not red" to objects, i.e. they prescribe a *method of speaking about things*. And their universal validity and certainty, their irrefutability, just derives from the fact that they say nothing at all about objects.

The same is to be said of all the other principles of logic. We shall presently return to this point. But first let us insert another consideration. We have previously maintained that there can be no material *a priori*, i.e. no *a priori* knowledge about matters of fact. For we cannot know the outcome of an observation before the latter takes place. We have made clear to ourselves that no material *a priori* is contained in the laws of contradiction and of excluded middle, since they say nothing about facts. There are those, however, who would perhaps admit that the nature of the laws of logic is as described, yet would insist that there is a material *a priori* elsewhere, e.g. in the statement "nothing is both red and blue" (of course what is meant is: at the same time and place) which is alleged to express real *a priori* knowledge about the nature of things. Even before having made any observation, they say, one can predict with absolute certainty that it will not disclose a thing which is both blue and red; and it is maintained that such *a priori* knowledge is obtained by "eidetic insight" or an intuitive grasp of the essence of colors. If one desires to adhere to our thesis that there is no kind of material *a priori*, one must somehow face statements like "nothing is both blue and red." I want to attempt this in a few suggestive words, though they cannot by any means do full justice to this problem which is not easy. It surely is correct that we can say with complete certainty before having made any observations: the latter will not show that a thing is both blue and red—just as we can say with complete certainty that no observation will yield the result that a thing is both red and not red, or that a snow rose is not a helleborus niger. The first statement, however, is not a case of a material *a priori* any more than the second and third. Like the statements "every snow rose is a helleborus niger":

and "nothing is both red and not red," the statement "nothing is both blue and red" says nothing at all about the nature of things; it likewise refers only to our proposed manner of speaking about objects, of applying designations to them. Earlier we said: there are some objects that we call "red," every other object we call "not red," and from this we derive the laws of contradiction and excluded middle. Now we say: some objects we call "red," some *other* objects we call "blue," and *other* objects again we call "green," etc. But if it is in this way that we ascribe color designations to objects, then we can say with certainty in advance: in this procedure no object is designated both as "red" and as "blue," or more briefly: no object is both red and blue. The reason why we can say this with certainty is that we have regulated the ascription of color designations to objects in just this way.

We see, then, that there are two totally different kinds of statements: those which really say something about objects, and those which do not say anything about objects but only stipulate rules for speaking about objects. If I ask "what is the color of Miss Erna's new dress?" and get the answer "Miss Erna's new dress is not both red and blue (all over)," then no information about this dress has been given to me at all. I have been made no wiser by it. But if I get the answer "Miss Erna's new dress is red," then I have received some genuine information about the dress.

Let us clarify this distinction in terms of one more example. A statement which really says something about the objects which it mentions, is the following: "If you heat this piece of iron up to 800°, it will turn red, if you heat it up to 1300°, it will turn white." What makes the difference between this statement and the statements cited above, which say nothing about facts? The application of temperature designations to objects is *independent* of the application of color designations, whereas the color designations "red" and "not red," or "red" and "blue" are applied to objects in *mutual dependence*. The statements "Miss Erna's new dress is either red or not red" and "Miss Erna's new dress is not both red and blue" merely express this dependence, hence make no assertion about that dress, and are for that reason absolutely certain and irrefutable. The above statement about the piece of iron, on the other hand, relates independently given designations, and therefore really says something about that piece of iron and is for just that reason not certain nor irrefutable by observation.

The following example may make the difference between these two kinds of statements particularly clear. If someone were to tell me: "I raised the temperature of this piece of iron to 800° but it did not turn red," then I would test his assertion; the result of the test may be that he was lying, or that he was the victim of an illusion, but perhaps it would turn out that—contrary to my previous beliefs—there are cases where a piece of iron heated to 800° does not become red-hot, and in that case I would just change my opinion about the reaction of iron to heating. But if someone tells me "I raised the temperature of this piece of iron to 800°, and this made it turn both red and not red" or "it became both red and white," then I will certainly make no test whatever. Nor will I say "he has told me a lie," or "he has become the victim of an illusion" and it is quite certain that I would not change my beliefs about the reaction of iron to heating. The point is—it is best to express it in language which any card player is familiar with—that the man has revoked: he has violated the rules in accordance with which we want to speak, and I shall refuse to speak with him any longer. It is as though one attempted in a game of chess to move the bishop orthogonally. In this case too, I would not make any tests, I would not change my beliefs about the behavior of things, but I would refuse to play chess with him any longer.

To sum up: we must distinguish two kinds of statements: those which say something about facts and those which merely express the way in which the rules which govern the application of words to facts depend upon each other. Let us call statements of the latter kind *tautologies:* they say nothing about objects and are for this very reason certain, universally valid, irrefutable by observation; whereas the statements of the former kind are not certain and are refutable by observation. The logical laws of contradiction and of the excluded middle are tautologies, likewise, e.g., the statement "nothing is both red and blue."

And now we maintain that in the same way all the other laws of logic are tautologies. Let us, therefore, return to logic once more in order to clarify the matter by an example. As we said, the designation "red" is applied to certain objects and the convention is adopted of applying the designation "not red" to any other object. It is this convention about the use of negation which is expressed by the laws of contradiction and of the excluded middle. Now we add the convention —still taking our examples from the domain of colors—that any object which is called "red" is also to be called "red or blue," "blue or red," "red or yellow," "yellow or red," etc., that every object which is called "blue," is also called "blue or red," "red or blue," "blue or yellow," "yellow or blue," etc., and so on. On the basis of this convention, we can again assert with complete certainty the proposition: "every red object is either red or blue." This is again a tautology. We do not speak about the objects, but only about our manner of talking about them.

If once more we remind ourselves of the way in which the designations "red," "not red," "blue," "red or blue," etc. are applied to objects, we can moreover assert with complete certainty and irrefutability: everything to which both designations "red or blue" and "not red" are applied, is also designated as "blue"—which is usually put more briefly: if a thing is red or blue and not red, then it is blue. Which is again a tautology. No information about the nature of things is contained in it, it only expresses the sense in which the logical words "not" and "or" are used.

Thus we have arrived at something fundamental: our conventions regarding the use of the words "not" and "or" is such that in asserting the two propositions "object A is either red or blue" and "object A is not red," I have implicitly already asserted "object A is blue." This is the essence of so-called *logical deduction*. It is not, then, in any way based on real connections between states of affairs, which we apprehend in thought. On the contrary, it has nothing at all to do with the nature of things, but derives from our manner of speaking about things. A person who refused to recognize logical deduction would not thereby manifest a different belief from mine about the behavior of things, but he would refuse to speak about things according to the same rules as I do. I could not convince him, but I would have to refuse to speak with him any longer, just as I should refuse to play chess with a partner who insisted on moving the bishop orthogonally.

What logical deduction accomplishes, then, is this: it makes us aware of all that we have implicitly asserted—on the basis of conventions regarding the use of language—in asserting a system of propositions, just as, in the above example, "object A is blue" is implicitly asserted by the assertion of the two propositions "object A is red or blue" and "object A is not red."

In saying this we have already suggested the answer to the question, which naturally must have forced itself on the mind of every reader who has followed our argument: if it is really the case that the propositions of logic are tautologies, that they say nothing about objects, what purpose does logic serve?

The logical propositions which were used as illustrations derived from conventions about the use of the words "not" and "or" (and it can be shown that the same holds for all the propositions of so-called propositional logic). Let us, then, first ask for what purpose the words "not" and "or" are introduced into language. Presumably the reason is that we are not ominiscient. If I am asked about the color of the dress worn by Miss Erna yesterday, I may not be able to remember its color. I cannot say whether it was red or blue or green; but perhaps I will be able to say at least "it was not yellow." Were I omniscient, I should know its color. There would be no need to say "it was not yellow"; I could say "it was red." Or again: my daughter has written to me that she received a cocker-spaniel as a present. As I have not seen it yet, I do not know its color; I cannot say "it is black" nor "it is brown"; but I *am* able to say "it is black or brown." Were I omniscient, I could do without this "or" and could say immediately "it is brown."

Thus logical propositions, though being purely tautologous, and logical deductions, though being nothing but tautological transformations, have significance for us because we are not omniscient. Our language is so constituted that in asserting such and such propositions we implicitly assert such and such other propositions—but we do not see immediately all that we have implicitly asserted in this manner. It is only logical deduction that makes us conscious of it. I assert, e.g., the propositions "the flower which Mr. Smith wears in his buttonhole, is either a rose or a carnation," "if Mr. Smith wears a carnation in his buttonhole, then it is white," "the flower which Mr. Smith wears in his buttonhole is not white." Perhaps I am not consciously aware that I have implicitly asserted also "the flower which Mr. Smith wears in his buttonhole is a rose"; but logical deduction brings it to my consciousness. To be sure, this does not mean that I know whether the flower which Mr. Smith wears in his buttonhole really is a rose; if I notice that it is not a rose, then I must not maintain my previous assertions —otherwise I sin against the rules of speaking, I revoke.

III

If I have succeeded in clarifying somewhat the role of logic, I may now be quite brief about the role of *mathematics*. The propositions of mathematics are of exactly the same kind as the propositions of logic: they are tautologous, they say nothing at all about the objects we want to talk about, but concern only the manner in which we want to speak of them. The reason why we can assert apodeictically with universal validity the proposition: $2 + 3 = 5$, why we can say even before any observations have been made, and can say it with complete certainty, that it will not turn out that $2 + 3 = 7$, is that by "$2 + 3$" we mean the same as by "5"—just as we mean the same by "helleborus niger" as by "snow rose." For this reason no botanical investigation, however subtle, could disclose that an instance of the species "snow rose" is not a *helleborus niger*. We become aware of meaning the same by "$2 + 3$" and by "5," by going back to the meanings of "2," "3," "5," "$+$," and making tautological transformations until we just see that "$2 + 3$" means the same as "5." It is such successive tautological transformation that is meant by "calculating"; the operations of addition and multiplication which are learnt in school are directives for such tautological transformation; every mathematical proof is a succession of such tautological transformations. Their utility, again, is due to the fact that, for example, we do not by any means see immediately that we mean by "24×31" the same as by "744"; but if we calculate the product "24×31," then we transform it step by step, in such a way that in each individual transformation we recognize that on the basis of the conventions regarding the use of the signs involved (in this case numerals and the signs "$+$" and "$\times$") what we mean after the transformation is still the same as what we meant before it, until finally we become consciously aware of meaning the same by "744" as by "24×31."

To be sure, the proof of the tautological character of mathematics is not yet complete in all details. This is a difficult and arduous task; yet we have no doubt that the belief in the tautological character of mathematics is essentially correct.

There has been prolonged opposition to the interpretation of mathematical statements as tautologies; Kant contested the tautological character of mathematics emphatically, and the great mathematician Henri Poincaré, to whom we are greatly indebted also for philosophical criticism, went so far as to argue that since mathematics cannot possibly be a huge tautology, it must somewhere contain an *a priori* principle. Indeed, at first glance it is difficult to believe that the whole of mathematics, with its theorems that it cost such labor to establish, with its results that so often surprise us, should admit of being resolved into tautologies. But there is just one little point which this argument overlooks: it overlooks the fact that we are not omniscient. An omniscient being, indeed, would at once know everything that is implicitly contained in the assertion of a few propositions. It would know immediately that on the basis of the conventions concerning the use of the numerals and the multiplication sign, "24×31" is synonymous with "744." An omniscient being has no need for logic and mathematics. We ourselves, however, first have to make ourselves conscious of this by successive tautological transformations, and hence it may prove quite surprising to us that in asserting a few propositions we have implicitly also asserted a proposition which seemingly is entirely different from them, or that we do mean the same by two complexes of symbols which are externally altogether different.

IV

And now let us be clear what a world-wide difference there is between our conception and the traditional—perhaps one may say: platonizing—conception, according to which the world is made in accordance with the laws of logic and mathematics ("God is perennially doing mathematics"), and our thinking, a feeble reflection of God's omniscience, is an instrument given to us for comprehending the eternal laws of the world. No! Our thinking cannot give insight into any sort of reality. It cannot bring us information of any fact in the world. It only refers to the manner in which we speak about the world. All it can do is to transform tautologically what has been said. There is no possibility of piercing through the sensible world disclosed by observation to a "world of true being": any metaphysics is impossible! Impossible, not because the task is too difficult for our human thinking, but because it is meaningless, because every attempt to do metaphysics is an attempt to speak in a way that contravenes the agreement as to how we wish to speak, comparable to the attempt to capture the queen (in a game of chess) by means of an orthogonal move of the bishop.

Let us return now to the problem which was our point of departure: what is the relationship between observation and theory in physics? We said that the usual view was roughly this: experience teaches us the validity of certain laws of nature, and since our thinking gives us insight into the most general laws of all being, we know that likewise anything which is deducible from these laws of nature by means of logical and mathematical reasoning must be found to exist. We see now that this view is untenable; for thinking does not grasp any sort of laws of being. Never and nowhere, then, can thought supply us with knowledge about facts that goes beyond the observed. But what, then, should we say about the discoveries made by means of theory on which, as we pointed out, the usual view so strongly relies for its support? Let us ask ourselves, e.g., what was involved in the computation of the position of the planet Neptune by Leverrier! Newton noticed that the familiar motions, celestial as well as terrestrial, can be well described in a unified way by the assumption that between any two mass points a force of attraction is exerted which is proportional to their masses and inversely proportional to the square of their distance. And it is because this assumption enables us to give a satisfactory description of the familiar motions, that he *made* it, i.e. he asserted tentatively, as an hypothesis, the law of gravitation: between any two mass points there is a force of attraction which is proportional to their masses and inversely proportional to the square of their distance. He could not pronounce this law as a *certainty*, but only as an hypothesis. For nobody can know that such is really the behavior of every pair of mass points —nobody can observe all mass points. But having asserted the law of gravitation, one has implicitly asserted many other propositions, that is, all propositions which are deducible from the law of gravitation (together with data immediately derivable from observation) by calculation and logical inference. It is the task of theoretical physicists and astronomers to make us conscious of everything we implicitly assert along with the law of gravitation. And Leverrier's calculations made people aware that the assertion of the law of gravitation implies that at a definite time and definite place in the heavens a hitherto unknown planet must be visible. People looked and actually saw that new planet —the hypothesis of the law of gravitation was confirmed. But it was not Leverrier's calculation that proved that this planet existed, but the looking, the observation. This observation could just as well have had a different result. It could just as well have happened that nothing was visible at the computed place in the heavens—in which case the law of gravitation would not have been confirmed and one would have begun to doubt whether it is really a suitable hypothesis for the description of the observable motions. Indeed, this is what actually happened later: in asserting the law of gravitation, one implicitly asserts that at a certain time the planet Mercury must be visible at a certain place in the heavens. Whether it would actually be visible at that time at that place, only observation could disclose; but observations showed that it was not visible at exactly the required position in the heavens. And what happened? They said: since in asserting the law of gravitation we implicitly assert propositions which are not true, we cannot maintain the hypothesis of the law of gravitation. Newton's theory of gravitation was replaced by Einstein's.

It is not the case, then, that we know through experience that certain laws of nature are valid, and—since by our thinking we grasp the most general laws of all being—therefore also know that whatever is deducible from these laws by reasoning must exist. On the contrary, the situation is this: there is not a single law of nature which we know to be valid; the laws of nature are *hypotheses* which we assert tentatively. But in asserting such laws of nature we implicitly assert also many other propositions, and it is the task of thinking to make us conscious of the implicitly asserted propositions. So long, now, as these implicitly asserted propositions, to the extent that they are about the directly observable, are confirmed by observation, these laws of nature are confirmed and we adhere to them; but if these implicitly asserted propositions are not confirmed by observation, then the laws of nature have not been confirmed and are replaced by others.

XII

C. L. STEVENSON

CHARLES STEVENSON (*b.* 1908) is Professor of Philosophy at the University of Michigan. Educated at Harvard and Cambridge universities, he has written one of the important books in ethics in the twentieth century, *Ethics and Language* (1944). He has also contributed important papers in aesthetics.

Stevenson's "The Emotive Meaning of Ethical Terms" (1937) is a refined variant on the emotive or expressive theory of ethical judgments advanced by the logical positivists. According to the emotive theory, value judgments in general and moral judgments in particular do not state any facts and may hence be said to be descriptively meaningless. Their function is not cognitive but rather the expression or evoking of emotion. G. E. Moore, according to this view, was right in rejecting the various earlier definitions of "good," but he was mistaken in thinking that "good" refers to any quality at all.

Stevenson, accepting the basic distinction between the cognitive and the emotive, contrasts the descriptive and the dynamic uses of words. Words, he points out, can be used to inform or to arouse feelings; and the meaning of a word can be construed as the psychological causes and effects with which its utterance tends to be associated. "This is good," consequently, does more than to express or to evince emotion. It subtly compels in that its power to command is implicit, whereas "I like this; do so as well," although close in meaning to "This is good," renders the command explicit. Ethical judgments function more as quasi-imperatives than as expressions or evocations of emotions. Though only hinted at in this essay, Stevenson later developed this important deviation from the early logical positivist conception of language.

The Emotive Meaning of Ethical Terms[1]

I

Ethical questions first arise in the form "Is so and so good?" or "Is this alternative better than that?" These questions are difficult partly because we don't quite know what we are seeking. We are asking, "Is there a needle in that haystack?" without even knowing just what a needle is. So the first thing to do is to examine the questions themselves. We must try to make them clearer, either by defining the terms in which they are expressed, or by any other method that is available.

The present paper is concerned wholly with this preliminary step of making ethical questions clear. In order to help answer the question "Is X good?" we must *substitute* for it a question which is free from ambiguity and confusion.

It is obvious that in substituting a clearer question we must not introduce some utterly different kind of question. It won't do (to take an extreme instance of a prevalent fallacy) to substitute for "Is X good?" the question "Is X pink with yellow trimmings?" and then point out how easy the question really is. This would beg the original question, not help answer it. On the other hand, we must not expect the substituted question to be strictly "identical" with the original one. The original question may embody hypostatization, anthropomorphism, vagueness, and all the other ills to which our ordinary discourse is subject. If our substituted question is to be clearer, it must remove these ills. The questions will be identical only in the sense that a child is identical with the man he later becomes. Hence we must not demand that the substitution strike us, on immediate introspection, as making no change in meaning.

Just how, then, must the substituted question be related to the original? Let us assume (inaccurately) that it must result from re-

1. This article first appeared in *Mind*, 1937. It is reprinted by the kind permission of Professor Stevenson and Yale University Press.

placing "good" by some set of terms which define it. The question then resolves itself to this: How must the defined meaning of "good" be related to its original meaning?

I answer that it must be *relevant*. A defined meaning will be called "relevant" to the original meaning under these circumstances: Those who have understood the definition must be able to say all that they then want to say by using the term in the defined way. They must never have occasion to use the term in the old, unclear sense. (If a person did have to go on using the word in the old sense, then to this extent his meaning would not be clarified, and the philosophical task would not be completed.) It frequently happens that a word is used so confusedly and ambiguously that we must give it *several* defined meanings, rather than one. In this case only the whole set of defined meanings will be called "relevant," and any one of them will be called "partially relevant." This is not a rigorous treatment of *relevance*, by any means; but it will serve for the present purposes.

Let us now turn to our particular task—that of giving a relevant definition of "good." Let us first examine some of the ways in which others have attempted to do this.

The word "good" has often been defined in terms of *approval*, or similar psychological attitudes. We may take as typical examples: "good" means *desired by me* (Hobbes); and "good" means *approved by most people* (Hume, in effect).[2] It will be convenient to refer to definitions of this sort as "interest theories," following Mr. R. B. Perry, although neither "interest" nor "theory" is used in the most usual way.

Are definitions of this sort relevant?

It is idle to deny their *partial* relevance. The most superficial inquiry will reveal that "good" is exceedingly ambiguous. To maintain that "good" is *never* used in Hobbes's sense, and never in Hume's, is only to manifest an insensitivity to the complexities of language. We must recognize, perhaps, not only these senses, but a variety of similar ones, differing both with regard to the kind of interest in question, and with regard to the people who are said to have the interest.

But this is a minor matter. The essential question is not whether interest theories are *partially* relevant, but whether they are *wholly* relevant. This is the only point for intelligent dispute. Briefly: Granted that some senses of "good" may relevantly be defined in terms of

---

2. [The author has requested that the following note be added here: For a more adequate treatment of Hume's views see my *Ethics and Language* (Yale University Press, 1944), Chap. XII, Sect. 5. In the present paper the references to Hume are to be taken as references to the general *family* of definitions of which Hume's is typical; but Hume's own definition is somewhat different from any that is here specifically stated. Perhaps the same should be said of Hobbes.]

interest, is there some *other* sense which is *not* relevantly so defined? We must give this question careful attention. For it is quite possible that when philosophers (and many others) have found the question "Is X good?" so difficult, they have been grasping for this *other* sense of "good," and not any sense relevantly defined in terms of interest. If we insist on defining "good" in terms of interest, and answer the question when thus interpreted, we may be begging *their* question entirely. Of course this *other* sense of "good" may not exist, or it may be a complete confusion; but that is what we must discover.

Now many have maintained that interest theories are *far* from being completely relevant. They have argued that such theories neglect the very sense of "good" which is most vital. And certainly, their arguments are not without plausibility.

Only . . . what *is* this "vital" sense of "good"? The answers have been so vague, and so beset with difficulties, that one can scarcely determine.

There are certain requirements, however, with which this "vital" sense has been expected to comply—requirements which appeal strongly to our common sense. It will be helpful to summarize these, showing how they exclude the interest theories.

In the first place, we must be able sensibly to *disagree* about whether something is "good." This condition rules out Hobbes's definition. For consider the following argument: "This is good." "That isn't so; it's not good." As translated by Hobbes, this becomes: "I desire this." "That isn't so, for *I* don't." The speakers are not contradicting one another, and think they are, only because of an elementary confusion in the use of pronouns. The definition, "good" means *desired by my community,* is also excluded, for how could people from different communities disagree?[3]

In the second place, "goodness" must have, so to speak, a magnetism. A person who recognizes X to be "good" must *ipso facto* acquire a stronger tendency to act in its favor than he otherwise would have had. This rules out the Humian type of definition. For according to Hume, to recognize that something is "good" is simply to recognize that the majority approve of it. Clearly, a man may see that the majority approve of X without having, himself, a stronger tendency to favor it. This requirement excludes any attempt to define "good" in terms of the interest of people *other* than the speaker.[4]

In the third place, the "goodness" of anything must not be verifiable solely by use of the scientific method. "Ethics must not be psy-

3. See G. E. Moore's *Philosophical Studies,* pp. 332-334.
4. See G. C. Field's *Moral Theory,* pp. 52, 56-57.

chology." This restriction rules out all of the traditional interest theories, without exception. It is so sweeping a restriction that we must examine its plausibility. What are the methodological implications of interest theories which are here rejected?

According to Hobbes's definition, a person can prove his ethical judgments, with finality, by showing that he is not making an introspective error about his desires. According to Hume's definition, one may prove ethical judgments (roughly speaking) by taking a vote. *This* use of the empirical method, at any rate, seems highly remote from what we usually accept as proof, and reflects on the complete relevance of the definitions which imply it.

But aren't there more complicated interest theories which are immune from such methodological implications? No, for the same factors appear; they are only put off for a while. Consider, for example, the definition: "X is good" means *most people would approve of X if they knew its nature and consequences.* How, according to this definition, could we prove that a certain X was good? We should first have to find out, empirically, just what X was like, and what its consequences would be. To this extent the empirical method, as required by the definition, seems beyond intelligent objection. But what remains? We should next have to discover whether most people would approve of the sort of thing we had discovered X to be. This couldn't be determined by popular vote—but only because it would be too difficult to explain to the voters, beforehand, what the nature and consequences of X really were. Apart from this, voting would be a pertinent method. We are again reduced to counting noses, as a *perfectly final* appeal.

Now we need not scorn voting entirely. A man who rejected interest theories as irrelevant might readily make the following statement: "If I believed that X would be approved by the majority, when they knew all about it, I should be strongly *led* to say that X was good." But he would continue: *"Need* I say that X was good, under the circumstances? Wouldn't my acceptance of the alleged 'final proof' result simply from my being democratic? What about the more aristocratic people? They would simply say that the approval of most people, even when they knew all about the object of their approval, simply had nothing to do with the goodness of anything, and they would probably add a few remarks about the low state of people's interests." It would indeed seem, from these considerations, that the definition we have been considering has presupposed democratic ideals from the start; it has dressed up democratic propaganda in the guise of a definition.

The omnipotence of the empirical method, as implied by interest theories and others, may be shown unacceptable in a somewhat different way. Mr. G. E. Moore's familiar objection about the open question is chiefly pertinent in this regard. No matter what set of scientifically knowable properties a thing may have (says Moore, in effect), you will find, on careful introspection, that it is an open question to ask whether anything having these properties is *good*. It is difficult to believe that this recurrent question is a totally confused one, or that it seems open only because of the ambiguity of "good." Rather, we must be using some sense of "good" which is not definable, relevantly, in terms of anything scientifically knowable. That is, the scientific method is not sufficient for ethics.[5]

These, then, are the requirements with which the "vital" sense of "good" is expected to comply: (1) goodness must be a topic for intelligent disagreement; (2) it must be "magnetic"; and (3) it must not be discoverable solely through the scientific method.

II

Let us now turn to my own analysis of ethical judgments. First let me present my position dogmatically, showing to what extent I vary from tradition.

I believe that the three requirements, given above, are perfectly sensible; that there is some *one* sense of "good" which satisfies all three requirements; and that no traditional interest theory satisfies them all. But this does not imply that "good" must be explained in terms of a Platonic Idea, or of a Categorical Imperative, or of an unique, unanalyzable property. On the contrary, the three requirements can be met by a *kind* of interest theory. *But we must give up a presupposition which all the traditional interest theories have made.*

Traditional interest theories hold that ethical statements are *descriptive* of the existing state of interests—that they simply *give information* about interests. (More accurately, ethical judgments are said to describe what the state of interests is, was, or will be, or to indicate what the state of interests *would* be under specified circumstances.) It is this emphasis on description, on information, which leads to their incomplete relevance. Doubtless there is always *some* element of description in ethical judgments, but this is by no means all. Their major use is not to indicate facts, but to *create an influence*. Instead of merely describing people's interests, they *change* or *intensify*

---

5. See G. E. Moore's *Principia Ethica,* Chap. i. I am simply trying to preserve the spirit of Moore's objection, and not the exact form of it.

them. They *recommend* an interest in an object, rather than state that the interest already exists.

For instance: When you tell a man that he oughtn't to steal, your object isn't merely to let him know that people disapprove of stealing. You are attempting, rather, to get *him* to disapprove of it. Your ethical judgment has a quasi-imperative force which, operating through suggestion, and intensified by your tone of voice, readily permits you to begin to *influence,* to *modify,* his interests. If in the end you do not succeed in getting *him* to disapprove of stealing, you will feel that you've failed to convince him that stealing is wrong. You will continue to feel this, even though he fully acknowledges that you disapprove of it, and that almost everyone else does. When you point out to him the consequences of his actions—consequences which you suspect he already disapproves of—these *reasons* which support your ethical judgment are simply a means of facilitating your influence. If you think you can change his interests by making vivid to him how others will disapprove of him, you will do so; otherwise not. So the consideration about other people's interest is just an additional means you may employ, in order to move him, and is not a part of the ethical judgment itself. Your ethical judgment doesn't merely describe interests to him, it directs his very interests. The difference between the traditional interest theories and my view is like the difference between describing a desert and irrigating it.

Another example: A munition maker declares that war is a good thing. If he merely meant that he approved of it, he would not have to insist so strongly, nor grow so excited in his argument. People would be quite easily convinced that he approved of it. If he merely meant that most people approved of war, or that most people would approve of it if they knew the consequences, he would have to yield his point if it were proved that this wasn't so. But he wouldn't do this, nor does consistency require it. He is not *describing* the state of people's approval; he is trying to *change* it by his influence. If he found that few people approved of war, he might insist all the more strongly that it was good, for there would be more changing to be done.

This example illustrates how "good" may be used for what most of us would call bad purposes. Such cases are as pertinent as any others. I am not indicating the *good* way of using "good." I am not influencing people, but am describing the way this influence sometimes goes on. If the reader wishes to say that the munition maker's influence is bad—that is, if the reader wishes to awaken people's disapproval of the man, and to make him disapprove of his own actions

—I should at another time be willing to join in this undertaking. But this is not the present concern. I am not using ethical terms, but am indicating how they *are* used. The munition maker, in his use of "good," illustrates the persuasive character of the word just as well as does the unselfish man who, eager to encourage in each of us a desire for the happiness of all, contends that the supreme good is peace.

Thus ethical terms are *instruments* used in the complicated interplay and readjustment of human interests. This can be seen plainly from more general observations. People from widely separated communities have different moral attitudes. Why? To a great extent because they have been subject to different social influences. Now clearly this influence doesn't operate through sticks and stones alone; words play a great part. People praise one another, to encourage certain inclinations, and blame one another, to discourage others. Those of forceful personalities issue commands which weaker people, for complicated instinctive reasons, find it difficult to disobey, quite apart from fears of consequences. Further influence is brought to bear by writers and orators. Thus social influence is exerted, to an enormous extent, by means that have nothing to do with physical force or material reward. The ethical terms facilitate such influence. Being suited for use in *suggestion*, they are a means by which men's attitudes may be led this way or that. The reason, then, that we find a greater similarity in the moral attitudes of one community than in those of different communities is largely this: ethical judgments propagate themselves. One man says "This is good"; this may influence the approval of another person, who then makes the same ethical judgment, which in turn influences another person, and so on. In the end, by a process of mutual influence, people take up more or less the same attitudes. Between people of widely separated communities, of course, the influence is less strong; hence different communities have different attitudes.

These remarks will serve to give a general idea of my point of view. We must now go into more detail. There are several questions which must be answered: How does an ethical sentence acquire its power of influencing people—why is it suited to suggestion? Again, what has this influence to do with the *meaning* of ethical terms? And finally, do these considerations really lead us to a sense of "good" which meets the requirements mentioned in the preceding section?

Let us deal first with the question about *meaning*. This is far from an easy question, so we must enter into a preliminary inquiry about meaning in general. Although a seeming digression, this will prove indispensable.

III

Broadly speaking, there are two different *purposes* which lead us to use language. On the one hand we use words (as in science) to record, clarify, and communicate *beliefs*. On the other hand we use words to give vent to our feelings (interjections), or to create moods (poetry), or to incite people to actions or attitudes (oratory).

The first use of words I shall call "descriptive"; the second, "dynamic." Note that the distinction depends solely upon the *purpose* of the *speaker*.

When a person says "Hydrogen is the lightest known gas," his purpose *may* be simply to lead the hearer to believe this, or to believe that the speaker believes it. In that case the words are used descriptively. When a person cuts himself and says "Damn," his purpose is not ordinarily to record, clarify, or communicate any belief. The word is used dynamically. The two ways of using words, however, are by no means mutually exclusive. This is obvious from the fact that our purposes are often complex. Thus when one says "I want you to close the door," part of his purpose, ordinarily, is to lead the hearer to believe that he has this want. To that extent the words are used descriptively. But the major part of one's purpose is to lead the hearer to *satisfy* the want. To that extent the words are used dynamically.

It very frequently happens that the same sentence may have a dynamic use on one occasion, and may not have a dynamic use on another; and that it may have different dynamic uses on different occasions. For instance: A man says to a visiting neighbor, "I am loaded down with work." His purpose may be to let the neighbor know how life is going with him. This would *not* be a dynamic use of words. He may make the remark, however, in order to drop a hint. This *would* be dynamic usage (as well as descriptive). Again, he may make the remark to arouse the neighbor's sympathy. This would be a *different* dynamic usage from that of hinting.

Or again, when we say to a man, "Of course you won't make those mistakes any more," we *may* simply be making a prediction. But we are more likely to be using "suggestion," in order to encourage him and hence *keep* him from making mistakes. The first use would be descriptive; the second, mainly dynamic.

From these examples it will be clear that we can't determine whether words are used dynamically or not, merely by reading the dictionary —even assuming that everyone is faithful to dictionary meanings. Indeed, to know whether a person is using a word dynamically, we must note his tone of voice, his gestures, the general circumstances under which he is speaking, and so on.

We must now proceed to an important question: What has the dynamic use of words to do with their *meaning?* One thing is clear —we must not define "meaning" in a way that would make meaning vary with dynamic usage. If we did, we should have no use for the term. All that we could say about such "meaning" would be that it is very complicated, and subject to constant change. So we must certainly distinguish between the dynamic use of words and their meaning.

It doesn't follow, however, that we must define "meaning" in some non-psychological fashion. We must simply restrict the psychological field. Instead of identifying meaning with *all* the psychological causes and effects that attend a word's utterance, we must identify it with those that it has a *tendency* (causal property, dispositional property) to be connected with. The tendency must be of a particular kind, moreover. It must exist for all who speak the language; it must be persistent; and must be realizable more or less independently of determinate circumstances attending the word's utterance. There will be further restrictions dealing with the interrelation of words in different contexts. Moreover, we must include, under the psychological responses which the words tend to produce, not only immediately introspectable experiences, but *dispositions* to react in a given way with appropriate stimuli. I hope to go into these matters in a subsequent paper. Suffice it now to say that I think "meaning" may be thus defined in a way to include "propositional" meaning as an important kind. Now a word may *tend* to have causal relations which in fact it sometimes doesn't; and it may sometimes have causal relations which it *doesn't tend* to have. And since the tendency of words which constitutes their meaning must be of a particular kind, and may include, as responses, dispositions to reactions, of which any of *several* immediate experiences may be a sign, then there is nothing surprising in the fact that words have a permanent meaning, in spite of the fact that the immediately introspectable experiences which attend their usage are so highly varied.

When "meaning" is defined in this way, meaning will not include dynamic use. For although words are sometimes accompanied by dynamic purposes, they do not *tend* to be accompanied by them in the way above mentioned. E.g., there is no tendency realizable independently of the determinate circumstances under which the words are uttered.

There will be a kind of meaning, however, in the sense above defined, which has an intimate relation to dynamic usage. I refer to "emotive" meaning (in a sense roughly like that employed by Ogden and Richards).[6] The emotive meaning of a word is a tendency of a

6. See *The Meaning of Meaning,* by C. K. Ogden and I. A. Richards. On p. 125, second edition, there is a passage on ethics which was the source of the ideas embodied in this paper.

word, arising through the history of its usage, to produce (result from) *affective* responses in people. It is the immediate aura of feeling which hovers about a word. Such tendencies to produce affective responses cling to words very tenaciously. It would be difficult, for instance, to express merriment by using the interjection "alas." Because of the persistence of such affective tendencies (among other reasons) it becomes feasible to classify them as "meanings."

Just *what* is the relation between emotive meaning and the dynamic use of words? Let us take an example. Suppose that a man is talking with a group of people which includes Miss Jones, aged 59. He refers to her, without thinking, as an "old maid." Now even if his purposes are perfectly innocent—even if he is using the words purely descriptively —Miss Jones won't think so. She will think he is encouraging the others to have contempt for her, and will draw in her skirts, defensively. The man might have done better if instead of saying "old maid" he had said "elderly spinster." The latter words could have been put to the same descriptive use, and would not so readily have caused suspicions about the dynamic use.

"Old maid" and "elderly spinster" differ, to be sure, only in emotive meaning. From the example it will be clear that certain words, because of their emotive meaning, are suited to a certain kind of dynamic use —so well suited, in fact, that the hearer is likely to be misled when we use them in any other way. The more pronounced a word's emotive meaning is, the less likely people are to use it purely descriptively. Some words are suited to encourage people, some to discourage them, some to quiet them, and so on.

Even in these cases, of course, the dynamic purposes are not to be identified with any sort of meaning; for the emotive meaning accompanies a word much more persistently than do the dynamic purposes. But there is an important contingent relation between emotive meaning and dynamic purpose: the former assists the latter. Hence if we define emotively laden terms in a way that neglects their emotive meaning, we are likely to be confusing. *We lead people to think that the terms defined are used dynamically less often than they are.*

IV

Let us now apply these remarks in defining "good." This word may be used morally or non-morally. I shall deal with the non-moral usage almost entirely, but only because it is simpler. The main points of the analysis will apply equally well to either usage.

As a preliminary definition, let us take an inaccurate approximation. It may be more misleading than helpful, but will do to begin with. Roughly, then, the sentence "X is good" means *We like X*. ("We" includes the hearer or hearers.)

At first glance this definition sounds absurd. If used, we should expect to find the following sort of conversation: A. "This is good." B. "But I *don't* like it. What led you to believe that I did?" The unnaturalness of B's reply, judged by ordinary word-usage, would seem to cast doubt on the relevance of my definition.

B's unnaturalness, however, lies simply in this: he is assuming that "We like it" (as would occur implicitly in the use of "good") is being used descriptively. This won't do. When "We like it" is to take the place of "This is good," the former sentence must be used not purely descriptively, but dynamically. More specifically, it must be used to promote a very subtle (and for the non-moral sense in question, a very easily resisted) kind of *suggestion*. To the extent that "we" refers to the hearer, it must have the dynamic use, essential to suggestion, of leading the hearer to *make* true what is said, rather than merely to believe it. And to the extent that "we" refers to the speaker, the sentence must have not only the descriptive use of indicating belief about the speaker's interest, but the quasi-interjectory, dynamic function of giving direct expression to the interest. (This immediate expression of feelings assists in the process of suggestion. It is difficult to disapprove in the face of another's enthusiasm.)

For an example of a case where "We like this" is used in the dynamic way that "This is good" is used, consider the case of a mother who says to her several children, "One thing is certain, *we all like to be neat*." If she really believed this, she wouldn't bother to say so. But she is not using the words descriptively. She is *encouraging* the children to like neatness. By telling them that they like neatness, she will lead them to *make* her statement true, so to speak. If, instead of saying "We all like to be neat" in this way, she had said "It's a good thing to be neat," the effect would have been approximately the same.

But these remarks are still misleading. Even when "We like it" is used for suggestion, it isn't quite like "This is good." The latter is more subtle. With such a sentence as "This is a good book," for example, it would be practically impossible to use instead "We like this book." When the latter is used, it must be accompanied by so exaggerated an intonation, to prevent its becoming confused with a descriptive statement, that the force of suggestion becomes stronger, and ludicrously more overt, than when "good" is used.

The definition is inadequate, further, in that the definiens has been restricted to dynamic usage. Having said that dynamic usage was different from meaning, I should not have to mention it in giving the *meaning* of "good."

It is in connection with this last point that we must return to emotive meaning. The word "good" has a pleasing emotive meaning which fits it especially for the dynamic use of suggesting favorable interest. But the sentence "We like it" has no such emotive meaning. Hence my definition has neglected emotive meaning entirely. Now to neglect emotive meaning is likely to lead to endless confusions, as we shall presently see; so I have sought to make up for the inadequacy of the definition by letting the restriction about dynamic usage take the place of emotive meaning. What I should do, of course, is to find a definiens whose emotive meaning, like that of "good," simply does *lead* to dynamic usage.

Why didn't I do this? I answer that it isn't possible, if the definition is to afford us increased clarity. No two words, in the first place, have quite the same emotive meaning. The most we can hope for is a rough approximation. But if we seek for such an approximation for "good," we shall find nothing more than synonyms, such as "desirable" or "valuable"; and these are profitless because they do not clear up the connection between "good" and favorable interest. If we reject such synonyms, in favor of non-ethical terms, we shall be highly misleading. For instance: "This is good" has something like the meaning of "I *do* like this; do so as well." But this is certainly not accurate. For the imperative makes an appeal to the conscious efforts of the hearer. Of course he can't like something just by trying. He must be led to like it through suggestion. Hence an ethical sentence differs from an imperative in that it enables one to make changes in a much more subtle, less fully conscious way. Note that the ethical sentence centers the hearer's attention not on his interests, but on the object of interest, and thereby facilitates suggestion. Because of its subtlety, moreover, an ethical sentence readily permits counter-suggestion, and leads to the give and take situation which is so characteristic of arguments about values.

Strictly speaking, then, it is impossible to define "good" in terms of favorable interest if emotive meaning is not to be distorted. Yet it is possible to say that "This is good" is *about* the favorable interest of the speaker and the hearer or hearers, and that it has a pleasing emotive meaning which fits the words for use in suggestion. This is a rough description of meaning, not a definition. But it serves the same clarifying function that a definition ordinarily does; and that, after all, is enough.

A word must be added about the moral use of "good." This differs from the above in that it is about a different kind of interest. Instead of being about what the hearer and speaker *like,* it is about a stronger sort of approval. When a person *likes* something, he is pleased when it prospers, and disappointed when it doesn't. When a person *morally approves* of something, he experiences a rich feeling of security when it prospers, and is indignant, or "shocked" when it doesn't. These are rough and inaccurate examples of the many factors which one would have to mention in distinguishing the two kinds of interest. In the moral usage, as well as in the non-moral, "good" has an emotive meaning which adapts it to suggestion.

And now, are these considerations of any importance? Why do I stress emotive meanings in this fashion? Does the omission of them really lead people into errors? I think, indeed, that the errors resulting from such omissions are enormous. In order to see this, however, we must return to the restrictions, mentioned in section I, with which the "vital" sense of "good" has been expected to comply.

V

The first restriction, it will be remembered, had to do with disagreement. Now there is clearly some sense in which people disagree on ethical points; but we must not rashly assume that all disagreement is modelled after the sort that occurs in the natural sciences. We must distinguish between "disagreement in belief" (typical of the sciences) and "disagreement in interest." Disagreement in belief occurs when A believes p and B disbelieves it. Disagreement in interest occurs when A has a favorable interest in X, when B has an unfavorable one in it, and when neither is content to let the other's interest remain unchanged.

Let me give an example of disagreement in interest. A. "Let's go to a cinema to-night." B. "I don't want to do that. Let's go to the symphony." A continues to insist on the cinema, B on the symphony. This is disagreement in a perfectly conventional sense. They can't agree on where they want to go, and each is trying to redirect the other's interest. (Note that imperatives are used in the example.)

It is disagreement in *interest* which takes places in ethics. When C says "This is good," and D says "No, it's bad," we have a case of suggestion and counter-suggestion. Each man is trying to redirect the other's interest. There obviously need be no domineering, since each may be willing to give ear to the other's influence; but each is trying to move the other nonetheless. It is in this sense that they disagree. Those who argue that certain interest theories make no provision for disagreement have been misled, I believe, simply because the traditional theories, in leaving out emotive meaning, give the impression that ethical judgments are used descriptively only; and of course when judgments are used purely descriptively, the only disagreement that can arise is disagreement *in belief*. Such disagreement may be disagreement in belief *about* interests; but this is not the same as disagreement *in* interest. My definition doesn't provide for disagreement in belief about interests, any more than does Hobbes's; but that is no matter, for there is no reason to believe, at least on common-sense grounds, that this kind of disagreement exists. There is only disagreement *in* interest. (We shall see in a moment that disagreement in interest does not remove ethics from sober argument—that this kind of disagreement may often be resolved through empirical means.)

The second restriction, about "magnetism," or the connection between goodness and actions, requires only a word. This rules out *only* those interest theories which do *not* include the interest of the speaker, in defining "good." My account does include the speaker's interest; hence is immune.

The third restriction, about the empirical method, may be met in a way that springs naturally from the above account of disagreement. Let us put the question in this way: When two people disagree over an ethical matter, can they completely resolve the disagreement through empirical considerations, assuming that each applies the empirical method exhaustively, consistently, and without error?

I answer that sometimes they can, and sometimes they cannot; and that at any rate, even when they can, the relation between empirical knowledge and ethical judgments is quite different from the one which traditional interest theories seem to imply.

This can best be seen from an analogy. Let's return to the example where A and B couldn't agree on a cinema or a symphony. The example differed from an ethical argument in that imperatives were used, rather than ethical judgments; but was analogous to the extent that each person was endeavoring to modify the other's interest. Now how would these people argue the case, assuming that they were too intelligent just to shout at one another?

Clearly, they would give "reasons" to support their imperatives. A might say, "But you know, Garbo is at the Bijou." His hope is that

B, who admires Garbo, will acquire a desire to go to the cinema when he knows what play will be there. B may counter, "But Toscanini is guest conductor tonight, in an all-Beethoven program." And so on. Each supports his imperative ("*Let's* do so and so") by reasons which may be empirically established.

To generalize from this: disagreement in interest may be rooted in disagreement in belief. That is to say, people who disagree in interest would often cease to do so if they knew the precise nature and consequences of the object of their interest. To this extent disagreement in interest may be resolved by securing agreement in belief, which in turn may be secured empirically.

This generalization holds for ethics. If A and B, instead of using imperatives, had said, respectively, "It would be *better* to go to the cinema," and "It would be better to go to the symphony," the reasons which they would advance would be roughly the same. They would each give a more thorough account of the object of interest, with the purpose of completing the redirection of interest which was begun by the suggestive force of the ethical sentence. On the whole, of course, the suggestive force of the ethical statement merely exerts enough pressure to start such trains of reasons, since the reasons are much more essential in resolving disagreement in interest than the persuasive effect of the ethical judgment itself.

Thus the empirical method is relevant to ethics simply because our knowledge of the world is a determining factor to our interests. But note that empirical facts are not inductive grounds from which the ethical judgment problematically follows. (This is what traditional interest theories imply.) If someone said "Close the door," and added the reason "We'll catch cold," the latter would scarcely be called an inductive ground of the former. Now imperatives are related to the reasons which support them in the same way that ethical judgments are related to reasons.

Is the empirical method *sufficient* for attaining ethical agreement? Clearly not. For empirical knowledge resolves disagreement in interest only to the extent that such disagreement is rooted in disagreement in belief. Not all disagreement in interest is of this sort. For instance: A is of a sympathetic nature, and B isn't. They are arguing about whether a public dole would be good. Suppose that they discovered all the consequences of the dole. Isn't it possible, even so, that A will say that it's good, and B that it's bad? The disagreement in interest may arise not from limited factual knowledge, but simply from A's sympathy and B's coldness. Or again, suppose, in the above argument, that

A was poor and unemployed, and that B was rich. Here again the disagreement might not be due to different factual knowledge. It would be
due to the different social positions of the men, together with their
predominant self-interest.

When ethical disagreement is not rooted in disagreement in belief,
is there *any* method by which it may be settled? If one means by
"method" a *rational* method, then there is no method. But in any case
there is a "way." Let's consider the above example, again, where disagreement was due to A's sympathy and B's coldness. Must they end
by saying, "Well, it's just a matter of our having different tempera-
ments"? Not necessarily. A, for instance, may try to *change* the temperament of his opponent. He may pour out his enthusiasms in such
a moving way—present the sufferings of the poor with such appeal—
that he will lead his opponent to see life through different eyes. He
may build up, by the contagion of his feelings, an influence which will
modify B's temperament, and create in him a sympathy for the poor
which didn't previously exist. This is often the only way to obtain
ethical agreement, if there is any way at all. It is persuasive, not empirical or rational; but that is no reason for neglecting it. There is no
reason to scorn it, either, for it is only by such means that our personalities are able to grow, through our contact with others.

The point I wish to stress, however, is simply that the empirical
method is instrumental to ethical agreement only to the extent that
disagreement in interest is rooted in disagreement in belief. There is
little reason to believe that all disagreement is of this sort. Hence the
empirical method is not sufficient for ethics. In any case, ethics is not
psychology, since psychology doesn't endeavor to *direct* our interests;
it discovers facts about the ways in which interests are or can be
directed, but that's quite another matter.

To summarize this section: my analysis of ethical judgments meets
the three requirements for the "vital" sense of "good" that were mentioned in section I. The traditional interest theories fail to meet these
requirements simply because they neglect emotive meaning. This neglect
leads them to neglect dynamic usage, and the sort of disagreement that
results from such usage, together with the method of resolving the
disagreement. I may add that my analysis answers Moore's objection
about the open question. Whatever scientifically knowable properties a
thing may have, it *is* always open to question whether a thing having
these (enumerated) qualities is good. For to ask whether it is good is
to ask for *influence*. And whatever I may know about an object, I can
still ask, quite pertinently, to be influenced with regard to my interest
in it.

VI

And now, have I really pointed out the "vital" sense of "good"?

I suppose that many will still say "No," claiming that I have simply failed to set down *enough* requirements which this sense must meet, and that my analysis, like all others given in terms of interest, is a way of begging the issue. They will say: "When we ask 'Is X good?' we don't want mere influence, mere advice. We decidedly don't want to be influenced through persuasion, nor are we fully content when the influence is supported by a wide scientific knowledge of X. The answer to our question will, of course, modify our interests. But this is only because an unique sort of *truth* will be revealed to us—a truth which must be apprehended *a priori*. We want our interests to be guided by this truth, and by nothing else. To substitute for such a truth mere emotive meaning and suggestion is to conceal from us the very object of our search."

I can only answer that I do not understand. What is this truth to be *about?* For I recollect no Platonic Idea, nor do I know what to *try* to recollect. I find no indefinable property, nor do I know what to look for. And the "self-evident" deliverances of reason, which so many philosophers have claimed, seem, on examination, to be deliverances of their respective reasons only (if of anyone's) and not of mine.

I strongly suspect, indeed, that any sense of "good" which is expected both to unite itself in synthetic *a priori* fashion with other concepts, and to influence interests as well, is really a great confusion. I extract from this meaning the power of influence alone, which I find the only intelligible part. If the rest is confusion, however, then it certainly deserves more than the shrug of one's shoulders. What I should like to do is to *account* for the confusion—to examine the psychological needs which have given rise to it, and to show how these needs may be satisfied in another way. This is *the* problem, if confusion is to be stopped at its source. But it is an enormous problem, and my reflections on it, which are at present worked out only roughly, must be reserved until some later time.

I may add that if "X is good" is essentially a vehicle for suggestion, it is scarcely a statement which philosophers, any more than many other men, are called upon to make. To the extent that ethics predicates the ethical terms of anything, rather than explains their meaning, it ceases to be a reflective study. Ethical statements are social instruments. They are used in a co-operative enterprise in which we are mutually adjusting ourselves to the interests of others. Philosophers have a part in this, as do all men, but not the major part.

XIII

C. G. HEMPEL

CARL HEMPEL (*b.* 1905) was a member of the Berlin group of physicists, mathematicians, and philosophers, which was closely linked to the Vienna Circle and was led by Hans Reichenbach. In 1937 Hempel joined Carnap at the University of Chicago. From there he went to Queens College, New York, and then to Yale University, and he is at present Professor of Philosophy at Princeton University. Author of many articles, he has also written *Fundamentals of Concept Formation in Empirical Science* (Volume II, Number 7, of International Encyclopedia of Unified Science) and *Aspects of Scientific Explanation* (Free Press, 1965).

Historians and philosophers of history have frequently held that the writing of history is concerned with particular events, not with general laws that govern human behavior and affairs, which are the province of science. From this contention it has been inferred that general laws play no role in the writing of history.

Hempel, in "The Function of General Laws in History" (1942), repudiates this rejection of law in historiography. Historical explanations, along with interpretations and descriptions, are "explanation sketches," which must be filled in by further empirical research. History, therefore, is analogous to the natural sciences in that in both the determination of general laws "form an indispensable instrument of . . . research."

Hempel's thesis, provocative as it is, has elicited a number of articles and books in which historical explanation, it is argued, differs radically from scientific or from "explanation sketches." One of these books is William Dray, *Laws and Explanation in History* (1957).

The Function of General Laws in History[1]

1. It is a rather widely held opinion that history, in contradistinction to the so-called physical sciences, is concerned with the description of particular events of the past rather than with the search for general laws which might govern those events. As a characterization of the type of problem in which some historians are mainly interested, this view probably can not be denied; as a statement of the theoretical function of general laws in scientific historical research, it is certainly unacceptable. The following considerations are an attempt to substantiate this point by showing in some detail that general laws have quite analogous functions in history and in the natural sciences, that they form an indispensable instrument of historical research, and that they even constitute the common basis of various procedures which are often considered as characteristic of the social in contradistinction to the natural sciences.

By a general law, we shall here understand a statement of universal conditional form which is capable of being confirmed or disconfirmed by suitable empirical findings. The term "law" suggests the idea that the statement in question is actually well confirmed by the relevant evidence available; as this qualification is, in many cases, irrelevant for our purpose, we shall frequently use the term "hypothesis of universal form" or briefly "universal hypothesis" instead of "general law," and state the condition of satisfactory confirmation separately, if necessary. In the context of this paper, a universal hypothesis may be assumed to assert a regularity of the following type: In every case where an event of a specified kind C occurs at a certain place and time, an event of a specified kind E will occur at a place and time which is related in a specified manner to the place and time of the occurrence of the first event. (The symbols "C" and "E" have been chosen to suggest the terms "cause" and "effect," which are often, though by no means always, applied to events related by a law of the above kind.)

1. Reprinted by kind permission of the author and the editors from *The Journal of Philosophy*, XXXIX (1942).

2.1 The main function of general laws in the natural sciences is to connect events in patterns which are usually referred to as *explanation* and *prediction*.

The explanation of the occurrence of an event of some specific kind E at a certain place and time consists, as it is usually expressed, in indicating the causes or determining factors of E. Now the assertion that a set of events—say, of the kinds $C_1, C_2, \ldots, C_n$—have caused the event to be explained, amounts to the statement that, according to certain general laws, a set of events of the kinds mentioned is regularly accompanied by an event of kind E. Thus, the scientific explanation of the event in question consists of

(1) a set of statements asserting the occurrence of certain events $C_1, \ldots C_n$ at certain times and places,
(2) a set of universal hypotheses, such that
   (*a*) the statements of both groups are reasonably well confirmed by empirical evidence,
   (*b*) from the two groups of statements the sentence asserting the occurrence of event E can be logically deduced.

In a physical explanation, group (1) would describe the initial and boundary conditions for the occurrence of the final event; generally, we shall say that group (1) states the *determining conditions* for the event to be explained, while group (2) contains the general laws on which the explanation is based; they imply the statement that whenever events of the kind described in the first group occur, an event of the kind to be explained will take place.

Illustration: Let the event to be explained consist in the cracking of an automobile radiator during a cold night. The sentences of group (1) may state the following initial and boundary conditions: The car was left in the street all night. Its radiator, which consists of iron, was completely filled with water, and the lid was screwed on tightly. The temperature during the night dropped from 39° F. in the evening to 25° F. in the morning; the air pressure was normal. The bursting pressure of the radiator material is so and so much. —Group (2) would contain empirical laws such as the following: Below 32° F., under normal atmospheric pressure, water freezes. Below 39.2° F., the pressure of a mass of water increases with decreasing temperature, if the volume remains constant or decreases; when the water freezes, the pressure again increases. Finally, this group would have to include a quantitative law concerning the change of pressure of water as a function of its temperature and volume.

From statements of these two kinds, the conclusion that the radiator cracked during the night can be deduced by logical reasoning; an explanation of the considered event has been established.

2.2 It is important to bear in mind that the symbols "E," "C," "C_1," "C_2," etc., which were used above, stand for kinds of properties of events, not for what is sometimes called individual events. For the object of description and explanation in every branch of empirical science is always the occurrence of an event of a certain *kind* (such as a drop in temperature by 14° F., an eclipse of the moon, a cell-division, an earthquake, an increase in employment, a political assassination) at a given place and time, or in a given empirical object (such as the radiator of a certain car, the planetary system, a specified historical personality, etc.) at a certain time.

What is sometimes called the complete description of an individual event (such as the earthquake of San Francisco in 1906 or the assassination of Julius Caesar) would require a statement of all the properties exhibited by the spatial region or the individual object involved, for the period of time occupied by the event in question. Such a task can never be completely accomplished.

A fortiori, it is impossible to explain an individual event in the sense of accounting for *all* its characteristics by means of universal hypotheses, although the explanation of what happened at a specified place and time may gradually be made more and more specific and comprehensive.

But there is no difference, in this respect, between history and the natural sciences: both can give an account of their subject-matter only in terms of general concepts, and history can "grasp the unique individuality" of its objects of study no more and no less than can physics or chemistry.

3. The following points result more or less directly from the above study of scientific explanation and are of special importance for the questions here to be discussed.

3.1 A set of events can be said to have caused the event to be explained only if general laws can be indicated which connect "causes" and "effect" in the manner characterized above.

3.2 No matter whether the cause-effect terminology is used or not, a scientific explanation has been achieved only if empirical laws of the kind mentioned under (2) in 2.1 have been applied.[2]

---

2. Maurice Mandelbaum, in his generally very clarifying analysis of relevance and causation in history (*The Problem of Historical Knowledge,* New York, 1938, Chs. 7, 8) seems to hold that there is a difference between the "causal analysis" or "causal explanation" of an event and the establishment of scientific laws governing it in the sense stated above. He argues that "scientific laws can only be formulated on the basis of causal analysis," but that "they are not substitutes for full causal explanations" (*loc. cit.,* p. 238). For the reasons outlined above, this distinction does not appear to be justified: every "causal explanation" is an "explanation by scientific laws"; for in no other way than by reference to empirical laws can the assertion of a causal connection between certain events be scientifically substantiated.

3.3 The use of universal empirical hypotheses as explanatory principles distinguishes genuine from pseudo-explanation, such as, say, the attempt to account for certain features of organic behavior by reference to an entelechy, for whose functioning no laws are offered, or the explanation of the achievements of a given person in terms of his "mission in history," his "predestined fate," or similar notions. Accounts of this type are based on metaphors rather than laws; they convey pictorial and emotional appeals instead of insight into factual connections; they substitute vague analogies and intuitive "plausibility" for deduction from testable statements and are therefore unacceptable as scientific explanations.

Any explanation of scientific character is amenable to objective checks; these include

(a) an empirical test of the sentences which state the determining conditions;

(b) an empirical test of the universal hypotheses on which the explanation rests;

(c) an investigation of whether the explanation is logically conclusive in the sense that the sentence describing the event to be explained follows from the statements of groups (1) and (2).

4. The function of general laws in *scientific prediction* can now be stated very briefly. Quite generally, prediction in empirical science consists in deriving a statement about a certain future event (for example, the relative position of the planets to the sun, at a future date) from (1) statements describing certain known (past or present) conditions (for example, the positions and momenta of the planets at a past or present moment), and (2) suitable general laws (for example, the laws of celestial mechanics). Thus, the logical structure of a scientific prediction is the same as that of a scientific explanation, which has been described in 2.1. In particular, prediction no less than explanation throughout empirical science involves reference to universal empirical hypotheses.

The customary distinction between explanation and prediction rests mainly on a pragmatical difference between the two: While in the case of an explanation, the final event is known to have happened, and its determining conditions have to be sought, the situation is reversed in the case of a prediction: here, the initial conditions are given, and their "effect"—which, in the typical case, has not yet taken place—is to be determined.

In view of the structural equality of explanation and prediction, it may be said that an explanation as characterized in 2.1 is not complete unless it might as well have functioned as a prediction: If the final event can be derived from the initial conditions and universal hypotheses stated in the explanation, then it might as well have been predicted, before it actually happened, on the basis of a knowledge of the initial conditions and the general laws. Thus, e.g., those initial conditions and general laws which the astronomer would adduce in explanation of a certain eclipse of the sun are such that they might also have served as a sufficient basis for a forecast of the eclipse before it took place.

However, only rarely, if ever, are explanations stated so completely as to exhibit this predictive character (which the test referred to under (c) in 3.3 would serve to reveal). Quite commonly, the explanation offered for the occurrence of an event is incomplete. Thus, we may hear the explanation that a barn burnt down "because" a burning cigarette was dropped in the hay, or that a certain political movement has spectacular success "because" it takes advantage of widespread racial prejudices. Similarly, in the case of the broken radiator, the customary way of formulating an explanation would be restricted to pointing out that the car was left in the cold, and the radiator was filled with water. —In explanatory statements like these, the general laws which confer upon the stated conditions the character of "causes" or "determining factors" are completely omitted (sometimes, perhaps, as a "matter of course"), and, furthermore, the enumeration of the determining conditions of group (1) is incomplete; this is illustrated by the preceding examples, but even by the earlier analysis of the broken-radiator case: as a closer examination would reveal, even that much more detailed statement of determining conditions and universal hypotheses would require amplification in order to serve as a sufficient basis for the deduction of the conclusion that the radiator broke during the night.

In some instances, the incompleteness of a given explanation may be considered as inessential. Thus, e.g., we may feel that the explanation referred to in the last example could be made complete if we so desired; for we have reasons to assume that we know the kind of determining conditions and of general laws which are relevant in this context.

Very frequently, however, we encounter "explanations" whose incompleteness can not simply be dismissed as inessential. The methodological consequences of this situation will be discussed later (especially in 5.3 and 5.4).

5.1 The preceding considerations apply to *explanation in history* as well as in any other branch of empirical science. Historical explanation, too, aims at showing that the event in question was not "a matter of chance," but was to be expected in view of certain antecedent or simultaneous conditions. The expectation referred to is not prophecy or divination, but rational scientific anticipation which rests on the assumption of general laws.

If this view is correct, it would seem strange that while most historians do suggest explanations of historical events, many of them deny the possibility of resorting to any general laws in history. It is, however, possible to account for this situation by a closer study of explanation in history, as may become clear in the course of the following analysis.

5.2 In some cases, the universal hypotheses underlying a historical explanation are rather explicitly stated, as is illustrated by the italicized passages in the following attempt to explain the tendency of government agencies to perpetuate themselves and to expand [italics the author's]:

As the activities of the government are enlarged, more people develop a vested interest in the continuation and expansion of governmental functions. *People who have jobs do not like to lose them; those who are habituated to certain skills do not welcome change; those who have become accustomed to the exercise of a certain kind of power do not like to relinquish their control—* if anything, *they want to develop greater power and correspondingly greater prestige.* . . .

Thus, government offices and bureaus, once created, in turn institute drives, not only to fortify themselves against assault, but to enlarge the scope of their operations.[3]

Most explanations offered in history or sociology, however, fail to include an explicit statement of the general regularities they presuppose; and there seem to be at least two reasons which account for this:

First, the universal hypotheses in question frequently relate to individual or social psychology, which somehow is supposed to be familiar to everybody through his everyday experience; thus, they are tacitly taken for granted. This is a situation quite similar to that characterized in 4.

Second, it would often be very difficult to formulate the underlying assumptions explicitly with sufficient precision and at the same time in such a way that they are in agreement with all the relevant empirical evidence available. It is highly instructive, in examining the adequacy of a suggested explanation, to attempt a reconstruction of the universal hypotheses on which it rests. Particularly, such terms as "hence," "therefore," "consequently," "because," "naturally," "obviously," etc., are often indicative of the tacit presupposition of some general law: they are used to tie up the initial conditions with the event to be explained; but that the latter was "naturally" to be expected as a "con-

3. Donald W. McConnell, *Economic Behavior,* New York, 1939; pp. 894-895.

sequence" of the stated conditions follows only if suitable general laws are presupposed. Consider, for example, the statement that the Dust Bowl farmers migrate to California "because" continual drought and sandstorms render their existence increasingly precarious, and because California seems to them to offer so much better living conditions. This explanation rests on some such universal hypothesis as that populations will tend to migrate to regions which offer better living conditions. But it would obviously be difficult accurately to state this hypothesis in the form of a general law which is reasonably well confirmed by all the relevant evidence available. Similarly, if a particular revolution is explained by reference to the growing discontent, on the part of a large part of the population, with certain prevailing conditions, it is clear that a general regularity is assumed in this explanation, but we are hardly in a position to state just what extent and what specific form the discontent has to assume, and what the environmental conditions have to be, to bring about a revolution. Analogous remarks apply to all historical explanations in terms of class struggle, economic or geographic conditions, vested interests of certain groups, tendency to conspicuous consumption, etc.: All of them rest on the assumption of universal hypotheses[4] which connect certain characteristics of individual or group ilfe with others; but in many cases, the content of the hypotheses which are tacitly assumed in a given explanation can be reconstructed only quite approximately.

5.3 It might be argued that the phenomena covered by the type of explanation just mehtioned are of a statistical character, and that therefore only probability hypotheses need to be assumed in their explanation, so that the question as to the "underlying general laws" would be based on a false premise. And indeed, it seems possible and justifiable to construe certain explanations offered in history as based on the assumption of probability hypotheses rather than of general "deterministic" laws, i.e., laws in the form of universal conditions. This claim may be extended to many of the explanations offered in other fields of empirical science as well. Thus, e.g., if Tommy comes down with the measles two weeks after his brother, and if he has not been in the company of other persons having the measles, we accept the explanation that he caught the disease from his brother. Now, there is a general hypothesis underlying this explanation; but it can hardly be said to be

---

4. What is sometimes, misleadingly, called an explanation by means of a certain *concept* is, in empirical science, actually an explanation in terms of *universal hypotheses* containing that concept. "Explanations" involving concepts which do not function in empirically testable hypotheses—such as "entelechy" in biology, "historic destination of a race" or "self-unfolding of absolute reason" in history—are mere metaphors without cognitive content.

a general law to the effect that any person who has not had the measles before will get them without fail if he stays in the company of somebody else who has the measles; that a contagion will occur can be asserted only with a high probability.

Many an explanation offered in history seems to admit of an analysis of this kind: if fully and explicitly formulated, it would state certain initial conditions, and certain probability hypotheses,[5] such that the occurrence of the event to be explained is made highly probable by the initial conditions in view of the probability hypotheses. But no matter whether explanations in history be construed as "causal" or as "probabilistic" in character, it remains true that in general the initial conditions and especially the universal hypotheses involved are not clearly indicated, and can not unambiguously be supplemented. (In the case of probability hypotheses, for example, the probability values involved will at best be known quite roughly.)

5.4 What the explanatory analyses of historical events offer is, then, in most cases not an explanation in one of the meanings developed above, but something that might be called an *explanation sketch*. Such a sketch consists of a more or less vague indication of the laws and initial conditions considered as relevant, and it needs "filling out" in order to turn into a full-fledged explanation. This filling-out requires further empirical research, for which the sketch suggests the direction. (Explanation sketches are common also outside of history; many explanations in psychoanalysis, for instance, illustrate this point.)

Obviously, an explanation sketch does not admit of an empirical test to the same extent as does a complete explanation; and yet, there is a difference between a scientifically acceptable explanation sketch and a pseudo-explanation (or a pseudo-explanation sketch). A scientifically acceptable explanation sketch needs to be filled out by more specific statements; but it points into the direction where these statemens are to be found; and concrete research may tend to confirm or to infirm those indications; i.e., it may show that the kind of initial conditions suggested are actually relevant; or it may reveal that factors of a quite different nature have to be taken into account in order to arrive at a satisfactory explanation.—The filling-out process required by an explanation sketch will, in general, assume the form of a gradually increasing precision of the formulations involved; but at any stage

5. E. Zilsel, in a very stimulating paper on "Physics and the Problem of Historico-Sociological Laws" (*Philosophy of Science,* Vol. 8, 1941, pp. 567-579), suggests that all specifically historical laws are of a statistical character similar to that of the "macro-laws" in physics. The above remarks, however, are not restricted to specifically historical laws since explanation in history rests to a large extent on non-historical laws (cf. section 8 of this paper).

of this process, those formulations will have some empirical import: it will be possible to indicate, at least roughly, what kind of evidence would be relevant in testing them, and what findings would tend to confirm them. In the case of non-empirical explanations or explanation sketches, on the other hand—say, by reference to the historical destination of a certain race, or to a principle of historical justice—the use of empirically meaningless terms makes it impossible even roughly to indicate the type of investigation that would have a bearing upon those formulations, and that might lead to evidence either confirming or infirming the suggested explanation.

5.5 In trying to appraise the soundness of a given explanation, one will first have to attempt to reconstruct as completely as possible the argument constituting the explanation or the explanation sketch. In particular, it is important to realize what the underlying explaining hypotheses are, and to judge of their scope and empirical foundation. A resuscitation of the assumptions buried under the gravestones "hence," "therefore," "because," and the like will often reveal that the explanation offered is poorly founded or downright unacceptable. In many cases, this procedure will bring to light the fallacy of claiming that a large number of details of an event have been explained when, even on a very liberal interpretation, only some broad characteristics of it have been accounted for. Thus, for example, the geographic or economic conditions under which a group lives may account for certain general features of, say, its art or its moral codes; but to grant this does not mean that the artistic achievements of the group or its system of morals has thus been explained in detail; for this would imply that from a description of the prevalent geographic or economic conditions alone, a detailed account of certain aspects of the cultural life of the group can be deduced by means of specifiable general laws.

A related error consists in singling out one of several important groups of factors which would have to be stated in the initial conditions, and then claiming that the phenomenon in question is "determined" by and thus can be explained in terms of that one group of factors.

Occasionally, the adherents of some particular school of explanation or interpretation in history will adduce, as evidence in favor of their approach, a successful historical prediction which was made by a representative of their school. But though the predictive success of a theory is certainly relevant evidence of its soundness, it is important to make sure that the successful prediction is in fact obtainable by means of the theory in question. It happens sometimes that the prediction is actually an ingenious guess which may have been influenced by the theoretical outlook of its author, but which can not be arrived at by means of his theory alone. Thus, an adherent of a quite metaphysical "theory" of history may have a sound feeling for historical developments and may be able to make correct predictions, which he will even couch in the terminology of his theory, though they could not have been attained by means of it. To guard against such pseudo-confirming cases would be one of the functions of test (c) in 3.3.

6. We have tried to show that in history no less than in any other branch of empirical inquiry, scientific explanation can be achieved only by means of suitable general hypotheses, or by theories, which are bodies of systematically related hypotheses. This thesis is clearly in contrast with the familiar view that genuine explanation in history is obtained by a method which characteristically distinguishes the social from the natural sciences, namely, *the method of empathetic understanding:* The historian, we are told, imagines himself in the place of the persons involved in the events which he wants to explain; he tries to realize as completely as possible the circumstances under which they acted, and the motives which influenced their actions; and by this imaginary self-identification with his heroes, he arrives at an understanding and thus at an adequate explanation of the events with which he is concerned.

This method of empathy is, no doubt, frequently applied by laymen and by experts in history. But it does not in itself constitute an explanation; it rather is essentially a heuristic device; its function is to suggest certain psychological hypotheses which might serve as explanatory principles in the case under consideration. Stated in crude terms, the idea underlying this function is the following: The historian tries to realize how he himself would act under the given conditions, and under the particular motivations of his heroes; he tentatively generalizes his findings into a general rule and uses the latter as an explanatory principle in accounting for the actions of the persons involved. Now, this procedure may sometimes prove heuristically helpful; but its use does not guarantee the soundness of the historical explanation to which it leads. The latter rather depends upon the factual correctness of the empirical generalizations which the method of understanding may have suggested.

Nor is the use of this method indispensable for historical explanation. A historian may, for example, be incapable of feeling himself into the rôle of a paranoiac historic personality, and yet he may well be able to explain certain of his actions; notably by reference to the principles of abnormal psychology. Thus, whether the historian is or is not in a position to identify himself with his historical hero, is irrelevant for the correctness of his explanation; what counts, is the soundness of the general hypotheses involved, no matter whether they were suggested by empathy or by a strictly behavioristic procedure. Much of the appeal of the "method of understanding" seems to be due to the fact that it tends to present the phenomena in question as some-how "plausible" or "natural" to us;[6] this is often done by means of attractively worded metaphors. But the kind of "understanding" thus conveyed must clearly be separated from scientific understanding. In history as anywhere else in empirical science, the explanation of a phe-nomenon consists in subsuming it under general empirical laws, and the criterion of its soundness is not whether it appeals to our imagina-tion, whether it is presented in suggestive analogies, or is otherwise made to appear plausible—all this may occur in pseudo-explanations as well—but exclusively whether it rests on empirically well confirmed as-sumptions concerning initial conditions and general laws.

7.1 So far, we have discussed the importance of general laws for explanation and prediction, and for so-called understanding in history. Let us now survey more briefly some other procedures of historical research which involve the assumption of universal hypotheses.

Closely related to explanation and understanding is the so-called *interpretation of historical phenomena* in terms of some particular approach or theory. The interpretations which are actually offered in history consist either in subsuming the phenomena in question under a scientific explanation or explanation sketch; or in an attempt to subsume them under some general idea which is not amenable to any empirical test. In the former case, interpretation clearly is explanation by means of universal hypotheses; in the latter, it amounts to a pseudo-explanation which may have emotive appeal and evoke vivid pictorial associations, but which does not further our theoretical under-standing of the phenomena under consideration.

7.2 Analogous remarks apply to the procedure of ascertaining the *"meaning"* of given historical events; its scientific import consists in determining what other events are relevantly connected with the event in question, be it as "causes," or as "effects"; and the statement of the relevant connections assumes, again, the form of explanations or explanation sketches which involve universal hypotheses; this will be seen more clearly in the subsequent section.

7.3 In the historical explanation of some social institutions great emphasis is laid upon an analysis of the *development* of the institution

---

6. For a criticism of this kind of plausibility, cf. Zilsel, *loc. cit.*, pp. 577-578, and sections 7 and 8 in the same author's "Problems of Empiricism," in *International Encyclopedia of Unified Science,* Vol. II, 8.

up to the stage under consideration. Critics of this approach have objected that a mere description of this kind is not a genuine explanation. This argument may be given a slightly different aspect in terms of the preceding reflections: A description of the development of an institution is obviously not simply a statement of *all* the events which temporally preceded it; only those events are meant to be included which are *"relevant"* to the formation of that institution. And whether an event is relevant to that development is not a question of the value attitude of the historian, but an objective question depending upon what is sometimes called a causal analysis of the rise of that institution.[7] Now, the causal analysis of an event consists in establishing an explanation for it, and since this requires reference to general hypotheses, so do assumptions about relevance, and, consequently, so does the adequate analysis of the historical development of an institution.

7.4 Similarly, the use of the notions of *determination* and of *dependence* in the empirical sciences, including history, involves reference to general laws.[8] Thus, e.g., we may say that the pressure of a gas depends upon its temperature and volume, or that temperature and volume determine the pressure, in virtue of Boyle's law. But unless the underlying laws are stated explicitly, the assertion of a relation of dependence or of determination between certain magnitudes or characteristics amounts at best to claiming that they are connected by some unspecified empirical law; and that is a very meager assertion indeed: If, for example, we know only that there is some empirical law connecting two metrical magnitudes (such as length and temperature of a metal bar), we can not even be sure that a change of one of the two will be accompanied by a change of the other (for the law may connect the same value of the "dependent" or "determined" magnitude with different values of the other), but only that with any specific

7. See the detailed and clear exposition of this point in M. Mandelbaum's book; *loc. cit.*, chs. 6-8.

8. According to Mandelbaum, history, in contradistinction to the physical sciences, consists "not in the formulation of laws of which the particular case is an instance, but in the description of the events in their actual determining relationships to each other; in seeing events as the products and producers of change" (*loc. cit.*, pp. 13-14). This is essentially a view whose untenability has been pointed out already by Hume; it is the belief that a careful examination of two specific events alone, without any references to similar cases and to general regularities, can reveal that one of the events produces or determines the other. This thesis does not only run counter to the scientific meaning of the concept of determination which clearly rests on that of general law, but it even fails to provide any objective criteria which would be indicative of the intended relationship of determination or production. Thus, to speak of empirical determination independently of any reference to general laws means to use a metaphor without cognitive content.

value of one of the variables, there will always be associated one and the same value of the other; and this is obviously much less than most authors mean to assert when they speak of determination or dependence in historical analysis.

Therefore, the sweeping assertion that economic (or geographic, or any other kind of) conditions "determine" the development and change of all other aspects of human society, has explanatory value only in so far as it can be substantiated by explicit laws which state just what kind of change in human culture will regularly follow upon specific changes in the economic (geographic, etc.) conditions. Only the establishment of concrete laws can fill the general thesis with scientific content, make it amenable to empirical tests, and confer upon it an explanatory function. The elaboration of such laws with as much precision as possible seems clearly to be the direction in which progress in scientific explanation and understanding has to be sought.

8. The considerations developed in this paper are entirely neutral with respect to the problem of *"specifically historical laws"*: neither do they presuppose a particular way of distinguishing historical from sociological and other laws, nor do they imply or deny the assumption that empirical laws can be found which are historical in some specific sense, and which are well confirmed by empirical evidence.

But it may be worth mentioning here that those universal hypotheses to which historians explicitly or tacitly refer in offering explanations, predictions, interpretations, judgments of relevance, etc., are taken from *various* fields of scientific research, in so far as they are not pre-scientific generalizations of everyday experiences. Many of the universal hypotheses underlying historical explanation, for instance, would commonly be classified as psychological, economical, sociological, and partly perhaps as historical laws; in addition, historical research has frequently to resort to general laws established in physics, chemistry, and biology. Thus, e.g., the explanation of the defeat of an army by reference to lack of food, adverse weather conditions, disease, and the like, is based on a—usually tacit—assumption of such laws. The use of tree rings in dating events in history rests on the application of certain biological regularities. Various methods of testing the authenticity of documents, paintings, coins, etc., make use of physical and chemical theories.

The last two examples illustrate another point which is relevant in this context: Even if a historian should propose to restrict his research to a *"pure description"* of the past, without any attempt at offering explanations, statements about relevance and determination, etc., he would continually have to make use of general laws. For the object of his studies would be the past—forever inaccessible to his direct examination. He would have to establish his knowledge by indirect methods: by the use of universal hypotheses which connect his present data with those past events. This fact has been obscured partly because some of the regularities involved are so familiar that they are not considered worth mentioning at all; and partly because of the habit of relegating the various hypotheses and theories which are used to ascertain knowledge about past events, to the "auxiliary sciences" of history. Quite probably, some of the historians who tend to minimize, if not to deny, the importance of general laws for history, are actuated by the feeling that only "genuinely historical laws" would be of interest for history. But once it is realized that the discovery of historical laws (in some specified sense of this very vague notion) would not make history methodologically autonomous and independent of the other branches of scientific research, it would seem that the problem of the existence of historical laws ought to lose some of its weight.

The remarks made in this section are but special illustrations of two broader principles of the theory of science: first, the separation of "pure description" and "hypothetical generalization and theory-construction" in empirical science is unwarranted; in the building of scientific knowledge the two are inseparably linked. And, second, it is similarly unwarranted and futile to attempt the demarcation of sharp boundary lines between the different fields of scientific research, and an autonomous development of each of the fields. The necessity, in historical inquiry, to make extensive use of universal hypotheses of which at least the overwhelming majority come from fields of research traditionally distinguished from history is just one of the aspects of what may be called the methodological unity of empirical science.

XIV

J. O. URMSON

JAMES O. URMSON (*b.* 1905), after teaching at Oxford and the University of St. Andrews, is at present Fellow of Corpus Christi College, Oxford. He is author of many articles on language, ethics, and aesthetics, in addition to his book *Philosophical Analysis* (1956).

Central to Logical Positivism was its doctrine of meaning: if a sentence is not verifiable and is not a truth-value tautology, it is cognitively meaningless. This doctrine ruled out a good deal of traditional philosophy. Only logic, mathematics, and the sciences could meet the positivist criterion. These three disciplines, however, it was held, are calculi, consisting of variables or constants and certain formation and transformation rules from which certain sentences can be constructed or derived. What, now, is the syntax of these calculi? The attempt to provide an answer to *this* question reconstituted itself as philosophical analysis. Philosophy became identified with analysis whose sole task is the systematic presentation of the logical syntax of the language of science. Carnap, more than any of the other positivists, worked out the details of this new program for analysis.

Urmson's *Philosophical Analysis* is a sustained critique of philosophical analysis as practiced by both the logical atomists and the logical positivists. The difference between them, as he sees it, is that the first is ontological, the second, not. Both, however, are subjected to rigorous scrutiny. In "Logical Positivism and Analysis" (reprinted below), Urmson summarizes, then rejects completely, the linguistic conception of analysis assumed in Logical Positivism.

Logical Positivism and Analysis[1]

The metaphysics of logical atomism and the conception of analysis which went with it had been, as we have seen, complementary. Roughly, the metaphysics had been the justification of the method of analysis, and the metaphysics had in turn determined the exact nature of the ideal to which analysis had to conform. It is important to realize that the logical positivists, while they rejected the metaphysics, took over the conception of analysis more or less complete. The actual practice of analysis went on always while the justification and characterization of it changed. Moore, after all, was neither a positivist nor an atomist, yet he practised the same sort of analysis as they did and was even regarded as the leading exponent of the technique. It was always obscurely felt that analysis, which overtly consisted in replacing one form of words by another with the same meaning, was a proper philosophical pursuit, and that there was good reason for preferring one form of words to another; it was only when it came to saying why analysis was a proper pursuit, why one form of words was preferable to another, that really serious differences arose. The atomists had given the justification that the new form of words better pictured the structure of reality; but that answer certainly could not be given by a positivist, though we may suspect that in fact this metaphysical view still had some power over him.

We must now, therefore, examine the accounts given by the positivists of the nature of analysis; we must see how they tried to show that analysis was a legitimate and, moreover, valuable activity without making any metaphysical presuppositions and without making any metaphysical statements. On a great deal there was virtual unanimity amongst the positivists, and it will be convenient to deal with that portion of their doctrine first. Then we must come to some questions which were of special difficulty for them, and at this point we shall notice some divergence of opinion.

---

1. From *Philosophical Analysis* (Oxford: Clarendon Press, 1956), Chap. 8. Reprinted by permission of the publishers.

We already know that the logical positivists, like Hume, claimed that all legitimate uses of language were either synthetic and *a posteriori*, i.e. empirical, or were tautologies. The empirical propositions were those of the natural sciences, understood to include the factual statements of everyday life; the tautologies are typically what we meet in the exact sciences such as mathematics. Wittgenstein had said, and the logical positivists agreed, that there were no special propositions of philosophy, metaphysical or otherwise. Philosophy was not a science alongside the natural sciences. Clearly therefore the philosopher does not make empirical statements. But analysis does not consist of empirical statements. The form of an analysis is the assertion of an equivalence between two expressions; we may say that 'The present King of France is bald' is equivalent to 'There is one and only one thing which, &c.', or that 'The average plumber earns £10 per week' is equivalent to 'The number of pounds earned each week by plumbers divided by the number of plumbers, &c.'. But a statement of an equivalence is, if correct, a tautology, if incorrect, a contradiction. So if a philosopher sticks to making analyses he will avoid either infringing on the preserves of natural science or attempting to make a special sort of philosophical statement. Philosophy is therefore to be identified with analysis. Analysis is the one and only legitimate activity of philosophers.

But the question now arises why analysis should be done. The logical atomist would have agreed that his analyses, if correct, had the verbal form of equivalences, but he said that the point of it was analysis of fact, the clarification of the structure and inter-relationships of facts, and thus of the world. But the logical positivists could not say this. Instead they simply denied any ulterior motive and claimed that philosophy was the analysis and clarification of language as such; or, since the purpose of a language is that we may make scientific statements, the clarification of the language of science.

Still conceiving a language to be a calculus with an added vocabulary—constants—to replace the variables of the calculus, the positivists envisaged their task in analysis as the exhibition in strings of tautologies of the structure of a language. There would be a set of sentences of simple form and containing only the basic vocabulary (such as the atomists had thought to picture basic facts) and out of them would be constructed the whole language of science; or to put the matter in reverse order, analysis would reduce the whole language of science to the basic elements out of which it was built. In the course of this analysis the relation between statements of observation, laws, hypotheses, and theories would be exhibited as would that of the more rarified, higher-order, concepts to the simpler ones. Most of the time of course the analyst would, in a less grandiose way, be attempting to straighten up the analysis of one portion of language at a comparatively high level; but Carnap, in his *Logische Aufbau der Welt*, went so far as to attempt to give a sketch of how the language of science could be analysed in terms of sentences containing only names of primitive experiences and the single relation *memory of similarity* (*Ähnlichkeitserinnerung*). If challenged for a reason for this activity the positivist claimed that apart from the intrinsic interest of his results two advantages were secured. First, an analysis of the language of science was likely to be of use to the scientist, especially in the frontier regions of progress—perhaps an earlier analysis would, for example, have revealed the ambiguity in the concept of simultaneity which it was left to Einstein to discover; this was a logical, not a physical discovery. Secondly, if we do not understand language thoroughly we are always liable to misuse it; in particular, we are liable to fall into metaphysics. Thus analysis will be a prophylactic against linguistic abuses. It can be no small thing to understand the tool of all sciences and all skills, and understanding of a language is achieved by analysis.

We have now added two principal theses of logical positivism to the rejection of metaphysics and the verification principle. First, philosophy is to be identified with analysis. This, of course, is not intended to deny that any but the most rigorous works will contain empirical statements about what other philosophers have said, about what the writer is going to discuss next, and so on. But these will be, strictly speaking, historical, not philosophical, sentences. Secondly, philosophy is nothing more and nothing less than the analysis of language; and since analysis is done in sets of equivalences, which are tautologies, philosophy is even to be equated with logic.

Thus the old activity of analysis can go on undisturbed. We can even continue to speak of logical constructions, since to say that *X*s are logical constructions out of *Y*s is but a way of saying that '*X*' is an incomplete symbol replaceable (though not simply replaceable) by '*Y*', i.e. it is in fact part of linguistic analysis and not really about *X*s and *Y*s at all. Though the positivist would now reject the atomists' account of the nature of analysis, Ayer, in his Preface to *Language, Truth and Logic*, was able to recognize even Moore's analysis as being the same task as he set himself. Thus the positivist who did not wish to break too finally with tradition could maintain that Hume in his analysis of causation, Berkeley in his analysis of physical objects, even Plato in, say, his analysis of knowledge in the *Theaetetus*, were doing philosophy as the positivists conceived it, even if they made mistakes of comparative detail in so doing and gave a wrong account of what they were doing. The business is still the old reductive analysis, even if it is under new management.

It might be thought that such a characterization of positivistic analysis embodied an illegitimate nostalgia, and was at least exaggerated. Not merely is a new rationale of analysis being given, but the new talk, when doing analysis, is of words, sentences, and the like —is talk about language, whereas the old analysis used metaphysical pseudo-concepts such as 'thing', 'fact', and the like. It was nonsensical, surely, according to the new régime, and that indicates a big difference. But as a matter of fact most positivists agreed that this difference was largely illusory, as can be shown by means of a new technical term evolved by Carnap in his *Logical Syntax of Language*. It is possible, said Carnap, to talk of language explicitly, by means of quotation marks. If one does so, then we have the formal mode of speech. But there is in ordinary language a device to enable us to talk about language without explicit mention of expressions and without the occurrence of quotation marks. This is the material mode of speech; and what it is can best be made clear by means of examples. Here is a collection of statements, all of which would be said by Carnap to be about language; those in the right-hand column will be so explicitly, and so in the formal mode of speech; those in the left-hand column will be in the material mode, and thus apparently about things other than words.

Material mode	*Formal mode*
A rose is a thing.	'Rose' is a thing-word (substantive, noun).
It is a fact that the rose is red.	'The rose is red' is a sentence (statement).
Redness is a quality.	'Red' is an adjective.
Five is a number.	'Five' is a numeral.

As we shall soon see, Carnap wished to use this distinction for purposes which did not satisfy all positivists; but most agreed in principle to it.

Thus the material mode of speech is a way of speaking which looks like talk about things but is in fact talk about words. If we accept this doctrine we can say that even formerly philosophers who apparently talked about facts, objects, and the like were talking about language, doing logical syntax, not talking metaphysics, even if they were sometimes not clear, or even positively mistaken, about what they were doing. It is only dangerous, not wrong, to use the material mode of speech. We are permitted, even by Carnap, to continue to use the material mode of speech, provided we do it very carefully and remember that we are doing so. He used it himself, not always too successfully. There are lots of statements in Carnap which certainly are neither empirical nor in the formal mode, and which we should presume are in the material mode; but they are very hard to translate, sometimes, into the formal mode.

Incidentally, Carnap thought that the existence of the material mode of speech was a potent source of metaphysics; philosophers, he considered, used the pseudo-concepts of the material mode (thing, quality, fact, &c.) as though they were genuine concepts. This metaphysical, nonsensical character could be brought out by attempting the translation into the formal mode which ought to be possible. He gave examples in *Logical Syntax of Language*. Thus Wittgenstein's famous mystical 'There is also the inexpressible' was translated into 'There are also words which are not words'. 'Some matters are beyond comprehension' would presumably become 'Some statements are not statements'. Of course a mere 'This matter is to me incomprehensible' goes intelligibly into the formal mode as 'I cannot understand this sentence'. This misuse of the material mode of speech was not, however, regarded as being by any means the only source of metaphysical error. There were other kinds of bad syntax into which we could fall.

That is the agreed part of the new rationale of analysis. Instead of clarifying the logical structure of the world by showing how all facts are complicated clusters of atomic, elementary, or basic facts, and exhibiting the logical structure of these facts and clusters, we now have a clarification of the structure of the language of science. And this clarification is achieved by showing how that language is built up out of the basic or protocol sentences, the logical derivation from which of all other kinds of sentence, including those containing the most complex concepts, must be exhibited and their epistemological relationships made clear. Language is still conceived of as truth-functional in character, and the most abstract of physical theories must therefore be shown to be reducible to basic, protocol statements, and to be validated by them.

But if we are clear what is to be done once we have our protocol statements, the question still remains how we are to identify the underived protocols among the mass of statements and which protocols are to be accepted and which are to be rejected. Now though there was disagreement among the positivists on the exact specifications of a basic protocol, just as there had been disagreement among the atomists on the exact specification of the basic propositions which pictured atomic facts, none the less they clearly wished to select as protocols those statements which had been selected as pictures of atomic facts by the atomists. The question was why these rather than others should be selected. Now Schlick, Ayer, and many other positivists answered substantially that sentences of this sort were to be accepted as protocols because direct reports of experience were of this type and that among protocols those which correctly recorded experience were to be accepted, the rest rejected. 'This is red' is the right sort of sentence to be a protocol because I might have an experience which could be recorded in those words, 'England is hypocritical' is not because it reports no direct experience; I choose between the possible protocols 'This is red' and 'This is .green' by seeing which correctly reports experience. Protocols are direct reports of the given and are justified with reference to the given. Whether these reports could be inaccurate, whether they were corrigible, was disputed even in this group, but their direct justification by experience was agreed. Without such a basis, it was maintained, the claim of logical positivism, alternatively styled logical empiricism, to be an empiricist position must be abandoned.

But this position was not acceptable to all positivists; notably Carnap and Neurath rejected it at the period we are now considering. Though the views of Carnap and Neurath are hardly part of the history of British philosophy, and few British philosophers, if any, followed them, this period of their views was such an instructive warning against an over-syntactical approach to philosophy, to British as to other philosophers, that we must consider what they had to say on this topic.

Let us consider the statement: 'Protocol statements are direct records of the given.' Is it a tautology? Surely not, if it is to serve the purpose for which it was intended. No doubt a protocol might be thus defined; but if one means by a protocol sentence a sentence from which other scientific sentences are logically derived but which is not itself derived from any other sentences, which is roughly the explanation usually given, and then, when asked how science gains its protocol sentences, answers that science accepts as protocols those sentences which are records of direct experience, this cannot be a tautology if it is to count as an answer at all. Is it then a statement of empirical science? But while a psychologist might talk of the causal relationship between the uttering of certain sentences and experience, this is a statement of a different kind; and philosophers have no business to be making empirical statements. It seems, then, that taken at face value it is metaphysics—nonsense. Moreover, it is that kind of metaphysics against which Wittgenstein gave an explicit warning (which he himself ignored), it is the attempt to talk about the relation of language to fact. *This* is not clarification of language. Faced with this difficulty most logical empiricists went on saying what they had said, hoping to find a way out of the dilemma. But there were no such half-way houses which suited Carnap and Neurath. They were determined to confine philosophy to logical syntax. Their extraordinarily unplausible attempts to do so must now be followed through. Lest parody be suspected we shall let them speak in their own words so far as possible. The critical comments also will be largely based on Ayer's contemporary paper, 'Verification and Experience'.[2]

In order [said Carnap[3]] to characterise a definite *language* it is necessary to give its *vocabulary* and *syntax*, i.e. the words which occur in it and the rules in accordance with which (1) sentences can be formed from those words and (2) such sentences can be transformed into other sentences, either of the same or of another language (the so-called rules of inference and rules for translation). But is it not also necessary, in order to understand the 'sense' of the sentences, to indicate the 'meaning' of the words? No; the demand thereby made in the material mode is satisfied by giving the formal rules which constitute its syntax. For the 'meaning' of a word is given either by translation or by definition. A translation is a rule for transforming a word from one language to another (e.g. 'cheval' = 'horse'); a definition is a rule for mutual transformation of words in the same language. This is true both of so-called nominal definitions (e.g. 'elephant' = 'animal with such and such distinguishing characteristics') and also, a fact usually forgotten, for so-called ostensive definitions e.g. 'elephant' = 'animal of the same kind as the animal in this or that position in space-time'); both definitions are translations of words.

We may pause here to observe that Carnap, in his anxiety not to allow that ostensive definition involves the pernicious comparison of language with fact, here perpetrates a first-class howler. Let us suppose that someone points to an elephant at Whipsnade and says 'That is an elephant', in order to let his hearer know the meaning of the word 'elephant'. Let us grant to Carnap that this is much the same as to say 'The animal just on the right of the entrance to Whipsnade now (or "on the 1st of January, 1954") is an elephant,' which it certainly is not. Even so the speaker is certainly not saying that the word 'elephant' means the same as 'animal of the same kind as the animal on the right of the entrance to Whipsnade on the 1st of January, 1954'. Yet Carnap says that a definition is a rule for mutual transformation of words in

---

2. *Proceedings of the Aristotelian Society,* 1936-7.
3. *Unity of Science (Psyche Miniatures),* p. 38.

the same language. But in any case the pointing and uttering of the word 'elephant' is not the equivalent of Carnap's sentence. One can teach a foreigner the meaning of the word 'elephant' by pointing to one and saying 'elephant', but not by verbally giving in English the spatio-temporal co-ordinates of an elephant with one's hands in one's pockets.

Having thus tried to establish that the meaning of words is something which one can study without going beyond the bounds of language, Carnap goes on[4] to say some of the forbidden things, but not inadvertently, for he has an explanation in waiting:

> Science is a system based on direct experience, and controlled by experimental verification. Verification is based on 'protocol statements', a term whose meaning will be made clearer in the course of further discussion. The term is understood to include statements belonging to the basic protocol or direct record of a scientist's experience. . . . A 'primitive' protocol will be understood to exclude all statements obtained indirectly by induction or otherwise and postulates therefore a sharp (theoretical) distinction between the raw material of scientific investigation and its organisation. . . . .

This may sound sufficiently compromising, but he apparently commits himself even more deeply by adding: 'The simplest statements in the *protocol-language* refer to the given, and describe directly given experience or phenomena, i.e. the simplest states of which knowledge may be had. The elements that are directly given are the simplest sensations and feelings.'

The explanation of Carnap's allowing himself to talk in this way is quite simple; he maintains that he is talking in the material mode of speech. He claims that though in appearance talking of the relation of language to the world he is really only talking about language. To make this clear he offers translations of some of the most difficult remarks in the formal mode. Thus he translates the last quotation we made from him as follows: 'The simplest statements in the *protocol-language* are protocol-statments, i.e. statements needing no justification and serving as foundation for all the remaining statements of science. Protocol statements are of the same kind as: "joy now", "here, now, blue", "there, red".'

At first sight this does not look too unreasonable, but we must look closer. When he says 'Protocol statements are of the same kind as: "joy now", "here, now, blue", "there, red" ', Carnap means, or ought to mean, that all protocol sentences are of the same syntactical type as

4. *Op. cit.*, p. 42.

'joy, now' and the rest. He does not mean, officially at any rate, statements which as directly report reality as does 'joy, now', but statements to which the same rules for the formation of sentences and their transformation into others apply. Bearing this in mind, we ought immediately to ask two obvious questions: Why does Carnap choose sentences of this syntactical form rather than any others to fulfil this particular basic role in language? And on what principles does one decide which of these protocols of the right syntactical form to accept and which to reject? Carnap cannot give the obvious answers that statements of this syntactical form are the kind which we use to report experience, and that we select those for acceptance which do as a matter of fact record experience accurately. For according to Carnap to say that a statement is of the kind which reports experience is just to say, in the material mode, that it is of this syntactical form.

The well-nigh incredible answers in fact given are these. It is purely a matter of convention that we select sentences of this syntactical form as the basic protocol statements; and we accept those protocols which are accepted by the accredited scientists and reject those which are not. Carnap says, for example,[5] 'Every concrete proposition belonging to the physicalist language-system can in suitable circumstances serve as a protocol proposition'. We could go on now to ask why we accept the protocols of accredited scientists, why they are accredited, and how we know within syntax that these or those are accepted by accredited scientists. But it is clearly not worth while to pursue this theory further. Philosophy cannot just be logical syntax, nor can a language be characterized by a vocabulary understood as a list of marks on paper with formation and transformation rules. Carnap and his fellows probably did as well as can be done by this thesis. But it is impossible; they could only make it appear plausible by relying on the natural meaning of what was supposed to be merely syntax in the material mode of speech. Carnap, of course, came to see this. He now acknowledges, and writes on, a branch of philosophy which he calls semantics and which deals with this forbidden topic of the relation of words to things. But on the credit side of the Carnap of other days it must be said that he was one of the few in the period of classical logical empiricism who honestly faced the need to maintain consistently that philosophy consisted solely of tautological transformations, of analytical equivalences. But for his errors the need for some revision of the doctrine would not have been seen so quickly.

The reader may very well wonder why to say that a statement is to be accepted because it records a fact was regarded as such a danger-

5. *Über Protokollsätze*, quoted by Ayer in 'Verification and Experience', p. 145.

ous thing, and why it was regarded as metaphysical. For it does not seem very similar to the more grandiose statements of speculative metaphysics. So far as Wittgenstein himself was concerned the matter is not so hard to understand. For (1) when Wittgenstein talked about a proposition picturing a fact he was certainly talking metaphysics, and intentionally. For this sort of fact was not just any fact but a very metaphysical variety. As Wittgenstein used the word it was probably not a fact that Queen Anne is dead, since Queen Anne was probably, like the rest of us, a logical construction, and not a genuine object or particular. One must be talking metaphysics whatever one says about this sort of fact. (2) If Wittgenstein's doctrine that a proposition is a picture of a fact is accepted, then it seems plain that one cannot talk about the relation of language to fact without violation of syntax; for one cannot produce a picture of the relation of a picture to what is pictured, the fact. This relation must show itself, and what is shown cannot be said. It seems that later logical positivists partly thought that all talk about facts must be as metaphysical as Wittgenstein's and partly accepted the consequences of the 'picture' theory of language from Wittgenstein somewhat uncritically even when they had abandoned the theory of language itself.

Probably, however, some more general, *a priori*, considerations played a great part. For example, the dichotomy 'tautological-empirical' seemed to be exhaustive to the positivists, and anything which could not be brought into these two categories was rejected as metaphysical. But philosophy had to be logical rather than empirical—one cannot carry on empirical studies in an arm-chair—and a logical inquiry is concerned, it seems, with statements and their relations to each other, not with the relation of language to fact. To some logical empiricists it seemed more tolerable to abandon, or to treat as in the material mode of speech, such statements as apparently involved extra-logical excursions than to allow any exception to the fundamental dichotomy 'logical-empirical'.

Our sketch of the salient features of logical empiricism, in its confident youth, and of the account it gave of the nature and point of analysis is now complete, though we shall have occasion later to consider some of the logical empiricists' views on some more detailed topics. We have not examined, and cannot examine, the contribution they made to many detailed problems which fall outside our main inquiry.

The two points that I have tried hardest to bring out about logical empiricism have been these: (1) while abandoning the metaphysics of logical atomism, at least officially and in intention, the logical empiricists retained substantially the same view of the scope and nature of analysis; but it was now conceived as revealing the logical structure of the language of science, of informative discourse, not of the facts with which science deals. Roughly the same propositions remained basic under both dispensations, whether they were said to picture facts or not, and roughly the same things remained as logical constructions. (2) The positivists all claimed that the sole legitimate propositions of philosophy were tautologies—verbal equivalences (Ayer, indeed, adds that empirical statements about the history of philosophy may be called philosophical, but this makes no real difference). Some maintained this thesis with considerable consistency but at the expense of intolerable paradox—for example, Carnap and the radical physicalists; others were more plausible but less consistent. Thus much of the criticism of Carnap which we have reproduced here is derived from the writings of Ayer, who maintained that we must be allowed to talk about the agreement of propositions with reality. Yet this is quite impossible on the general account of the nature of philosophy given by Ayer in *Language, Truth and Logic,* where he maintains that, apart from history of philosophy, all philosophical statements must be tautological equivalences. Whatever defect we may find in these and other doctrines of the logical empiricists, their services in arousing philosophy from dogmatic slumbers and in making philosophers look really carefully at such problems as the nature of metaphysics and significance cannot be over-estimated. 'Classical' logical positivism may be dead, but it did not live in vain.

It will be recalled that we considered that logical atomism came to be abandoned for two reasons; the first was the general rejection of metaphysics, including a *fortiori* logical atomism, the second that on examination a number of flaws were discovered in the metaphysics of atomism which made it less attractive as metaphysics. We have now examined in some detail the first of these reasons, and the consequential change of attitude towards analysis. We must now turn to examine the more detailed objections to the metaphysics. We cannot possibly discuss them all or go into them fully, but we must look at some of the more important ones, saving the most important, from our point of view, to the last. These more detailed flaws which were found in logical atomism undoubtedly led to a speedier and wider acceptance of logical positivism than would otherwise have occurred. Many who accepted it would have at least hesitated longer if, as metaphysics, logical atomism had appeared impeccable.

CONCEPTUAL ELUCIDATION

JOHN WISDOM

JOHN WISDOM (*b.* 1904) was a student of Moore, under whose influence he wrote *Problems of Mind and Matter* (1934). Later, under the tutelage of Ludwig Wittgenstein, he published a number of articles, the main ideas of which he cautiously attributed to Wittgenstein. A practitioner of philosophical analysis, he soon became one of its severest and most important critics. At present he is Professor of Philosophy at Cambridge University.

Wisdom's "Philosophical Perplexity" (1936), as the title suggests, attempts to provide a general account of the many puzzles and paradoxes of traditional philosophy. This essay has become a landmark in the recent history of philosophy because it exhibits the notion that the task of philosophy is the "resolution of puzzles" and not the answering of problems.

Philosophical questions, Wisdom claims, are really requests for a ruling on the use of sentences in matters where ordinary usage has no univocal answer. Furthermore, philosophical answers are really verbal recommendations regarding these requests. As such, they attempt to clarify ordinary language: "Philosophical theories exhibit both linguistic confusion and linguistic penetration." In a series of illuminating examples, Wisdom shows the force of his insight into the nature of philosophy.

Philosophical Perplexity[1]

1. *Philosophical statements are really verbal.*—I have inquired elsewhere the real nature of philosophical requests such as 'Can we know what is going on in someone else's mind?' 'Can we really know the causes of our sensations?' 'What is a chair?' and of philosophical answers such as 'We can never really know the causes of our sensations', 'A chair is nothing but our sensations', or 'A chair is something over and above our sensations', 'The goodness of a man, of a picture, of an argument is something over and above our feelings of approval and over and above those features of the man, the picture or the argument, which "determine" its goodness'. There is no time to repeat the inquiry here and I have to say dogmatically:

A philosophical answer is really a verbal recommendation in response to a request which is really a request with regard to a sentence which lacks a conventional use whether there occur situations which could conventionally be described by it. The description, for example 'I know directly what is going on in Smith's mind', is not a jumble like 'Cat how is up', nor is it in conflict with conventional usage like 'There are two white pieces and three black so there are six pieces on the board'. It just lacks a conventional usage. To call both 'Can $2 + 3 = 6$?' and 'Can I know what is going on in the minds of others?' nonsensical questions serves to bring out the likeness between them. But if one were to deny that there is a difference between them it would be an instance of that disrespect for other people which we may platitudinously say, so often damages philosophical work. A disrespect which blinds one to the puzzles they raise—in this instance the puzzle of the philosophical *can* which somehow seems between 'Can $2 + 3$ make 6?' and 'Can terriers catch hares?' Compare 'Can persons be in two places at once?' 'Do we have unconscious wishes?' 'Can you play chess without the queen?' (W).[2]

---

1. From: *Proceedings of the Aristotelian Society*, 1936-37. Reprinted by permission of the Editor.

2. Wittgenstein has not read this over-compressed paper and I warn people

283

Even to say that 'I know directly what is going on in Smith's mind' is *meaningless*, is dangerous, especially if you have just said that 'There are two white pieces and three black so there are six' is meaningless.

It is not even safe to say that 'I know directly what is going on in Smith's mind' lacks a use or meaning and leave it at that. For though it has no meaning it tends to have a meaning, like 'All whifley was the tulgey wood', though of course it is unlike this last example in the important respect that it does not lack a meaning because its constituent words are unknown. Nor does it lack meaning because its syntax is unknown. This makes it puzzling and makes it resemble the logical case. It is clear that for these reasons it would be even more illuminating and more misleading to say that 'God exists' and 'Men are immortal' are meaningless—especially just after saying $2 + 3 = 6$ is meaningless.

2. *Philosophical statements are not verbal.*—I have said that philosophers' questions and theories are really verbal. But if you like we will not say this or we will say also the contradictory.[3] For of course (*a*) philosophic statements usually have not a verbal air. On the contrary they have a non-verbal air like 'A fox's brush is really a tail'. (W). And their non-verbal air is not an unimportant feature of them because on it very much depends their puzzlingness.

And (*b*) though really verbal a philosopher's statements have not a merely verbal point. Unlike many statements the primary point of uttering them is not to convey the information they convey but to do something else. Consequently all attempts to explain their peculiar status by explaining the peculiar nature of their subject-matter, fail. For their subject-matter is not peculiar; their truth or falsity, in so far as these are appropriate to them at all, is fixed by facts about words, e.g. Goodness is not approval by the majority, because 'The majority sometimes approve what is bad' is not self-contradictory. But the point of philosophical statements is peculiar. It is the illumination of the ultimate structure of facts, i.e. the relations between different categories of being or (we must be in the mode) the relations between different sub-languages within a language.

The puzzles of philosophical propositions, of fictional propositions,

against supposing it a closer imitation of Wittgenstein than it is. On the other hand I can hardly exaggerate the debt I owe to him and how much of the good in this work is his—not only in the treatment of this philosophical difficulty and that but in the matter of how to do philosophy. As far as possible I have put a W against examples I owe to him. It must not be assumed that they are used in a way he would approve.

3. I do not wish to suggest that Wittgenstein would approve of *this* sort of talk nor that he would disapprove of it.

eneral propositions, negative propositions, propositions about the future, propositions about the past, even the puzzle about psychological propositions, are not removed by explaining the peculiar nature of the subject-matter of the sentences in which they are expressed but by reflecting upon the peculiar manner in which those sentences work. Mnemonic slogan: It's not the stuff, it's the style that stupefies.

3. *The divergence of point from content.*—The divergence of point from content which is found in necessary and near necessary propositions can be explained here only briefly.

Suppose a decoder, though still utterly ignorant of the meaning of both of two expressions 'monarchy' and 'set of persons ruled by the same king', has after prolonged investigation come to the conclusion that they mean the same in a certain code. He will say to his fellow-decoder ' "Monarchy" means the same as "set of persons ruled by the same king" '. The translator, and the philosopher also, may say the same. They all use the same form of words because what they say is the same. But the point of what they say is very different. The decoder's point can be got by anyone who knows the meaning of 'means the same as'; the translator does what he wants with the sentence only if his hearer knows the meaning either of 'monarchy' or of 'set of persons ruled by the same king'; the philosopher does what he wants with the sentence only if his hearer already uses, i.e. understands, i.e. knows the meaning of, *both* 'monarchy' and 'set of persons ruled by the same king'. This condition makes the case of the philosopher curious; for it states that he can do what he wants with the sentence only if his hearer already knows what he is telling him. But this is true in the required sense. The philosopher draws attention to what is already known with a view to giving insight into the structure of what 'monarchy', say, means, i.e. bringing into connection the sphere in which the one expression is used with that in which the other is. Compare the man who says 'I should have the change from a pound after spending five shillings on a book, one and sevenpence-halfpenny on stamps and two and twopence-halfpenny at the grocer's, so I should have eleven shillings and twopence'. This is Moore's example and I beg attention for it. It is tremendously illuminating in the *necessary synthetic* group of puzzles and in a far, far wider field than this, because it illuminates the use of 'means the same'—a phrase which stops so many. When on first going to France I learn the exchange rate for francs, do I know the meaning of 'worth 100 francs' or do I come to know this after staying three weeks?

The philosopher is apt to say 'A monarchy is a set of people under a king' rather than ' "Monarchy" means the same as "a set of people

under a king" ' . By using the former sentence he intimates his point
Now shall we say "A monarchy is a set of people under a king' means
the same as ' "Monarchy" means "a set of people under a king" ' or
not? My answer is 'Say which you like. But if you say "Yes" be careful, etc., and if you say "No" be careful, etc.'

If we decide to describe the difference between the two as a difference of meaning we must not say that the difference in meaning is a
difference of subjective intension, nor that it is a difference of emotional
significance merely. For these are not adequate accounts of the difference between the two—and not an adequate account of the difference
between the use of '3 plus 5 plus 8' and the use of '16'.

4. *Philosophy, truth, misleadingness and illumination.*—Now that we
have seen that the philosopher's intention is to bring out relations between categories of being, between spheres of language, we shall be
more prepared to allow that false statements about the usage of words
may be philosophically very useful and even adequate provided their
falsity is realized and there is no confusion about what they are being
used for.

The nature of the philosopher's intention explains how it is that
one may call a philosophical theory such as *A proposition is a sentence,*
certainly false, and yet feel that to leave one's criticism at that is to
attend to the letter and not the spirit of the theory criticized.

The nature of the philosopher's intention explains also how it is
that one cannot say of a philosopher's theory that it is false when he
introduces it in his own terminology, while yet one often feels that such
theories are somehow philosophically bad. Thus (W) suppose the word
'sense-datum' has never been used before and that someone says 'When
Jones sees a rabbit, has an illusion of a rabbit, has an hallucination of
a rabbit, dreams of a rabbit, he has a sense-datum of a rabbit'. One
cannot protest that this is false, since no statement has been made, only
a recommendation. But the recommendation purports to be enlightening
and one may well protest if it is, on the contrary, misleading. This
particular recommendation is liable to suggest that sense-data are a
special sort of thing, *extremely* thin coloured pictures, and thus liable
to raise puzzles, such as 'How are sense-data related to material things?'
We can abuse a philosopher as much as we like if we use the right
adjectives. *Good is an ultimate predicate* is useless, *A proposition is a
subsistent entity* is useless and pretentious,[4] *We can never know the
real cause of our sensations* is misleading. And we can praise him although he speaks falsely or even nonsensically. People have considered

4. Neither of these theories is entirely useless. They are for one thing good antitheses to the naturalistic error.

whether it is true that 'an event is a pattern of complete, particular, pecific facts and a complete, particular, specific fact is an infinitely thin lice out of an event'.[5]

You may say 'How absurd of them since the statement is nonsense'. Certainly the statement is nonsense and so, if you like, it was absurd of them. But it was better than saying it was nonsense and ignoring it. Suppose I say 'The thoroughbred is a neurotic woman on four legs'. This is nonsense, but it is not negligible.[6]

5. *Provocation and Pacification.*—So far, however, little or nothing has been said to explain what sort of things make a philosophical statement misleading and what make it illuminating. Only a short answer is possible here.

In the first place there is the misleading feature which nearly all philosophical statements have—a non-verbal air. The philosopher *laments* that we can never really know what is going on in someone else's mind, that we can never really know the causes of our sensations, that inductive conclusions are never really justified. He laments these things as if he can dream of another world where we can see our friends and tables face to face, where scientists can justify their conclusions and terriers can catch hares. This enormous source of confusion we cannot study now.

Secondly philosophical statements mislead when by the use of like expressions for different cases, they suggest likenesses which do not exist, and by the use of different expressions for like cases, they conceal likenesses which do exist.

Philosophical theories are illuminating in a corresponding way, namely when they suggest or draw attention to a terminology which reveals likenesses and differences concealed by ordinary language.

I want to stress the philosophical usefulness of metaphysical surprises such as 'We can never really know the causes of our sensations', 'We can never know the real causes of our sensations', 'Inductive conclusions are never really justified', 'The laws of mathematics are really rules of grammar'. I believe that too much fun has been made of philosophers who say this kind of thing. Remember what Moore said about 1924—words to this effect: When a philosopher says that really something is so we are warned that what he says is really so is not so really. With horrible ingenuity Moore can rapidly reduce any metaphysical

5. *Problems of Mind and Matter,* p. 32.

6. The matter can be put in terms of truth and falsehood. A philosophical theory involves an explicit claim, an equation, and an implicit claim that the equation is not misleading and is illuminating. The explict claim may be false and the implicit true on one or both counts, or vice versa.

theory to a ridiculous story. For he is right, they are false—only ther
is good in them, poor things. This shall be explained.

Wittgenstein allows importance to these theories. They are for hir
expressions of deep-seated puzzlement. It is an important part of th
treatment of a puzzle to develop it to the full.

But this is not enough. Wittgenstein allows that the theories ar
philosophically important not merely as specimens of the whopper
philosophers can tell. But he too much represents them as merely symp
toms of linguistic confusion. I wish to represent them as also symptom
of linguistic penetration.

Wittgenstein gives the impression that philosophical remarks eithe
express puzzlement or if not are remarks such as Wittgenstein himsel
makes with a view to curing puzzlement.

This naturally gives rise to the question 'If the proper business o
philosophy is the removal of puzzlement, would it not be best done b
giving a drug to the patient which made him entirely forget the state
ments puzzling him or at least lose his uneasy feelings?'

This of course will never do. And what we say about the philoso
pher's purposes must be changed so that it shall no longer seem to lea
to such an absurd idea.

The philosopher's purpose is to gain a grasp of the relations betwee
different categories of being, between expressions used in *differen
manners*.[7] He is confused about what he wants and he is confused b
the relations between the expressions, so he is very often puzzled. Bu
only such treatment of the puzzles as increases a grasp of the relation
between different categories of being is philosophical. And not all th
philosopher's statements are either complaints of puzzlement or pacif
icatory. Philosophers who say 'We never know the real causes of ou
sensations', 'Only my sensations are real', often bring out these 'theo
ries' with an air of triumph (with a misleading air of empirical dis
covery indeed). True the things they say are symptoms of confusio
even if they are not of puzzlement. But they are also symptoms o
penetration, of noticing what is not usually noticed. Philosophical prog
ress has two aspects, provocation and pacification.

6. *Example of the pointless doubts: (a) how misleading they are*.—
Let us consider this with examples. Take first the philosopher who says
to the plain man: 'We do not really know that there is cheese on the
table; for might not all the sense evidence suggest this and yet there
be no cheese—remember what happened at Madame Tussaud's'.

Our assertion with confidence that there is cheese on the table or
our assertion that we know that there is cheese on the table raises at

---

7. See 'different level' in *Proc. Aris. Soc.* Supp. Vol. XIII, p. 66.

last these three puzzles: (1) *the category puzzle,* which finds expression in 'We ought not to speak of a cheese (of the soul) but of bundles of sense-data'; (2) *the knowledge puzzle,* which finds expression in 'We ought not to say "I know there is cheese on the table" but "Very, very probably there is cheese on the table" '; (3) *the justification puzzle,* which finds expression in 'Empirical conclusions are not really justified'.

We cannot here speak of all these. We are considering (2) the *knowledge* or *pointless doubt* puzzle. There are a group of pointless doubt puzzles including the following: 'We don't really know that there is cheese on the table'; 'We ought to say only "It is probable that there is cheese on the table" '; 'It is improper to say "I know that there is cheese on the table" '; 'It would be well if we prefixed every remark about material things with "probably" '.

All these suggestions are misleading—they all suggest that it has been discovered that we have been over-confident about material things. They should have slightly different treatment but I have only just *realized* this multiplicity. Let us take the puzzle in the crude form 'Couldn't there be no cheese here although all the sense-evidence suggests there is?'

Wittgenstein explains that this sentence though of the verbal form we associate with doubt and though it may be uttered with the intonation, expression and gestures we associate with doubt is not *used* as a sentence expressing doubt. To utter it is to raise a pseudo doubt. People say 'We ought not to say "There *is* cheese on the table" but "Probably there is cheese on the table" or "The sense-evidence suggests ever so strongly that there is cheese on the table". For whatever we do we never observe a cheese, we have to rely upon our senses. And we may be suffering from a joint hallucination of all the senses or a consistent dream. Remember how people are deceived at Madame Tussaud's. And we may see and touch cheesy patches, smell cheesy smells, obtain cheesy pictures from cameras and cheesy reactions from mice and yet the stuff to-morrow be soap in our mouth. And then to-morrow we shall say "Yesterday we were mistaken". So our "knowledge" to-day that there is cheese here is not real knowledge. Every one ought really to whisper "Possibly hallucinatory" after *every* sentence about material things however much he has made sure that he is right'.

What those who recommend this should notice is how not merely unusual but pointless a use of words they recommend. As language is at present used, I raise my hungry friends' hopes if I say 'There is cheese on the table', and I damp them if I add 'unless it is hallucinatory'. But this additional clause has its effect only because I do *not always* use it. If a parent adds 'be very careful' to everything he says to a child he will soon find his warnings ineffective. If I prefix every statement about material things with 'probably' this doubt-raiser will soon cease to frighten hungry friends, that is cease to function as it now does. Consequently in order to mark those differences which I now mark by saying in one case 'Probably that is cheese on the table' and in another case 'I know that is cheese on the table', I shall have to introduce a new notation, one to do the work the old did. 'To do the work the old did!' that is, to claim what I formerly claimed with 'know!'

It may now be said 'In the ordinary use of "know" we may know that that is cheese on the table, but this knowledge is not real knowledge'.

This gives the misleading idea that the philosopher has envisaged some kind of knowing which our failing faculties prevent us from attaining. Terriers cannot catch hares, men cannot really know the causes of their sensations. Nothing of the kind, however. For when we say to the philosopher 'Go on, describe this real knowledge, tell us what stamp of man you want and we will see if we can buy or breed one' then he can never tell us.

It may now be said, 'No, no, the point is this: There is some inclination to use[8] "know" strictly so that we do not know that insulin cures diabetes, that the sun will rise to-morrow, because these propositions are only probable inferences from what we have observed. There is some inclination to use "know" only when what is known is observed or is entailed by something known for certain. Now you do not know in this sense that you will not have to correct yourself to-morrow and say "I was mistaken yesterday, that was not cheese", since nothing you know for certain to-day is incompatible with this. And if you do not know but what you may have to correct yourself to-morrow you do not know that you are right to-day'.

But what is meant by 'certain'? I should claim to know for certain that that is cheese on the table now. And as the objector rightly points out this entails that I shall not have to correct myself to-morrow. I therefore know in the strict sense that I shall not have to correct myself to-morrow.

It will be said that it is not *absolutely* certain that that is cheese on the table. But I should reply that it is.

It will be said that it is not *senseless to doubt* that that is cheese on the table, not even after the most exhaustive tests. I should reply that it is.

---

8. Another form would be: 'It is proper' as opposed to 'usual' to use 'know' so that, etc.

But, of course, by now I see what the sceptic is driving at. It is not senseless to doubt that that is cheese on the table, in the sense in which it is senseless to doubt 'I am in pain', 'I hear a buzzing'—not even after the most exhaustive tests—indeed the exhaustive tests make no difference to this. For, in this sense, it is not senseless to doubt that that is cheese on the table provided only that 'He says that that is cheese but perhaps he is mistaken' has a use in English. You see, 'He says he is in pain, but perhaps he is mistaken' has no use in English. Hence we may be 'absolutely certain' that he is not mistaken[9] about his pain, in the very special sense that 'He is mistaken' makes no sense in this connection.

Thus the sceptic's pretended doubts amount to pointing out that, unlike statements descriptive of sensations, statements about material things make sense with 'perhaps he is mistaken'. And the sceptic proposes to mark this by an extraordinary use of 'know' and 'probably'. He proposes that we should not say that we know that that is cheese on the table unless it is entailed by statements with regard to which a doubt is not merely out of the question but unintelligible, i.e. such that where S is P is one of them then 'S is P unless I am mistaken' raises a titter like 'I am in pain unless I am mistaken'. 'That is cheese on the table' is not such a statement and so of course it does not follow from such statements—otherwise a doubt with regard to it would be unintelligible, i.e. it would be absolutely certain in the strict, philosophic sense.

The sceptic's doubts become then a recommendation to use 'know' only with statements about sense-experience and mathematics and to prefix *all* other statements with 'probably'.[10]

This is very different talk and much less misleading. But still it is misleading unless accompanied by the explanation given above of the astounding certainty of statements about sense-experience. Even with the explanation the suggestion is highly dangerous, involving as it does a new and *'manner*—indicating' use of the familiar words 'know' and 'probable'. Without the explanation it suggests that there is a difference in degree of certainty between statements about material things and statements about sense-data, a difference in certainty dependent upon their subject-matter, in a sense analogous to that in which we say 'I am certain about what happened in Hyde Park—I was there—but I am not certain about what happened in Spain—I was not an eye-witness'.

9. Of course he may be *lying*.

10. Compare the tendency to use 'what ought to be done' irrevocably. People who do this lament thus: 'What one ought to do is always for the best, but unfortunately we never know what we really ought to do'. Others lament thus: 'We can know what we ought to do but unfortunately this does not always turn out for the best'.

This suggests that I know what it would be like to be an eye-witness of cheese, but am in fact unfortunately obliged to *rely upon the testimony of* my senses.

Now the difference between statements about sense-experiences and statements about material things is not at all like this. The difference is not one of subject-matter (stuff) but of a different manner of use (style). And statements about sense-experiences are certain only because it makes no sense to say that they may be wrong.[11] Notice the connection between 'He says he is in pain but I think he is mistaken' and 'He cries "Ow!" but I think he is mistaken'. The difference between sense-statements and thing-statements cannot be adequately explained here. And consequently the full misleadingness of such a use of 'probably' as is recommended in what we may call the last form of the pseudo-doubt, cannot be adequately explained here.

But I hope I have said enough to bring out in good measure the misleadingness of saying such things as 'O dear, we can never know the causes of our sensations', and even 'It would be philosophically excellent to put "probably" before all statements about material things'.

7. *Example of the pointless doubts: (b) how importantly illuminating they are.*—But though the recommended use of 'probably' would be pointless as a cautionary clause and would thus be extremely misleading, the recommendation to use it so is not pointless, is not prompted wholly by confusion, but partly by penetration. The philosopher says to the plain man 'You do not really know that that is a cheese on the table'. We have pacified those who are opposed to this statement by bringing out the sources of their reluctance to agree with it. But the philosopher must pacify everyone and we must now pacify those philosophers who are pleased with, it and complete the pacification of those who are puzzled by it, being tempted to deny it and at the same time tempted to assert it. What *is* the point behind the misleading statement 'We can never know statements about material things'? The answer has been given already by the method of forcing reformulations. But we may now approach the answer by a different route. Under what circumstances are such things usually said?

It is when after considering hallucinations, illusions, etc., one wishes to emphasize (1) the likeness between such cases and cases in which there was 'something really there', and to emphasize the continuity between (*a*) cases in which one says 'I think that is cheese on the table', 'I believe that is a real dagger', 'Probably that is a snake, not a branch' and (*b*) cases in which one says 'That *is* cheese on the table', 'I found that it *was* a snake'; and to emphasize (2) the unlikeness between even

---

11. This, I realize, stands very much in need of pacifying explanation.

so well assured a statement as 'This is my thumb' and such a statement as 'I see a pinkish patch', 'I feel a softish patch', 'I am in pain'.

It is not at all easy at first to see how in being revocable and correctable by others the most assured statement about a thing is more like the most precarious statement about another thing than it is to a statement descriptive of one's sensations. Ordinary language conceals these things because in ordinary language we speak both of some favourable material-thing-statements and of statements about our sensations, as certain, while we speak of other statements about material things as merely probable. This leads to pseudo-laments about the haunting uncertainty of even the best material-thing-statements and pseudo-congratulations upon the astounding certainty of statements about our sensations.

We are all, when our attention is drawn to those cases so often described in which it looks for all the world as if our friend is standing in the room although he is dying two thousand miles away, or in which we think we see a banana and it turns out to be a reflection in a greengrocer's mirror, we are all, in such cases, inclined to say 'Strictly we ought always to add "unless it is a queer looking stick and not a banana, or a reflection or an hallucination or an illusion" '.[12] We do not stop to consider what would happen if we did always add this. Horrified at the deceptions our senses have practised upon us we feel we must abuse them somehow and so we say that they never *prove* anything, that we never *know* what is based on them.

The continuity and the difference which are concealed by ordinary language would be no longer concealed but marked if we used 'probably' in the way recommended. But what an unfortunate way of obtaining this result! And in what a misleading way was the recommendation made! I do not really know that this is a thumb. The huntsman's coat is not really pink. A fox's brush is really a tail. (W).

8. *Other Examples.*—Now many other examples should be given. 'What is a mathematical proposition?' 'Do inductive arguments give any probability to their conclusions?' These other puzzles should be re-created; the temptations to give the answers which have been given should be re-created. But this cannot be done in this paper. Without bringing up the puzzles and temptations the following accounts are half dead, but I offer them for what they are worth.

Take "The laws of mathematics and logic are really rules of grammar'. With this instructive incantation people puzzle themselves to death. Is it or isn't it true? And if false what amendment will give us the truth? If not rules then what? The answer is 'They are what they

---

12. Then every statement would be tautologous but *absolutely* certain!

are, etc. Is a donkey a sort of horse but with *very* long ears?' People are puzzled because of course it isn't true that the laws of mathematics are rules of grammar (more obvious still that they are not commands). And yet they cannot bring themselves to lose the advantages of this falsehood. For this falsehood draws attention to (1) an unlikeness and (2) a likeness concealed by ordinary language; (1) an unlikeness to the laws of hydraulics and an unlikeness in this unlikeness to the unlikeness between the laws of hydraulics and those of aeronautics; for it is an unlikeness not of subject-matter but of manner of functioning —and (2) a likeness but not an exact likeness to the functioning of rules.

Again 'Inductive arguments do not really give any probability to their conclusions' gives the misleading idea that the scientists have been found out at last, that our confidence in our most careful research workers is entirely misplaced, their arguments being no better than those of the savage. Nothing of the kind of course. What is at the back of this lament is this: In ordinary language we speak of Dr. So and So's experiment with a group of 100 children whose teeth improved after six months extra calcium' as having very much increased the probability of the proposition that bad teeth are due to calcium deficiency. We also say that my having drawn 90 white balls from a bag which we know to contain 100 balls, each either white or black, has very much increased the probability of the proposition that all the balls in that bag are white. We even speak numerically in connection with empirical probability—we not only argue *a priori* and say 'There were six runners, there are now only five, we still know nothing of any of them, so it is now 4-1 against the dog from trap 1' but we also argue empirically and say 'It was 5-1 against the dog from trap 1; but I hear a rumour that each of the others has been provided with a cup of tea, and I think we may now take 4-1 against him'.

The similarity in the way we speak of these cases leads us when asked how empirical arguments give probability to their conclusions to try to assimilate them to the formal cases, balls in bags, dice, etc. But when this attempt is made it begins to appear that the investigation of nature is much less like the investigation of balls in a bag than one is at first apt to think.

At the same time is revealed the shocking continuity between the scientist's arguments by the method of difference and the savage's *post hoc ergo propter hoc*,[13] between the method of agreement and the reflexes of rats, and struck by the difference and the continuity and how they are concealed by ordinary language we provoke attention to

13. See Keynes, *A Treatise on Probability*.

them with 'Even the best established scientific results are nothing but specially successful superstitions'. We say this although we have made no shocking discovery of scientists faking figures, although the scientist's reasons for his belief in insulin still differ from my landlady's reasons for belief in Cure-all, in exactly the way which, in the ordinary use of language, makes us call the one belief scientifically grounded and the other a superstition. Similarly we may say, having seen a butterfly die or been told the age of an oak 'The strongest of us have really only a short time to live'. We say this although we have made no discovery of impending disaster, or we may say 'Man is nothing but a complicated parasite' when we watch the arrival of the 9.5 at the Metropolis.

¶ Conclusion

The plain man has come to expect of philosophers paradoxical, provoking statements such as 'We can never really know the causes of our sensations', 'Causation is really nothing more than regular sequence', 'Inductive conclusions are really nothing but lucky superstitions', 'The laws of logic are ultimately rules of grammar'. Philosophers know that the statements are provocative; this is why they so often put in some apologetic word such as 'really' or 'ultimately'.

These untruths persist. This is not merely because they are symptoms of an intractable disorder but because they are philosophically useful. The curious thing is that their philosophical usefulness depends upon their paradoxicalness and thus upon their falsehood. They are false because they are needed where ordinary language fails, though it must not be supposed that they are or should be in some perfect language. They are in a language not free from the same sort of defects as those from the effects of which they are designed to free us.

To invent a special word to describe the status of, for example, mathematical propositions would do no good. There is a phrase already, 'necessary yet synthetic'. It is, of course, perfectly true that mathematical propositions are 'necessary synthetics'—it should be true since the expression was made to measure. True but no good. We are as much inclined to ask 'What are necessary synthetic propositions?' as we were to ask 'What are mathematical propositions?' 'What is an instinct?' An innate disposition certainly. But philosophically that answer is useless. No—what is wanted is some device for bringing out the relations between the manner in which mathematical (or dispositional) sentences are used and the manners in which others are used—so as to give their place on the language map. This cannot be done with a plain answer, a single statement. We may try opposite falsehoods or we may say, 'Be careful that this expression "mathematical proposition" does not suggest certain analogies at the expense of others. Do not let it make you think that the difference between mathematical propositions and others is like that between the propositions of hydraulics and those of aeronautics. Do notice how like to rules, etc., and yet, etc.'

If you will excuse a suspicion of smartness: Philosophers should be continually trying to say what cannot be said.

GILBERT RYLE

RYLE's *The Concept of Mind* (1949) is the best single example in contemporary philosophy of the change from philosophy as analysis to philosophy as elucidation of concepts. Even the title indicates that the primary concern is with the concept, not the nature, of mind. Ryle's preoccupaion is with the logical mapping of central mental concepts or expressions. His basic claim, which pervades the book, is that the description of the logical behavior of mental concepts constitutes the whole philosophical story of the mind; and neither in plot nor in character is it the story as narrated by the orthodox, classical amalgam of traditional theories, from Descartes to Russell, that Ryle collectively calls "Cartesianism."

The book has four main theses: (1) The philosophy of mind is fundamentally the logical elucidation of mental concepts and expressions and the logical mapping of their "cross-bearings"; (2) statements about mental phenomena are logically, at least, irreducibly threefold: categorical, hypothetical, and mongrel-categorical; (3) the mind is not an extra, metaphysically hidden entity affixed to the body—a "Ghost in the Machine"—but a "person's abilities, liabilities, and inclinations to do and undergo certain sorts of things, and of the doing and undergoing of these things in the ordinary world"; (4) Cartesianism, in all its versions, is fundamentally a *logical* mistake in that it reduces certain crucial mind-statements which are not and cannot be categorical to categorical ones.

Chapter I, "Descartes' Myth" (reprinted below), states the fourth thesis: Cartesianism is a category-mistake.

Descartes' Myth[1]

¶ (1) THE OFFICIAL DOCTRINE

There is a doctrine about the nature and place of minds which is so prevalent among theorists and even among laymen that it deserves to be described as the official theory. Most philosophers, psychologists and religious teachers subscribe, with minor reservations, to its main articles and, although they admit certain theoretical difficulties in it, they tend to assume that these can be overcome without serious modifications being made to the architecture of the theory. It will be argued here that the central principles of the doctrine are unsound and conflict with the whole body of what we know about minds when we are not speculating about them.

The official doctrine, which hails chiefly from Descartes, is something like this. With the doubtful exceptions of idiots and infants in arms every human being has both a body and a mind. Some would prefer to say that every human being is both a body and a mind. His body and his mind are ordinarily harnessed together, but after the death of the body his mind may continue to exist and function.

Human bodies are in space and are subject to the mechanical laws which govern all other bodies in space. Bodily processes and states can be inspected by external observers. So a man's bodily life is as much a public affair as are the lives of animals and reptiles and even as the careers of trees, crystals and planets.

But minds are not in space, nor are their operations subject to mechanical laws. The workings of one mind are not witnessable by other observers; its career is private. Only I can take direct cognisance of the states and processes of my own mind. A person therefore lives through two collateral histories, one consisting of what happens in and to his body, the other consisting of what happens in and to his mind.

1. From *The Concept of Mind* (London: Hutchinson, 1949), Chap. I. Reprinted by permission of the publishers, Hutchinson, London, and Barnes·and Noble, New York.

The first is public, the second private. The events in the first history are events in the physical world, those in the second are events in the mental world.

It has been disputed whether a person does or can directly monitor all or only some of the episodes of his own private history; but, according to the official doctrine, of at least some of these episodes he has direct and unchallengeable cognisance. In consciousness, self-consciousness and introspection he is directly and authentically apprised of the present states and operations of his mind. He may have great or small uncertainties about concurrent and adjacent episodes in the physical world, but he can have none about at least part of what is momentarily occupying his mind.

It is customary to express this bifurcation of his two lives and of his two worlds by saying that the things and events which belong to the physical world, including his own body, are external, while the workings of his own mind are internal. This antithesis of outer and inner is of course meant to be construed as a metaphor, since minds, not being in space, could not be described as being spatially inside anything else, or as having things going on spatially inside themselves. But relapses from this good intention are common and theorists are found speculating how stimuli, the physical sources of which are yards or miles outside a person's skin, can generate mental responses inside his skull, or how decisions framed inside his cranium can set going movements of his extremities.

Even when 'inner' and 'outer' are construed as metaphors, the problem how a person's mind and body influence one another is notoriously charged with theoretical difficulties. What the mind wills, the legs, arms and the tongue execute; what affects the ear and the eye has something to do with what the mind perceives; grimaces and smiles betray the mind's moods and bodily castigations lead, it is hoped, to moral improvement. But the actual transactions between the episodes of the private history and those of the public history remain mysterious, since by definition they can belong to neither series. They could not be reported among the happenings described in a person's autobiography of his inner life, but nor could they be reported among those described in some one else's biography of that person's overt career. They can be inspected neither by introspection nor by laboratory experiment. They are theoretical shuttlecocks which are forever being bandied from the physiologist back to the psychologist and from the psychologist back to the physiologist.

Underlying this partly metaphorical representation of the bifurcation of a person's two lives there is a seemingly more profound and philosophical assumption. It is assumed that there are two different kinds of existence or status. What exists or happens may have the status of physical existence, or it may have the status of mental existence. Somewhat as the faces of coins are either heads or tails, or somewhat as living creatures are either male or female, so, it is supposed, some existing is physical existing, other existing is mental existing. It is a necessary feature of what has physical existence that it is in space and time, it is a necessary feature of what has mental existence that it is in time but not in space. What has physical existence is composed of matter, or else is a function of matter; what has mental existence consists of consciousness, or else is a function of consciousness.

There is thus a polar opposition between mind and matter, an opposition which is often brought out as follows. Material objects are situated in a common field, known as 'space', and what happens to one body in one part of space is mechanically connected with what happens to other bodies in other parts of space. But mental happenings occur in insulated fields, known as 'minds', and there is, apart maybe from telepathy, no direct causal connection between what happens in one mind and what happens in another. Only through the medium of the public physical world can the mind of one person make a difference to the mind of another. The mind is its own place and in his inner life each of us lives the life of a ghostly Robinson Crusoe. People can see, hear and jolt one another's bodies, but they are irremediably blind and deaf to the workings of one another's minds and inoperative upon them.

What sort of knowledge can be secured of the workings of a mind? On the one side, according to the official theory, a person has direct knowledge of the best imaginable kind of the workings of his own mind. Mental states and processes are (or are normally) conscious states and processes, and the consciousness which irradiates them can engender no illusions and leaves the door open for no doubts. A person's present thinkings, feelings and willings, his perceivings, rememberings and imaginings are intrinsically 'phosphorescent'; their existence and their nature are inevitably betrayed to their owner. The inner life is a stream of consciousness of such a sort that it would be absurd to suggest that the mind whose life is that stream might be unaware of what is passing down it.

True, the evidence adduced recently by Freud seems to show that there exist channels tributary to this stream, which run hidden from their owner. People are actuated by impulses the existence of which they vigorously disavow; some of their thoughts differ from the thoughts which they acknowledge; and some of the actions which they think they will to perform they do not really will. They are

thoroughly gulled by some of their own hypocrisies and they successfully ignore facts about their mental lives which on the official theory
ought to be patent to them. Holders of the official theory tend, however, to maintain that anyhow in normal circumstances a person must
be directly and authentically seized of the present state and workings
of his own mind.

Besides being currently supplied with these alleged immediate data
of consciousness, a person is also generally supposed to be able to
exercise from time to time a special kind of perception, namely inner
perception, or introspection. He can take a (non-optical) 'look' at
what is passing in his mind. Not only can he view and scrutinize a
flower through his sense of sight and listen to and discriminate the
notes of a bell through his sense of hearing; he can also reflectively
or introspectively watch, without any bodily organ of sense, the current
episodes of his inner life. This self-observation is also commonly supposed to be immune from illusion, confusion or doubt. A mind's reports
of its own affairs have a certainty superior to the best that is possessed
by its reports of matters in the physical world. Sense-perceptions can,
but consciousness and introspection cannot, be mistaken or confused.

On the other side, one person has no direct access of any sort to
the events of the inner life of another. He cannot do better than make
problematic inferences from the observed behaviour of the other person's body to the states of mind which, by analogy from his own conduct, he supposes to be signalised by that behaviour. Direct access to
the workings of a mind is the privilege of that mind itself; in default
of such privileged access, the workings of one mind are inevitably occult
to everyone else. For the supposed arguments from bodily movements
similar to their own to mental workings similar to their own would
lack any possibility of observational corroboration. Not unnaturally,
therefore, an adherent of the official theory finds it difficult to resist
this consequence of his premisses, that he has no good reason to believe
that there do exist minds other than his own. Even if he prefers to
believe that to other human bodies there are harnessed minds not unlike his own, he cannot claim to be able to discover their individual
characteristics, or the particular things that they undergo and do.
Absolute solitude is on this showing the ineluctable destiny of the
soul. Only our bodies can meet.

As a necessary corollary of this general scheme there is implicitly
prescribed a special way of construing our ordinary concepts of mental
powers and operations. The verbs, nouns and adjectives, with which
in ordinary life we describe the wits, characters and higher-grade performances of the people with whom we have do, are required to be

construed as signifying special episodes in their secret histories, or else as signifying tendencies for such episodes to occur. When someone is described as knowing, believing or guessing something, as hoping, dreading, intending or shirking something, as designing this or being amused at that, these verbs are supposed to denote the occurrence of specific modifications in his (to us) occult stream of consciousness. Only his own privileged access to this stream in direct awareness and introspection could provide authentic testimony that these mental-conduct verbs were correctly or incorrectly applied. The onlooker, be he teacher, critic, biographer or friend, can never assure himself that his comments have any vestige of truth. Yet it was just because we do in fact all know how to make such comments, make them with general correctness and correct them when they turn out to be confused or mistaken, that philosophers found it necessary to construct their theories of the nature and place of minds. Finding mental-conduct concepts being regularly and effectively used, they properly sought to fix their logical geography. But the logical geography officially recommended would entail that there could be no regular or effective use of these mental-conduct concepts in our descriptions of, and prescriptions for, other people's minds.

¶ (2) THE ABSURDITY OF THE OFFICIAL DOCTRINE

Such in outline is the official theory. I shall often speak of it, with deliberate abusiveness, as 'the dogma of the Ghost in the Machine'. I hope to prove that it is entirely false, and false not in detail but in principle. It is not merely an assemblage of particular mistakes. It is one big mistake and a mistake of a special kind. It is, namely, a category-mistake. It represents the facts of mental life as if they belonged to one logical type or category (or range of types or categories), when they actually belong to another. The dogma is therefore a philosopher's myth. In attempting to explode the myth I shall probably be taken to be denying well-known facts about the mental life of human beings, and my plea that I aim at doing nothing more than rectify the logic of mental-conduct concepts will probably be disallowed as mere subterfuge.

I must first indicate what is meant by the phrase 'Category-mistake'. This I do in a series of illustrations.

A foreigner visiting Oxford or Cambridge for the first time is shown a number of colleges, libraries, playing fields, museums, scientific departments and administrative offices. He then asks 'But where is the University? I have seen where the members of the Colleges live, where the Registrar works, where the scientists experiment and the rest. But

I have not yet seen the University in which reside and work the members of your University.' It has then to be explained to him that the University is not another collateral institution, some ulterior counterpart to the colleges, laboratories and offices which he has seen. The University is just the way in which all that he has already seen is organized. When they are seen and when their co-ordination is understood, the University has been seen. His mistake lay in his innocent assumption that it was correct to speak of Christ Church, the Bodleian Library, the Ashmolean Museum *and* the University, to speak, that is, as if 'the University' stood for an extra member of the class of which these other units are members. He was mistakenly allocating the University to the same category as that to which the other institutions belong.

The same mistake would be made by a child witnessing the march-past of a division, who, having had pointed out to him such and such battalions, batteries, squadrons, etc., asked when the division was going to appear. He would be supposing that a division was a counterpart to the units already seen, partly similar to them and partly unlike them. He would be shown his mistake by being told that in watching the battalions, batteries and squadrons marching past he had been watching the division marching past. The march-past was not a parade of battalions, batteries, squadrons *and* a division; it was a parade of the battalions, batteries and squadrons *of* a division.

One more illustration. A foreigner watching his first game of cricket learns what are the functions of the bowlers, the batsmen, the fielders, the umpires and the scorers. He then says 'But there is no one left on the field to contribute the famous element of team-spirit. I see who does the bowling, the batting and the wicket-keeping; but I do not see whose role it is to exercise *esprit de corps*.' Once more, it would have to be explained that he was looking for the wrong type of thing. Team-spirit is not another cricketing-operation supplementary to all of the other special tasks. It is, roughly, the keenness with which each of the special tasks is performed, and performing a task keenly is not performing two tasks. Certainly exhibiting team-spirit is not the same thing as bowling or catching, but nor is it a third thing such that we can say that the bowler first bowls *and* then exhibits team-spirit or that a fielder is at a given moment *either* catching *or* displaying *esprit de corps*.

These illustrations of category-mistakes have a common feature which must be noticed. The mistakes were made by people who did not know how to wield the concepts *University, division* and *team-spirit*. Their puzzles arose from inability to use certain items in the English vocabulary.

The theoretically interesting category-mistakes are those made by people who are perfectly competent to apply concepts, at least in the situations with which they are familiar, but are still liable in their abstract thinking to allocate those concepts to logical types to which they do not belong. An instance of a mistake of this sort would be the following story. A student of politics has learned the main differences between the British, the French and the American Constitutions, and has learned also the differences and connections between the Cabinet, Parliament, the various Ministries, the Judicature and the Church of England. But he still becomes embarrassed when asked questions about the connections between the Church of England, the Home Office and the British Constitution. For while the Church and the Home Office are institutions, the British Constitution is not another institution in the same sense of that noun. So inter-institutional relations which can be asserted or denied to hold between the Church and the Home Office cannot be asserted or denied to hold between either of them and the British Constitution. 'The British Constitution' is not a term of the same logical type as 'the Home Office' and 'the Church of England'. In a partially similar way, John Doe may be a relative, a friend, an enemy or a stranger to Richard Roe; but he cannot be any of these things to the Average Taxpayer. He knows how to talk sense in certain sorts of discussions about the Average Taxpayer, but he is baffled to say why he could not come across him in the street as he can come across Richard Roe.

It is pertinent to our main subject to notice that, so long as the student of politics continues to think of the British Constitution as a counterpart to the other institutions, he will tend to describe it as a mysteriously occult institution; and so long as John Doe continues to think of the Average Taxpayer as a fellow-citizen, he will tend to think of him as an elusive insubstantial man, a ghost who is everywhere yet nowhere.

My destructive purpose is to show that a family of radical category-mistakes is the source of the double-life theory. The representation of a person as a ghost mysteriously ensconced in a machine derives from this argument. Because, as is true, a person's thinking, feeling and purposive doing cannot be described solely in the idioms of physics, chemistry and physiology, therefore they must be described in counter-part idioms. As the human body is a complex organised unit, so the human mind must be another complex organised unit, though one made of a different sort of stuff and with a different sort of structure. Or, again, as the human body, like any other parcel of matter, is a field of causes and effects, so the mind must be another field of causes and effects, though not (Heaven be praised) mechanical causes and effects.

¶ (3) THE ORIGIN OF THE CATEGORY-MISTAKE

One of the chief intellectual origins of what I have yet to prove to be the Cartesian category-mistake seems to be this. When Galileo showed that his methods of scientific discovery were competent to provide a mechanical theory which should cover every occupant of space, Descartes found in himself two conflicting motives. As a man of scientific genius he could not but endorse the claims of mechanics, yet as a religious and moral man he could not accept, as Hobbes accepted, the discouraging rider to those claims, namely that human nature differs only in degree of complexity from clockwork. The mental could not be just a variety of the mechanical.

He and subsequent philosophers naturally but erroneously availed themselves of the following escape-route. Since mental-conduct words are not to be construed as signifying the occurrence of mechanical processes, they must be construed as signifying the occurrence of non-mechanical processes; since mechanical laws explain movements in space as the effects of other movements in space, other laws must explain some of the non-spatial workings of minds as the effects of other non-spatial workings of minds. The difference between the human behaviours which we describe as intelligent and those which we describe as unintelligent must be a difference in their causation; so, while some movements of human tongues and limbs are the effects of mechanical causes, others must be the effects of non-mechanical causes, i.e. some issue from movements of particles of matter, others from workings of the mind.

The differences between the physical and the mental were thus represented as differences inside the common framework of the categories of 'thing', 'stuff', 'attribute', 'state', 'process', 'change', 'cause' and 'effect'. Minds are things, but different sorts of things from bodies; mental processes are causes and effects, but different sorts of causes and effects from bodily movements. And so on. Somewhat as the foreigner expected the University to be an extra edifice, rather like a college but also considerably different, so the repudiators of mechanism represented minds as extra centres of causal processes, rather like machines but also considerably different from them. Their theory was a para-mechanical hypothesis.

That this assumption was at the heart of the doctrine is shown by the fact that there was from the beginning felt to be a major theoretical difficulty in explaining how minds can influence and be influenced by bodies. How can a mental process, such as willing, cause spatial movements like the movements of the tongue? How can a physical change in the optic nerve have among its effects a mind's perception of a flash of light? This notorious crux by itself shows the logical mould into which Descartes pressed his theory of the mind. It was the self-same mould into which he and Galileo set their mechanics. Still unwittingly adhering to the grammar of mechanics, he tried to avert disaster by describing minds in what was merely an obverse vocabulary. The workings of minds had to be described by the mere negatives of the specific descriptions given to bodies; they are not in space, they are not motions, they are not modifications of matter, they are not accessible to public observation. Minds are not bits and the laws it obeys are not those known to ordinary engineers.

As thus represented, minds are not merely ghosts harnessed to machines, they are themselves just spectral machines. Though the human body is an engine, it is not quite an ordinary engine, since some of its workings are governed by another engine inside it—this interior governor-engine being one of a very special sort. It is invisible, inaudible and it has no size or weight. It cannot be taken to bits and the laws it obeys are not those known to ordinary engineers. Nothing is known of how it governs the bodily engine.

A second major crux points the same moral. Since, according to the doctrine, minds belong to the same category as bodies and since bodies are rigidly governed by mechanical laws, it seemed to many theorists to follow that minds must be similarly governed by rigid non-mechanical laws. The physical world is a deterministic system, so the mental world must be a deterministic system. Bodies cannot help the modifications that they undergo, so minds cannot help pursuing the careers fixed for them. *Responsibility, choice, merit* and *demerit* are therefore inapplicable concepts—unless the compromise solution is adopted of saying that the laws governing mental processes, unlike those governing physical processes, have the congenial attribute of being only rather rigid. The problem of the Freedom of the Will was the problem how to reconcile the hypothesis that minds are to be described in terms drawn from the categories of mechanics with the knowledge that higher-grade human conduct is not of a piece with the behaviour of machines.

It is an historical curiosity that it was not noticed that the entire argument was broken-backed. Theorists correctly assumed that any sane man could already recognise the differences between, say, rational and non-rational utterances or between purposive and automatic behaviour. Else there would have been nothing requiring to be salved from mechanism. Yet the explanation given presupposed that one person could in principle never recognise the difference between the rational and the irrational utterances issuing from other human bodies, since he could never get access to the postulated immaterial causes of some of their utterances. Save for the doubtful exception of himself, he could never tell the difference between a man and a Robot. It would have to be conceded, for example, that, for all that we can tell, the inner lives of persons who are classed as idiots or lunatics are as rational as those of anyone else. Perhaps only their overt behaviour is disappointing; that is to say, perhaps 'idiots' are not really idiotic, or 'lunatics' lunatic. Perhaps, too, some of those who are classed as sane are really idiots. According to the theory, external observers could never know how the overt behaviour of others is correlated with their mental powers and processes and so they could never know or even plausibly conjecture whether their applications of mental-conduct concepts to these other people were correct or incorrect. It would then be hazardous or impossible for a man to claim sanity or logical consistency even for himself, since he would be debarred from comparing his own performances with those of others. In short, our characterisations of persons and their performances as intelligent, prudent and virtuous or as stupid, hypocritical and cowardly could never have been made, so the problem of providing a special causal hypothesis to serve as the basis of such diagnoses would never have arisen. The question, 'How do persons differ from machines?' arose just because everyone already knew how to apply mental-conduct concepts before the new causal hypothesis was introduced. This causal hypothesis could not therefore be the source of the criteria used in those applications. Nor, of course, has the causal hypothesis in any degree improved our handling of those criteria. We still distinguish good from bad arithmetic, politic from impolitic conduct and fertile from infertile imaginations in the ways in which Descartes himself distinguished them before and after he speculated how the applicability of these criteria was compatible with the principle of mechanical causation.

He had mistaken the logic of his problem. Instead of asking by what criteria intelligent behaviour is actually distinguished from non-intelligent behaviour, he asked 'Given that the principle of mechanical causation does not tell us the difference, what other causal principle will tell it us?' He realised that the problem was not one of mechanics and assumed that it must therefore be one of some counterpart to mechanics. Not unnaturally psychology is often cast for just this role.

When two terms belong to the same category, it is proper to construct conjunctive propositions embodying them. Thus a purchaser may say that he bought a left-hand glove and a right-hand glove, but not that he bought a left-hand glove, a right-hand glove and a pair of gloves. 'She came home in a flood of tears and a sedan-chair' is a well-known joke based on the absurdity of conjoining terms of different types. It would have been equally ridiculous to construct the disjunction 'She came home either in a flood of tears or else in a sedan-chair'. Now the dogma of the Ghost in the Machine does just this. It maintains that there exist both bodies and minds; that there occur physical processes and mental processes; that there are mechanical causes of corporeal movements and mental causes of corporeal movements. I shall argue that these and other analogous conjunctions are absurd; but, it must be noticed, the argument will not show that either of the illegitimately conjoined propositions is absurd in itself. I am not, for· example, denying that there occur mental processes. Doing long division is a mental process and so is making a joke. But I am saying that the phrase 'there occur mental processes' does not mean the same sort of thing as 'there occur physical processes', and, therefore, that it makes no sense to conjoin or disjoin the two.

If my argument is successful, there will follow some interesting consequences. First, the hallowed contrast between Mind and Matter will be dissipated, but dissipated not by either of the equally hallowed absorptions of Mind by Matter or of Matter by Mind, but in quite a different way. For the seeming contrast of the two will be shown to be as illegitimate as would be the contrast of 'she came home in a flood of tears' and 'she came home in a sedan-chair'. The belief that there is a polar opposition between Mind and Matter is the belief that they are terms of the same logical type.

It will also follow that both Idealism and Materialism are answers to an improper question. The 'reduction' of the material world to mental states and processes, as well as the 'reduction' of mental states and processes to physical states and processes, presuppose the legitimacy of the disjunction 'Either there exist minds or there exist bodies (but not both)'. It would be like saying, 'Either she bought a left-hand and a right-hand glove or she bought a pair of gloves (but not both)'.

It is perfectly proper to say, in one logical tone of voice, that there exist minds and to say, in another logical tone of voice, that there exist bodies. But these expressions do not indicate two different species of existence, for 'existence' is not a generic word like 'coloured' or 'sexed'. They indicate two different senses of 'exist', somewhat as 'rising' has different senses in 'the tide is rising', 'hopes are rising', and 'the average age of death is rising'. A man would be thought to be making a poor joke who said that three things are now rising, namely the tide, hopes and the average age of death. It would be just as good or bad a joke to say that there exist prime numbers and Wednesdays and public opinions and navies; or that there exist both minds and bodies. In the succeeding chapters I try to prove that the official theory does rest on a batch of category-mistakes by showing that logically absurd corollaries follow from it. The exhibition of these absurdities will have the constructive effect of bringing out part of the correct logic of mental-conduct concepts.

¶ (4) HISTORICAL NOTE

It would not be true to say that the official theory derives solely from Descartes' theories, or even from a more widespread anxiety about the implications of seventeenth century mechanics. Scholastic and Reformation theology had schooled the intellects of the scientists as well as of the laymen, philosophers and clerics of that age. Stoic-Augustinian theories of the will were embedded in the Calvinist doctrines of sin and grace; Platonic and Aristotelian theories of the intellect shaped the orthodox doctrines of the immortality of the soul. Descartes was reformulating already prevalent theological doctrines of the soul in the new syntax of Galileo. The theologian's privacy of conscience became the philosopher's privacy of consciousness, and what had been the bogy of Predestination reappeared as the bogy of Determinism.

It would also not be true to say that the two-worlds myth did no theoretical good. Myths often do a lot of theoretical good, while they are still new. One benefit bestowed by the para-mechanical myth was that it partly superannuated the then prevalent para-political myth. Minds and their Faculties had previously been described by analogies with political superiors and political subordinates. The idioms used were those of ruling, obeying, collaborating and rebelling. They survived and still survive in many ethical and some epistemological discussions. As, in physics, the new myth of occult Forces was a scientific improvement on the old myth of Final Causes, so in anthropological and psychological theory, the new myth of hidden operations, impulses and agencies was an improvement on the old myth of dictations, deferences and disobediences.

XVII

LUDWIG WITTGENSTEIN

LUDWIG WITTGENSTEIN (1889-1951) was born in Vienna. Educated at home until he was fourteen, he then attended school at Linz and Berlin-Charlottenburg. In 1908 he went to England where, later that year, he became an engineering student at the University of Manchester. While at Manchester he read Russell's *Principles of Mathematics* and thereupon decided to give up engineering to study with Russell at Cambridge University. In Cambridge, during 1912-13, he began the research that led to the *Tractatus Logico-Philosophicus*. In 1913 he left England for Norway, where he lived as a recluse until the First World War when he volunteered for the Austrian Army. After the war, Wittgenstein taught in a small village school in Austria. In 1929 he returned to Cambridge where, after several more sojourns to the continent, he became Moore's successor to the Chair of Philosophy at Cambridge in 1939. He taught from 1939 to 1947, when he retired to devote his last years to writing.

Wittgenstein, whose engrossing life has been eloquently narrated by one of his pupils and friends, Norman Malcolm (*see* Bibliography), wrote two books, *Tractatus Logico-Philosophicus* (1922) and *Philosophical Investigations* (1953, published posthumously), that in content and influence are as important as any in twentieth century philosophy.

In the Preface to *Philosophical Investigations*, Wittgenstein writes: "The thoughts which I publish in what follows are the precipitate of philosophical investigations which have occupied me for the last sixteen years. They concern many subjects: the concepts of meaning, of understanding, of a proposition, of logic, the foundations of mathematics, states of consciousness, and other things. I have written down all these thoughts as *remarks*, short paragraphs, of which there is sometimes a fairly long chain about the same subject, while I sometimes make a sudden change, jumping from one topic to another."

One of these fairly long chains about the same subject is Wittgenstein's discussion of pain (reprinted below). It not only exemplifies the philosophical style and techniques of the *Investigations*, but also serves as a superb example of his doctrine that mental concepts do not refer to inner private states, hence, cannot be said to function as names in a uniquely private language. Elucidation of the concept of pain, i.e., of the "logical grammar" of "pain" —of its actual role in human life and the actual conditions under which "pain" plays that role, serves to remind us of the social or public character of this concept, consequently, to prove that the criteria for its correct use cannot be equated with private rules for its application because the very notion of a private rule is self-contradictory.

Pain and Private Language[1]

243. A human being can encourage himself, give himself orders, obey, blame and punish himself; he can ask himself a question and answer it. So we could imagine human beings who spoke only in monologue; who accompanied their activities by talking to themselves. —An explorer who watched them and listened to their talk might succeed in translating their language into ours. (This would enable him to predict these people's actions correctly, for he also hears them making resolutions and decisions.)

But could we also imagine a language in which a person could write down or give vocal expression to his inner experiences—his feelings, moods, and the rest—for his private use?——Well, can't we do so in our ordinary language?—But that is not what I mean. The individual words of this language are to refer to what can only be known to the person speaking; to his immediate private sensations. So another person cannot understand the language.

244. How do words *refer* to sensations?—There doesn't seem to be any problem here; don't we talk about sensations every day, and give them names? But how is the connexion between the name and the thing named set up? This question is the same as: how does a human being learn the meaning of the names of sensations?—of the word "pain" for example. Here is one possibility: words are connected with the primitive, the natural, expressions of the sensation and used in their place. A child has hurt himself and he cries; and then adults talk to him and teach him exclamations and, later, sentences. They teach the child new pain-behaviour.

"So you are saying that the word 'pain' really means crying?"—On the contrary: the verbal expression of pain replaces crying and does not describe it.

245. For how can I go so far as to try to use language to get between pain and its expression?

---

1. From *Philosophical Investigations* (Oxford: Basil Blackwell, 1953), pp. 88e–104e. Translated by G. E. M. Anscombe. Reprinted by permission of the publishers.

246. In what sense are my sensations *private?*—Well, only I can know whether I am really in pain; another person can only surmise it.—In one way this is false, and in another nonsense. If we are using the word "to know" as it is normally used (and how else are we to use it?), then other people very often know when I am in pain.— Yes, but all the same not with the certainty with which I know it myself!—It can't be said of me at all (except perhaps as a joke) that I *know* I am in pain. What is it supposed to mean—except perhaps that I *am* in pain?

Other people cannot be said to learn of my sensations *only* from my behaviour,—for *I* cannot be said to learn of them. I *have* them.

The truth is: it makes sense to say about other people that they doubt whether I am in pain; but not to say it about myself.

247. "Only you can know if you had this intention." One might tell someone this when one was explaining the meaning of the word "intention" to him. For then it means: *that* is how we use it.

(And here "know" means that the expression of uncertainty is senseless.)

248. The proposition "Sensations are private" is comparable to: "One plays patience by oneself".

249. Are we perhaps over-hasty in our assumption that the smile of an unweaned infant is not a pretence?—And on what experience is our assumption based?

(Lying is a language-game that needs to be learned like any other one.)

250. Why can't a dog simulate pain? Is he too honest? Could one teach a dog to simulate pain? Perhaps it is possible to teach him to howl on particular occasions as if he were in pain, even when he is not. But the surroundings which are necessary for this behaviour to be real simulation are missing.

251. What does it mean when we say: "I can't imagine the opposite of this" or "What would it be like, if it were otherwise?"—For example, when someone has said that my images are private, or that only I myself can know whether I am feeling pain, and similar things.

Of course, here "I can't imagine the opposite" doesn't mean: my powers of imagination are unequal to the task. These words are a defence against something whose form makes it look like an empirical proposition, but which is really a grammatical one.

But why do we say: "I can't imagine the opposite"? Why not: "I can't imagine the thing itself"?

Example: "Every rod has a length." That means something like: we call something (or *this*) "the length of a rod"—but nothing "the length of a sphere." Now can I imagine 'every rod having a length'? Well, I simply imagine a rod. Only this picture, in connexion with this proposition, has a quite different role from one used in connexion with the proposition "This table has the same length as the one over there". For here I understand what it means to have a picture of the opposite (nor need it be a mental picture).

But the picture attaching to the grammatical proposition could only shew, say, what is called "the length of a rod". And what should the opposite picture be?

((Remark about the negation of an *a priori* proposition.))

252. "This body has extension." To this we might reply: "Nonsense!"—but are inclined to reply "Of course!"—Why is this?

253. "Another person can't have my pains."—Which are *my* pains? What counts as a criterion of identity here? Consider what makes it possible in the case of physical objects to speak of "two exactly the same", for example, to say "This chair is not the one you saw here yesterday, but is exactly the same as it".

In so far as it makes *sense* to say that my pain is the same as his, it is also possible for us both to have the same pain. (And it would also be imaginable for two people to feel pain in the same—not just the corresponding—place. That might be the case with Siamese twins, for instance.)

I have seen a person in a discussion on this subject strike himself on the breast and say: "But surely another person can't have THIS pain!"—The answer to this is that one does not define a criterion of identity by emphatic stressing of the word "this". Rather, what the emphasis does is to suggest the case in which we are conversant with such a criterion of identity, but have to be reminded of it.

254. The substitution of "identical" for "the same" (for instance) is another typical expedient in philosophy. As if we were talking about shades of meaning and all that were in question were to find words to hit on the correct nuance. That is in question in philosophy only where we have to give a psychologically exact account of the temptation to use a particular kind of expression. What we 'are tempted to say' in such a case is, of course, not philosophy; but it is its raw material. Thus, for example, what a mathematician is inclined to say about the objectivity and reality of mathematical facts, is not a philosophy of mathematics, but something for philosophical *treatment*.

255. The philosopher's treatment of a question is like the treatment of an illness.

256. Now, what about the language which describes my inner experiences and which only I myself can understand? *How* do I use

words to stand for my sensations?—As we ordinarily do? Then are my words for sensations tied up with my natural expressions of sensation? In that case my language is not a 'private' one. Someone else might understand it as well as I.—But suppose I didn't have my natural expression of sensation, but only had the sensation? And now I simply *associate* names with sensations and use these names in descriptions.—

257. "What would it be like if human beings shewed no outward signs of pain (did not groan, grimace, etc.)? Then it would be impossible to teach a child the use of the word 'tooth-ache'."—Well, let's assume the child is a genius and itself invents a name for the sensation! —But then, of course, he couldn't make himself understood when he used the word.—So does he understand the name, without being able to explain its meaning to anyone?—But what does it mean to say that he has 'named his pain'?—How has he done this naming of pain?! And whatever he did, what was its purpose?—When one says "He gave a name to his sensation" one forgets that a great deal of stage-setting in the language is presupposed if the mere act of naming is to make sense. And when we speak of someone's having given a name to pain, what is presupposed is the existence of the grammar of the word "pain"; it shews the post where the new word is stationed.

258. Let us imagine the following case. I want to keep a diary about the recurrence of a certain sensation. To this end I associate it with the sign "E" and write this sign in a calendar for every day on which I have the sensation.——I will remark first of all that a definition of the sign cannot be formulated.—But still I can give myself a kind of ostensive definition.—How? Can I point to the sensation? Not in the ordinary sense. But I speak, or write the sign down, and at the same time I concentrate my attention on the sensation—and so, as it were, point to it inwardly.—But what is this ceremony for? for that is all it seems to be! A definition surely serves to establish the meaning of a sign.—Well, that is done precisely by the concentrating of my attention; for in this way I impress on myself the connexion between the sign and the sensation.—But "I impress it on myself" can only mean: this process brings it about that I remember the connexion *right* in the future. But in the present case I have no criterion of correctness. One would like to say: whatever is going to seem right to me is right. And that only means that here we can't talk about 'right'.

259. Are the rules of the private language *impressions* of rules?— The balance on which impressions are weighed is not the *impression* of a balance.

260. "Well, I *believe* that this is the sensation E again."—Perha
you *believe* that you believe it!

Then did the man who made the entry in the calendar make a no
of *nothing whatever?*—Don't consider it a matter of course that
person is making a note of something when he makes a mark—say
a calendar. For a note has a function, and this "E" so far has nor

(One can talk to oneself.—If a person talks when no one else
present, does that mean he is talking to himself?)

261. What reason have we for calling "E" the sign for a *sensatior*
For "sensation" is a word of our common language, not of one inte
ligible to me alone. So the use of this word stands in need of a justific
tion which everybody understands.—And it would not help either
say that it need not be a *sensation;* that when he writes "E", he h
something—and that is all that can be said. "Has" and "somethin₁
also belong to our common language.—So in the end when one is doi₁
philosophy one gets to the point where one would like just to emit ₁
inarticulate sound.—But such a sound is an expression only as it occu
in a particular language-game, which should now be described.

262. It might be said: if you have given yourself a private defir
tion of a word, then you must inwardly *undertake* to use the word
such-and-such a way. And how do you undertake that? Is it to ₁
assumed that you invent the technique of using the word; or that y₄
found it ready-made?

263. "But I can (inwardly) undertake to call THIS 'pain' in t₁
future."—"But is it certain that you have undertaken it? Are you su
that it was enough for this purpose to concentrate your attention ₄
your feeling?" A queer question.—

264. "Once you know *what* the word stands for, you understand ₁
you know its whole use."

265. Let us imagine a table (something like a dictionary) th
exists only in our imagination. A dictionary can be used to justi
the translation of a word X by a word Y. But are we also to call
a justification if such a table is to be looked up only in the imagir
tion?—"Well, yes; then it is a subjective justification."—But justific
tion consists in appealing to something independent.—"But surely
can appeal from one memory to another. For example, I don't knc
if I have remembered the time of departure of a train right and
check it I call to mind how a page of the time-table looked. Isn't
the same here?"—No; for this process has got to produce a memo₁
which is actually *correct*. If the mental image of the time-table cou
not itself be *tested* for correctness, how could it confirm the correctne
of the first memory? (As if someone were to buy several copies of t₁

morning paper to assure himself that what it said was true.)

Looking up a table in the imagination is no more looking up a table than the image of the result of an imagined experiment is the result of an experiment.

266. I can look at the clock to see what time it is: but I can also look at the dial of a clock in order to *guess* what time it is; or for the same purpose move the hand of a clock till its position strikes me as right. So the look of a clock may serve to determine the time in more than one way. (Looking at the clock in imagination.)

267. Suppose I wanted to justify the choice of dimensions for a bridge which I imagine to be building, by making loading tests on the material of the bridge in my imagination. This would, of course, be to imagine what is called justifying the choice of dimensions for a bridge. But should we also call it justifying an imagined choice of dimensions?

268. Why can't my right hand give my left hand money?—My right hand can put it into my left hand. My right hand can write a deed of gift and my left hand a receipt.—But the further practical consequences would not be those of a gift. When the left hand has taken the money from the right, etc., we shall ask: "Well, and what of it?" And the same could be asked if a person had given himself a private definition of a word; I mean, if he has said the word to himself and at the same time has directed his attention to a sensation.

269. Let us remember that there are certain criteria in a man's behaviour for the fact that he does not understand a word, that it means nothing to him; that he can do nothing with it. And criteria for his 'thinking he understands', attaching some meaning to the word, but not the right one. And, lastly, criteria for his understanding the word right. In the second case one might speak of a subjective understanding. And sounds which no one else understands but which I *'appear to understand'* might be called a "private language".

270. Let us now imagine a use for the entry of the sign "E" in my diary. I discover that whenever I have a particular sensation a manometer shews that my blood-pressure rises. So I shall be able to say that my blood-pressure is rising without using any apparatus. This is a useful result. And now it seems quite indifferent whether I have recognized the sensation *right* or not. Let us suppose I regularly identify it wrong, it does not matter in the least. And that alone shews that the hypothesis that I make a mistake is mere show. (We as it were turned a knob which looked as if it could be used to turn on some part of the machine; but it was a mere ornament, not connected with the mechanism at all.)

And what is our reason for calling "E" the name of a sensation here? Perhaps the kind of way this sign is employed in this language-game.—And why a "particular sensation," that is, the same one every time? Well, aren't we supposing that we write "E" every time?

271. "Imagine a person whose memory could not retain *what* the word 'pain' meant—so that he constantly called different things by that name—but nevertheless used the word in a way fitting in with the usual symptoms and presuppositions of pain"—in short he uses it as we all do. Here I should like to say: a wheel that can be turned though nothing else moves with it, is not part of the mechanism.

272. The essential thing about private experience is really not that each person possesses his own exemplar, but that nobody knows whether other people also have *this* or something else. The assumption would thus be possible—though unverifiable—that one section of mankind had one sensation of red and another section another.

273. What am I to say about the word "red"?—that it means something 'confronting us all' and that everyone should really have another word, besides this one, to mean his *own* sensation of red? Or is it like this: the word "red" means something known to everyone; and in addition, for each person, it means something known only to him? (Or perhaps rather: it *refers* to something known only to him.)

274. Of course, saying that the word "red" "refers to" instead of "means" something private does not help us in the least to grasp its function; but it is the more psychologically apt expression for a particular experience in doing philosophy. It is as if when I uttered the word I cast a sidelong glance at the private sensation, as it were in order to say to myself: I know all right what I mean by it.

275. Look at the blue of the sky and say to yourself "How blue the sky is!"—When you do it spontaneously—without philosophical intentions—the idea never crosses your mind that this impression of colour belongs only to *you*. And you have no hesitation in exclaiming that to someone else. And if you point at anything as you say the words you point at the sky. I am saying: you have not the feeling of pointing-into-yourself, which often accompanies 'naming the sensation' when one is thinking about 'private language'. Nor do you think that really you ought not to point to the colour with your hand, but with your attention. (Consider what it means "to point to something with the attention".)

276. But don't we at least *mean* something quite definite when we look at a colour and name our colour-impression? It is as if we detached the colour-*impression* from the object, like a membrane. (This ought to arouse our suspicions.)

277. But how is it even possible for us to be tempted to think that we use a word to *mean* at one time the colour known to everyone—and at another the 'visual impression' which *I* am getting *now?* How can there be so much as a temptation here?——I don't turn the same kind of attention on the colour in the two cases. When I mean the colour impression that (as I should like to say) belongs to me alone I immerse myself in the colour—rather like when I 'cannot get my fill of a colour'. Hence it is easier to produce this experience when one is looking at a bright colour, or at an impressive colour-scheme.

278. "I know how the colour green looks to *me*"—that makes sense!—Certainly: which use of the proposition are you thinking of?

279. Imagine someone saying: "But I know how tall I am!" and laying his hand on top of his head to prove it.

280. Someone paints a picture in order to shew how he imagines a theatre scene. And now I say: "This picture has a double function: it informs others, as pictures or words inform——but for the one who gives the information it is a representation (or piece of information?) of another kind: for him it is the picture of his image, as it can't be for anyone else. To him his private impression of the picture means what he has imagined, in a sense in which the picture cannot mean this to others."—And what right have I to speak in this second case of a representation or piece of information—if these words were rightly used in the *first* case?

281. "But doesn't what you say come to this: that there is no pain, for example, without *pain-behaviour?*"—It comes to this: only of a living human being and what resembles (behaves like) a living human being can one say: it has sensations; it sees; is blind; hears; is deaf; is conscious or unconscious.

282. "But in a fairy tale the pot too can see and hear!" (Certainly; but it *can* also talk.)

"But the fairy tale only invents what is not the case: it does not talk *nonsense*."—It is not as simple as that. Is it false or nonsensical to say that a pot talks? Have we a clear picture of the circumstances in which we should say of a pot that it talked? (Even a nonsense-poem is not nonsense in the same way as the babbling of a child.)

We do indeed say of an inanimate thing that it is in pain: when playing with dolls for example. But this use of the concept of pain is a secondary one. Imagine a case in which people ascribed pain *only* to inanimate things; pitied *only* dolls! (When children play at trains their game is connected with their knowledge of trains. It would nevertheless be possible for the children of a tribe unacquainted with trains to learn this game from others, and to play it without knowing that it was copied from anything. One might say that the game did not make the same *sense* to them as to us.)

283. What gives us *so much as the idea* that living beings, things, can feel?

Is it that my education has led me to it by drawing my attention to feelings in myself, and now I transfer the idea to objects outside myself? That I recognize that there is something there (in me) which I can call "pain" without getting into conflict with the way other people use this word?—I do not transfer my idea to stones, plants, etc.

Couldn't I imagine having frightful pains and turning to stone while they lasted? Well, how do I know, if I shut my eyes, whether I have not turned into a stone? And if that has happened, in what sense will *the stone* have the pains? In what sense will they be ascribable to the stone? And why need the pain have a bearer at all here?!

And can one say of the stone that it has a soul and *that* is what has the pain? What has a soul, or pain, to do with a stone?

Only of what behaves like a human being can one say that it *has* pains.

For one has to say it of a body, or, if you like of a soul which some body *has*. And how can a body *have* a soul?

284. Look at a stone and imagine it having sensations.—One says to oneself: How could one so much as get the idea of ascribing a *sensation* to a *thing*? One might as well ascribe it to a number!—And now look at a wriggling fly and at once these difficulties vanish and pain seems able to get a foothold here, where before everything was, so to speak, too smooth for it.

And so, too, a corpse seems to us quite inaccessible to pain.—Our attitude to the living is not the same as to the dead. All our reactions are different.—If anyone says: "That cannot simply arise from the fact that a living thing moves in such and such ways and a dead one not then I want to intimate to him that this is a case of the transition 'from quantity to quality'.

285. Think of the recognition of *facial expressions*. Or of the description of facial expressions—which does not consist in giving the measurements of the face! Think, too, how one can imitate a man's face without seeing one's own in a mirror.

286. But isn't it absurd to say of a *body* that it has pain?——And why does one feel an absurdity in that? In what sense is it true that my hand does not feel pain, but I in my hand?

What sort of issue is: Is it the *body* that feels pain?—How is it to be decided? What makes it plausible to say that it is *not* the body?—

Vell, something like this: if someone has a pain in his hand, then the and does not say so (unless it writes it) and one does not comfort he hand, but the sufferer: one looks into his face.

287. How am I filled with pity *for this man?* How does it come ut what the object of my pity is? (Pity, one may say, is a form of onviction that someone else is in pain.)

288. I turn to stone and my pain goes on.—Suppose I were in rror and it was no longer *pain?*——But I can't be in error here; t means nothing to doubt whether I am in pain!—That means: if nyone said "I do not know if what I have got is a pain or something lse", we should think something like, he does not know what the English word "pain" means; and we should explain it to him.—How? Perhaps by means of gestures, or by pricking him with a pin and saying: "See, that's what pain is!" This explanation, like any other, he might understand right, wrong, or not at all. And he will shew which he does by his use of the word, in this as in other cases.

If he now said, for example: "Oh, I know what 'pain' means; what I don't know is whether *this*, that I have now, is pain"—we should merely shake our heads and be forced to regard his words as a queer reaction which we have no idea what to do with. (It would be rather as if we heard someone say seriously: "I distinctly remember that some time before I was born I believed . . . . .".)

That expression of doubt has no place in the language-game; but if we cut out human behaviour, which is the expression of sensation, it looks as if I might *legitimately* begin to doubt afresh. My temptation to say that one might take a sensation for something other than what it is arises from this: if I assume the abrogation of the normal language-game with the expression of a sensation, I need a criterion of identity for the sensation; and then the possibility of error also exists.

289. "When I say 'I am in pain' I am at any rate justified *before myself*."—What does that mean? Does it mean: "If someone else could know what I am calling 'pain', he would admit that I was using the word correctly"?

To use a word without a justification does not mean to use it without right.

290. What I do is not, of course, to identify my sensation by criteria: but to repeat an expression. But this is not the *end* of the language-game: it is the beginning.

But isn't the beginning the sensation—which I describe?—Perhaps this word "describe" tricks us here. I say "I describe my state of mind" and "I describe my room". You need to call to mind the differences between the language-games.

291. What we call *"descriptions"* are instruments for particular uses. Think of a machine-drawing, a cross-section, an elevation with measurements, which an engineer has before him. Thinking of description as a word-picture of the facts has something misleading about it: one tends to think only of such pictures as hang on our walls which seem simply to portray how a thing looks, what it is like. (These pictures are as it were idle.)

292. Don't always think that you read off what you say from the facts; that you portray these in words according to rules. For even so you would have to apply the rule in the particular case without guidance.

293. If I say of myself that it is only from my own case that I know what the word "pain" means—must I not say the same of other people too? And how can I generalize the *one* case so irresponsibly?

Now someone tells me that *he* knows what pain is only from his own case!——Suppose everyone had a box with something in it: we call it a "beetle". No one can look into anyone else's box, and everyone says he knows what a beetle is only by looking at *his* beetle.—Here it would be quite possible for everyone to have something different in his box. One might even imagine such a thing constantly changing.—But suppose the word "beetle" had a use in these people's language?—If so it would not be used as the name of a thing. The thing in the box has no place in the language-game at all; not even as *a something* for the box might even be empty.—No, one can 'divide through' by the thing in the box; it cancels out, whatever it is.

That is to say: if we construe the grammar of the expression of sensation on the model of 'object and name' the object drops out of consideration as irrelevant.

294. If you say he sees a private picture before him, which he is describing, you have still made an assumption about what he has before him. And that means that you can describe it or do describe it more closely. If you admit that you haven't any notion what kind of thing it might be that he has before him—then what leads you into saying, in spite of that, that he has something before him? Isn't it as if I were to say of someone: "He *has* something. But I don't know whether it is money, or debts, or an empty till."

295. "I know . . . . only from my *own* case"—what kind of proposition is this meant to be at all? An experiential one? No.—A grammatical one?

Suppose everyone does say about himself that he knows what pain is only from his own pain.—Not that people really say that, or are even prepared to say it. But *if* everybody said it——it might be a kind of exclamation. And even if it gives no information, still it is a picture, and why should we not want to call up such a picture? Imagine an allegorical painting taking the place of those words.

When we look into ourselves as we do philosophy, we often get to see just such a picture. A full-blown pictorial representation of our grammar. Not facts; but as it were illustrated turns of speech.

296. "Yes, but there is *something* there all the same accompanying my cry of pain. And it is on account of that that I utter it. And this something is what is important—and frightful."—Only whom are we informing of this? And on what occasion?

297. Of course, if water boils in a pot, steam comes out of the pot and also pictured steam comes out of the pictured pot. But what if one insisted on saying that there must also be something boiling in the pictured pot?

298. The very fact that we should so much like to say: *"This* is the important thing"—while we point privately to the sensation— is enough to shew how much we are inclined to say something which gives no information.

299. Being unable—when we surrender ourselves to philosophical thought—to help saying such-and-such; being irresistibly inclined to say it—does not mean being forced into an *assumption,* or having an immediate perception or knowledge of a state of affairs.

300. It is—we should like to say—not merely the picture of the behaviour that plays a part in the language-game with the words "he is in pain", but also the picture of the pain. Or, not merely the paradigm of the behaviour, but also that of the pain.—It is a misunderstanding to say "The picture of pain enters into the language-game with the word 'pain'." The image of pain is not a picture and *this* image is not replaceable in the language-game by anything that we should call a picture.—The image of pain certainly enters into the language game in a sense; only not as a picture.

301. An image is not a picture, but a picture can correspond to it.

302. If one has to imagine someone else's pain on the model of one's own, this is none too easy a thing to do: for I have to imagine pain which I *do not feel* on the model of the pain which I *do feel.* That is, what I have to do is not simply to make a transition in imagination from one place of pain to another. As, from pain in the hand to pain in the arm. For I am not to imagine that I feel pain in some region of his body. (Which would also be possible.)

Pain-behaviour can point to a painful place—but the subject of pain is the person who gives it expression.

303. "I can only *believe* that someone else is in pain, but I *know* it

if I am."—Yes: one can make the decision to say "I believe he is in pain" instead of "He is in pain". But that is all.——What looks like an explanation here, or like a statement about a mental process, is in truth an exchange of one expression for another which, while we are doing philosophy, seems the more appropriate one.

Just try—in a real case—to doubt someone else's fear or pain.

304. "But you will surely admit that there is a difference between pain-behaviour accompanied by pain and pain-behaviour without any pain?"—Admit it? What greater difference could there be?—"And yet you again and again reach the conclusion that the sensation itself is a *nothing*."—Not at all. It is not a *something*, but not a *nothing* either! The conclusion was only that a nothing would serve just as well as a something about which nothing could be said. We have only rejected the grammar which tries to force itself on us here.

The paradox disappears only if we make a radical break with the idea that language always functions in one way, always serves the same purpose: to convey thoughts—which may be about houses, pains, good and evil, or anything else you please.

305. "But you surely cannot deny that, for example, in remembering, an inner process takes place."—What gives the impression that we want to deny anything? When one says "Still, an inner process does take place here"—one wants to go on: "After all, you *see* it." And it is this inner process that one means by the word "remembering".—The impression that we wanted to deny something arises from our setting our faces against the picture of the 'inner process'. What we deny is that the picture of the inner process gives us the correct idea of the use of the word "to remember". We say that this picture with its ramifications stands in the way of our seeing the use of the word as it is.

306. Why should I deny that there is a mental process? But "There has just taken place in me the mental process of remembering . . . ." means nothing more than: "I have just remembered . . . .". To deny the mental process would mean to deny the remembering; to deny that anyone ever remembers anything.

307. "Are you not really a behaviourist in disguise? Aren't you at bottom really saying that everything except human behaviour is a fiction?"—If I do speak of a fiction, then it is of a *grammatical* fiction.

308. How does the philosophical problem about mental processes and states and about behaviourism arise?——The first step is the one that altogether escapes notice. We talk of processes and states and leave their nature undecided. Sometime perhaps we shall know more

bout them—we think. But that is just what commits us to a particular
way of looking at the matter. For we have a definite concept of what
it means to learn to know a process better. (The decisive movement
in the conjuring trick has been made, and it was the very one that
we thought quite innocent.)—And now the analogy which was to make
us understand our thoughts falls to pieces. So we have to deny the yet
uncomprehended process in the yet unexplored medium. And now it
looks as if we had denied mental processes. And naturally we don't
want to deny them.

309. What is your aim in philosophy?—To shew the fly the way out
of the fly-bottle.

310. I tell someone I am in pain. His attitude to me will then be
that of belief; disbelief; suspicion; and so on.

Let us assume he says: "It's not so bad."—Doesn't that prove that
he believes in something behind the outward expression of pain?——
His attitude is a proof of his attitude. Imagine not merely the words
"I am in pain" but also the answer "It's not so bad" replaced by
instinctive noises and gestures.

311. "What difference could be greater?"—In the case of pain I
believe that I can give myself a private exhibition of the difference.
But I can give anyone an exhibition of the difference between a broken
and an unbroken tooth.—But for the private exhibition you don't
have to give yourself actual pain; it is enough to *imagine* it—for
instance, you screw up your face a bit. And do you know that what you
are giving yourself this exhibition of is pain and not, for example, a
facial expression? And how do you know what you are to give yourself
an exhibition of before you do it? This *private* exhibition is an illusion.

312. But again, *aren't* the cases of the tooth and the pain similar?
For the visual sensation in the one corresponds to the sensation of
pain in the other. I can exhibit the visual sensation to myself as little
or as well as the sensation of pain.

Let us imagine the following: The surfaces of the things around us
(stones, plants, etc.) have patches and regions which produce pain
in our skin when we touch them. (Perhaps through the chemical composition of these surfaces. But we need not know that.) In this case
we should speak of pain-patches on the leaf of a particular plant just
as at present we speak of red patches. I am supposing that it is useful
to us to notice these patches and their shapes; that we can infer important properties of the objects from them.

313. I can exhibit pain, as I exhibit red, and as I exhibit straight
and crooked and trees and stones.—*That* is what we *call* "exhibiting".

314. It shews a fundamental misunderstanding, if I am inclined to

study the headache I have now in order to get clear about the philo sophical problem of sensation.

315. Could someone understand the word "pain", who had *never* felt pain?—Is experience to teach me whether this is so or not?— And if we say "A man could not imagine pain without having sometime felt it"—how do we know? How can it be decided whether it is true?

316. In order to get clear about the meaning of the word "think" we watch ourselves while we think; what we observe will be what the word means!—But this concept is not used like that. (It would be as if without knowing how to play chess, I were to try and make out what the word "mate" meant by close observation of the last move of some game of chess.)

317. Misleading parallels: the expression of pain is a cry—the expression of thought, a proposition.

As if the purpose of the proposition were to convey to one person how it is with another: only, so to speak, in his thinking part and not in his stomach.

XVIII

JOHN AUSTIN

JOHN AUSTIN (1911-60) WAS until his death White's Professor of Moral Philosophy at the University of Oxford. Educated at Balliol College, Oxford, he became a Fellow of All Souls' College, then moved to Magdalen College until 1952, when he was elected to the Chair of Moral Philosophy. During his lifetime he published important papers, among them his classic, "Other Minds" (1946), and a translation of Frege's *Foundations of Arithmetic* (1950). After his death, two important sets of lectures were collected and edited by G. Warnock and J. O. Urmson. His influence upon philosophy in Anglo-Saxon countries has been very great, comparable with that of Wittgenstein.

For Austin, as for others, the central task of philosophy—the "begin-all" if not the "end-all"—is the careful elucidation of some of the concepts of ordinary language. But unlike Wittgenstein (and others), this elucidation is regarded as valuable for its own sake, not simply for the alleviation of philosophical puzzlement. Clarification of the subtle distinctions embodied in ordinary language illuminates equally subtle discriminata in the world: "When we examine what we would say when, what words we should use in what situations, we are looking again not *merely* at words (or "meanings," whatever they may be) but also at the realities we use the words to talk about: we are using a sharpened awareness of words to sharpen our perception of, though not as the final arbiter of, the phenomena."

Austin's "A Plea for Excuses" (1956) provides an excellent account of some of his aims, techniques, and results. Central to the concept of excuses is responsibility. What, among other things, Austin asks, is involved in this notion? If we turn from the nature or analysis of responsibility and traditional theories of free will to our ordinary ways of assessing human responsibility, we find an amazing array of related terms: "deliberately," "intentionally," "on purpose," "knowingly," "voluntarily," "accidentally," "by mistake," "inadvertently," "unwittingly," "involuntarily," and "under duress." All of these terms and the acts or situations they mark out or qualify must come into any adequate philosophical account of responsibility and the making of excuses.

A Plea for Excuses[1]

The subject of this paper, *Excuses,* is one not to be treated, but only to be introduced, within such limits. It is, or might be, the name of a whole branch, even a ramiculated branch, of philosophy, or at least of one fashion of philosophy. I shall try, therefore, first to state *what* the subject is, *why* it is worth studying, and *how* it may be studied, all this at a regrettably lofty level: and then I shall illustrate, in more congenial but desultory detail, some of the methods to be used, together with their limitations, and some of the unexpected results to be expected and lessons to be learned. Much, of course, of the amusement, and of the instruction, comes in drawing the coverts of the microglot, in hounding down the minutiae, and to this I can do no more here than incite you. But I owe it to the subject to say, that it has long afforded me what philosophy is so often thought, and made, barren of—the fun of discovery, the pleasures of cooperation, and the satisfaction of reaching agreement.

What, then, is the subject? I am here using the word "excuses" *for a title,* but it would be unwise to freeze too fast to this one noun and its partner verb: indeed for some time I used to use "extenuation" instead. Still, on the whole "excuses" is probably the most central and embracing term in the field, although this includes others of importance —"plea," "defense," "justification," and so on. When, then, do we "excuse" conduct, our own or somebody else's? When are "excuses" proffered?

In general, the situation is one where someone is *accused* of having done something, or (if that will keep it any cleaner) where someone is *said* to have done something which is bad, wrong, inept, unwelcome, or in some other of the numerous possible ways untoward. Thereupon he, or someone on his behalf, will try to defend his conduct or to get him out of it.

One way of going about this is to admit flatly that,he, X, did do

1. The Presidential Address to the Aristotelian Society, 1956, *Proceedings of the Aristotelian Society,* 1956-57. Reprinted by permission of the Editor.

that very thing, A, but to argue that it was a good thing, or the right or sensible thing, or a permissible thing to do, either in general or at least in the special circumstances of the occasion. To take this line is to *justify* the action, to give reasons for doing it: not to say, to brazen it out, to glory in it, or the like.

A different way of going about it is to admit that it wasn't a good thing to have done, but to argue that it is not quite fair or correct to say *baldly* "X did A." We may say it isn't fair just to say X did it; perhaps he was under somebody's influence, or was nudged. Or, it isn't fair to say baldly he *did* A; it may have been partly accidental, or an unintentional slip. Or, it isn't fair to say he did simply A—he was really doing something quite different and A was only incidental, or he was looking at the whole thing quite differently. Naturally these arguments can be combined or overlap or run into each other.

In the one defense, briefly, we accept responsibility but deny that it was bad: in the other, we admit that it was bad but don't accept full, or even any, responsibility.

By and large, justifications can be kept distinct from excuses, and I shall not be so anxious to talk about them because they have enjoyed more than their fair share of philosophical attention. But the two certainly can be confused, and can *seem* to go very near to each other, even if they do not perhaps actually do so. You dropped the tea tray: Certainly, but an emotional storm was about to break out: or, Yes, but there was a wasp. In each case the defense, very soundly, insists on a fuller description of the event in its context; but the first is a justification, the second an excuse. Again, if the objection is to the use of such a dyslogistic verb as "murdered," this may be on the ground that the killing was done in battle (justification) or on the ground that it was only accidental if reckless (excuse). It is arguable that we do not use the terms "justification" and "excuse" as carefully as we might; a miscellany of even less-clear terms, such as "extenuation," "palliation," "mitigation," hovers uneasily between partial justification and partial excuse; and when we plead, say, provocation, there is genuine uncertainty or ambiguity as to what we mean—is *he* partly responsible, because he roused a violent impulse or passion in me, so that it wasn't truly or merely me acting "of my own accord" (excuse)? Or is it rather that, he having done me such injury, I was entitled to retaliate (justification)? Such doubts merely make it the more urgent to clear up the usage of these various terms. But that the defenses I have for convenience labeled "justification" and "excuse" are in principle distinct can scarcely be doubted.

This then is the sort of situation we have to consider under "excuses." I will only further point out how very wide a field it covers. We have, of course, to bring in the opposite numbers of excuses—the expressions that *aggravate,* such as "deliberately," "on purpose," and so on, if only for the reason that an excuse often takes the form of a rebuttal of one of these. But we have also to bring in a large number of expressions which at first blush look not so much like excuses as like accusations—"clumsiness," "tactlessness," "thoughtlessness," and the like. Because it has always to be remembered that few excuses get us out of it *completely*: the average excuse, in a poor situation, gets us only out of the fire into the frying-pan—but still, of course, any frying-pan in a fire. If I have broken your dish or your romance, maybe the best defense I can find will be clumsiness.

Why, if this is what "excuses" are, should we trouble to investigate them? It might be thought reason enough that their production has always bulked so large among human activities. But to moral philosophy in particular a study of them will contribute in special ways, both positively towards the development of a cautious, latter-day version of conduct, and negatively towards the correction of older and hastier theories.

In ethics we study, I suppose, the good and the bad, the right and the wrong, and this must be for the most part in some connection with conduct or the doing of actions. Yet before we consider what actions are good or bad, right or wrong, it is proper to consider first what is meant by, and what not, and what is included under, and what not, the expression "doing an action" or "doing something." These are expressions still too little examined on their own account and merits, just as the general notion of "saying something" is still too lightly passed over in logic. There is indeed a vague and comforting idea in the background that, after all, in the last analysis, doing an action must come down to the making of physical movements with parts of the body; but this is about as true as that saying something must, in the last analysis, come down to making movements of the tongue.

The beginning of sense, not to say wisdom, is to realize that "doing an action," as used in philosophy,[2] is a highly abstract expression—it is a stand-in used in the place of any (or almost any?) verb with a personal subject, in the same sort of way that "thing" is a stand-in for any (or when we remember, almost any) noun substantive, and "quality" a stand-in for the adjective. Nobody, to be sure, relies on such dummies quite implicitly quite indefinitely. Yet notoriously it is possible to arrive at, or to derive the idea for, an oversimplified metaphysics

---

2. This use has little to do with the more down-to-earth occurrences of "action" in ordinary speech.

from the obsession with "things" and their "qualities." In a similar way, less commonly recognized even in these semi-sophisticated times, we fall for the myth of the verb. We treat the expression "doing an action" no longer as a stand-in for a verb with a personal subject, as which it has no doubt some uses, and might have more if the range of verbs were not left unspecified, but as a self-explanatory, ground-level description, one which brings adequately into the open the essential features of everything that comes, by simple inspection, under it. We scarcely notice even the most patent exceptions or difficulties (is to think something, or to say something, or to try to do something, to do an action?), any more than we fret, in the *ivresse des grandes profondeurs*, as to whether flames are things or events. So we come easily to think of our behavior over any time, and of a life as a whole, as consisting in doing now action A, next action B, then action C, and so on, just as elsewhere we come to think of the world as consisting of this, that, and the other substance or material thing, each with its properties. All "actions" are, as actions (meaning what?), equal, composing a quarrel with striking a match, winning a war with sneezing: worse still, we assimilate them one and all to the supposedly most obvious and easy cases, such as posting letters or moving fingers, just as we assimilate all "things" to horses or beds.

If we are to continue to use this expression in sober philosophy, we need to ask such questions as: Is to sneeze to do an action? Or is to breathe, or to see, or to checkmate, or each one of countless others? In short, for what range of verbs, as used on what occasions, is "doing an action" a stand-in? What have they in common, and what do those excluded severally lack? Again we need to ask how we decide what is the correct name for "the" action that somebody did—and what, indeed, are the rules for the use of "the" action, "an" action, "one" action, a "part" or "phase" of an action and the like. Further, we need to realize that even the "simplest" named actions are not so simple—certainly are not the mere makings of physical movements, and to ask what more, then, comes in (intentions? conventions?) and what does not (motives?), and what is the detail of the complicated internal machinery we use in "acting"—the receipt of intelligence, the appreciation of the situation, the invocation of principles, the planning, the control of execution and the rest.

In two main ways the study of excuses can throw light on these fundamental matters. First, to examine excuses is to examine cases where there has been some abnormality or failure: and as so often, the abnormal will throw light on the normal, will help us to penetrate the blinding veil of ease and obviousness that hides the mechanisms of the natural successful act. It rapidly becomes plain that the breakdowns signalized by the various excuses are of radically different kinds, affecting different parts or stages of the machinery, which the excuses consequently pick out and sort out for us. Further, it emerges that not *every* slip-up occurs in connection with *every*thing that could be called an "action," that not every excuse is apt with every verb—far indeed from it: and this provides us with one means of introducing some classification into the vast miscellany of "actions." If we classify them according to the particular selection of breakdowns to which each is liable, this should assign them their places in some family group or groups of actions, or in some model of the machinery of acting.

In this sort of way, the philosophical study of conduct can get off to a positive fresh start. But by the way, and more negatively, a number of traditional cruces or mistakes in this field can be resolved or removed. First among these comes the problem of Freedom. While it has been the tradition to present this as the "positive" term requiring elucidation, there is little doubt that to say we acted "freely" in the philosopher's use, which is only faintly related to the everyday use) is to say only that we acted *not* unfreely, in one or another of the many heterogeneous ways of so acting (under duress, or what not). Like "real," "free" is only used to rule out the suggestion of some or all of its recognized antitheses. As "truth" is not a name for a characteristic of assertions, so "freedom" is not a name for a characteristic of actions, but the name of a dimension in which actions are assessed. In examining all the ways in which each action may not be "free," i.e., the cases in which it will not do to say simply "X did A," we may hope to dispose of the problem of Freedom. Aristotle has often been chidden for talking about excuses or pleas and overlooking "the real problem": in my own case, it was when I began to see the injustice of this charge that I first became interested in excuses.

There is much to be said for the view that, philosophical tradition apart, Responsibility would be a better candidate for the role here assigned to Freedom. If ordinary language is to be our guide, it is to evade responsibility, or full responsibility, that we most often make excuses, and I have used the word myself in this way above. But in fact "responsibility" too seems not really apt in all cases: I do not exactly evade responsibility when I plead clumsiness or tactlessness, nor, often, when I plead that I only did it unwillingly or reluctantly, and still less if I plead that I had in the circumstances no choice: here I was constrained and have an excuse (or justification), yet may accept responsibility. It may be, then, that at least two key terms, Freedom and Responsibility, are needed: the relation between them is not clear, and it may be hoped that the investigation of excuses will contribute towards its clarification.[3]

So much, then, for ways in which the study of excuses may throw light on ethics. But there are also reasons why it is an attractive subject methodologically, at least if we are to proceed from "ordinary language," that is, by examining *what we should say when,* and so why and what we should mean by it. Perhaps this method, at least as *one* philosophical method, scarcely requires justification at present—too evidently, there is gold in them thar hills: more opportune would be a warning about the care and thoroughness needed if it is not to fall into disrepute. I will, however, justify it very briefly.

First, words are our tools, and, as a minimum, we should use clean tools: we should know what we mean and what we do not, and we must forearm ourselves against the traps that language sets us. Secondly, words are not (except in their own little corner) facts or things: we need therefore to prize them off the world, to hold them apart from and against it, so that we can realize their inadequacies and arbitrariness, and can relook at the world without blinkers. Thirdly, and more hopefully, our common stock of words embodies all the distinctions men have found worth drawing, and the connections they have found worth making, in the lifetimes of many generations: these surely are likely to be more numerous, more sound, since they have stood up to the long test of the survival of the fittest, and more subtle, at least in all ordinary and reasonably practical matters, than any that you or I are likely to think up in our armchairs of an afternoon—the most favored alternative method.

In view of the prevalence of the slogan "ordinary language," and of such names as "linguistic" or "analytic" philosophy or "the analysis of language," one thing needs specially emphasizing to counter misunderstandings. When we examine what we should say when, what words we should use in what situations, we are looking again not *merely* at words (or "meanings," whatever they may be) but also at the realities we use the words to talk about: we are using a sharpened awareness of words to sharpen our perception of, though not as the final arbiter of,

---

3. Another well-flogged horse in these same stakes is Blame. At least two things seem confused together under this term. Sometimes when I blame X for doing A, say for breaking the vase, it is a question simply or mainly of my disapproval of A, breaking the vase, which unquestionably X did: but sometimes it is, rather, a question simply or mainly of how far I think X responsible for A, which unquestionably was bad. Hence if somebody says he blames me for something, I may answer by giving a *justification,* so that he will cease to disapprove of what I did, or else by giving an *excuse,* so that he will cease to hold me, at least entirely and in every way, responsible for doing it.

the phenomena. For this reason I think it might be better to use, for this way of doing philosophy, some less misleading name than those given above—for instance, "linguistic phenomenology," only that is rather a mouthful.

Using, then, such a method, it is plainly preferable to investigate a field where ordinary language is rich and subtle, as it is in the pressingly practical matter of Excuses, but certainly is not in the matter, say, of Time. At the same time we should prefer a field which is not too much trodden into bogs or tracks by traditional philosophy, for in that case even "ordinary" language will often have become infected with the jargon of extinct theories, and our own prejudices too, as the upholders or imbibers of theoretical views, will be too readily, and often insensibly, engaged. Here too, Excuses form an admirable topic; we can discuss at least clumsiness, or absence of mind, or inconsiderateness, even spontaneousness, without remembering what Kant thought, and so progress by degrees even to discussing deliberation without for once remembering Aristotle or self-control without Plato. Granted that our subject is, as already claimed for it, neighboring, analogous, or germane in some way to some notorious center of philosophical trouble, then, with these two further requirements satisfied, we should be certain of what we are after: a good site for *field work* in philosophy. Here at last we should be able to unfreeze, to loosen up and get going on agreeing about discoveries, however small, and on agreeing about how to reach agreement.[4] How much it is to be wished that similar field work will soon be undertaken in, say, aesthetics; if only we could forget for a while about the beautiful and get down instead to the dainty and the dumpy.

There are, I know, or are supposed to be, snags in "linguistic" philosophy, which those not very familiar with it find, sometimes not without glee or relief, daunting. But with snags, as with nettles, the thing to do is to grasp them—and to climb above them. I will mention two in particular, over which the study of excuses may help to encourage us. The first is the snag of Loose (or Divergent or Alternative) Usage; and the second the crux· of the Last Word. Do we all say the same, and only the same, things in the same situations? Don't usages differ? And, Why should what we all ordinarily say be the only or the best or final way of putting it? Why should it even be true?

Well, people's usages do vary, and we do talk loosely, and we do say different things apparently indifferently. But first, not nearly as much as one would think. When we come down to cases, it transpires in the

---

4. All of which was seen and claimed by Socrates, when he first betook himself to the way of Words.

very great majority that what we had thought was our wanting to say different things of and in *the same* situation was really not so—we had simply imagined the situation *slightly* differently: which is all too easy to do, because of course no situation (and we are dealing with *imagined* situations) is ever "completely" described. The more we imagine the situation in detail, with a background of story—and it is worth employing the most idiosyncratic or, sometimes, boring means to stimulate and to discipline our wretched imaginations—the less we find we disagree about what we should say. Nevertheless, *sometimes* we do ultimately disagree: sometimes we must allow a usage to be, though appalling, yet actual; sometimes we should genuinely use either or both of two different descriptions. But why should this daunt us? All that is happening is entirely explicable. If our usages disagree, then you use "X" where I use "Y," or more probably (and more intriguingly) your conceptual system is different from mine, though very likely it is at least equally consistent and serviceable: in short, we can find *why* we disagree—you choose to classify in one way, I in another. If the usage is loose, we can understand the temptation that leads to it, and the distinctions that it blurs: if there are "alternative" descriptions, then the situation can be described or can be "structured" in two ways, or perhaps it is one where, for current purposes, the two alternatives come down to the same. A disagreement as to what we should say is not to be shied off, but to be pounced upon: for the explanation of it can hardly fail to be illuminating. If we light on an electron that rotates the wrong way, that is a discovery, a portent to be followed up, not a reason for chucking physics: and by the same token, a genuinely loose or eccentric talker is a rare specimen to be prized.

As practice in learning to handle this bogey, in learning the essential *rubrics,* we could scarcely hope for a more promising exercise than the study of excuses. Here, surely, is just the sort of situation where people will say "almost anything," because they are so flurried, or so anxious to get off. "It was a mistake," "It was an accident"—how readily these can *appear* indifferent, and even be used together. Yet, a story or two, and everybody will not merely agree that they are completely different, but even discover for himself what the difference is and what each means.[5]

---

5. You have a donkey, so have I, and they graze in the same field. The day comes when I conceive a dislike for mine. I go to shoot it, draw a bead on it, fire: the brute falls in its tracks. I inspect the victim, and find to my horror that it is *your* donkey. I appear on your doorstep with the remains and say—what? "I say, old sport, I'm awfully sorry, etc., I've shot your donkey *by accident*"? Or *"by mistake"*? Then again, I go to shoot my donkey as before, draw a bead on it, fire—but as I do so, the beasts move, and to my horror yours falls. Again the scene on the door-step—what do I say? "By mistake"? Or "by accident"?

Then, for the Last Word. Certainly ordinary language has no claim to be the last word, if there is such a thing. It embodies, indeed, something better than the metaphysics of the Stone Age, namely, as was said, the inherited experience and acumen of many generations of men. But then, that acumen has been concentrated primarily upon the practical business of life. If a distinction works well for practical purposes in ordinary life (no mean feat, for even ordinary life is full of hard cases), then there is sure to be something in it, it will not mark nothing: yet this is likely enough to be not the best way of arranging things if our interests are more extensive or intellectual than the ordinary. And again, that experience has been derived only from the sources available to ordinary men throughout most of civilized history: it has not been fed from the resources of the microscope and its successors. And it must be added too, that superstition and error and fantasy of all kinds do become incorporated in ordinary language and even sometimes stand up to the survival test (only, when they do, why should we not detect it?). Certainly, then, ordinary language is *not* the last word: in principle it can everywhere be supplemented and improved upon and superseded. Only remember, it *is* the *first* word.[6]

For this problem too the field of Excuses is a fruitful one. Here is matter both contentious and practically important for everybody, so that ordinary language is on its toes: yet also, on its back it has long had a bigger flea to bite it, in the shape of the Law, and both again have lately attracted the attentions of yet another, and at least a healthily growing, flea, in the shape of psychology. In the law a constant stream of actual cases, more novel and more tortuous than the mere imagination could contrive, are brought up *for decision*—that is, formulas for docketing them must somehow be found. Hence it is necessary first to be careful with, but also to be brutal with, to torture, to fake, and to override, ordinary language: we cannot here evade or forget the whole affair. (In ordinary life we dismiss the puzzles that crop up about time, but we cannot do that indefinitely in physics.) Psychology likewise produces novel cases, but it also produces new methods for bringing phenomena under observation and study: moreover, unlike the law, it has an unbiased interest in the totality of them and is unpressed for decision. Hence its own special and constant need to supplement, to revise and to supersede the classifications of both ordinary life and the law. We have, then, ample material for practice in learning to handle the bogey of the Last Word, however it should be handled.

Suppose, then, that we set out to investigate excuses, what are the methods and resources initially available? Our object is to imagine

6. And forget, for once and for a while, that other curious question "Is it true?" May we?

the varieties of situation in which we make excuses, and to examine the expressions used in making them. If we have a lively imagination, together perhaps with an ample experience of dereliction, we shall go far, only we need system: I do not know how many of you keep a list of the kinds of fool you make of yourselves. It is advisable to use systematic aids, of which there would appear to be three at least. I list them here in order of availability to the layman.

First we may use the dictionary—quite a concise one will do, but the use must be *thorough*. Two methods suggest themselves, both a little tedious, but repaying. One is to read the book through, listing all the words that seem relevant; this does not take as long as many suppose. The other is to start with a widish selection of obviously relevant terms, and to consult the dictionary under each: it will be found that, in the explanations of the various meanings of each, a surprising number of other terms occur, which are germane though of course not often synonymous. We then look up each of *these*, bringing in more for our bag from the "definitions" given in each case; and when we have continued for a little, it will generally be found that the family circle begins to close, until ultimately it is complete and we come only upon repetitions. This method has the advantage of grouping the terms into convenient clusters—but of course a good deal will depend upon the comprehensiveness of our initial selection.

Working the dictionary, it is interesting to find that a high percentage of the terms connected with excuses prove to be *adverbs*, a type of word which has not enjoyed so large a share of the philosophical limelight as the noun, substantive or adjective, and the verb: this is natural because, as was said, the tenor of so many excuses is that I did it but only *in a way*, not just flatly like that—i.e., the verb needs modifying. Besides adverbs, however, there are other words of all kinds, including numerous abstract nouns, "misconception," "accident," "purpose," and the like, and a few verbs too, which often hold key positions for the grouping of excuses into classes at a high level ("couldn't help," "didn't mean to," "didn't realize," or again "intend," and "attempt"). In connection with the nouns another neglected class of words is prominent, namely, prepositions. Not merely does it matter considerably which preposition, often of several, is being used with a given substantive, but further the prepositions deserve study on their own account. For the question suggests itself, Why are the nouns in one group governed by "under," in another by "on," in yet another by "by" or "through" or "from" or "for" or "with," and so on? It will be disappointing if there prove to be no good reasons for such groupings.

Our second sourcebook will naturally be the law. This will provide us with an immense miscellany of untoward cases, and also with a useful list of recognized pleas, together with a good deal of acute analysis of both. No one who tries this resource will long be in doubt, I think, that the common law, and in particular the law of tort, is the richest storehouse; crime and contract contribute some special additions of their own, but tort is altogether more comprehensive and more flexible. But even here, and still more with so old and hardened a branch of the law as crime, much caution is needed with the arguments of counsel and the dicta or decisions of judges: acute though these are, it has always to be remembered that, in legal cases, (1) there is the overriding requirement that a decision be reached, and a relatively black or white decision—guilty or not guilty—for the plaintiff or for the defendant; (2) there is the general requirement that the charge or action and the pleadings be brought under one or another of the heads and procedures that have come in the course of history to be accepted by the courts (These, though fairly numerous, are still few and stereotyped in comparison with the accusations and defenses of daily life. Moreover contentions of many kinds are beneath the law, as too trivial, or outside it, as too purely moral—for example, inconsiderateness); (3) there is the general requirement that we argue from and abide by precedents (The value of this in the law is unquestionable, but it can certainly lead to distortions of ordinary beliefs and expressions). For such reasons as these, obviously closely connected and stemming from the nature and function of the law, practicing lawyers and jurists are by no means so careful as they might be to give to our ordinary expressions their ordinary meanings and applications. There is special pleading and evasion, stretching and strait-jacketing, besides the invention of technical terms, or technical senses for common terms. Nevertheless, it is a perpetual and salutary surprise to discover how much is to be learned from the law; and it is to be added that if a distinction drawn is a sound one, even though not yet recognized in law, a lawyer can be relied upon to take note of it, for it may be dangerous not to—if he does not, his opponent may.

Finally, the third sourcebook is psychology, with which I include such studies as anthropology and animal behavior. Here I speak with even more trepidation than about the Law. But this at least is clear, that some varieties of behavior, some ways of acting or explanations of the doing of actions, are here noticed and classified which have not been observed or named by ordinary men and hallowed by ordinary language, though perhaps they often might have been so if they had been of more practical importance. There is real danger in contempt for the "jargon" of psychology, at least when it sets out to supplement, and at least sometimes when it sets out to supplant, the language of ordinary life.

With these sources, and with the aid of the imagination, it will go hard if we cannot arrive at the meanings of large numbers of expressions and at the understanding and classification of large numbers of "actions." Then we shall comprehend clearly much that, before, we only made use of *ad hoc*. Definition, I would add, explanatory definition, should stand high among our aims: it is not enough to show how clever we are by showing how obscure everything is. Clarity, too, I know, has been said to be not enough: but perhaps it will be time to go into that when we are within measurable distance of achieving clarity on some matter.

So much for the cackle. It remains to make a few remarks, not, I am afraid, in any very coherent order, about the types of significant result to be obtained and the more general lessons to be learned from the study of Excuses.

1. *No modification without aberration.* When it is stated that X did A, there is a temptation to suppose that given some, indeed perhaps *any*, expression modifying the verb we shall be entitled to insert either it or its opposite or negation in our statement: that is, we shall be entitled to ask, typically, "Did X do A Mly or not Mly?" (e.g., "Did X murder Y voluntarily or involuntarily?"), and to answer one or the other. Or as a minimum it is supposed that if X did A there must be at least *one* modifying expression that we could, justifiably and informatively, insert with the verb. In the great majority of cases of the use of the great majority of verbs ("murder" perhaps is not one of the majority) such suppositions are quite unjustified. The natural economy of language dictates that for the *standard* case covered by any normal verb—not, perhaps, a verb of omen such as "murder," but a verb like "eat" or "kick" or "croquet"—no modifying expression is required or even permissible. Only if we do the action named in some *special* way or circumstances, different from those in which such an act is naturally done (and of course both the normal and the abnormal differ according to what verb in particular is in question), is a modifying expression called for, or even in order. I sit in my chair, in the usual way—I am not in a daze or influenced by threats or the like: here, it will not do to say either that I sat in it intentionally or that I did not sit in it intentionally,[7] nor yet that I sat in it automatically or from habit or what you will. It is bedtime, I am alone, I yawn: but I do not yawn involuntarily (or voluntarily!), nor yet deliberately. To yawn in any such peculiar way is just not to just yawn.

2. *Limitation of application.* Expressions modifying verbs, typically adverbs, have limited ranges of application. That is, given any adverb

---

7. Caveat or hedge: of course we can say "I did *not* sit in it 'intentionally' " as a way simply of repudiating the suggestion that I sat in it intentionally.

of excuse, such as "unwittingly" or "spontaneously" or "impulsively," it will not be found that it makes good sense to attach it to any and every verb of "action" in any and every context: indeed, it will often apply only to a comparatively narrow range of such verbs. Something in the lad's upturned face appealed to him, he threw a brick at it— "spontaneously"? The interest then is to discover why some actions can be excused in a particular way but not others, particularly perhaps the latter.[8] This will largely elucidate the meaning of the excuse, and at the same time will illuminate the characteristics typical of the group of "actions" it picks out: very often too it will throw light on some detail of the machinery of "action" in general (see 4), or on our standards of acceptable conduct (see 5). It is specially important in the case of some of the terms most favored by philosophers or jurists to realize that at least in ordinary speech (disregarding backseepage of jargon) they are not used so universally or so dichotomistically. For example, take "voluntarily" and "involuntarily": we may join the army or make a gift voluntarily, we may hiccough or make a small gesture involuntarily, and the more we consider further actions which we might naturally be said to do in either of these ways, the more circumscribed and unlike each other do the two classes become, until we even doubt whether there is *any* verb with which both adverbs are equally in place. Perhaps there are some such; but at least sometimes when we may think we have found one it is an illusion, an apparent exception that really does prove the rule. I can perhaps "break a cup" voluntarily, *if* that is done, say, as an act of self-impoverishment: and I can perhaps break another involuntarily, *if*, say, I make an involuntary movement which breaks it. Here, plainly, the two acts described each as "breaking a cup" are really very different, and the one is similar to acts typical of the "voluntary" class, the other to acts typical of the "involuntary" class.

3. *The importance of Negations and Opposites.* "Voluntarily" and "involuntarily," then, are not opposed in the obvious sort of way that they are made to be in philosophy or jurisprudence. The "opposite," or rather "opposites," of "voluntarily" might be "under constraint" of some sort, duress or obligation or influence;[9] the opposite of "involuntarily" might be "deliberately" or "on purpose" or the like. Such divergences in opposites indicate that "voluntarily" and "involuntarily," in spite of their apparent connection, are fish from very different kettles.

---

8. For we are sometimes not so good at observing what we *can't* say as what we can, yet the first is pretty regularly the more revealing.

9. But remember, when I sign a check in the normal way, I do *not* do so *either* "voluntarily" *or* "under constraint."

In general, it will pay us to take nothing for granted or as obvious about negations and opposites. It does not pay to assume that a word must have an opposite, or one opposite, whether it is a "positive" word like "wilfully" or a "negative" word like "inadvertently." Rather, we should be asking ourselves such questions as why there is no use for the adverb "advertently." For above all it will not do to assume that the "positive" word must be around to wear the trousers; commonly enough the "negative" (looking) word marks the (positive) abnormality, while the "positive" word, *if* it exists, merely serves to rule out the suggestion of that abnormality. It is natural enough, in view of what was said in (1) above, for the "positive" word not to be found at all in some cases. I do an act A_1 (say, crush a snail) *inadvertently* if, in the course of executing by means of movements of my bodily parts some other act A_2 (say, in walking down the public path), I fail to exercise such meticulous supervision over the courses of those movements as would have been needed to ensure that they did not bring about the untoward event (here, the impact on the snail).[10] By claiming that A_1 was inadvertent we place it, where we imply it belongs, on this special level, in a class of incidental happenings which must occur in the doing of any physical act. To lift the act out of this class, we need and possess the expression "not . . . inadvertently": "advertently," if used for this purpose, would suggest that, if the act was not done inadvertently, then it must have been done noticing what I was doing, which is far from necessarily the case (e.g., if I did it absent-mindedly), or at least that there is *something* in common to the ways of doing all acts not done inadvertently, which is not the case. Again, there is no use for "advertently" at the *same* level as "inadvertently": in passing the butter I do not knock over the cream-jug, though I do (inadvertently) knock over the teacup—yet I do not by-pass the cream-jug *advertently;* for at this level, below supervision in detail, *anything* that we do is, if you like, inadvertent, though we only call it so, and indeed only call it something we have done, if there is something untoward about it.

A further point of interest in studying so-called "negative" terms is the manner of their formation. Why are the words in one group formed with *un-* or *in-,* those in another with *-less* ("aimless," "reckless," "heedless," etc.), and those in another with *mis-* ("mistake," "misconcep-

---

10. Or analogously: I do an act A_1 (say, divulge my age, or imply you are a liar) *inadvertently* if, in the course of executing by the use of some medium of communication some other act A_2 (say, reminiscing about my war service), I fail to exercise such meticulous supervision over the choice and arrangement of the signs as would have been needed to ensure that. . . . It is interesting to note how such adverbs lead parallel lives, one in connection with physical actions ("doing") and the other in connection with acts of communication ("saying"), or sometimes also in connection with acts of "thinking" ("inadvertently assumed").

tion," "misjudgment," etc.)? Why care*less*ly but *in*attentively? Perhaps care and attention, so often linked, are rather different. Here are re-munerative exercises.

4. *The machinery of action.* Not merely do adverbial expressions pick out classes of actions, they also pick out the internal detail of the machinery of doing actions, or the departments into which the business of doing actions is organized. There is for example the stage at which we have actually to *carry out* some action upon which we embark—perhaps we have to make certain bodily movements or to make a speech. In the course of actually *doing* these things (getting weaving) we have to pay (some) attention to what we are doing and to take (some) care to guard against (likely) dangers: we may need to use judgment or tact: we must exercise sufficient control over our bodily parts: and so on. Inattention, carelessness, errors of judgment, tactless-ness, clumsiness, all these and others are ills (with attendant excuses) which affect one specific stage in the machinery of action, the *executive* stage, the stage where we *muff* it. But there are many other departments in the business too, each of which is to be traced and mapped through its cluster of appropriate verbs and adverbs. Obviously there are de-partments of intelligence and planning, of decision and resolve, and so on: but I shall mention one in particular, too often overlooked, where troubles and excuses abound. It happens to us, in military life, to be in receipt of excellent intelligence, to be also in self-conscious possession of excellent principles (the five golden rules for winning victories), and yet to hit upon a plan of action which leads to disaster. One way in which this can happen is through failure at the stage of *appreciation* of the situation, that is at the stage where we are required to cast our excellent intelligence into such a form, under such heads and with such weights attached, that our equally excellent principles can be brought to bear on it properly, in a way to yield the right answer.[11] So too in real, or rather civilian, life, in moral or practical affairs, we can know the facts and yet look at them mistakenly or perversely, or not fully realize or appreciate something, or even be under a total misconception. Many expressions of excuse indicate failure at this particularly tricky stage: even thoughtlessness, inconsiderateness, lack of imagination, are perhaps less matters of failure in intelligence or planning than might be supposed, and more matters of failure to appreciate the situation. A course of E. M. Forster and we see things differently: yet perhaps we know no more and are no cleverer.

5. *Standards of the unacceptable.* It is characteristic of excuses to

---

11. We know all about how to do quadratics: we know all the needful facts about pipes, cisterns, hours and plumbers: yet we reach the answer "3¾ men." We have failed to cast our facts correctly into mathematical form.

be "unacceptable": given, I suppose, almost any excuse, there will be cases of such a kind or of such gravity that "we will not accept" it. It is interesting to detect the standards and codes we thus invoke. The extent of the supervision we exercise over the execution of any act can never be quite unlimited, and usually is expected to fall within fairly definite limits ("due care and attention") in the case of acts of some general kind, though of course we set very different limits in different cases. We may plead that we trod on the snail inadvertently: but not on a baby —you ought to look where you are putting your great feet. Of course it *was* (*really*), if you like, inadvertence: but that word constitutes a plea, which is not going to be allowed, because of standards. And if you try it on, you will be subscribing to such dreadful standards that your last state will be worse than your first. Or again, we set different standards, and will accept different excuses, in the case of acts which are rule-governed, like spelling, and which we are expected absolutely to get right, from those we set and accept for less stereotyped actions: a wrong spelling may be a slip, but hardly an accident, a winged beater may be an accident, but hardly a slip.

6. *Combination, dissociation, and complication.* A belief in opposites and dichotomies encourages, among other things, a blindness to the combinations and dissociations of adverbs that are possible, even to such obvious facts as that we can act at once on impulse and intentionally, or that we can do an action intentionally yet for all that not deliberately, still less on purpose. We walk along the cliff, and I feel a sudden impulse to push you over, which I promptly do: I acted on impulse, yet I certainly intended to push you over, and may even have devised a little ruse to achieve it: yet even then I did not act deliberately, for I did not (stop to) ask myself whether to do it or not.

It is worth bearing in mind, too, the general rule that we must not expect to find simple labels for complicated cases. If a mistake results in an accident, it will not do to ask whether "it" was an accident or a mistake, or to demand some briefer description of "it." Here the natural economy of language operates: if the words already available for simple cases suffice in combination to describe a complicated case, there will be need for special reasons before a special new word is invented for the complication. Besides, however well-equipped our language, it can never be forearmed against all possible cases that may arise and call for description: fact is richer than diction.

7. *Regina* v. *Finney.* Often the complexity and difficulty of a case is considerable. I will quote the case of *Regina* v. *Finney*:[12]

---

12. A somewhat distressing favorite in the class that Hart used to conduct with me in the years soon after the war. The italics are mine.

Shrewsbury Assizes.   1874.   12 Cox 625.

Prisoner was indicted for the manslaughter of Thomas Watkins.

The Prisoner was an attendant at a lunatic asylum. Being in charge of a lunatic, who was bathing, he turned on hot water into the bath, and thereby scalded him to death. The facts appeared to be truly set forth in the statement of the prisoner made before the committing magistrate, as follows: "I had bathed Watkins, and had loosed the bath out. *I intended putting in a clean bath,* and asked Watkins if he would get out. At this time *my attention was drawn* to the next bath by the new attendant, who was asking me a question; and *my attention was taken from the bath* where Watkins was. I put my hand down to turn water on in the bath where Thomas Watkins was. *I did not intend to turn the hot water,* and *I made a mistake in the tap. I did not know what I had done until* I heard Thomas Watkins shout out; and *I did not find my mistake out till* I saw the steam from the water. You cannot get water in this bath when they are drawing water at the other bath; but at other times it shoots out like a water gun when the other baths are not in use...."

(It was proved that the lunatic had such possession of his faculties as would enable him to understand what was said to him, and to get out of the bath.)

A. Young (for Prisoner). The death *resulted from accident.* There was no such *culpable negligence* on the part of the prisoner as will support this indictment. A *culpable mistake,* or some degree of *culpable negligence,* causing death, will not support a charge of manslaughter; unless the *negligence* be so gross as to be *reckless.* (*R. v. Noakes.*)

Lush, J. To render a person liable for *neglect of duty* there must be such a degree of culpability as to amount to *gross negligence* on his part. If you accept the prisoner's own statement, you find no such amount of *negligence* as would come within this definition. It is not every little *trip or mistake* that will make a man so liable. It was the duty of the attendant not to let hot water into the bath while the patient was therein. According to the prisoner's own account, *he did not believe that* he was letting the hot water in while the deceased remained there. The lunatic was, we have heard, a man capable of getting out by himself and of understanding what was said to him. He was told to get out. A new attendant who had come on this day, was at an adjoining bath and he *took off the prisoner's attention.* Now, if the prisoner, knowing that the man was in the bath, had turned on the tap, and turned on the hot instead of the cold water, I should have said there was gross negligence; for he ought to have looked to see. But from his own account he had told the deceased to get out, and *thought he had got out*. If you think that indicates gross *carelessness,* then you should find the prisoner guilty of manslaughter. But if you think it *inadvertence* not amounting to culpability—i.e., what is properly termed an *accident*—then the prisoner is not liable.

Verdict, Not guilty.

In this case there are two morals that I will point. (1) Both counsel and judge make very free use of a large number of terms of excuse, using several as though they were, and even stating them to be, indifferent or equivalent when they are not, and presenting as alternatives those that are not. (2) It is constantly difficult to be sure *what* act it is that counsel or judge is suggesting might be qualified by what expression of excuse. The learned judge's concluding direction is a paradigm of these faults.[13] Finney, by contrast, stands out as an evident master of the Queen's English. He is explicit as to each of his acts and states, mental and physical: he uses different, and the correct, adverbs in connection with each: and he makes no attempt to boil down.

8. *Small distinctions, and big too.* It should go without saying that terms of excuse are not equivalent, and that it matters which we use: we need to distinguish inadvertence not merely from (save the mark) such things as mistake and accident, but from such nearer neighbors as, say, aberration and absence of mind. By imagining cases with vividness and fullness we should be able to decide in which precise terms to describe, say, Miss Plimsoll's action in writing, so carefully, "DAIRY" on her fine new book: we should be able to distinguish between sheer, mere, pure, and simple mistake or inadvertence. Yet unfortunately, at least when in the grip of thought, we fail not merely at these stiffer hurdles. We equate even—I have seen it done—"inadvertently" with "automatically": as though to say I trod on your toe inadvertently means to say I trod on it automatically. Or we collapse succumbing to temptation into losing control of ourselves—a bad patch, this, for telescoping.[14]

---

13. Not but what he probably manages to convey his meaning somehow or other. Judges seem to acquire a knack of conveying meaning, and even carrying conviction, through the use of a pithy Anglo-Saxon which sometimes has literally no meaning at all. Wishing to distinguish the case of shooting at a post in the belief that it was an enemy, as *not* an "attempt," from the case of picking an empty pocket in the belief that money was in it, which *is* an "attempt," the judge explains that in shooting at the post "the man is never on the thing at all."

14. Plato, I suppose, and after him Aristotle, fastened this confusion upon us, as bad in its day and way as the later, grotesque, confusion of moral weakness with

All this is not so much a *lesson* from the study of excuses as the very object of it.

9. *The exact phrase and its place in the sentence.* It is not enough, either, to attend simply to the "key" word: notice must also be taken of the full and exact form of the expression used. In considering mistakes, we have to consider seriatim "by mistake," "owing to a mistake," "mistakenly," "it was a mistake to," "to make a mistake in or over or about," "to be mistaken about," and so on: in considering purpose, we have to consider "on," "with the," "for the," etc., besides "purposeful," "purposeless," and the like. These varying expressions may function quite differently—and usually do, or why should we burden ourselves with more than one of them?

Care must be taken too to observe the precise position of an adverbial expression in the sentence. This should of course indicate what verb it is being used to modify: but more than that, the position can also affect the *sense* of the expression, i.e., the way in which it modifies that verb. Compare, for example:

> a_1 He clumsily trod on the snail.
> a_2 Clumsily he trod on the snail.
> b_1 He trod clumsily on the snail.
> b_2 He trod on the snail clumsily.

Here, in a_1 and a_2 we describe his treading on the creature at all as a piece of clumsiness, incidental, we imply, to his performance of some other action: but with b_1 and b_2 to tread on it is, very likely, his aim or policy, what we criticize is his execution of the feat.[15] Many adverbs, though far from all (not, for example, "purposely") are used in these two typically different ways.

10. *The style of performance.* With some adverbs the distinction between the two senses referred to in the last paragraph is carried a stage further. "He ate his soup deliberately" may mean, like "He deliberately ate his soup," that his eating his soup was a deliberate act,

---

weakness of will. I am very partial to ice cream, and a bombe is served divided into segments corresponding one to one with the persons at High Table: I am tempted to help myself to two segments and do so, thus succumbing to temptation and even conceivably (but why necessarily?) going against my principles. But do I lose control of myself? Do I raven, do I snatch the morsels from the dish and wolf them down, impervious to the consternation of my colleagues? Not a bit of it. We often succumb to temptation with calm and even with finesse.

15. As a matter of fact, most of these examples *can* be understood the other way, especially if we allow ourselves inflections of the voice, or commas, or contexts. a_2 might be a poetic inversion for b_2: b_1, perhaps with commas round the "clumsily," might be used for a_1: and so on. Still, the two senses are clearly enough distinguishable.

one perhaps that he thought would annoy somebody, as it would more commonly if he deliberately ate *my* soup, and which he decided to do: but it will often mean that he went through the performance of eating his soup in a noteworthy manner or *style*—pause after each mouthful, careful choice of point of entry for the spoon, sucking of moustaches, and so on. That is, it will mean that he ate *with* deliberation rather than *after* deliberation. The style of the performance, slow and unhurried, is understandably called "deliberate" because each movement *has the typical look* of a deliberate act: but it is scarcely being said that the making of each motion *is* a deliberate act or that he is "literally" deliberating. This case, then, is more extreme than that of "clumsily," which does in both uses describe literally a manner of performing.

It is worth watching out for this secondary use when scrutinizing any particular adverbial expression: when it definitely does not exist, the reason is worth inquiring into. Sometimes it is very hard to be sure whether it does exist or does not: it does, one would think, with "carelessly," it does not with "inadvertently," but does it or does it not with "absent-mindedly" or "aimlessly"? In some cases a word akin to but distinct from the primary adverb is used for this special role of describing a style of performance: we use "purposefully" in this way, but never "purposely."

11. *What modifies what?* The judge in *Regina* v. *Finney* does not make clear what event is being excused in what way. "If you think that indicates gross carelessness, then.... But if you think it inadvertence not amounting to culpability—i.e., what is properly called an accident—then...." Apparently he means that Finney may have *turned on the hot tap* inadvertently:[16] does he mean also that the tap may have been turned accidentally, or rather that *Watkins may have been scalded* and killed accidentally? And was the carelessness in turning the tap or in thinking Watkins had got out? Many disputes as to what excuse we should properly use arise because we will not trouble to state explicitly *what* is being excused.

To do so is all the more vital because it is in principle always open

---

16. What Finney says is different: he says he "made a mistake in the tap." This is the basic use of "mistake," where we simply, and not necessarily accountably, take the wrong one. Finney here attempts to account for his mistake, by saying that his attention was distracted. But suppose the order is "Right turn" and I turn left: no doubt the sergeant will insinuate that my attention was distracted, or that I cannot distinguish my right from my left—but it was not and I can; this was a simple, pure mistake. As often happens. Neither I nor the sergeant will suggest that there was any accident, or any inadvertence either. If Finney had turned the hot tap inadvertently, then it would have been knocked, say, in reaching for the cold tap: a different story.

to us, along various lines, to describe or refer to "what I did" in so many different ways. This is altogether too large a theme to elaborate here. Apart from the more general and obvious problems of the use of "tendentious" descriptive terms, there are many special problems in the particular case of "actions." Should we say, are we saying, that he took her money, or that he robbed her? That he knocked a ball into a hole, or that he sank a putt? That he said "Done," or that he accepted an offer? How far, that is, are motives, intentions, and conventions to be part of the description of actions? And more especially here, what is *an* or *one* or *the* action? For we can generally split up what might be named as one action in several distinct ways, into different *stretches* or *phases* or *stages*. Stages have already been mentioned: we can dismantle the machinery of the act, and describe (and excuse) separately the intelligence, the appreciation, the planning, the decision, the execution, and so forth. Phases are rather different: we can say that he painted a picture or fought a campaign, or else we can say that first he laid on this stroke of paint and then that, first he fought this action and then that. Stretches are different again: a single term descriptive of what he did may be made to cover either a smaller or a larger stretch of events, those excluded by the narrower description being then called "consequences" or "results" or "effects" or the like of his act. So here we can describe Finney's act *either* as turning on the hot tap, which he did by mistake, with the result that Watkins was scalded, *or* as scalding Watkins, which he did *not* do by mistake.

It is very evident that the problems of excuses and those of the different descriptions of actions are throughout bound up with each other.

12. *Trailing clouds of etymology.* It is these considerations that bring us up so forcibly against some of the most difficult words in the whole story of Excuses, such words as "result," "effect," and "consequence," or again as "intention," "purpose," and "motive." I will mention two points of method which are, experience has convinced me, indispensable aids at these levels.

One is that a word never—well, hardly ever—shakes off its etymology and its formation. In spite of all changes in and extensions of and additions to its meanings, and indeed rather pervading and governing these, there will still persist the old idea. In an *accident* something befalls: by *mistake* you take the wrong one: in *error* you stray: when you act *deliberately* you act after weighing it up (*not* after thinking out ways and means). It is worth asking ourselves whether we know the etymology of "result" or of "spontaneously," and worth remembering that "unwillingly" and "involuntarily" come from very different sources.

And the second point is connected with this. Going back into the

history of a word, very often into Latin, we come back pretty commonly to pictures or *models* of how things happen or are done. These
models may be fairly sophisticated and recent, as is perhaps the case
with "motive" or "impulse," but one of the commonest and most primitive types of model is one which is apt to baffle us through its very
naturalness and simplictiy. We take *some very simple action*, like shov-
ing a stone, usually as done by and viewed by oneself, and use *this*,
with the features distinguishable in it, as our model in terms of which
to talk about other actions and events: and we continue to do so,
scarcely realizing it, even when these other actions are pretty remote
and perhaps much more interesting to us in their own right than the
acts originally used in constructing the model ever were, and even when
the model is really distorting the facts rather than helping us to observe
them. In primitive cases we may get to see clearly the differences between, say, "results," "effects," and "consequences," and yet discover
that these differences are no longer clear, and the terms themselves no
longer of real service to us, in the more complicated cases where we had
been bandying them about most freely. A model must be recognized for
what it is. "Causing," I suppose, was a notion taken from a man's own
experience of doing simple actions, and by primitive man every event
was construed in terms of this model: every event has a cause, that is,
every event is an action done by somebody—if not by a man, then by
a quasi-man, a spirit. When, later, events which are *not* actions are
realized to be such, we still say that they must be "caused," and the
word snares us: we are struggling to ascribe to it a new, unanthropomor-
phic meaning, yet constantly, in searching for its analysis, we unearth
and incorporate the lineaments of the ancient model. As happened even
to Hume, and consequently to Kant. Examining such a word historically, we may well find that it has been extended to cases that have by
now too tenuous a relation to the model case, that it is a source of
confusion and superstition.

There is too another danger in words that invoke models, half-
forgotten or not. It must be remembered that there is no necessity whatsoever that the various models used in creating our vocabulary,
primitive or recent, should all fit together neatly as parts into one single,
total model or scheme of, for instance, the doing of actions. It is possible,
and indeed highly likely, that our assortment of models will include
some, or many, that are overlapping, conflicting, or more generally
simply *disparate*.[17]

---

17. This is by way of a general warning in philosophy. It seems to be too readily
assumed that if we can only discover the true meanings of each of a cluster of key
terms, usually historic terms, that we use in some particular field (as, for example,

13. In spite of the wide and acute observation of the phenomena of action embodied in ordinary speech, modern scientists have been able, it seems to me, to reveal its inadequacy at numerous points, if only because they have had access to more comprehensive data and have studied them with more catholic and dispassionate interest than the ordinary man, or even the lawyer, has had occasion to do. I will conclude with two examples.

Observation of animal behavior shows that regularly, when an animal is embarked on some recognizable pattern of behavior but meets in the course of it with an insuperable obstacle, it will betake itself to energetic, but quite unrelated, activity of some wild kind, such as standing on its head. This phenomenon is called "displacement behavior" and is well identifiable. If now, in the light of this, we look back at ordinary human life, we see that displacement behavior bulks quite large in it: yet we have apparently no word, or at least no clear and simple word, for it. If, when thwarted, we stand on our heads or wiggle our toes, than we are not exactly *just* standing on our heads, don't you know, in the ordinary way, yet is there any convenient adverbial expression we can insert to do the trick? "In desperation"?

Take, again, "compulsive" behavior, however exactly psychologists define it, compulsive washing for example. There are of course hints in ordinary speech that we do things in this way—"just feel I have to," "shouldn't feel comfortable unless I did," and the like: but there is no adverbial expression satisfactorily pre-empted for it, as "compulsively" is. This is understandable enough, since compulsive behavior, like displacement behavior, is not in general going to be of great practical importance.

Here I leave and commend the subject to you.

"right," "good," and the rest in morals), then it must without question transpire that each will fit into place in some single, interlocking, consistent, conceptual scheme. Not only is there no reason to assume this, but all historical probability is against it, especially in the case of a language derived from such various civilizations as ours is. We may cheerfully use, and with weight, terms which are not so much head-on incompatible as simply disparate, which just do not fit in or even on. Just as we cheerfully subscribe to, or have the grace to be torn between, simply disparate ideals —why *must* there be a conceivable amalgam, the Good Life for Man?

XIX

H. L. A. HART
and A. M. HONORÉ

HERBERT LIONEL ADOLPHUS HART (*b.* 1907) was educated at Oxford. After a time in London as a lawyer, he returned to Oxford as a Fellow of New College. In 1952 he became Professor of Jurisprudence at the University of Oxford.

Anthony Maurice Honoré (*b.* 1921) is Rhodes Reader in Roman-Dutch Law at the University of Oxford.

Causation in the Law (1955) is an extensive examination of the concept of causation and of its applications to the law as well as, by implication, to history and the social sciences. Believing as they do that the legal uses of causal language are rooted in the ordinary concept of causation, Hart and Honoré devote the whole of the first part of their book to an elucidation of that concept.

Ordinary causal language is varied and complex. Causes must be distinguished from consequences, conditions, results, effects, and reasons, although of course all of these also are intimately related in many different ways. Nevertheless, central in our ordinary concept of causation is the idea of purposive manipulation of objects by people.

This notion of an action that makes a difference, which presupposes, although it is not the same as, the concept of uniformity or regular sequence of events, the authors develop in three main ways: (1) natural events that make a difference come to be called causes by analogy with human actions that make a difference; (2) omissions of actions, where these omissions or lack of action are harmful; and (3) interpersonal transactions, i.e., situations in which one man gets another to do something by means of threats, bribes, inducements, commands, advice, or statements.

It is the discussion of these interpersonal transactions, in which reasons and causes are distinguished and related in clear, mixed, and borderline cases, that is reproduced here. This discussion, the authors claim, shows the inadequacy of the Humean or regularity theory of causation to cover these transactions.

Reasons and Causes in the Law[1]

So far our analysis has been concerned with cases where some event, other than human action, is said to be the effect, result, or consequence of some other event or of some human act or omission. We have not considered cases where one human being is said, either by words or deeds, to cause another to act, nor the important and very varied field of cases where one human action is said to be done 'in consequence of', 'because of', or 'as the result of' another, as, for example, where one man induces another to do something. We have reserved this topic for separate treatment because we have here a set of principles different, in certain ways, from those involved in the central type of causation of physical events and occurrences other than human actions. In this field of relationship between two human actions we have to deal with the concept of *reasons* for action rather than *causes* of events; yet there are many transitional cases for, while the contrast between these concepts is important, it shades off in many directions.

The range of notions under examination in this section is exemplified in the standard use of such expressions as 'He made me do it', 'He persuaded me to do it', 'He induced me to do it', 'I did it because he ordered me to do it', 'I did it because he offered me a reward', 'I did it because he threatened to hit me', 'I did it on his advice'. We shall call these cases 'interpersonal transactions'. There are indeed many differences within this group of notions but also important common features: of these the most important is that such relationships between two persons' actions, though often and intelligibly called causal connexion, especially by legal writers,[2] do not

---

1. From *Causation in the Law* (Oxford: Clarendon Press, 1955), pp. 48-54. Reprinted by permission of the publishers.

2. Street, *The Law of Torts,* p. 357: 'There has been much discussion of the difference between advice and persuasion but the problem . . . presents just the same difficulties on the facts as other problems of causation in torts.' Prosser (*Torts,* p. 550) speaks of 'causal connection in such cases taking the form of inducement' but does not draw attention to any differences between these and ordinary cases of causation.

depend upon 'regular connexion' or sequence as the causal relations between physical events do. Hence the assertion that one person, for example, induced another to act is not 'covertly' general even in the modified sense discussed in section IV. Generalizations have a place here but a less central one.

It would be somewhat unnatural in the informal discourse of ordinary life to describe any of this range of cases by saying that one person *caused* another to act; and in some cases this description would be positively misleading, 'He caused me to act' would be merely unnatural (and 'He made me do it' natural) in those cases where one person is induced to act by threats, coercion, the exercise of authority, or false statements; it would be positively misleading in those cases where one person merely advised, or tempted, or requested another to act, or procured his action by offering a reward. The special factors which are entailed by the expressions 'causing' another to act or 'making' him do something are that the first person should intend the second to do the act in question, and should use means of persuasion or inducement (e.g. threats) which render it not wholly voluntary.

There is a temptation to assimilate the relationships between human actions here under discussion to those exhibited in ordinary cases of causal connexion, and so to think of cases where one person induces another to act, and cases where the impact of one body on another causes it to move, as different examples of the same causal relationship, differing only because, in the first case, the terms related are human actions involving psychological and mental factors; whereas in the second, more familiar case the terms related are merely physical events. Hypnosis and many cases of the infliction of nervous shock *are* cases where the difference from familiar cases of causation consists simply in the fact that psychological elements are involved; they do not involve the *radical* differences which separate 'He induced me to do it' from 'His blow caused the victim's death'. The temptation to ignore the more radical differences between these two types of relationship has many roots; there are important similarities as well as differences, which are sometimes expressed by saying that a reason for action is just a cause 'looked at from the inside'. Many important causal idioms are appropriate for the description both of such relationships between human actions and ordinary causal sequences; when one person induces another to act we correctly say that the latter acted 'because of', or 'as the result of', what the first person said or did, and these expressions are often apt to describe the effect of the impact of one body on another. Further, an important and characteristic use of such statements as 'X induced Y to steal' is to provide an explanation as an answer to the question 'Why did Y steal?' So, just like ordinary causal statements, discovery of the relationship between two actions may have an explanatory force. Moreover, these relationships constitute an important element in different sorts of legal and moral responsibility, criminal or civil liability; and special *exemptions* from these forms of liability often depend, for example, on whether one person coerced or induced someone into doing some action. Hence references to such relationships between two human actions appear scattered throughout every branch of most legal systems.

Four common features demand attention in the various relationships of this type. (i) In all of them the second actor knows of and understands the significance of what the first actor has said or done; (ii) the first actor's words or deeds are part of the second actor's reasons for acting; (iii) the second actor forms the intention to do the act in question only after the first actor's intervention; (iv) except in the case where the first actor has merely advised the second act, he intends the second actor to do the act in question.

1. In all the cases under discussion one essential requirement, if such a relationship is to exist, is that words spoken or actions done by one person must have been known to the second person, and in the case of words they must not only have been known[3] but understood. They do not 'affect' the second person merely as so much noise, for he recognizes their meaning. One person can only be 'induced' to act by another if he knows and understands what that other has said. In this sense the relationship between the two actions in such cases is 'through the mind' of the second person. Precisely what the second person's mental attitude to the action or words of the first person must be, depends on what form of relationship is said to exist. In the case of deceit and false pretence it is necessary that he should have understood and also believed what was said to him; in the case of threats or bribes he must not merely know of and understand what is said to him, but at least think there is some chance that what is threatened or offered will be forthcoming. Even in the case of certain gross forms of persuasion where non-rational means are used to incite another to act, it must at least be the case that any words used, for example, in inflammatory speeches, should be understood, and to

3. One person *knowing, understanding,* and in some cases *believing* what another has said is essential where the act of the first person consists in his saying something. This is one necessary stage to be distinguished from the further stage where the second person acts *because* of what he has understood or believed. Even if the first stage is (as some analysts of the notion of communication hold) a causal connexion of the familiar kind, the second is not.

the extent that the incitement consists of non-rational stimuli (shrieks, groans, gestures) the second person must at least be aware of them. These last cases where, as we say, the first person 'works on' the feelings of the second come very close to cases of ordinary causal connexion.

2. In nearly all these cases the first actor's words or deeds constitute at least part of the second actor's *reasons* for doing the act in question; and in all cases but those of disinterested advice and the grosser forms of incitement by non-rational means, the reason is of a special kind; for it entails that the first actor should by his words or deeds have done something to render some course of action more *eligible* in the eyes of the second actor than it would otherwise have been. This element is most obvious in the cases where one person induces another to act by bribes, threats or offers of reward. Here the second actor is led to believe that, if he acts as required, he will obtain, through the agency of the first actor, something he wants or escape something he dislikes. In this way the action in question is rendered more eligible: he has an extra reason for doing the action, in addition to any reason he might have had independently of the first actor. So it is often said that the first act has 'provided a motive' for doing the second act, and this expression is only misleading to the extent that it conceals the fact that normally in such cases the second actor will have had a pre-existing wish to seek, for example, material benefits or to avoid pain, in conjunction with which the first actor's offers or threats constitute a reason for acting. In some cases, however, there need not be a pre-existing disposition of this sort, since the first actor may both arouse the second's desires or cupidity and also make offers to satisfy it contingently on his doing some action.

Where inducement takes the form of false statements the action is rendered more eligible in the eyes of the second actor simply because he is led to believe that he will gain in a way which he had not thought of; but, unless the false statement takes the form of a prediction by the first actor of his own future conduct or a statement of his own intentions, the benefits which the second actor is led to expect are independent of the agency of the first actor. This is one of the main ways in which inducement by false statement differs from inducement by threats or offers of reward.

Mere advice differs from inducement in that the role of the first person is primarily that of drawing the attention of the second to reasons for or against doing some action. This is to advise another *upon* or *about* some contemplated action. To advise another *to do* an action, of course, goes beyond this discussion of the pro's and con's.

In saying 'I advise you to do this' the speaker personally commends the action, and his doing this may of itself render it eligible in the eyes of someone who trusts or respects him. Hence, if the advice is taken, the mere giving of the advice may be the second person's reason for acting; in other cases the merits of the action which have emerged in the course of the discussion may also have weighed with him in deciding to do it.

3. Whenever it is appropriate to say that one person has acted in consequence of what another has done or said (whether this constitutes inducement or merely advice), it must be the case that the person so acting should have made up his mind to act only after the first actor's intervention by words or deeds. If before this intervention the second actor had already intended to do the act in question, all such relationships are excluded; for in such cases the intervention could not be the second actor's reason for doing what he did do.

It is often said that if the first actor's words or deeds are to be accepted as the second actor's reasons for doing what he did, the first must be a condition *sine qua non* of the second, i.e. it must be true that he would not have acted in the way he did, had the first actor not said or done what he did. Even if this is true (and in certain contexts legal and non-legal statements of an actor's reasons seem not to have this implication) it is wrong to conclude that, if this relationship between two actions is to subsist, the first person's words or deeds must have the general connexion with the act of the second which is characteristic of causal relationships between physical events. The statement that one person did something because, for example, another threatened him, carries no implication or covert assertion that if the circumstances were repeated the same action would follow; nor does such a statement require for its defence, as ordinary singular causal statements do, a generalization of the kind discussed in section IV. This is most obvious if we consider not a third person's statements about the case where someone has done something because of another's threats, but the threatened person's own statement that he acted because of those threats. It would be absurd to call upon him to show that there really was this connexion between the threats and his action, by showing that generally he or other persons complied when threats were made. This general statement might be quite untrue and yet his statement of his reasons might be true: the assertion that he acted because of the threats carries no implication that, given similar circumstances, he would act again in this way or that, in similar circumstances, he or other persons had always acted in that way. By contrast, if he had said that a blow had caused a bruise, where no statement of *reasons* for acting is involved, evidence of what experience has shown to be generally the case would be required to show that this was a case of *propter hoc* not *post hoc*.

The question, whether or not a given person acted on a given occasion for a given reason, is primarily a question as to the way in which the agent reaches his decision to do the act in question: whether the thought of a given reason weighed with him as he made up his mind, and whether or not in doing the action he consciously adapted the manner of its execution accordingly. These are questions primarily about the agent's experience in contemplating, deciding upon and carrying out the action in question, and for this reason the agent's own declarations about his reasons have a special primacy or importance. This is recognized in the law as well as in ordinary life. If asked to make sure, in giving evidence, that his reasons for acting were as he claims, an honest witness will not be expected to produce generalizations, but to attempt to reconstruct the deliberative situation or his 'state of mind' at the time.

Of course generalizations about the way in which either the person in question or other persons respond, e.g. to threats, or by what reasons they are or are not actuated, have an important place in such cases. They may be used as *evidence* that a person in saying he acted from a certain reason was not speaking the truth (or was forgetful), because it was 'out of character' for him, or is rare for anyone to act for such a reason. Such generalizations are built up from knowledge of many individual cases where we have found that a person acted (or did not act) from a given reason, and we now use them in a new case to confirm or throw doubt on the agent's statement that he did act for this reason. But the instances out of which such generalizations are constructed were themselves cases where it was found that an individual had a certain reason for action, and this was known independently of such generalizations. On the other hand, a singular causal statement asserting that one physical event was the cause of another depends on generalizations in a different way: here the latter are not merely *evidence* that in the particular case the events are causally related; they are *part* of what is meant by causal connexion; and the instances from which these causal generalizations are constructed were not already recognized *apart* from such generalizations as cases of causal connexion but only as cases of succession between events.

The matter is, however, complicated by one point. Though there is no implication of uniform sequence in asserting that a person acted for a given reason, what we recognise as a possible reason is not independent of how in a general very broad sense most people act. If a person said he left the room 'because Caesar died in 44 B.C.' we should not understand him. Roughly speaking, we recognize as a reason for action (and therefore as a given person's reason on a particular occasion) something which is relevant to the promotion of some purpose known to be pursued by human beings and so renders an action eligible by human beings as we know them. The concept of reasons therefore *presupposes* that, in general, human beings respond to certain situations in such ways as fleeing from danger, or conforming with social rules or conventions, &c. Yet this presupposition of broad similarity in human behaviour, without which we could not have the concept of a reason for action, does not mean that, when on a particular occasion we assert that a person acted for a particular reason (e.g. to avoid threatened danger), we are committed to any assertion that, if the circumstances were repeated, the same action would follow: it may be that neither he nor anyone else would act so again in such circumstances. All that is required is that, if the case is to be one of a person acting for a reason, we must understand how it promoted some objective analogous at least in some way to those which human beings are known to pursue by action.

In some of the relationships considered here the intermediate act may be fully voluntary. This will be the case, for example, if the first actor has done no more than advise the second actor or offer him a reward for acting; whereas in cases where the first actor resorts to threats or gives orders which the second is under some duty to obey the second action is less than fully voluntary. It is this second class of case that would be expressed by saying that the first actor 'caused' the second to act or 'made him act' as he did. A more detailed analysis of the use in criminal law of the expression 'causing something to be done' is given in Chapter XIV.

KURT BAIER

Kurt Baier (*b.* 1917) was educated at the University of Vienna, the University of Melbourne, and Oxford University. He is at present Professor of Philosophy at the University of Pittsburgh. He is author of *The Moral Point of View* (1958), in addition to many articles.

Contemporary analytic philosophy is often accused of rejecting, neglecting, or trivializing the perennial problems of philosophy, of saying nothing about certain basic problems that concern all of us. Whatever the force of this objection may be, it is perhaps more salutary to answer the charge by a vigorous counterexample than to debate its truth or falsity. In *The Meaning of Life* (1957), Kurt Baier deals straightforwardly with one of the perennial problems of philosophy. Human life, he argues in no uncertain terms, *is* meaningful; and people who claim it is meaningless if God does not exist, simply confuse purposes *in* life with the purpose *of* life. Baier clarifies these two senses of purpose and attempts to show in great detail that much of human life can be said to be purposeful, worthwhile, and meaningful.

The Meaning of Life[1]

Tolstoy, in his autobiographical work, "A Confession", reports how, when he was fifty and at the height of his literary success, he came to be obsessed by the fear that life was meaningless.

At first I experienced moments of perplexity and arrest of life, as though I did not know what to do or how to live; and I felt lost and became dejected. But this passed, and I went on living as before. Then these moments of perplexity began to recur oftener and oftener, and always in the same form. They were always expressed by the questions: What is it for? What does it lead to? At first it seemed to me that these were aimless and irrelevant questions. I thought that it was all well known, and that if I should ever wish to deal with the solution it would not cost me much effort; just at present I had no time for it, but when I wanted to, I should be able to find the answer. The questions however began to repeat themselves frequently, and to demand replies more and more insistently; and like drops of ink always falling on one place they ran together into one black blot.[2]

A Christian living in the Middle Ages would not have felt any serious doubts about Tolstoy's questions. To him it would have seemed quite certain that life had a meaning and quite clear what it was. The medieval Christian world picture assigned to man a highly significant, indeed the central part in the grand scheme of things. The universe was made for the express purpose of providing a stage on which to enact a drama starring Man in the title role.

To be exact, the world was created by God in the year 4004 B.C. Man was the last and the crown of this creation, made in the likeness of God, placed in the Garden of Eden on earth, the fixed centre of the

1. From Inaugural Lecture at Canberra University College, 1957, *The Meaning of Life*, pp. 3-4, 18-29. Reprinted by kind permission of the author and the Registrar, The School of General Studies, The Australian National University.

2. Count Leo Tolstoy, "A Confession", reprinted in *A Confession, The Gospel in Brief, and What I Believe*, No. 229, The World's Classics (London: Geoffrey Cumberlege, 1940).

universe, round which revolved the nine heavens of the sun, the moon, the planets and the fixed stars, producing as they revolved in their orbits the heavenly harmony of the spheres. And this gigantic universe was created for the enjoyment of man, who was originally put in control of it. Pain and death were unknown in paradise. But this state of bliss was not to last. Adam and Eve ate of the forbidden tree of knowledge, and life on this earth turned into a death-march through a vale of tears. Then, with the birth of Jesus, new hope came into the world. After He had died on the cross, it became at least possible to wash away with the purifying water of baptism some of the effects of Original Sin and to achieve salvation. That is to say, on condition of obedience to the law of God, man could now enter heaven and regain the state of everlasting, deathless bliss, from which he had been excluded because of the sin of Adam and Eve.

To the medieval Christian the meaning of human life was therefore perfectly clear. The stretch on earth is only a short interlude, a temporary incarceration of the soul in the prison of the body, a brief trial and test, fated to end in death, the release from pain and suffering. What really matters, is the life after the death of the body. One's existence acquires meaning not by gaining what this life can offer but by saving one's immortal soul from death and eternal torture, by gaining eternal life and everlasting bliss.

The scientific world picture which has found ever more general acceptance from the beginning of the modern era onwards is in profound conflict with all this. At first, the Christian conception of the world was discovered to be erroneous in various important details. The Copernican theory showed up the earth as merely one of several planets revolving round the sun, and the sun itself was later seen to be merely one of many fixed stars each of which is itself the nucleus of a solar system similar to our own. Man, instead of occupying the centre of creation, proved to be merely the inhabitant of a celestial body no different from millions of others. Furthermore, geological investigations revealed that the universe was not created a few thousand years ago, but was probably millions of years old.

Disagreements over details of the world picture, however, are only superficial aspects of a much deeper conflict. The appropriateness of the whole Christian outlook is at issue. For Christianity, the world must be regarded as the "creation" of a kind of Superman, a person possessing all the human excellences to an infinite degree and none of the human weaknesses, Who has made man in His image, a feeble, mortal, foolish copy of Himself. In creating the universe, God acts as a sort of playwright-cum-legislator-cum-judge-cum-executioner. In the capacity of playwright, He creates the historical world process, including man. He erects the stage and writes, in outline, the plot. He creates the *dramatis personae* and watches over them with the eye partly of a father, partly of the law. While on stage, the actors are free to extemporise, but if they infringe the divine commandments, they are later dealt with by their creator in His capacity of judge and executioner.

Within such a framework, the Christian attitudes towards the world are natural and sound: it is natural and sound to think that all is arranged for the best even if appearances belie it; to resign oneself cheerfully to one's lot; to be filled with awe and veneration in regard to anything and everything that happens; to want to fall on one's knees and worship and praise the Lord. These are wholly fitting attitudes within the framework of the world view just outlined. And this world view must have seemed wholly sound and acceptable because it offered the best explanation which was then available of all the observed phenomena of nature.

As the natural sciences developed, however, more and more things in the universe came to be explained without the assumption of a supernatural creator. Science, moreover, could explain them better, that is, more accurately and more reliably. The Christian hypothesis of a supernatural maker, whatever other needs it was capable of satisfying, was at any rate no longer indispensable for the purpose of explaining the existence or occurrence of anything. In fact, scientific explanations do not seem to leave any room for this hypothesis. The scientific approach demands that we look for a natural explanation of anything and everything. The scientific way of looking at and explaining things has yielded an immensely greater measure of understanding of, and control over, the universe than any other way. And when one looks at the world in this scientific way, there seems to be no room for a personal relationship between human beings and a supernatural perfect being ruling and guiding men. Hence many scientists and educated men have come to feel that the Christian attitudes towards the world and human existence are inappropriate. They have become convinced that the universe and human existence in it are without a purpose and therefore devoid of meaning.[3]

¶ THE PURPOSE OF MAN'S EXISTENCE

Our conclusion in the previous section [omitted here, ed.] has been that science is in principle able to give complete and real explanations

---

3. See e.g. Edwyn Bevan, *Christianity*, pp. 211-227. See also H. J. Paton, *The Modern Predicament* (London: George Allen and Unwin Ltd., 1955), pp. 103-116, 374.

of every occurrence and thing in the universe. This has two important corollaries: (i) Acceptance of the scientific world picture cannot be *one's reason* for the belief that the universe is unintelligible and therefore meaningless, though coming to accept it, after having been taught the Christian world picture, may well have been, in the case of many individuals, *the only or the main cause* of their belief that the universe and human existence are meaningless. (ii) It is not in accordance with reason to reject this pessimistic belief on the grounds that scientific explanations are only provisional and incomplete and must be supplemented by religious ones.

In fact, it might be argued that the more clearly we understand the explanations given by science, the more we are driven to the conclusion that human life has no purpose and therefore no meaning. The science of astronomy teaches us that our earth was not specially created about 6,000 years ago, but evolved out of hot nebulae which previously had whirled aimlessly through space for countless ages. As they cooled, the sun and the planets formed. On one of these planets at a certain time the circumstances were propitious and life developed. But conditions will not remain favourable to life. When our solar system grows old, the sun will cool, our planet will be covered with ice, and all living creatures will eventually perish. Another theory has it that the sun will explode and that the heat generated will be so great that all organic life on earth will be destroyed. That is the comparatively short history and prospect of life on earth. Altogether it amounts to very little when compared with the endless history of the inanimate universe.

Biology teaches us that the species man was not specially created but is merely, in a long chain of evolutionary changes of forms of life, the last link, made in the likeness not of God but of nothing so much as an ape. The rest of the universe, whether animate or inanimate, instead of serving the ends of man, is at best indifferent, at worst savagely hostile. Evolution to whose operation the emergence of man is due is a ceaseless battle among members of different species, one species being gobbled up by another, only the fittest surviving. Far from being the gentlest and most highly moral, man is simply the creature best fitted to survive, the most efficient if not the most rapacious and insatiable killer. And in this unplanned, fortuitous, monstrous, savage world man is madly trying to snatch a few brief moments of joy, in the short intervals during which he is free from pain, sickness, persecution, war or famine until, finally, his life is snuffed out in death. Science has helped us to know and understand this world, but what purpose or meaning can it find in it?

Complaints such as these do not mean quite the same to everybody, but one thing, I think, they mean to most people: science shows life to be meaningless, because life is without purpose. The medieval world picture provided life with a purpose, hence medieval Christians could believe that life had a meaning. The scientific account of the world takes away life's purpose and with it its meaning.

There are, however, two quite different senses of "purpose". Which one is meant? Has science deprived human life of purpose in both senses? And if not, is it a harmless sense, in which human existence has been robbed of purpose? Could human existence still have meaning if it did not have a purpose in that sense?

What are the two senses? In the first and basic sense, purpose is normally attributed only to persons or their behaviour as in "Did you have a purpose in leaving the ignition on?" In the second sense, purpose is normally attributed only to things, as in "What is the purpose of that gadget you installed in the workshop?" The two uses are intimately connected. We cannot attribute a purpose to a thing without implying that someone did something, in the doing of which he had some purpose, namely, to bring about the thing with the purpose. Of course, *his* purpose is not identical with *its* purpose. In hiring labourers and engineers and buying materials and a site for a factory and the like, the entrepreneur's purpose, let us say, is to manufacture cars, but the purpose of cars is to serve as a means of transportation.

There are many things that a man may do, such as buying and selling, hiring labourers, ploughing, felling trees, and the like, which it is foolish, pointless, silly, perhaps crazy, to do if one has no purpose in doing them. A man who does these things without a purpose is engaging in inane, futile pursuits. Lives crammed full with such activities devoid of purpose are pointless, futile, worthless. Such lives may indeed be dismissed as meaningless. But it should also be perfectly clear that acceptance of the scientific world picture does not force us to regard our lives as being without a purpose in this sense. Science has not only not robbed us of any purpose which we had before, but it has furnished us with enormously greater power to achieve these purposes. Instead of praying for rain or a good harvest or offspring, we now use ice pellets, artificial manure, or artificial insemination.

By contrast, having or not having a purpose, in the other sense, is value neutral. We do not think more or less highly of a thing for having or not having a purpose. "Having a purpose", in this sense, confers no kudos, "being purposeless" carries no stigma. A row of trees growing near a farm may or may not have a purpose: it may or may not be a windbreak, may or may not have been planted or deliberately left standing there in order to prevent the wind from sweeping across the fields. We do not in any way disparage the trees if we say they have no purpose, but have just grown that way. They are as beautiful, made of as good wood, as valuable, as if they had a purpose. And, of course, they break the wind just as well. The same is true of living creatures. We do not disparage a dog when we say that it has no purpose, is not a sheep dog or a watch dog or a rabbiting dog, but just a dog that hangs around the house and is fed by us.

Man is in a different category, however. To attribute to a human being a purpose in that sense is not neutral, let alone complimentary: it is offensive. It is degrading for a man to be regarded as merely serving a purpose. If, at a garden party, I ask a man in livery, "What is your purpose?" I am insulting him. I might as well have asked, "What are you *for*?" Such questions reduce him to the level of a gadget, a domestic animal, or perhaps a slave. I imply that *we* allot to *him* the tasks, the goals, the aims which he is to pursue; that *his* wishes and desires and aspirations and purposes are to count for little or nothing. We are treating him, in Kant's phrase, merely as a means to our ends, not as an end in himself.

The Christian and the scientific world pictures do indeed differ fundamentally on this point. The latter robs man of a purpose in this sense. It sees him as a being with no purpose allotted to him by anyone but himself. It robs him of any goal, purpose, or destiny appointed for him by any outside agency. The Christian world picture, on the other hand, sees man as a creature, a divine artefact, something halfway between a robot (manufactured) and an animal (alive), a homunculus, or perhaps Frankenstein, made in God's laboratory, with a purpose or task assigned him by his Maker.

However, lack of purpose in this sense does not in any way detract from the meaningfulness of life. I suspect that many who reject the scientific outlook because it involves the loss of purpose of life, and therefore meaning, are guilty of a confusion between the two senses of "purpose" just distinguished. They confusedly think that if the scientific world picture is true, then their lives must be futile because that picture implies that man has no purpose given him from without. But this is muddled thinking, for, as has already been shown, pointlessness is implied only by purposelessness in the other sense, which is not at all implied by the scientific picture of the world. These people mistakenly conclude that there can be no purpose *in* life because there is no purpose *of* life; that *men* cannot themselves adopt and achieve purposes because *man*, unlike a robot or a watchdog, is not a creature with a purpose.[4]

---

4. See e.g. "Is Life Worth Living?" B.B.C. Talk by the Rev. John Sutherland Bonnell in *Asking Them Questions,* Third Series, ed. by R. S. Wright (London: Geoffrey Cumberlege, 1950).

However, not all people taking this view are guilty of the above confusion. Some really hanker after a purpose of life in this sense. To some people the greatest attraction of the medieval world picture is the belief in an omnipotent, omniscient, and all-good Father, the view of themselves as His children who worship Him, of their proper attitude to what befalls them as submission, humility, resignation in His will, and what is often described as the "creaturely feeling".[5] All these are attitudes and feelings appropriate to a being that stands to another in the same sort of relation, though of course on a higher plane, in which a helpless child stands to his progenitor. Many regard the scientific picture of the world as cold, unsympathetic, unhomely, frightening, because it does not provide for any appropriate object of this creaturely attitude. There is nothing and no one in the world, as science depicts it, in which we can have faith or trust, on whose guidance we can rely, to whom we can turn for consolation, whom we can worship or submit to—except other human beings. This may be felt as a keen disappointment, because it shows that the meaning of life cannot lie in submission to His will, in acceptance of whatever may come, and in worship. But it does not imply that life can have *no* meaning. It merely implies that it must have a different meaning from that which it was thought to have. Just as it is a great shock for a child to find that he must stand on his own feet, that his father and mother no longer provide for him, so a person who has lost his faith in God must reconcile himself to the idea that he has to stand on his own feet, alone in the world except for whatever friends he may succeed in making.

But is not this to miss the point of the Christian teaching? Surely, Christianity can tell us the meaning of life because it tells us the grand and noble end for which God has created the universe and man. No human life, however pointless it may seem, is meaningless because in being part of God's plan, every life is assured of significance.

This point is well taken. It brings to light a distinction of some importance: we call a person's life meaningful not only if it is worthwhile, but also if he has helped in the realization of some plan or purpose transcending his own concerns. A person who knows he must soon die a painful death, can give significance to the remainder of his doomed life by, say, allowing certain experiments to be performed on him which will be useful in the fight against cancer. In a similar way, only on a much more elevated plane, every man, however humble or plagued by suffering, is guaranteed significance by the knowledge that he is participating in God's purpose.

5. See e.g. Rudolf Otto, *The Idea of the Holy,* pp. 9-11. See also C. A. Campbell, *On Selfhood and Godhood* (London: George Allen & Unwin Ltd., 1957) p. 246, and H. J. Paton, *The Modern Predicament,* pp. 69-71.

What, then, on the Christian view, is the grand and noble end for which God has created the world and man in it? We can immediately dismiss that still popular opinion that the smallness of our intellect prevents us from stating meaningfully God's design in all its imposing grandeur.[6] This view cannot possibly be a satisfactory answer to our question about the purpose of life. It is, rather, a confession of the impossibility of giving one. If anyone thinks that this "answer" can remove the sting from the impression of meaninglessness and insignificance in our lives, he cannot have been stung very hard.

If, then, we turn to those who are willing to state God's purpose in so many words, we encounter two insuperable difficulties. The first is to find a purpose grand and noble enough to explain and justify the great amount of undeserved suffering in this world. We are inevitably filled by a sense of bathos when we read statements such as this: ". . . history is the scene of a divine purpose, in which the whole of history is included, and Jesus of Nazareth is the centre of that purpose, both as revelation and as achievement, as the fulfilment of all that was past, and the promise of all that was to come . . . If God is God, and if He made all these things, why did He do it? . . . God created a universe, bounded by the categories of time, space, matter, and causality, because He desired to enjoy for ever the society of a fellowship of finite and redeemed spirits which have made to His love the response of free and voluntary love and service."[7] Surely this cannot be right? Could a God be called omniscient, omnipotent, *and* all-good who, for the sake of satisfying his desire to be loved and served, imposes (or has to impose) on his creatures the amount of undeserved suffering we find in the world?

There is, however, a much more serious difficulty still: God's purpose in making the universe must be stated in terms of a dramatic story

---

6. For a discussion of this issue, see the eighteenth century controversy between Deists and Theists, for instance, in Sir Leslie Stephen's *History of English Thought in the Eighteenth Century* (London: Smith, Elder & Co., 1902) pp. 112-119 and pp. 134-163. See also the attacks by Toland and Tindal on "the mysterious" in *Christianity not Mysterious* and *Christianity as Old as the Creation, or the Gospel a Republication of the Religion of Nature,* resp., parts of which are reprinted in Henry Bettenson's *Doctrines of the Christian Church,* pp. 426-431. For modern views maintaining that mysteriousness is an essential element in religion, see Rudolf Otto, *The Idea of the Holy,* esp. pp. 25-40, and most recently M. B. Foster, *Mystery and Philosophy* (London: S.C.M. Press, 1957) esp. Chs. IV. and VI. For the view that statements about God must be nonsensical or absurd, see e.g. H. J. Paton, op. cit. pp. 119-120, 367-369. See also "Theology and Falsification" in *New Essays in Philosophical Theology,* ed. by A. Flew and A. MacIntyre (London: S.C.M. Press, 1955) pp. 96-131; also N. McPherson, "Religion as the Inexpressible", ibid., esp. pp. 137-143.

7. Stephen Neill, *Christian Faith To-day* (London: Penguin Books, 1955) pp. 240-241.

many of whose key incidents symbolize religious conceptions and prac-
tices which we no longer find morally acceptable: the imposition of a
taboo on the fruits of a certain tree, the sin and guilt incurred by
Adam and Eve by violating the taboo, the wrath of God,[8] the curse of
Adam and Eve and all their progeny, the expulsion from Paradise, the
Atonement by Christ's bloody sacrifice on the cross which makes available by way of the sacraments God's Grace by which alone men can
be saved (thereby, incidentally, establishing the valuable power of
priests to forgive sins and thus alone make possible a man's entry to
heaven,[9]) Judgment Day on which the sheep are separated from the
goats and the latter condemned to eternal torment in hell-fire.

Obviously it is much more difficult to formulate a purpose for creating the universe and man that will justify the enormous amount of
undeserved suffering which we find around us, if that story has to be
fitted in as well. For now we have to explain not only why an omnipotent, omniscient, and all-good God should create such a universe and
such a man, but also why, foreseeing every move of the feeble, weak-
willed, ignorant, and covetous creature to be created, He should nevertheless have created him and, having done so, should be incensed and
outraged by man's sin, and why He should deem it necessary to sacrifice His own son on the cross to atone for this sin which was, after all,
only a disobedience of one of his commands, and why this atonement
and consequent redemption could not have been followed by man's
return to Paradise—particularly of those innocent children who had not
yet sinned—and why, on Judgment Day, this merciful God should condemn some to eternal torment.[10] It is not surprising that in the face of
these and other difficulties, we find, again and again, a return to the
first view: that God's purpose cannot meaningfully be stated.

It will perhaps be objected that no Christian to-day believes in the
dramatic history of the world as I have presented it. But this is not so.

---

8. It is difficult to feel the magnitude of this first sin unless one takes seriously
the words "Behold, the man has eaten of the fruit of the tree of knowledge of good
and evil, and is become as one of us; and now, may he not put forth his hand, and
take also of the tree of life, and eat, and live forever?" Genesis iii, 22.

9. See in this connection the pastoral letter of 2nd February, 1905, by Johannes
Katschtaler, Prince Bishop of Salzburg on the honour due to priests, contained in
Quellen zur Geschichte des Papsttums, by Mirbt, pp. 497-9, translated and reprinted
in *The Protestant Tradition,* by J. S. Whale (Cambridge: University Press, 1955)
pp. 259-262.

10. How impossible it is to make sense of this story has been demonstrated beyond
any doubt by Tolstoy in his famous "Conclusion of A Criticism of Dogmatic Theology", reprinted in *A Confession, The Gospel in Brief, and What I Believe.*

It is the official doctrine of the Roman Catholic, the Greek Orthodox, and a large section of the Anglican Church.[11] Nor does Protestantism substantially alter this picture. In fact, by insisting on "Justification by Faith Alone" and by rejecting the ritualistic, magical character of the medieval Catholic interpretation of certain elements in the Christian religion, such as indulgences, the sacraments, and prayer, while at the same time insisting on the necessity of grace, Protestantism undermined the moral element in medieval Christianity expressed in the Catholics' emphasis on personal merit.[12] Protestantism, by harking back to St. Augustine, who clearly realized the incompatibility of grace and personal merit,[13] opened the way for Calvin's doctrine of Predestination (the intellectual parent of that form of rigid determinism which is usually blamed on science) and Salvation or Condemnation from all eternity.[14] Since Roman Catholics, Lutherans, Calvinists, Presbyterians and Baptists officially subscribe to the views just outlined, one can justifiably claim that the overwhelming majority of professing Christians hold or ought to hold them.

It might still be objected that the best and most modern views are wholly different. I have not the necessary knowledge to pronounce on the accuracy of this claim. It may well be true that the best and most modern views are such as Professor Braithwaite's who maintains that Christianity is, roughly speaking, "morality plus stories", where the stories are intended merely to make the strict moral teaching both more easily understandable and more palatable.[15] Or it may be that one or the other of the modern views on the nature and importance of the dramatic story told in the sacred Scriptures is the best. My reply is that, even if it is true, it does not prove what I wish to disprove, that one can extract a sensible answer to our question, "What is the meaning of life?" from the kind of story subscribed to by the overwhelming majority of Christians, who would, moreover, reject any such modernist

---

11. See "The Nicene Creed", "The Tridentine Profession of Faith", "The Syllabus of Errors", reprinted in *Documents of the Christian Church*, pp. 34, 373 and 380 resp.

12. See e.g. J. S. Whale, *The Protestant Tradition*, Ch. IV., esp. pp. 48-56.

13. See ibid., pp. 61 ff.

14. See "The Confession of Augsburg" esp. Articles II., IV., XVIII., XIX., XX.; "Christianae Religionis Institutio", "The Westminster Confession of Faith", esp. Articles III., VI., IX., X., XI., XVI., XVII.; "The Baptist Confession of Faith", esp. Articles III., XXI., XXIII., reprinted in *Documents of the Christian Church*, pp. 294 ff., 298 ff., 344 ff., 349 ff.

15. See e.g. his *An Empiricist's View of the Nature of Religious Belief* (Eddington Memorial Lecture).

interpretation at least as indignantly as the scientific account. More-over, though such views can perhaps avoid some of the worst absurd-ities of the traditional story, they are hardly in a much better position to state the purpose for which God has created the universe and man in it, because they cannot overcome the difficulty of finding a purpose grand and noble enough to justify the enormous amount of undeserved suffering in the world.

Let us, however, for argument's sake, waive all these objections. There remains one fundamental hurdle which no form of Christianity can overcome: the fact that it demands of man a morally repugnant attitude towards the universe. It is now very widely held[16] that the basic element of the Christian religion is an attitude of worship towards a being supremely worthy of being worshipped and that it is religious feelings and experiences which apprise their owner of such a being and which inspire in him the knowledge or the feeling of complete depend-ence, awe, worship, mystery, and self-abasement. There is, in other words, a bi-polarity (the famous "I-Thou relationship") in which the object, "the wholly-other", is exalted whereas the subject is abased to the limit. Rudolf Otto has called this the "creature-feeling"[17] and he quotes as an expression of it, Abraham's words when venturing to plead for the men of Sodom: "Behold now, I have taken upon me to speak unto the Lord, which am but dust and ashes". (Gen. XVIII.27). Chris-tianity thus demands of men an attitude inconsistent with one of the presuppositions of morality: that man is not wholly dependent on something else, that man has free will, that man is in principle capable of responsibility. We have seen that the concept of grace is the Chris-tian attempt to reconcile the claim of total dependence and the claim of individual responsibility (partial independence), and it is obvious that such attempts must fail. We may dismiss certain doctrines, such as the doctrine of original sin or the doctrine of eternal hellfire or the doctrine that there can be no salvation outside the Church as extrava-gant and peripheral, but we cannot reject the doctrine of total depend-ence without rejecting the characteristically Christian attitude as such.

¶ THE MEANING OF LIFE

Perhaps some of you will have felt that I have been shirking the real problem. To many people the crux of the matter seems as follows. How

16. See e.g. the two series of Gifford Lectures most recently published: *The Modern Predicament* by H. J. Paton (London: George Allen & Unwin Ltd., 1955) pp. 69 ff., and *On Selfhool and Godhood* by C. A. Campbell (London: George Allen & Unwin Ltd., 1957) pp. 231-250.

17. Rudolf Otto, *The Idea of the Holy*, p. 9.

can there be any meaning in our life if it ends in death? What meaning can there be in it that our inevitable death does not destroy? How can our existence be meaningful if there is no after-life in which perfect justice is meted out? How can life have any meaning if all it holds out to us are a few miserable earthly pleasures and even these to be enjoyed only rarely and for such a piteously short time?

I believe this is the point which exercises most people most deeply. Kirilov, in Dostoevsky's novel, *The Possessed,* claims, just before committing suicide, that as soon as we realize that there is no God, we cannot live any longer, we must put an end to our lives. One of the reasons which he gives is that when we discover that there is no paradise, we have nothing to live for.

". . . there was a day on earth, and in the middle of the earth were three crosses. One on the cross had such faith that He said to another, 'To-day thou shalt be with me in paradise'. The day came to an end, both died, and they went, but they found neither paradise nor resurrection. The saying did not come true. Listen: that man was the highest of all on earth . . . There has never been any one like Him before or since, and never will be . . . And if that is so, if the laws of Nature did not spare even *Him,* and made even Him live in the midst of lies and die for a lie, then the whole planet is a lie and is based on a lie and a stupid mockery. So the very laws of the planet are a lie and a farce of the devil. What, then, is there to live for?"[18] And Tolstoy, too, was nearly driven to suicide when he came to doubt the existence of God and an after-life.[19] And this is true of many.

What, then, is it that inclines us to think that if life is to have a meaning, there would have to be an after-life? It is this. The Christian world view contains the following three propositions. The first is that since the Fall, God's curse of Adam and Eve, and the expulsion from Paradise, life on earth for mankind has not been worth while, but a vale of tears, one long chain of misery, suffering, unhappiness, and injustice. The second is that a perfect after-life is awaiting us after the death of the body. The third is that we can enter this perfect life only on certain conditions, among which is also the condition of enduring our earthly existence to its bitter end. In this way, our earthly existence which, in itself, would not (at least for many people if not all) be worth living, acquires meaning and significance: only if we endure it, can we gain admission to the realm of the blessed.

It might be doubted whether this view is still held to-day. How-

---

18. Fyodor Dostoyevsky, *The Devils* (London: The Penguin Classics, 1953) pp. 613-614.

19. Leo Tolstoy, *A Confession, The Gospel in Brief, and What I Believe,* The World's Classics, p. 24.

ever, there can be no doubt that even to-day we all imbibe a good deal
of this view with our earliest education. In sermons, the contrast between the perfect life of the blessed and our life of sorrow and drudgery
is frequently driven home and we hear it again and again that Christianity has a message of hope and consolation for all those "who are
weary and heavy laden".[20]

It is not surprising, then, that when the implications of the scientific
world picture begin to sink in, when we come to have doubts about the
existence of God and another life, we are bitterly disappointed. For if
there is no afterlife, then all we are left is our earthly life which we
have come to regard as a necessary evil, the painful fee of admission
to the land of eternal bliss. But if there is no eternal bliss to come and
if this hell on earth is all, why hang on till the horrible end?

Our disappointment therefore arises out of these two propositions,
that the earthy life is not worth living, and that there is another perfect
life of eternal happiness and joy which we may enter upon if we satisfy
certain conditions. We can regard our lives as meaningful, if we believe
both. We cannot regard them as meaningful if we believe merely the first
and not the second. It seems to me inevitable that people who are taught
something of the history of science, will have serious doubts about the
second. If they cannot overcome these, as many will be unable to do,
then they must either accept the sad view that their life is meaningless
or they must abandon the first proposition: that this earthly life is not
worth living. They must find the meaning of their life in this earthly
existence. But is this possible?

A moment's examination will show us that the Christian evaluation
of our earthly life as worthless, which we accept in our moments of
pessimism and dissatisfaction, is not one that we normally accept.
Consider only the question of murder and suicide. On the Christian
view, other things being equal, the most kindly thing to do would be
for every one of us to kill as many of our friends and dear ones as still
have the misfortune to be alive, and then to commit suicide without
delay, for every moment spent in this life is wasted. On the Christian
view, God has not made it that easy for us. He has forbidden us to
hasten others or ourselves into the next life. Our bodies are his private
property and must be allowed to wear themselves out in the way decided
by Him, however painful and horrible that may be. We are, as it were,
driving a burning car. There is only one way out, to jump clear and
let it hurtle to destruction. But the owner of the car has forbidden it
on pain of eternal tortures worse than burning. And so we do better
to burn to death inside.

---

20. See for instance J. S. Whale, *Christian Doctrine*, pp. 171, 176-178, &c. See also
Stephen Neill, *Christian Faith To-day*, p. 241.

On this view, murder is a less serious wrong than suicide. For murder can always be confessed and repented and therefore forgiven, suicide cannot—unless we allow the ingenious way out chosen by the heroine of Graham Greene's play, The Living Room, who swallows a slow but deadly poison and, while awaiting its taking effect, repents having taken it. Murder, on the other hand, is not so serious because, in the first place, it need not rob the victim of anything but the last lap of his march in the vale of tears, and, in the second place, it can always be forgiven. Hamlet, it will be remembered, refrains from killing his uncle during the latter's prayers because, as a true Christian, he believes that killing his uncle at that point, when the latter has purified his soul by repentance, would merely be doing him a good turn, for murder at such a time would simply despatch him to undeserved and everlasting happiness.

These views strike us as odd, to say the least. They are the logical consequence of the official medieval evaluation of this our earthly existence. If this life is not worth living, then taking it is not robbing the person concerned of much. The only thing wrong with it is the damage to God's property, which is the same both in the case of murder and suicide. We do not take this view at all. Our view, on the contrary, is that murder is the most serious wrong because it consists in taking away from some one else against his will his most precious possession, his life. For this reason, when a person suffering from an incurable disease asks to be killed, the mercy killing of such a person is regarded as a much less serious crime than murder because, in such a case, the killer is not robbing the other of a good against his will. Suicide is not regarded as a real crime at all, for we take the view that a person can do with his own possessions what he likes.

However, from the fact that these are our normal opinions, we can infer nothing about their truth. After all, we could easily be mistaken. Whether life is or is not worthwhile, is a value judgment. Perhaps all this is merely a matter of opinion or taste. Perhaps no objective answer can be given. Fortunately, we need not enter deeply into these difficult and controversial questions. It is quite easy to show that the medieval evaluation of earthly life is based on a misguided procedure.

Let us remind ourselves briefly of how we arrive at our value judgments. When we determine the merits of students, meals, tennis players, bulls, or bathing belles, we do so on the basis of some criteria and some standard or norm. Criteria and standards notoriously vary from field to field and even from case to case. But that does not mean that we have *no* idea about what are the appropriate criteria or standards to use. It would not be fitting to apply the criteria for judging bulls to the judgment of students or bathing belles. They score on quite different points. And even where the same criteria are appropriate as in the judgment of students enrolled in different schools and universities, the standards will vary from one institution to another. Pupils who would only just pass in one, would perhaps obtain honours in another. The higher the standard applied, the lower the marks, that is, the merit conceded to the candidate.

The same procedure is applicable also in the evaluation of a life. We examine it on the basis of certain criteria and standards. The medieval Christian view uses the criteria of the ordinary man: a life is judged by what the person concerned can get out of it: the balance of happiness over unhappiness, pleasure over pain, bliss over suffering. Our earthly life is judged not worthwhile because it contains much unhappiness, pain, and suffering, little happiness, pleasure, and bliss. The next life is judged worth while because it provides eternal bliss and no suffering.

Armed with these criteria, we can compare the life of this man and that, and judge which is more worth while, which has a greater balance of bliss over suffering. But criteria alone enable us merely to make comparative judgments of value, not absolute ones. We can say which is more and which is less worth while, but we cannot say which is worth while and which is not. In order to determine the latter, we must introduce a standard. But what standard ought we to choose?

Ordinarily, the standard we employ is the average of the kind. We call a man and a tree tall if they are well above the average of their kind. We do not say that Jones is a short man because he is shorter than a tree. We do not judge a boy a bad student because his answer to a question in the Leaving Examination is much worse than that given in reply to the same question by a young man sitting for his finals for the Bachelor's degree.

The same principles must apply to judging lives. When we ask whether a given life was or was not worth while, then we must take into consideration the range of worthwhileness which ordinary lives normally cover. Our end poles of the scale must be the best possible and the worst possible life that one finds. A good and worthwhile life is one that is well above average. A bad one is one well below.

The Christian evaluation of earthly lives is misguided because it adopts a quite unjustifiably high standard. Christianity singles out the major shortcomings of our earthly existence: there is not enough happiness; there is too much suffering; the good and bad points are quite unequally and unfairly distributed; the underprivileged and underendowed do not get adequate compensation; it lasts only a short time. It then quite accurately depicts the perfect or ideal life as that which does not have any of these shortcomings. Its next step is to promise the believer that he will be able to enjoy this perfect life later on. And then it adopts as its standard of judgment the perfect life, dismissing as inadequate anything that falls short of it. Having dismissed earthly life as miserable, it further damns it by characterizing most of the pleasures of ,which earthly existence allows as bestial, gross, vile, and sinful, or alternatively as not really pleasurable.

This procedure is as illegitimate as if I were to refuse to call anything tall unless it is infinitely tall, or anything beautiful unless it is perfectly flawless, or any one strong unless he is omnipotent. Even if it were true that there is available to us an after-life which is flawless and perfect, it would still not be legitimate to judge earthly lives by this standard. We do not fail every candidate who is not an Einstein. And if we do not believe in an after-life, we must of course use ordinary earthly standards.

I have so far only spoken of the worthwhileness, only of what a person can get out of a life. There are other kinds of appraisal. Clearly, we evaluate people's lives not merely from the point of view of what they yield to the persons that lead them, but also from that of other men on whom these lives have impinged. We judge a life more significant if the person has contributed to the happiness of others, whether directly by what he did for others, or by the plans, discoveries, inventions, and work he performed. Many lives that hold little in the way of pleasure or happiness for its owner are highly significant and valuable, deserve admiration and respect on account of the contributions made.

It is now quite clear that death is simply irrelevant. If life can be worthwhile at all, then it can be so even though it be short. And if it is not worthwhile at all, then an eternity of it is simply a nightmare. It may be sad that we have to leave this beautiful world, but it is so only if and because it is beautiful. And it is no less beautiful for coming to an end. I rather suspect that an eternity of it might make us less appreciative, and in the end it would be tedious.

It will perhaps be objected now that I have not really demonstrated that life has a meaning, but merely that it can be worthwhile or have value. It must be admitted that there is a perfectly natural interpretation of the question, "What is the meaning of life?" on which my view actually proves that life has no meaning. I mean the interpretation discussed in section 2 of this lecture [omitted here, ed.], where I attempted to show that, if we accept the explanations of natural science, we cannot believe that living organisms have appeared on earth in accordance with the deliberate plan of some intelligent being. Hence, on this view, life cannot be said to have a purpose, in the sense in which man-made things have a purpose. Hence it cannot be said to have a meaning or significance in that sense.

However, this conclusion is innocuous. People are disconcerted by the thought that *life as such* has no meaning in that sense only because they very naturally think it entails that no individual life can have meaning either. They naturally assume that *this* life or *that* can have meaning only if *life as such* has meaning. But it should by now be clear that your life and mine may or may not have meaning (in one sense) even if life as such has none (in the other). Of course, it follows from this that your life may have meaning while mine has not. The Christian view guarantees a meaning (in one sense) to every life, the scientific view does not (in any sense). By relating the question of the meaningfulness of life to the particular circumstances of an individual's existence, the scientific view leaves it an open question whether an individual's life has meaning or not. It is, however, clear that the latter is the important sense of "having a meaning". Christians, too, must feel that their life is wasted and meaningless if they have not achieved salvation. To know that even such lost lives have a meaning in another sense is no consolation to them. What matters is not that life should have a guaranteed meaning, whatever happens here or here-after, but that, by luck (Grace) or the right temperament and attitude (Faith) or a judicious life (Works) a person should make the most of his life.

"But here lies the rub," it will be said. "Surely, it makes all the difference whether there is an after-life. This is where morality comes in." It would be a mistake to believe that. Morality is not the meting out of punishment and reward. To be moral is to refrain from doing to others what, if they followed reason, they would not do to themselves, and to do for others what, if they followed reason, they would want to have done. It is, roughly speaking, to recognize that others, too, have a right to a worthwhile life. Being moral does not make one's own life worthwhile, it helps others to make theirs so.

¶ CONCLUSION

I have tried to establish three points: (i) that scientific explanations render their explicanda as intelligible as pre-scientific explanations; they differ from the latter only in that, having testable implications and being more precisely formulated, their truth or falsity can be determined with a high degree of probability; (ii) that science does not rob human life of purpose, in the only sense that matters, but, on the contrary, renders many more of our purposes capable of realization; (iii) that common sense, the Christian world view, and the scientific approach agree on the criteria but differ on the standard to be employed in the evaluation of human lives; judging human lives by the standards of perfection, as Christians do, is unjustified; if we abandon this excessively high standard and replace it by an everyday one, we have no longer any reason for dismissing earthly existence as not worthwhile.

On the basis of these three points I have attempted to explain why so many people come to the conclusion that human existence is meaningless and to show that this conclusion is false. In my opinion, this pessimism rests on a combination of two beliefs, both partly true and partly false: the belief that the meaningfulness of life depends on the satisfaction of at least three conditions, and the belief that this universe satisfies none of them. The conditions are, first, that the universe is intelligible, second, that life has a purpose, and third, that all men's hopes and desires can ultimately be satisfied. It seemed to medieval Christians and it seems to many Christians to-day that Christianity offers a picture of the world which can meet these conditions. To many Christians and non-Christians alike it seems that the scientific world picture is incompatible with that of Christianity, therefore with the view that these three conditions are met, therefore with the view that life has a meaning. Hence they feel that they are confronted by the dilemma of accepting either a world picture incompatible with the discoveries of science or the view that life is meaningless.

I have attempted to show that the dilemma is unreal because life can be meaningful even if not all of these conditions are met. My main conclusion, therefore, is that acceptance of the scientific world picture provides no reason for saying that life is meaningless, but on the contrary every reason for saying that there are many lives which are meaningful and significant. My subsidiary conclusion is that one of the reasons frequently offered for retaining the Christian world picture, namely, that its acceptance gives us a guarantee of a meaning for human existence, is unsound. We can see that our lives can have a meaning even if we abandon it and adopt the scientific world picture instead. I have, moreover, mentioned several reasons for rejecting the Christian world picture: (i) the biblical explanations of the details of our universe are often simply false; (ii) the so-called explanations of the whole universe are incomprehensible or absurd; (iii) Christianity's low evaluation of earthly existence (which is the main cause of the belief in the meaninglessness of life) rests on the use of an unjustifiably high standard of judgment.

BIBLIOGRAPHY

¶ I. Source Books and Surveys

General surveys of the history of twentieth century analytic philosophy are to be found in J. Passmore, *A Hundred Years of Philosophy* (London: G. Duckworth, 1957); G. Warnock, *English Philosophy since 1900* (London: Oxford Univ. Press, 1958); and W. P. Alston and G. Nakhnikian (eds.), *Readings in Twentieth Century Philosophy* (New York: Free Press, 1963). Alston's and Nakhnikian's Introductions to the selections from Moore, Russell, logical positivism, and ordinary language philosophy are especially informative. An excellent short account is A. Quinton, "Contemporary British Philosophy," *A Critical History of Western Philosophy* (New York: Free Press, 1964). Edited by D. J. O'Connor, this volume also contains essays on Moore, Russell, and the logical positivists. J. O. Urmson, *Philosophical Analysis* (Oxford: Clarendon Press, 1956), more restricted in scope than the other general surveys, is a critical scrutiny of logical analysis and logical positivism between the two world wars. Besides the anthologies listed above, the following collections are of great value: H. Feigl and W. Sellars (eds.), *Readings in Philosophical Analysis* (New York: Appleton-Century-Crofts, 1949); M. Black (ed.), *Philosophical Analysis* (Ithaca: Cornell Univ. Press, 1950); A. Flew (ed.), *Logic and Language*, First and Second Series (Oxford: Blackwell, 1952, 1953); and *Essays in Conceptual Analysis* (London: Macmillan, 1956). *Contemporary British Philosophy*, First and Second Series, ed. J. H. Muirhead (London: Macmillan, 1924, 1925) and Third Series, ed. H. D. Lewis (London: Macmillan, 1956), contain valuable essays by Russell, Moore, C. D. Broad, G. Ryle, and F. Waismann, among others. *The Philosophy of G. E. Moore* (Evanston: Northwestern Univ. Press, 1942); *The Philosophy of Bertrand Russell* (Evanston: Northwestern Univ. Press, 1944), reissued as Harper Torchback, 2 vols.; and *The Philosophy of Rudolf Carnap* (La Salle, Ill.: Open Court, 1963); all ed. P. A. Schilpp, contain mostly essays about the philosophers indicated but also individual autobiographies as well as replies to their critics represented in the volumes. Another short survey is *The Revolution in Philosophy* (London: Macmillan, 1956), which consists of broadcast talks on contemporary philosophers by A. J. Ayer, W. C. Kneale, G. A. Paul, D. F. Pears, P. F. Strawson, G. J.

Warnock, and R. A. Wollheim, with an introduction by G. Ryle. A. J. Ayer (ed.), *Logical Positivism* (New York: Free Press, 1959) includes classics of logical positivism and important papers by analytic philosophers not usually classified as logical positivists, as well as a superb bibliography of everyone remotely connected with analytic philosophy in the twentieth century.

The autobiographies or biographies of some of the major philosophers represented in this volume are: G. E. Moore, "An Autobiography," *The Philosophy of G. E. Moore, op. cit.;* Bertrand Russell, "My Mental Development," *The Philosophy of Bertrand Russell, op. cit.; My Philosophical Development* (New York: Simon and Schuster, 1959); "Obituary," *The Listener,* 1937, reprinted in *Unpopular Essays* (New York: Simon and Schuster, 1950), which is a Russellian spoof; Alan Wood, *Bertrand Russell: The Passionate Sceptic* (London: Allen & Unwin, 1957); Rudolf Carnap, "Intellectual Autobiography," *The Philosophy of Rudolf Carnap, op. cit.;* Norman Malcolm, *Ludwig Wittgenstein:* a memoir, with a biographical sketch by G. H. von Wright (London: Oxford Univ. Press, 1958); and G. Pitcher, *The Philosophy of Wittgenstein* (Englewood Cliffs: Prentice-Hall, 1964). N. Malcolm also covers Wittgenstein's life and J. O. Urmson, John Austin's, in the forthcoming *Encyclopedia of Philosophy,* ed. P. Edwards (New York: Macmillan-Free Press).

¶ II. WORKS BY AND COMMENTARIES ON INDIVIDUAL PHILOSOPHERS REPRESENTED IN THE PRESENT VOLUME

Some other major works of the philosophers included in this volume are: G. E. Moore, "The Nature of Judgment," *Mind,* 1899; "Necessity," *Mind,* 1900; *Principia Ethica* (Cambridge: Cambridge Univ. Press, 1903); *Ethics* (London: Home Univ. Library, 1912); *Philosophical Studies* (London: Routledge & Kegan Paul, 1922); "Proof of an External World," 1939, reprinted in *Philosophical Papers* (London: Macmillan, 1959), available as Collier paperback; "Russell's 'Theory of Descriptions' "; *The Philosophy of Bertrand Russell, op. cit.,* reprinted in *Philosophical Papers, op. cit.;* and *Some Main Problems of Philosophy* (London: Allen & Unwin, 1953), available as Collier paperback.

Bertrand Russell, *The Philosophy of Leibniz* (Cambridge: Cambridge Univ. Press, 1900); *The Principles of Mathematics* (Cambridge: Cambridge Univ. Press, 1903); "On Denoting," *Mind,* 1905, reprinted in H. Feigl and W. Sellars (eds.), *Readings in Philosophical Analysis, op. cit.; Principia Mathematica,* 3 vols., written with A. N. Whitehead (Cambridge: Cambridge Univ. Press, 1910-13); *Philosophical Essays* (London: Longmans, Green, 1910); *The Problems of Philosophy* (London: Home Univ. Library, 1912);

Our Knowledge of the External World (London: Allen & Unwin, 1914), available as paperback; "Philosophy of Logical Atomism," *Monist*, 1918-19, reprinted in the R. C. Marsh (ed.), *Logic and Knowledge* (London: Allen & Unwin, 1956); *The Analysis of Mind* (London: Allen & Unwin, 1921); *The Analysis of Matter* (London: Kegan Paul, Trench, Trubner, 1927), available as 'paperback; *An Inquiry into Meaning and Truth* (New York: Norton, 1940), available as paperback; and *Human Knowledge: Its Scope and Limits* (New York: Simon and Schuster, 1948).

Arthur Lovejoy, *et al.*, *Essays in Critical Realism* (New York: Macmillan, 1920); *The Revolt Against Dualism* (Chicago: Open Court, 1930); *The Great Chain of Being* (Cambridge, Mass.: Harvard University Press, 1936). For other references, see R. M. Chisholm (ed.), *Realism and the Background of Phenomenology* (New York: The Free Press, 1960).

Gilbert Ryle, "Are There Propositions?," *Proc. Arist. Soc.*, 1929-30; "Phenomenology," *Proc. Arist. Soc.*, 1937-38; *Philosophical Arguments* Oxford: Oxford University Press, 1945); *The Concept of Mind* (London: Hutchinson's; New York: Barnes & Noble, 1949); and *Dilemmas* (Cambridge: Cambridge Univ. Press, 1954). For other references, see A. Ayer (ed.), *Logical Positivism, op. cit.*, pp. 434-35.

Rudolf Carnap, *Der logische Aufbau der Welt* (Berlin: Weltkreis-Verlag, 1928); *Logical Syntax of Language* (London: Kegan Paul, 1937); "Testability and Meaning," *Philosophy of Science*, reprinted, New Haven: Yale Graduate Philosophy Club. For other references, see A. Ayer (ed.), *Logical Positivism, op. cit.*, pp. 383-84, 400-402.

Charles L. Stevenson, *Ethics and Language* (New Haven: Yale Univ. Press, 1945), available as paperback.

C. G. Hempel, "Fundamentals of Concept Formation in Empirical Science," *Inter. Ency. of Unified Science* (Chicago: Univ. of Chicago Press, 1952).

John Wisdom, "Logical Constructions, I-V," *Mind*, 1931-33; *Problems of Mind and Matter* (Cambridge: Cambridge Univ. Press, 1934), available as paperback; *Other Minds* (Oxford: Blackwell, 1952), *Philosophy and Psycho-analysis* (Oxford: Blackwell, 1953).

Ludwig Wittgenstein, *Tractatus Logico-Philosophicus* (London: Kegan Paul, 1921, new translation, London: Routledge & Kegan Paul, 1961); *Philosophical Investigations* (Oxford: Blackwell, 1953); *Remarks on the Foundations of Mathematics* (Oxford: Blackwell, 1956); *The Blue and the Brown Books* (Oxford: Blackwell, 1958); *Notebooks, 1914-1916* (Oxford: Blackwell, 1961); "Some Remarks on Logical Form," *Proc. Arist. Soc.*, Suppl. vol., 1929; "A Lecture on Ethics," *Philosophical Review*, 1965.

John Austin, *Philosophical Papers* (Oxford: Clarendon Press, 1961); *How to do Things with Words* (Oxford: Clarendon Press, 1962); *Sense and Sensibilia* (Oxford: Clarendon Press, 1962).

Herbert L. A. Hart, *Definition and Theory in Jurisprudence* (Oxford: Clarendon Press, 1953), *The Concept of Law* (Oxford: Clarendon Press, 1961), "The Ascription of Responsibility and Rights," *Proc. Arist. Soc.*,

1948-49, reprinted in A. Flew (ed.), *Logic and Language, op. cit.*, First Series,

Kurt Baier, *The Moral Point of View* (Ithaca: Cornell Univ. Press, 1958).

Some of the major commentaries on the individual philosophers of this volume are: A. White, *G. E. Moore: A Critical Exposition* (Oxford: Blackwell, 1958); G. E. M. Anscombe, *An Introduction to Wittgenstein's Tractatus* (London: Hutchinson, 1959); E. Stenius, *Wittgenstein's Tractatus* (Oxford: Blackwell, 1960); J. Griffin, *Wittgenstein's Logical Atomism* (Oxford: Clarendon Press, 1964); G. Pitcher, *The Philosophy of Wittgenstein* (Englewood Cliffs: Prentice-Hall, 1964); M. Black, *A Companion to Wittgenstein's Tractatus* (Ithaca: Cornell Univ. Press, 1964); N. Malcolm, Review of *Philosophical Investigations, Philosophical Review*, 1954, reprinted, *Knowledge and Certainty* (Englewood Cliffs: Prentice-Hall, 1963). There are no large-scale commentaries on Russell, Lovejoy, Ryle, Carnap, Stevenson, Wisdom, or Austin, among the others of this anthology, although there are various essays on certain aspects of their work which will be listed below as they relate to the author's essays.

¶ III. WORKS BY OTHER PHILOSOPHERS OF THE SAME PERIOD

English and American Realists

S. Alexander, *Space, Time and Deity*, 2 vols. (London: Macmillan, 1918); G. F. Stout, *Mind and Matter* (London: Macmillan, 1931); H. H. Price, *Perception* (New York: McBride, 1933); E. B. Holt, *et al., The New Realism* (New York: Macmillan, 1912); R. B. Perry, *Present Philosophical Tendencies* (New York: Longmans, Green, 1912); Durant Drake, *et al., Essays in Critical Realism: A Cooperative Study of the Problem of Knowledge* (New York: Macmillan, 1920); G. Santayana, *Scepticism and Animal Faith* (New York: Scribners, 1923); W. T. Stace, *The Theory of Knowledge and Existence* (London: Oxford Univ. Press, 1932).

Logical Analysts

C. D. Broad, "Critical and Speculative Philosophy," *Contemporary British Philosophy, op. cit.*, First Series, *Scientific Thought* (London: Kegan Paul, 1923); John Wisdom, "Is Analysis a Useful Method in Philosophy?," *Proc. Arist. Soc.*, Suppl. vol., 1934, reprinted in *Philosophy and Psychoanalysis, op. cit.;* Frank Ramsey, *The Foundations of Mathematics and Other Logical Essays* (London: Kegan Paul, 1931); L. Susan Stebbing, "The Method of Analysis in Metaphysics," *Proc. Arist. Soc.*, 1932-33, *Logical Positivism and Analysis* (London: Oxford Univ. Press, 1933); M. Black, "Philosophical Analysis," *Proc. Arist. Soc.*, Suppl. vol., 1934; *The Nature of Mathematics* (London: Kegan Paul, 1933); *Language and Phi-*

losophy (Ithaca: Cornell Univ. Press, 1949); *Problems of Analysis* (London: Routledge & Kegan Paul, 1954); *Models and Metaphors* (Ithaca: Cornell Univ. Press, 1962); W. V. Quine, "On What There Is," *Review of Metaphysics*, 1948, reprinted, *From a Logical Point of View* (Cambridge: Harvard Univ. Press, 1953); and with N. Goodman, "Steps Toward a Constructive Nominalism," *Journal of Symbolic Logic*, 1947.

Logical Positivists

A. J. Ayer, *Language, Truth and Logic* (London: Gollancz, 1946), available as paperback; G. Bergmann, *The Metaphysics of Logical Positivism* (London: Longmans, Green, 1954); H. Feigl, "Logical Empiricism," in D. D. Runes (ed.), *Twentieth Century Philosophy* (New York: Philosophical Library, 1943), reprinted, H. Feigl and W. Sellars, *Readings in Philosophical Analysis, op. cit.;* P. Frank, *Between Physics and Philosophy* (Cambridge: Harvard Univ. Press, 1941); J. Jorgensen, "The Development of Logical Empiricism," *Int. Ency. Unified Science* (Chicago: Univ. of Chicago Press, 1951); O. Neurath, *et al., Wissenschaftliche Weltauffassung: Der Wiener Kreis* (Vienna: Wolf, 1929); H. Reichenbach, *Experience and Prediction: An Analysis of the Foundations and Structure of Knowledge* (Chicago: Univ. of Chicago Press, 1938); M. Schlick, *Gesammelte Aufsätze* (Vienna: Gerold, 1938); *Problems of Ethics* (Englewood Cliffs: Prentice-Hall, 1939). K. R. Popper, *The Logic of Scientific Discovery* (London: Hutchinson, 1958), although critical of logical positivism, stems from the Vienna Circle.

Conceptual Analysts

I. Berlin, "Logical Translation," *Proc. Arist. Soc.*, 1949-50; "Empirical Propositions and Hypothetical Statements," *Mind*, 1950; S. Hampshire, *Thought and Action* (London: Chatto & Windus, 1959); R. M. Hare, *The Language of Morals* (Oxford: Clarendon Press, 1952); G. A. Paul, "Is There a Problem about Sense-Data?," *Proc. Arist. Soc.*, Suppl. vol., 1936, reprinted, A. Flew (ed.), *Logic and Language, op. cit.*, First Series; P. F. Strawson, "On Referring," *Mind*, 1950; F. Waismann, "How I See Philosophy," *Contemporary British Philosophy, op. cit.*, Third Series.

¶ IV. Discussions of Major Issues

Internal Relations

B. Russell, *Principles of Mathematics, op. cit.*, Ch. 26; "The Monistic Doctrine of Truth," *Proc. Arist. Soc.*, 1906-7, reprinted, *Philosophical Essays, op. cit.;* "Some Explanations in Reply to Mr. Bradley," *Mind*, 1910; G. E. Moore, "External and Internal Relations," *Proc. Arist. Soc.*, 1918-19, reprinted, *Philosophical Studies, op. cit.;* B. Blanshard, *The Nature of Thought*, 2 vols. (London: Allen & Unwin, 1930); A. C. Ewing, *Idealism* (London: Methuen, 1933); E. Nagel, *Sovereign Reason* (New York: Free Press, 1954);

A. J. Ayer and G. Ryle, "Internal Relations," *Proc. Arist. Soc.*, Suppl. vol., 1935; R. B. Perry, "The Ego-centric Predicament," *The Journal of Philosophy*, 1910; and W. T. Stace, "The Refutation of Realism," *Mind*, 1934.

Role of Analysis in Moore

A. White, *G. E. Moore, op. cit.;* C. H. Langford, "Moore's Notion of Analysis"; *The Philosophy of G. E. Moore, op. cit.;* Moore, "Reply" to Langford, *Phil. of G. E. Moore, op. cit.*

Role of Analysis in Russell

M. Weitz, "Analysis and the Unity of Russell's Philosophy"; *The Philosophy of Bertrand Russell, op. cit.*

Dualism of Universals and Particulars

G. E. Moore, *Some Main Problems of Philosophy, op. cit.;* B. Russell, *The Problems of Philosophy, op. cit., An Inquiry into Meaning and Truth, op. cit.;* A. D. Woozley, *Theory of Knowledge* (London: Hutchinson, 1949); and H. H. Price, *Thinking and Experience* (London: Hutchinson, 1953).

Dualism of Mind and Matter

Moore, *Some Main Problems of Philosophy, op. cit.;* Russell, *The Problems of Philosophy, op. cit.;* G. Ryle, *The Concept of Mind, op. cit.;* and C. D. Broad, *The Mind and Its Place in Nature* (London: Kegan Paul, 1925).

Sense-Data and Perception

G. E. Moore, "Reply" to O. K. Bouwsma and A. Murphy, *The Philosophy of G. E. Moore, op. cit.* (The essays by Bouwsma and Murphy are in this volume along with Moore's "Reply.") This "Reply" and his essay, "Visual Data," *British Philosophy in the Mid-Century, op. cit.*, are the most convincing defenses of the theory of sense-data in recent philosophy. A. J. Ayer, *The Problem of Knowledge* (London: Macmillan, 1956) and the classic, H. H. Price, *Perception, op. cit.*, also defend the theory that there are sense-data. Among the important recent critiques of the theory are G. Paul, "Is There a Problem about Sense-Data?," *op. cit.;* G. Ryle, *The Concept of Mind, op. cit.;* "Sensation," *Contemporary British Philosophy, op. cit.*, Third Series; and J. Austin, *Sense and Sensibilia, op. cit.*

Moore's Ethics

B. Russell, "The Elements of Ethics," *Philosophical Essays, op. cit.*, also reprinted in W. Sellars and J. Hospers, (eds.), *Readings in Ethical Theory* (New York: Appleton-Century-Crofts, 1952); and, by way of influential criticism of both Moore and Russell, G. Santayana, "Hypostatic Ethics," *Winds of Doctrine* (New York: Scribners, 1913).

Moore's Defence of Common Sense

Moore, "Proof of an External World," *Philosophical Papers, op. cit.;* N. Malcolm, "Moore and Ordinary Language," *The Philosophy of G. E. Moore, op. cit.;* "Certainty and Empirical Statements," *Mind,* 1942; and for a recent criticism of Malcolm's interpretation of Moore, A. White, *G. E. Moore, op. cit.*

Russell's Theory of Descriptions

B. Russell, "On Denoting," *op. cit.,* "Philosophy of Logical Atomism," *op. cit.,* and, more technically, *Principia Mathematica, op. cit.,* vol. I, section 14. The importance of the theory is discussed in F. Ramsey, *The Foundations of Mathematics, op. cit.;* L. Wittgenstein, *Tractatus Logico-Philosophicus, op. cit.;* G. Ryle, "Systematically Misleading Expressions," *op. cit.;* W. V. Quine, "On What There Is," *op. cit.;* and P. F. Strawson, "On Referring," *op. cit.* Strawson's essay is as important to the repudiation of philosophy as contextual definition as Russell's theory is to the formulation of the theory of analysis as contextual definition.

Assessment of Logical Analysis

L. S. Stebbing, "Moore's Influence"; *The Philosophy of G. E. Moore, op. cit.;* J. Wisdom, "Philosophical Perplexity"; and for a brilliant summary, J. O. Urmson, *Philosophical Analysis, op. cit.*

Assessment of Logical Atomism

J. Wisdom, "Logical Constructions," *op. cit.;* J. Urmson, *Philosophical Analysis, op. cit.;* G. Pitcher, *The Philosophy of Wittgenstein, op. cit.;* J. Griffin, *Wittgenstein's Logical Atomism, op. cit.* Urmson especially explores the differences between Russell's and Wittgenstein's logical atomism.

Constructionism

E. Nagel, "Russell's Philosophy of Science," *The Philosophy of Bertrand Russell, op. cit.;* is an incisive statement and criticism of Russell's version of logical constructionism as a method for dealing with scientific concepts. C. Fritz, *Bertrand Russell's Construction of the External World* (New York: Humanities Press, 1952) is an extensive summary and critique of Russell's constructionism.

The Verification Theory of Meaning

C. G. Hempel, "The Empiricist Criterion of Meaning," *Revue Internationale de Philosophie,* 1950, reprinted, A. J. Ayer (ed.), *Logical Positivism, op. cit.,* surveys the entire gamut of positivists' formulations of meaning as verifiability and testability; it contains all the requisite references to the history of the positivist theory. G. Warnock, "Verification and the Use of Language," *Revue Internationale de Philosophie,* 1951, reprinted in P. Edwards and A. Pap, (eds.), *A Modern Introduction to Philosophy,* 2nd Ed. (New York: The Free Press, 1965), is a general criticism of the verification theory; G. Ryle, Review of R. Carnap, *Meaning and Necessity,* in *Philosophy,* 1949, is a criticism of Carnap's theory of meaning.

Carnap's Theory of Analysis

R. Carnap, *The Logical Syntax of Language, op. cit.;* and for a critique, J. Urmson, *Philosophical Analysis, op. cit.*

The Statements of Mathematics and Logic as Tautologies

L. Wittgenstein, *Tractatus Logico-Philosophicus, op. cit.,* is acknowledged as the source of the doctrine. C. G. Hempel, "The Nature of Mathematical Truth" and "Geometry and Empirical Science," both reprinted in H. Feigl and W. Sellars (eds.), *Readings in Philosophical Analysis, op. cit.,* are succinct defenses of the doctrine. For a criticism, E. J. Nelson, "The Relation of Logic to Metaphysics," *Philosophical Review,* 1949. For a reply to Nelson and to ontological theories of mathematics and logic, E. Nagel, "Logic Without Ontology," reprinted, *Logic Without Metaphysics* (New York: Free Press, 1956) and H. Feigl and W. Sellars (eds.), *Readings in Philosophical Analysis, op. cit.* For a far-reaching criticism of both the ontological and conventional theories, W. V. Quine, "Two Dogmas of Empiricism," reprinted in *From a Logical Point of View, op. cit.*

The Emotive Theory of Ethics

A. J. Ayer, *Language, Truth and Logic, op. cit.;* C. L. Stevenson, *Ethics and Language, op. cit.* Critiques have ranged from the hysterical, such as C. E. M. Joad, *A Critique of Logical Positivism* (Chicago: Univ. of Chicago Press, 1950) to the rejections of the linguistic assumptions of the emotive theory, such as R. M. Hare, *The Language of Morals, op. cit.* For a history of the emotive theory, M. Warnock, *Ethics since 1900* (London: Oxford Univ. Press, 1960).

The Origins of Philosophy as Conceptual Elucidation

G. Warnock, *English Philosophy since 1900, op. cit.;* J. Urmson, *Philosophical Analysis, op. cit.;* L. Wittgenstein, *The Blue and the Brown Books, op. cit.;* and P. F. Strawson, "Construction and Analysis," in A. Ayer, *et al., The Revolution in Philosophy, op. cit.*

Examples of Conceptual Elucidation

Examples other than those of the present anthology are P. F. Strawson, "On Referring," *op. cit.;* G. Ryle, "The Theory of Meaning," in C. A. Mace (ed.), *British Philosophy in the Mid-Century, op. cit.;* J. O. Urmson, *Philosophical Analysis, op. cit.;* and any of the essays in the volumes edited by A. Flew, *Logic and Language, op. cit.,* First and Second Series; and *Essays in Conceptual Analysis, op. cit.*

INDEX